GOVERNMENT & POLITICS
OF TEXAS

Seventh Edition

GOVERNMENT & POLITICS OF TEXAS

A Comparative View

Gary M. Halter
Texas A&M University

Mc Graw Hill **Higher Education**

Boston   Burr Ridge, IL   Dubuque, IA   New York   San Francisco   St. Louis
Bangkok   Bogotá   Caracas   Kuala Lumpur   Lisbon   London   Madrid   Mexico City
Milan   Montreal   New Delhi   Santiago   Seoul   Singapore   Sydney   Taipei   Toronto

Higher Education

GOVERNMENT & POLITICS OF TEXAS, SEVENTH EDITION

Published by McGraw-Hill, an imprint of The McGraw-Hill Companies, Inc., 1221 Avenue of the Americas, New York, NY 10020. Copyright © 2009, 2008, 2005, 2003, 2001, 1999, 1997. All rights reserved. No part of this publication may be reproduced or distributed in any form or by any means, or stored in a database or retrieval system, without the prior written consent of The McGraw-Hill Companies, Inc., including, but not limited to, in any network or other electronic storage or transmission, or broadcast for distance learning.

This book is printed on acid-free paper.

1 2 3 4 5 6 7 8 9 0 CCW/CCW 0 9 8

ISBN: 978-0-07-337898-5
MHID: 0-07-337898-4

Editor in Chief: *Michael Ryan*
Publisher: *Beth Mejia*
Sponsoring Editor: *Mark Georgiev*
Marketing Manager: *Bill Minick*
Developmental Editor: *Kate Scheinman*
Production Editor: *Regina Ernst*
Manuscript Editor: *Margaret Hines*
Cover Designer: *Laurie Entringer*
Photo Research: *Natalia Peschiera*
Production Supervisor: *Rich DeVitto*
Composition: *10/12 Minion by Macmillan Publishing Solutions*
Printing: *PMS 335, 45# New Era Matte Plus, Courier*

Cover: Courtesy of the author

Photo Credits: **Page 2:** Archives Division-Texas State Library; **8:** Courtesy of the author; **11:** © Brand X Pictures/PunchStock; **14:** Courtesy of the author; **18:** Larry Brownstein/Getty Images; **19:** Will Van Overbeek; **32:** Texas Senate Media Services; **44, 51:** © Bob Daemmrich/PhotoEdit, Inc.; **55:** © Bettmann/Corbis; **57:** © John Nourok/PhotoEdit, Inc.; **79:** Courtesy of the author; **82:** © Bettmann/Corbis; **83:** Bob Daemmrich Photography, Inc.; **90:** AP Photo/Charles Rex Arbogast; **100:** © Barbara Davidson/TEXAS & SOUTHWEST_NSW/Dallas Morning News/Corbis; **109:** Courtesy of the author; **118:** (both) Aker/Zvonkovic Photography; **144, 145:** www.senate.state.tx.us; **160:** (top) Aker/Zvonkovic Photography, (bottom) Bob Daemmrich Photography, Inc.; **161:** (both) Archives Division-Texas State Library; **163:** © Bettmann/Corbis; **194, 221:** Aker/Zvonkovic Photography; **262:** © Walter Bibikow/JAI/Corbis

Library of Congress Cataloging-in-Publication Data

Halter, Gary M.
   Government and politics of Texas / Gary Halter. — 7th ed.
      p. cm.
      Previous eds. used ampersand in title.
      Includes index.
      ISBN-13: 978-0-07-337898-5 (alk. paper)
      ISBN-10: 0-07-337898-4 (alk. paper)
      1. Texas—Politics and government—1951—Textbooks. I. Title. II. Title: Government & politics of Texas.
   JK4816.H35 2008
   320.9764—dc22

                                                                2008033126

The Internet addresses listed in the text were accurate at the time of publication. The inclusion of a Web site does not indicate an endorsement by the authors or McGraw-Hill, and McGraw-Hill does not guarantee the accuracy of the information presented at these sites.

Contents

PREFACE

Studying Texas politics is not something most college students voluntarily agree to do. In 1947 the Texas legislature decided that all students graduating from a Texas college or university must take two courses in American government. One of these courses is to emphasize the government and politics of Texas. While many students dread the study of government, for some who remember their high school civics class taught by the coach it can be an enjoyable subject. This book is aimed at fulfilling this state course requirement and making the study of Texas state government an enjoyable experience.

To help students understand the government and politics of the Lone Star State, this book adds a comparative perspective. Some books on Texas government confine their discussion to Texas. This textbook, in contrast, attempts to explain how and why Texas is different from and similar to other states in the nation. Placing the study of state government in a broader national context will enhance the student's understanding of Texas.

In addition to being comparative in its approach, this book also stresses the concept of political culture as a way to enhance the student's understanding of how and why things work in Texas. A knowledge of the historical and cultural development of Texas helps students understand the reasons behind current affairs and how historical forces in the state have contributed to modern-day Texas politics and policies.

Government & Politics of Texas also attempts to examine the changing nature of politics in the state, a political climate that may bring about the end to Republican majorities in the state and move Texas toward being a true two-party state. This change may be part of a national decline of the Republican majority as well as a rise in the participation of minority interests, especially among Mexican Americans. Students should be aware of these changes and how they will affect their lives.

Some scholars of government have noted that controversy and conflict are essential in a free and democratic society. This book addresses a number of controversial issues, for example, the traditionalistic culture of Texas that depicts policies of the state as protective of the status quo while neglecting the needs of the rising minority and underclasses in the state. Another controversial example is the new Republican leadership in Texas that seems more concerned about protecting their power than in addressing issues in the state. Some readers might find this coverage offensive. Every effort has been made to provide balanced discussions of such issues.

New to this seventh edition, Chapter 12, "Public Policy in Texas," covers a number of policies that have an impact on college students. I hope that students will develop an understanding of how significant changes in state policy can have a direct impact on their lives and their pocketbooks. I also hope that students will enjoy reading this book and, more importantly, that they will come away from it with an understanding of the government and politics of the Lone Star State and with an appreciation of how other states operate.

I wish to thank several people who helped with the development of this book. My wife, Linda, assisted in proofreading some of the early drafts, and our marriage has survived. Charles Johnson, former chair of the Political Science Department at Texas A&M

University, was extremely generous with his encouragement and resources, which made it possible to write the first edition of the text in a timely manner. My departmental colleagues Charles Wiggins, Harvey Tucker, Norm Luttbeg, Jon Bond, and James Anderson all assisted in various ways in bringing this project to a close.

I would also like to thank the following reviewers for their insightful comments in the development of this seventh edition of *Government and Politics of Texas:* Jeffrey C. Berry, South Texas College; Robert A. Carp, University of Houston; Neal Coates, Abilene Christian University; Warren A. Dixon, Texas A&M University; Terence M. Garrett, The University of Texas at Brownsville; Charles M. Miles, Austin Community College; Steven J. Showalter, Lee College; Mavis J. (Jim) Startin, University of Texas at San Antonio; Harvey J. Tucker, Texas A&M University; and Ronald W. Vardy, University of Houston.

ABOUT THE AUTHOR

Gary M. Halter is a native of Amarillo and Wichita Falls, Texas. He earned his BA degree from Midwestern University and his PhD from the University of Maryland. He is a Professor of Political Science at Texas A&M University in College Station, Texas. He served as a member of the city council for five years and as mayor for six years. He has worked as a consultant to many city councils in Texas and other states on goal setting and policy making. With Harvey Tucker, he is co-author of the *Texas Legislative Almanac* published by Texas A&M Press in 1997 and 2001.

To my wife, Linda,
my daughter, Katie Mitchell,
my granddaughter, Chloe Mitchell,
and my son, Lee Halter.

CHAPTER 1

INTRODUCTION TO TEXAS GOVERNMENT

Although this book is primarily about the government and politics of Texas, it is also a study of other state governments. It is important to understand Texas government, yet it is also important to understand the governments of other states. This book will explain how and why Texas is different from other states and how and why Texas is similar to the other forty-nine states. While each state is unique, there are many similarities. Each state has a unique history that influences its government and politics, and regional differences within the United States affect state policies. As we will see, Texas's history and southern heritage very much influence its government, politics, and policies.

A **comparative approach** will give students a better understanding of Texas government. They will be able to see that Texas is very much influenced by the actions of other states and at the same time influences what other states do. As the second most populous state, Texas is also a leader in influencing national policies. A broad comparative perspective is important if we are to understand the government and politics of the Lone Star State.

comparative approach
Study of state government by comparing Texas with other states.

✦ TEXAS: A LAND OF CONTRASTS

Several years ago, Texas state tourism promotion literature used the theme "Texas, a Land of Contrasts." Texas is very much **a land of contrasts,** and this is reflected in its government and politics. Texas is rural and urban, southern and western, Anglo, African American, and Hispanic. A southern state with a southern heritage, Texas is also a

a land of contrasts
Texas as a mixture of many peoples and cultures.

Texas Capitol, 1888.

western state with a western heritage and a very strong Spanish and Mexican heritage. The southern culture of East Texas is different from the western culture of the lower plains and high plains regions. Both are different from the Hispanic culture of the Rio Grande Valley and the San Antonio area.

The diversity of Texas history is reflected in the name of a popular theme park in the Dallas/Fort Worth area—*Six Flags over Texas*. Texas has been a Spanish colony, partially under French control; a Mexican state; an independent republic; a state in the United States; and a Confederate state. Each of these periods of its history has influenced what the state is today.

✦ SETTLEMENT PATTERNS IN TEXAS HISTORY

settlement patterns in Texas
The many origins of first settlers to the state.

These contrasts are better understood and take on meaning if we examine the history of **settlement patterns** in the state. Settlement patterns have a significant impact on Texas politics today. This large state (268,601 square miles) has been a crossroads where the cultures of Mexico, the Old South, the West, and the Midwest have met and clashed. (See figure 1.1.)

The Tejanos or Mexican Settlers

The Rio Grande Valley was the first area of the state to be settled by Europeans. In the late 1600s, Spaniards developed settlements along the Rio Grande and as far north and east as San Antonio. Of the Spanish settlements in other parts of the state, only Nacogdoches lasted for more than a few years. Although permanent Spanish settlements did not penetrate much beyond San Antonio, the influence of Spain extends throughout the state. Most of the major rivers have Spanish names: the Rio Grande, Pecos, Nueces, Frio,

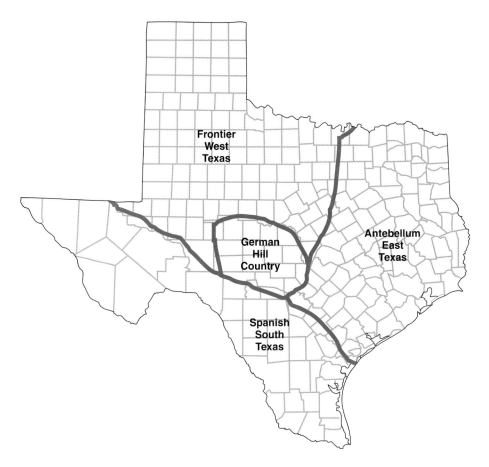

FIGURE 1.1   *Settlement Patterns in Texas.*

SOURCE: D. W. Meining, *Imperial Texas: An Interpretive Essay in Cultural Geography* (Austin: University of Texas Press, 1969).

San Antonio, Guadalupe, Lavaca, Colorado, Brazos, and San Jacinto, for example. Many other geographic features and a number of cities and counties also have Spanish names. Texas state laws are still very much influenced by past Spanish law, especially laws on land ownership and rights.

Anglo Settlers

Southern Anglos and African Americans began settling East Texas in the 1820s. The southern white Protestant settlers were decidedly different from the resident Spanish Catholic settlers. These two groups clashed in 1836 during the Texas Revolutionary War, with many of the Spanish remaining loyal to Mexico while the Anglos formed the Republic of Texas (1836–45).

The settlements of Anglo southerners did not extend west much beyond a line running from the Red River to present-day Fort Worth and south through Waco and Austin to San Antonio. This line is a natural geological feature, known as the Balcones Escarpment, which separates the Coastal Plain and pine forest regions of Texas from the middle and High Plains (*Llano Estacado,* which translates as "staked plains") regions of the state. For two reasons most of the areas west of this line were not settled until after the Civil War. First, Comanche, Lipan Apache, Kiowa, and Tonkawa Indians inhabited this region. In the 1850s, the U.S. Army attempted to control this region by constructing a series of forts on the edge of the Cross Timbers area. These were Forts Belknap, Cooper, Phantom Hill, Chadborne, McKavett, and Terrett. During the Civil War the U.S. government abandoned these forts, and the Indian presence in this region reemerged. Indian domination of the area did not end until 1875, when Chief Quanah Parker was captured in Palo Duro Canyon near present-day Amarillo. The second reason for the lack of settlement was that the southern wood, water, and plantation culture was not adaptable to the dry, arid, treeless plains west of the Balcones Escarpment (Grande Prairie, Cross Timbers, lower plains, and High Plains).

Settlement in this area increased after 1875 and took the form of large ranches and, later, small farms. Many of these settlers migrated from northern states, mostly from the Midwest, and from foreign countries. These settlers lacked the southern culture and traditions that dominated East Texas.

German Immigrants

Adelsverein Society

An organization that promoted German immigration to Texas in the 1840s.

One other early immigrant group also contributed to the character of Texas politics and warrants mention. Due to the efforts of the **Adelsverein Society** (established to promote German immigrants), Germans began to immigrate to Texas in the 1840s. By 1847 the society had brought more than seven thousand Germans to Texas, most settling in and around the town of Fredericksburg.[1] By 1850 German settlers made up 5.4 percent of the state population.[2]

These German immigrants were not slave owners and objected to that institution. They lived apart from and often shunned contact with non-Germans. During the Civil War, many young German men refused to fight, and some fled to Mexico. From Reconstruction until the 1960s, a majority of the votes for Republicans cast in Texas were in areas settled by Germans.

Thus, Texas has four distinct and contrasting settlement periods and regions: Spanish South Texas, antebellum East Texas, frontier West Texas, and the German Fredericksburg Hill Country area. As we will see later, these regional differences still have an influence on Texas politics today.

✦ URBAN AND RURAL CONTRASTS

Texas is the second most populous state, and over 80 percent of its 22 million people live in 53 urban counties. The remaining 20 percent live in the other 201 counties. Texas has three of the ten largest cities in the United States (Houston, Dallas, and San Antonio).

Texas is also a rural state. One does not have to travel far from an urban center to see the contrast. The young urban professional living in Dallas has very little in common with someone working in a sawmill in Diboll. If the urban professional and the mill worker were to meet, they might have little to converse about other than the Dallas Cowboys football team.

These contrasts often frame the conflicts of Texas politics. East Texas Anglos demanding English-only amendments to the state constitution view demands for bilingual education by South Texas Hispanics with contempt. High Plains Republicans from Amarillo often clash with East Texas traditional Democrats. The urban legislator from Austin might see things quite differently than a colleague from Muleshoe in West Texas does.

These regional, urban, and rural contrasts are less severe today than they were twenty-five years ago, but they are still important for understanding the unique character of politics in the Lone Star State.

✦ POPULATION GROWTH AND THE CHANGING CLIMATE OF TEXAS POLITICS

For the last thirty years Texas has experienced a migration of people from other states, due partly to its strategic location in the Sunbelt and its proximity to Mexico. The 1970s Texas oil boom and economic decline in the industrial Midwest also contributed to this migration. Some people migrated out of the state in 1987–89, but by 1990 the population had increased to almost 17 million, up from 11.2 million in 1970. In 1996 the population of Texas was estimated to be 18.6 million, and by the year 2000 the population had reached 20.9 million. Today's estimate is 22 million.

Many of these newcomers to Texas have caused a **changing political climate** in significant ways. From the end of Reconstruction until the mid-1970s, the Democratic party dominated Texas politics, with only one person (U.S. Senator John Tower) winning statewide office as a Republican. The term *Yellow Dog Democrat* was used to describe the voting habits of many Texans ("He would vote for a yellow dog if it ran as a Democrat"). From the 1880s until the 1960s, straight ticket party voting was also necessitated by the absence of meaningful competition from Republicans in the November general election. Many new immigrants to the state, however, brought with them their Republican traditions and strengthened the Republican party in the state. This, coupled with changing national politics, made it respectable to vote Republican.

changing political climate
Population growth changing the politics of the state.

HIGHLIGHT

State Symbols

Most states have a few state symbols, such as official state flowers or state birds. Texas has an abundance of state symbols. Some are obvious, but clearly politics are involved in getting something declared a state symbol. Some symbols are political "hot potatoes" that the legislature won't touch. For example, what should the state sport be? Football jumps to mind, but the bass fishers, golfers, baseball players, basketball fans, and others might object.

Bird	Mockingbird	Musical Instrument	Guitar
Dinosaur	Brachiosaur Sauropod,	Native Pepper	Chiltepin
	Pleurocoelus	Pepper	Jalapeno
Dish	Chili	Plant	Prickly Pear Cactus
Fiber and Fabric	Cotton	Plays	*The Lone Star, Texas, Beyond*
Fish	Guadalupe Bass		*the Sundown, Fandangle*
Flower	Bluebonnet	Reptile	Horned Lizard
Flower Song	"Bluebonnets"	Seashell	Lightning Whelk
Flying Mammal	Mexican Free-Tailed Bat	Ship	U.S.S. *Texas*
Folk Dance	Square Dance	Small Mammal	Armadillo
Fruit	Red Grapefruit	Song	"Texas, Our Texas"
Gem	Blue Topaz	Sport	Rodeo
Gemstone Cut	Lone Star Cut	Stone	Petrified Palmwood
Grass	Sideoats Grama	Tree	Pecan Tree
Insect	Monarch Butterfly	Vegetable	Texas Sweet Onion
Large Mammal	Longhorn		
Motto	"Friendship"		

Source: Texas Fact Book 2006. Texas Legislative Budget Board (www.lbb.state.tx.us).

✦ MINORITY GROUPS

Minority groups play a significant role in Texas politics today. Higher birth rates for minorities and migration to urban areas, coupled with white migration to suburban areas, contributed to the concentration of minority groups in major cities of the state. Corpus Christi, Dallas, El Paso, Houston, and San Antonio have **majority-minority** populations.

Official estimates have projected that by the early twenty-first century the majority of the state's population will be Mexican American and African American and that Anglos will be a minority. (See figure 1.2.) School enrollments are already majority-minority according to the Texas Education Agency. In 1987 Anglos made up 52.5 percent of all school attendees in Texas. In 2004, Anglos made up 39 percent of the school population.[3] These changes in majority and minority status will have many implications for the politics of the state and public policy decisions.

In the past thirty years Texas has experienced tremendous growth in its population. This growth is due both to birth rates and to immigration of citizens from other states and countries. The largest growing segment of the population is the Mexican Americans. The growth in Texas population is also due to growth among southern states as can be seen on page 7. Also, many northeastern states are losing population. Figure 1.3 shows how Texas compares with the fourteen other most populous states.

Hispanics

Hispanic immigration from Mexico to Texas has been a factor in population increases and in state politics. In 1960 Hispanics were 15 percent of the total population of Texas. Their percentage increased to 18 percent by 1970, to 21 percent in 1980, to 25 percent in

majority-minority
Minority groups that make up a majority of the population of the state. Anglos are no longer a majority.

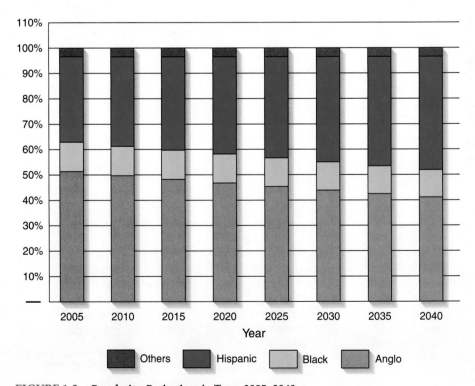

FIGURE 1.2   *Population Projections in Texas 2005–2040.*

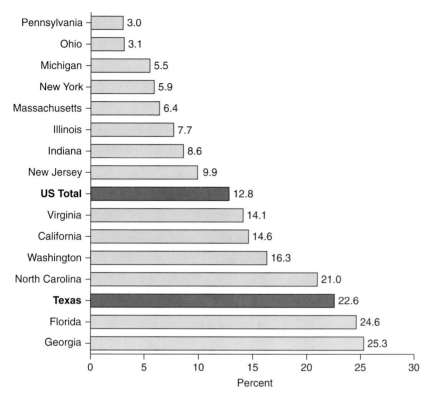

FIGURE 1.3   *Percentage Change in Population from 1994 to 2002.*

SOURCE: *Texas Fact Book 2004 (www.lbb.state.tx.us).*

1990, and was 32.1 percent in 2000. With liberalized voter registration procedures, Hispanics have begun to dominate politics in the border areas, in some sections of the Gulf Coast, and in the San Antonio area. They have been successful in electing local officials to city and county government and school boards, to the state legislature, and to Congress. Dan Morales was elected state's attorney general in 1990 and served until 1999. Raul Gonzales was appointed to serve on the Texas Supreme Court in 1984 and served until 1999.[4] Victor Morales, a newcomer to politics, won the Democratic party nomination for the U.S. Senate in April 1996 to run against Senator Phil Gramm. The Hispanic vote will continue to be a major force in state politics in the future. In the 2002 governor's race, Tony Sanchez was the first Hispanic candidate for governor in a major party. The expectation was that Sanchez would produce a great increase in Hispanic votes. This did not happen, and he was soundly defeated. In fact, there is some evidence that Anglo voters, who would normally vote for Democratic candidates, failed to vote for Sanchez.

Despite Sanchez's loss, Hispanic voters remain a potential force in Texas politics in the years ahead. By 2036 Hispanics will outnumber Anglos and should be a major force in Texas politics.

African Americans

Unlike the Hispanic population, which has steadily increased as a percentage of the total population since the 1960s, the African American population has remained at about 10 to 12 percent since 1950. African Americans tend to be concentrated in three metropolitan

A midwestern family, early settlers to the High Plains of Texas.

areas—Houston, Dallas/Fort Worth, and Austin. They have had some political success at electing officials to local offices (school boards, city councils, and county offices), to the state legislature, and to a few seats in the U.S. Congress. Only one African American, Morris Overstreet, has been elected to statewide office. From 1990 to 1999, Judge Overstreet served on the Texas Court of Criminal Appeals, the Supreme Court for criminal matters in the state. In 2002, Ron Kirk, a popular mayor of Dallas, ran for the U.S. Senate seat. While polls showed Kirk to be in a dead heat with John Cornyn, he lost this race. Voting among African Americans was low, and some Anglos, who normally support Democrats, voted for Republican Cornyn.

Asian Americans

Asian Americans constituted less than 1 percent of the population of Texas in 1980; by 1990 they were 1.9 percent. Projections are that by the year 2020 the Asian American population of Texas will increase to 4.5 percent. Most Asian Americans are concentrated in the Houston area. One section of Houston has such a large concentration of Chinese Americans that the City of Houston has placed Chinese writing on some of the street signs there. Asian Americans in the Houston area have had some success in electing local officials, including one city council member and a county judge. In 2002, the Houston area elected Martha Wong to the Texas state house. She is only the second Asian to serve in the Texas house and the first Republican of Asian background. In 2004 voters elected a Vietnamese, Hubert Vo, a close race for state representative.

political culture
A system of beliefs and values that define the role of government and the role of citizens in that government.

→ THE POLITICAL CULTURE OF TEXAS

Thus far we have discussed the historic settlement patterns, the changing makeup of the current population, and the ethnic mix of the population in the state. These factors contribute to what is called **political culture.** To understand politics, one must understand political culture. The first step is to define government as the process by which values in a society are authoritatively allocated.[5] Government, in the political process, decides which of the competing values regarding the role of government will be upheld. The predominant values that government supports are the values held by most citizens. These dominant values are called the political culture. Thus, political culture is the attitudes, values, and beliefs that most people in a state have about the proper role of government. Most people might not know much about government or how it works, but most do have views and values, sometimes poorly defined, about what government should and should not do.

Daniel J. Elazar, in his book *American Federalism: A View from the States*, developed a system for applying the idea of political culture to the fifty states. Elazar found that there were three distinctive political subcultures in the United States—moralistic, individualistic, and traditionalistic. The map in figure 1.4 shows the political cultures in the fifty states.[6]

In the **moralistic subculture,** politics "is considered one of the great activities of [people in their] search for the good society . . . an effort to exercise power for the betterment of the commonwealth."[7] Government is a positive instrument for change and a means of promoting the general welfare of all citizens. Politics becomes the responsibility of all citizens, who have an obligation to participate in government. People serve in

moralistic subculture
Government viewed as a positive force to achieve a common good for all citizens.

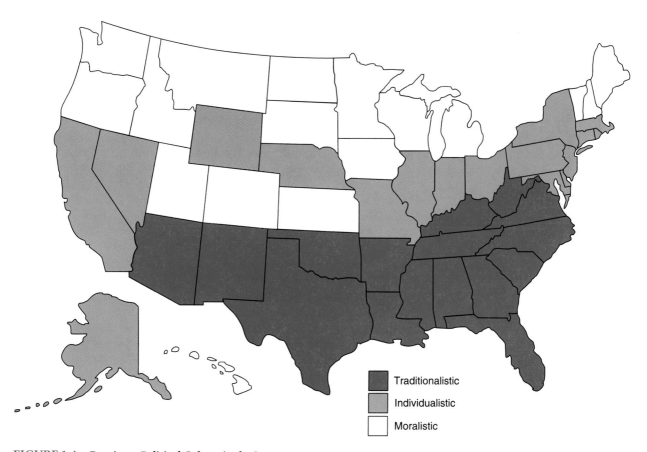

FIGURE 1.4 *Dominent Political Culture in the States.*

SOURCE: Daniel J. Elazar, *American Federalism: A View from the States* (New York: HarperCollins, 1984), 124–25.

government, not for personal gain, but out of a sense of serving the public. The government has a right, an obligation, to intervene in the private affairs of citizens when it is necessary for the "public good or the well-being of the community."[8]

individualistic subculture
Government that benefits the individual rather than society in general.

The **individualistic subculture** "emphasizes the conception of the democratic order as a marketplace. In its view, a government is created for strictly utilitarian reasons, to handle those functions demanded by the people it is created to serve."[9] Government is not concerned with the creation of a "good society," and government intervention in the private sector should be kept to a minimum. Politics is viewed, not as a profession of high calling, but as something that should be left to those willing to dirty their hands. Participation is a necessary evil but not an obligation of each citizen.

traditionalistic subculture
Government that maintains existing political order for the benefit of a small elite.

The **traditionalistic subculture** has as its primary function the maintenance of the existing political order, and participation is confined to a small, self-perpetuating elite. The public has only limited power and influence. Policies that benefit the public are enacted only when the elite allows them to be. Most policies enacted by government benefit the ruling elite and not the public. Political participation by the public is discouraged. A class-based social structure helps to maintain the existing order.

As can be seen in figure 1.4, most of the old southern states have traditionalistic or individualistic political cultures. Southern Anglo settlers of East Texas brought with them a strong traditionalistic culture. Settlers in West Texas in the late nineteenth century and early twentieth century were from midwestern states where the individualistic political culture predominates.

These two political cultures (traditionalistic and individualistic) coexist and blend together in the state. They share some common views regarding the role of government. Both see a limited role for government and discourage broad-based citizen participation in political processes. Both share a conservative view of government: Individuals should do for themselves whenever possible, and government should do only those things that individuals cannot do for themselves—such as pave the roads, keep the peace, and put out fires—and leave the rest to the private sector. Government should keep taxes low, limit social services, and limit the advancement of civil rights. However, most government institutions and political processes are much more consistent with the traditionalistic political culture than with the individualistic political culture.

Immigrants to East Texas from the lower South (Louisiana, Arkansas, Alabama, Georgia, South Carolina, and Florida) supported the traditionalistic idea of rule by an elite as a natural extension of slavery. After the Civil War this culture was maintained, even in the absence of slavery.

Immigrants from the upper South (Missouri, Tennessee, Kentucky, southern Illinois, southern Ohio, and parts of Pennsylvania) tended to support the individualistic political culture. Most were of German, Scotch-Irish, and English ethnic origins; few were slave owners, but almost all were hard-core individualists. The many settlers from the upper South far outnumbered the slave owners from the lower South.[10] Similar immigrant patterns persisted among the late-nineteenth-century settlers to West Texas, contributing an individualistic political culture to that area of the state.

Thus, the first Anglo settlers to Texas brought with them individualistic and traditionalistic views on the role of government. These beliefs remain dominant in modern-day Texas politics.

German immigrants also contributed an individualistic element to the political culture of Texas. These people came to Texas in search of individual opportunities and viewed government as having a limited role.[11] Mexican American immigrants contributed a traditionalistic view to the Texas political culture. Spanish culture in the eighteenth

Longhorn cattle are still a symbol of the ranching heritage of Texas.

century was dominated by a landed aristocracy, a small elite that controlled government for its own benefit, and possessing traditionalistic views:

> Elements of this traditionalistic Mexican culture have remained vital well into the late twentieth century—both in Mexico itself and in the United States among Mexican Americans. A great respect for the extended family is one of those elements. A rigid role structure for family members, such as husbands and wives, is a second element. Adherence to the Catholic faith is a third. Indeed, some scholars have argued that Mexican culture still places considerably more emphasis on family and religious values than on individual achievement.[12]

Mexicans in Texas have also been subjected to domination by a traditionalistic Anglo culture for a large part of their history in the state. This has reinforced their pre-ordained view of the role of government. Their segregation from Anglo society and their limited access to political processes, due to restrictive voter registration procedures, also have reinforced their traditional Mexican cultural predispositions. Some have argued that this is a defensive reaction to Anglo domination.[13]

African Americans were participants in a traditionalistic political culture by force during pre-Civil War days. After the Civil War, especially at the end of Reconstruction in 1876, they were subjected to similar restraints. Their involvement in Texas political processes was effectively restricted until the late 1960s and early 1970s with the passage of the 1965 Federal Voting Rights Act and its application to Texas in the 1970s. The poll tax, the Democratic party white primary (only Anglos were allowed to vote), and fear and intimidation severely limited their participation in Texas politics. Segregated public schools and housing laws also reinforced the traditionalistic political culture.

Patterns of political culture are slow to change and persist for very long periods of time. For example, these were the primary planks of the **party platform** of the Democratic governors in the 1940s and 1950s:

1. Opposition to expanding civil rights
2. Limits on the role of the federal government in state affairs

party platform
Statement of primary beliefs and goals of a political party.

3. Opposition to federal control over natural resources (oil and gas)
4. Opposition to organized labor unions
5. No new taxes[14]

Except for minor differences, most of these planks would fit well into the platforms of former Republican Governor George W. Bush in 1994 and 1998 and Governor Rick Perry in 2002 and 2004. Also, a review of the platform of the Republican party in Texas in 2004 showed support for all these points (*www.texasgop.org*). The party in control of the governor's mansion and most statewide offices has a different name; the political culture has not changed. In the year 2004 it is safe to say that in the past twenty-five years, Texas has gone from a state dominated by the Democratic party to a state dominated by the Republican party with no change in philosophy, ideology, or policy. The concept of political culture helps us understand how and why state governments differ on important determinants. Political culture influences the basic structure of state government, defines government policy, and influences the degree of citizen involvement in government.

The basic structure of state government in Texas fits the traditionalistic/individualistic model quite well. Government is limited. Power is divided among many elected officials. Executive authority is weak, and most power rests with the state legislature. Few state regulations are placed on business, and many of those that exist benefit specific businesses. Regulation of the environment is modest. Despite the repeal of the poll tax, intervention by the federal government, and the passage of the Voting Rights Act, voter participation in Texas is still quite low, ranking near the bottom of the fifty states in terms of percentage of population voting. Political corruption is often tolerated as the necessary cost of doing the business of government. Except on rare occasions, the state legislature protects the status quo and places few restrictions on lobbying and other activities of interest groups. The office of governor is formally very weak. The state bar and business interest groups heavily control the selection of the state judiciary in partisan elections. State finances reflect the philosophy of limited government; Texas often ranks near the bottom of the fifty states on expenditures. Limited state expenditures are financed with a regressive tax system that relies on property taxes and sales taxes. (See Chapter 10.)

In conclusion, the political culture of Texas supports a conservative, limited government. Later chapters will expand on these ideas to demonstrate the differences and similarities between Texas and other states.

✦ The Economy of Texas

The economy of a state also plays a role in its politics. The economy of Texas has changed greatly in the past twenty to thirty years. Texas is no longer a rural state with an economy dominated by cattle, cotton, and oil, although these are still important elements in the economy.

Land has always been an important factor in Texas economy and politics. Many settlers were lured to Texas by offers of free land. The Spanish and later the Mexican government provided generous grants of land to any family that settled in the state. Each family could receive one *sitio* or *legua* (Spanish for "league"), about 4,428 acres of land. A single person could receive 1,500 acres of land. In the 1820s it took such a generous incentive to get people to live in Texas, given the hardships of travel and simple survival. General P. H. Sheridan, best known for his remark, "The only good Indian I ever saw was dead," said in a letter from Fort Clark, Texas, dated 1855, "If I owned Hell and Texas, I'd rent out Texas and live in Hell."[15] Other people supposedly came to Texas from more comfortable environments to escape the law. "GTT" (Gone to Texas) was supposedly a common sign left by those escaping the long arm of the sheriff.

Land issues drove the Texas revolution in 1836 and the annexation of Texas by the United States in 1845. When Texas entered the Union, it kept its public debt and its public lands. The U.S. government had to purchase from Texans all land that was to be federal land. The U.S. government also purchased lands that were formerly the west and northwest parts of Texas and that now make up much of present-day New Mexico and some of Colorado, Utah, and Wyoming.[16]

For most of its history the Lone Star State has had a **land-based economy.** Cotton farming dominated from the 1820s to the 1860s. After the Civil War, cattle became the economic mainstay. In the early twentieth century, abundant oil was discovered in East Texas. Only in the past thirty to forty years has the economy begun to diversify and become less dependent on the land and its cotton, cattle, and oil. Some regions of the state remain more dependent on land economies than others, and vast differences can be found from one region to another.

The State of Texas Comptroller's Office has divided Texas into a number of **economic regions** as a convenient way to collect data for a wide variety of purposes. For purposes of discussion, these have been combined into six regions. These regions are shown in figure 1.5.

The East Texas or Piney Woods region was traditionally dominated by agriculture, timber, and oil. Today, agriculture is less important and oil is declining. Timber is still important. Some diversification has occurred, with manufacturing becoming a more important element in the economy.

land-based economy
An economic system in which most wealth is derived from the use of the land.

economic regions
Divisions of the state based on dominant economic activity.

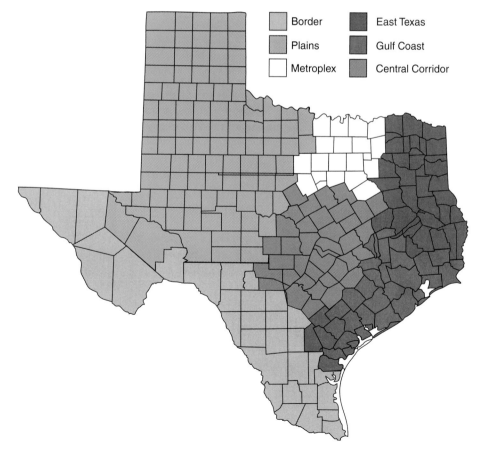

FIGURE 1.5   *Economic Regions of Texas.*

Wheat harvest on the High Plains near Amarillo in the 1920s.

The Plains region of the state, with Lubbock and Amarillo as the major cities, was dominated by agriculture (especially cotton, wheat, and maize) and by ranching and cattle feedlots. In recent years, the economy of this region has become more diversified and less dominated by agriculture.

The Gulf Coast region, extending from Corpus Christi to Beaumont/Port Arthur/Orange, and including Houston, is dominated by petrochemical industries, manufacturing, shipping, and fishing. In recent years this area has diversified into manufacturing and high-tech industries. It is also the area with the highest concentration of organized labor unions in the entire state.

The border area of South Texas and the Rio Grande Valley, stretching from Brownsville to El Paso, is noted primarily for its agricultural production of citrus fruits and vegetables. In recent years, trade with Mexican border cities has diversified the economy of this region, and with the passage of the North American Free Trade Agreement (NAFTA) this process has increased. Some writers would distinguish the El Paso area and the border area as separate economic units because the two regions are several hundred miles apart, and their economic contact is limited. Many citizens of El Paso often feel that they are not a part of Texas and feel more closely associated with New Mexico.

The Metroplex or Dallas/Fort Worth area is considered the financial center of the state. This economic region is the most diversified in the state, with a combination of banking, manufacturing, high-tech, and aerospace industries.

The Central Corridor or midstate region is an area roughly stretching from College Station in the east to Waco in the north and Austin and San Antonio in the southwest. This economic area is dominated by two large state universities (Texas A&M University and the University of Texas at Austin), high-tech industries in Austin and San Antonio, and major military bases in the Waco/Temple/Killeen and San Antonio areas. During the 1970s and early 1980s the state economy experienced tremendous growth due to the increase in the price of oil. In the mid-1980s the price of oil declined, and with it the economy of the entire state declined. The price of oil also greatly affected the economy of Mexico, which in turn affected economic growth in Texas. Although it had benefited earlier from the increase in oil prices and inflation, Texas faced budgetary shortfalls as the economy fell into a deep recession.

To many, the economic recession of the early 1980s showed a need for more **economic diversity** for the state. It was felt that the old land-based economy could not carry the state into the twenty-first century. Since 1988 there has been significant restructuring of the state economy. NAFTA promised some significant economic growth due to increases in trade with Mexico, and new high-tech industries, especially in Austin, Dallas, and Houston, have significantly influenced the Texas economy.

economic diversity
An economy based on many types of economic activity rather than one or a few activities.

When Texas entered the twenty-first century, the economy of the state was far more diverse than even twenty years ago. While energy and agriculture are still important elements in the state's economy, they are balanced by many new elements. This trend will continue for some time.

✦ CONCLUSIONS

People from other states are often bored with Texans who brag about their state. Some Texans think they have the right to brag, because the history and diversity of the state are unique, and the state is truly a land of contrasts. Others might say that Texas is also a land of contradictions and that Texans have no right to brag. Texas is still one of the lowest ranking states on many factors such as school expenditures, levels of voter participation, and fair treatment of all citizens. These contrasts and the contradictions have contributed to and can be partially explained by its cultural legacy. As we will see in later chapters, these cultural patterns and clashes help explain much of what occurs in the legislative, executive, and judicial branches of the state government.

Texas is no longer a rural backwater state dependent upon a land-based economy. It is now a large urban industrial state and a major player in national politics. The expanding population of the state and the increase in minority groups in the state will continue to contribute to the challenges facing state government. The challenges facing Texas today are many and varied. Only time will tell how well the government of Texas deals with them.

INTERNET RESOURCES

Texas Facts Book: *www.lbb.state.tx.us*
> Gives information on Texas past and present. Good source of data on state budget.

State of Texas Home Page: *www.state.tx.us/#government*
> General guide to state agencies.

Comptroller of Public Accounts: *www.window.state.tx.us/*
> Good source on the state expenditures and on economic regions of the state.

State newspapers: *www.usnpl.com/txnews.php*
> Information on Texas newspapers.

KEY TERMS

a land of contrasts (p. 1)
Adelsverein Society (p. 4)
changing political climate (p. 5)
comparative approach (p. 1)
economic diversity (p. 15)

economic regions (p. 13)
individualistic subculture (p. 10)
land-based economy (p. 13)
majority-minority (p. 6)
moralistic subculture (p. 9)

party platform (p. 11)
political culture (p. 8)
settlement patterns in Texas (p. 2)
traditionalistic subculture (p. 10)

Notes

1. Terry G. Jordan, *German Seed in Texas Soil: Immigrant Farmers in Nineteenth Century Texas* (Austin: University of Texas Press, 1966).

2. Robert A. Calvert and Arnold DeLeon, *The History of Texas* (Arlington Heights, Ill.: Harland Davidson, 1990), 99–100.

3. http://texaseducationinfo.org/tea.tpeir.web/tpeirpage/Resources.html

4. Raul Gonzales was appointed by Governor Mark White to the Texas Supreme Court in 1984. He has subsequently been elected and reelected to the court.

5. David Easton, *The Political System* (New York: Knopf, 1953), 129.

6. Daniel J. Elazar, *American Federalism: A View from the States* (New York: HarperCollins, 1984).

7. Ibid., 90.

8. Ibid.

9. Ibid., 86.

10. See Elazar, *American Federalism;* and Terry Jordan, "The Imprint of the Upper and Lower South on Mid-Nineteenth Century Texas," *Annals of the Association of American Geographers* 57 (December 1967): 667–90.

11. Jordan, "Imprint of the Upper and Lower South," 668.

12. Kenneth R. Mladenka and Kim Q. Hill, *Texas Government: Politics and Economics,* 2d ed. (Pacific Grove, Calif.: Brooks/Cole, 1989), 56.

13. Joan W. Moore and Harry Pachon, *Mexican Americans,* 2d ed. (Englewood Cliffs, N.J.: Prentice Hall, 1976), 135–36.

14. Platforms of Beauford Jester, 1946 and 1948; Allan Shivers, 1950, 1952, and 1954; Price Daniel, 1956, 1958, and 1960. See James R. Soukup, Clifton McCleskey, and Harry Holloway, *Party and Factional Division in Texas* (Austin: University of Texas Press, 1964).

15. Roy Morris, *Sheridan: The Life and Wars of General Phil Sheridan* (New York: Crown, 1992).

16. T. R. Fehrendbach, *Lone Star: A History of Texas and the Texans* (New York: Collier, 1980), 276–77.

CHAPTER 2

THE STATE CONSTITUTION AND THE AMERICAN FEDERAL SYSTEM

All states and the national government have written constitutions that provide the broad outlines of government. These constitutions are contracts between the government and the people, and they stand as a measure against which governments must act. Constitutions also reveal something about a state. In the previous chapter we discussed the traditionalistic/individualistic political culture of Texas. The **Texas Constitution** is very much an embodiment of this culture. It reflects the conservative nature of the state, the distrust of government, the desire to limit the government's ability to act, and the desire to protect some special interests.

Texas Constitution
The basic document that provides a framework for government and limits what the government can do.

The Alamo, in San Antonio, has long been a symbol of the struggle for Texas independence.

An examination of the several constitutions that have governed Texas helps us understand the importance of political culture and its impact on the formal structure of government. Texas has been governed by seven constitutions, five since it entered the Union in 1845.

In addition, in this chapter we will examine how Texas and other states operate within a federal system of government—American federalism. This system both limits and enhances what state and local governments can do and is one of the great compromises in American history.

✦ CONSTITUTIONS UNDER THE REPUBLIC OF MEXICO

The first constitution to govern Anglos in Texas was the Republic of Mexico's constitution of 1824. This constitution was federalist in concept and a clear break with the Spanish centralist tradition.[1] Under the 1824 national constitution, Texas was governed by a provincial constitution of the state of Coahuila y Tejas that was approved in 1827. The 1827 constitution provided for a unicameral legislature, and Texas elected two representatives to the provincial legislature. This constitution, which lacked a bill of rights, provided a government structure with which the Anglos were comfortable. Texans ignored sections of the constitution of 1827, most notably those that required Catholicism as the state religion and those that did not recognize slavery.

The suspension of the Mexican national constitution of 1824, and with it the provincial constitution of 1827, by Mexican president Santa Anna was a factor that led to the Texas revolution. One of the early Texas flags, supposedly flown at the Alamo, had the numbers *1824* superimposed on a red, green, and white emblem of the Mexican flag. This was a demand that the constitution of 1824 be restored.[2]

The Texas Declaration of Independence was signed in February and March 1836 in a building like this replica at the Washington-on-the-Brazos State Park.

✦ THE REPUBLIC OF TEXAS CONSTITUTION OF 1836

In 1836, when Texas declared itself a republic independent of Mexico, a new constitution was adopted. This document was a composite of the U.S. Constitution and the constitutions of several southern states. It provided for a unitary, rather than federal, form of government. Signs of the distrust of government by the traditionalistic southerners who wrote the document are evident. They limited the term of the president to one 3-year term with prohibitions against consecutive reelection. The president was also prohibited from raising an army without the consent of the congress. There were other features, such as freedom of religion and property rights protection, that had been absent in the 1824 and 1827 constitutions. Slavery, which had been ignored by the Mexican government, was legalized.[3]

✦ STATEHOOD CONSTITUTION OF 1845

When Texas joined the Union in 1845, a state constitution was adopted. This document also reflected the traditionalistic southern culture, with a few notable exceptions that were adaptations of Spanish law. Women were granted property rights equal to those of men, especially in marriage, where women were given half the value of all property acquired during the marriage (community property). In addition, a person's homestead was protected from forced sale to pay debts. These ideas were later adopted by many other states.

The 1845 constitution also provided for limited executive authority, biennial sessions of the legislature, and two-year terms for most officials. Most of these features were included in later constitutions.

✦ THE CIVIL WAR AND RECONSTRUCTION CONSTITUTIONS OF 1861, 1866, AND 1869

In 1861, when Texas joined the Confederacy, another constitution was adopted. It was essentially the same as the 1845 document, with the exception of a prohibition against the emancipation of slaves, a provision to secede from the Union, and a provision to join the Confederacy.

In 1866, a third state constitution was approved as a condition for rejoining the Union following the Civil War. This document abolished slavery, nullified the ordinances of secession, renounced the right of future secession, and repudiated the wartime debts of the state. This constitution of 1866 was short-lived and overturned by Reconstruction acts of the U.S. Congress.

Military rule was again imposed on Texas, and a new constitution was adopted in 1869. This fourth state constitution, which was approved under the supervision of the federal government's military rule, is called the Reconstruction constitution or the "carpetbagger's constitution." It represented a radical departure from past and future documents and reflected the centralization aspirations of the national Republicans. A four-year term was provided for the governor, who was also given strong appointive authority. The governor could appoint most state and many local officials. County courts were abolished, and much local authority and control were removed from the planter class. Public schools were centralized under state control and funded with a poll tax and the sale of public lands. African Americans were given the right to vote, and whites who had participated in the "rebellion" (Civil War) were disenfranchised.[4]

✦ THE CONSTITUTION OF 1876

The current constitution was written in 1875 at the end of Reconstruction and approved by the voters in 1876. The constitutional convention was assembled in 1875. "Not one man who had written the constitution of 1869 sat in this delegation." As T. R. Fehrenbach put it, these men were

> mostly old Texans: John Henry Brown, Sterling C. Robertson, sons of empresarios, Rip Ford (Texas Ranger), John H. Reagan, (Ex-Postmaster General of the Confederacy, and a bevy of generals who has worn the grey. Of the ninety members, more than twenty held high rank in the C.S.A. This was a restoration convention. . . . It was a landowners' group, including forty members of the Grange. . . . This was an antigovernment instrument: too many Texans had seen what government could do, not for them but to them. It tore up previous frameworks, and its essential aim was to try and bind all state government within tight confines.[5]

These men were landowners who had objected strongly to the centralist government under Reconstruction. The document reflected the antigovernment sentiments of the traditionalistic/individualistic political culture of the state. The new document reimposed shorter terms of office, reestablished many statewide and local elected offices, and severely restricted the ability of government to act. The powers of both the legislature and the governor were restricted.[6]

None of these changes were especially controversial. The controversial issues were the poll tax payment for the right to vote, women's suffrage, and public schools. The centralized state school system was abolished and replaced by local control of schools with some state funding provided. In addition, provisions were made for a state-funded university system.[7]

Thus, Texas has been governed by a number of state constitutions. The Spanish constitutions contributed several key elements, including community property rights for women, which was a clear departure from English laws. The 1845 constitution provided for limited government with little centralized power. The constitutions of 1861 and 1866 continued these principles of limited government. The present constitution, approved in 1876, not only reinstated but expanded the ideas of limited government. Only the Reconstruction constitution of 1869, which provided for a strong, centralized government, was a departure from these ideas. Its swift repeal at the end of Reconstruction indicates how utterly the southern whites rejected these concepts. Many Texans today would not accept these concepts. In 1999 voters rejected two amendments that would have expanded the power of the governor to appoint and remove minor state officials.

✦ Culture Drives Institutions

To a large degree **political culture drives institutions.** The Reconstruction constitution of 1869 was a fundamental departure from earlier constitutions and in conflict with the political culture of the state. This document centralized power in state government and reduced the authority of local governments, provided for four-year terms for many officeholders, and gave the governor the power to appoint most state and many local officials, including the state judiciary. In addition it provided for annual sessions of the legislature, gave African Americans the right to vote, and provided for state-controlled schools and a state police system. Most of these provisions are not supported by a traditionalistic/individualistic political culture that calls for decentralized, weak government while discouraging political participation and nonelite involvement in government.

Except for the four-year terms for governor and other statewide officials, most of these ideas (gubernatorial appointment of state and local officials, annual sessions of the legislature, and state control of local affairs) have little support in Texas today. The voters have rejected annual sessions of the legislature on several occasions, and despite great decentralization of local schools, there is demand for even greater decentralization of decisions down to the local level. Culture drives institutions by influencing the basic structure and organization of government. Thus the current constitution is very compatible with the political culture of the state.

political culture drives institutions
The basic structure and organization of state government are molded by the political culture of the state.

✦ Principles of Constitutional Government

Most generally, history, culture, and traditions have an impact on constitutions, but several important principles specifically underpin the general idea of constitutional government. The first of these is the idea of **popular sovereignty,** the idea that all power rests with the people.[8] Constitutions are written by a popularly elected convention of citizens and not by state legislatures. Thus the citizens must also approve any changes in state constitutions—except in Delaware, where the state legislature can amend the state constitution. The current Texas Constitution supports this idea very strongly in its preamble and bill of rights.

Second, **constitutions are a contract** or compact between the citizens and the government and cannot be violated. The laws passed by legislatures must fit within the framework of the constitution.

Third, **constitutions are a limitation upon the power of government.** The assumption here is that the government can do anything not prohibited by the constitution, and thus it is necessary to expressly limit the power of government. As has been

popular sovereignty
The idea that power granted in state constitutions rests with the people.

constitutions are a contract
State constitutions are contracts between the citizen and the government that limit the power of government.

constitutions are a limitation on the power of government
State constitutions limit what government can do. Without limitations governments can do anything.

pointed out, the current (1876) Texas Constitution is very much an example of limitations upon the power of state government. When the current constitution was drafted in 1874–75, Governor Richard Coke said to the assembled constitutional convention:

> The accepted theory of American constitutional government is that State Constitutions are limitations upon, rather than grants of power: and as a rule, not without its exceptions, that power not prohibited exists in State government. Therefore, express prohibitions are necessary upon the power of state government . . . these restrictions . . . have multiplied in the more recently created instruments of fundamental law.

Some would say that Governor Coke was "preaching to the choir" with this opening statement. The men (women could not vote until 1920 in Texas) who assembled in a constitutional convention of 1875 had as their primary aim limiting the power of state government. The actions of the Radical Republicans during Reconstruction may have intensified the desires of these men to weaken and limit government, but they were predisposed to this philosophy even before the Civil War. While the Texas Constitution embraces all these principles, the idea of a limited government is wholeheartedly embraced.

✦ CHARACTERISTICS COMMON TO STATE CONSTITUTIONS

Separation of Powers

separation of powers
Power divided between the legislative, executive, and judicial branches of government.

Besides the ideals of popular sovereignty, compact or contract theory, and limited government, there are some common characteristics of state constitutions. First, all state constitutions embrace the idea of **separation of powers** provided in the U.S. Constitution. Power is divided among an elected executive, an elected legislature, and the judiciary. The separation of powers provides a check on the actions of government. Fear of concentration of power in a single person led the framers of the U.S. Constitution to separate powers. Fragmented power was safer. All state constitutions embrace this idea. Fear of strong executive authority, experienced in Texas under Governor Edmund J. Davis and the Radical Republicans, led the framers of the 1876 document to fragment executive power. The voters elect a governor, a lieutenant governor, a comptroller, an attorney general, a commissioner of the land office, and, at that time, a state treasurer. The agricultural commissioner, railroad commissioners, and a state board of education were added later. The office of treasurer was abolished in 1995.

Bill of Rights

bill of rights
A list of individual rights and freedoms granted to citizens within the state constitution.

Like the U.S. Constitution, most state constitutions have very strong statements on civil liberties that grant basic freedoms. Most of the civil liberties protections in state constitutions duplicate those found in the U.S. document, but many state constitutions are more generous in the granting of liberties than is the U.S. Constitution. The Texas Constitution is no exception in this regard. The average citizen, upon reading the **bill of rights** section of the Texas Constitution, might well conclude that it is a very liberal document. Besides those rights provided by the federal document, the Texas Constitution also grants equalities under the law to all citizens regardless of "sex, race, color, creed or national origin."[9] This is almost the exact wording of the failed Equal Rights Amendment to the U.S. Constitution. Citizens often have more freedoms provided in their state constitutions than in the national constitution, but most are unaware of this. Attention is often focused on the national Bill of Rights and not the state bill of rights.

For most of the twentieth century citizens relied on the Federal Bill of Rights for protection and filed suit in Federal court when rights were violated. In recent years, state courts have played a more active role in protecting the rights of citizens. For example in Texas the issue of equity in school finance (discussed in Chapter 11) was litigated in the state courts, and the Texas Supreme court forced the state legislature to change the system of school financing.

Supreme Law of the State

Article 6 of the U.S. Constitution contains the **supremacy clause.** This makes the U.S. Constitution the supreme law of the land. Most state constitutions have a similar statement that makes the state constitution superior to state law and actions by local governments. Any state or local law that conflicts with the state constitution is invalid.

supremacy clause
A clause that makes a state constitution superior to state and local laws.

A recent example of local laws potentially conflicting with a state law involves the state's issuing of permits to citizens to carry concealed handguns. Many local governments (cities, counties, and metropolitan transit authorities) passed regulations prohibiting the carrying of concealed handguns in some public places. Supporters of the "concealed carry law" have charged that these local regulations violate the state law. The state court system determined that these local regulations did not violate the concept of "supreme law of the state."

✧ Comparing the Structure of State Constitutions

Although they have some common characteristics, there are vast differences among state constitutions. According to legal experts and political theorists, there are some ideal characteristics that constitutions should possess and against which constitutions can be compared. Ideally, a constitution should be brief and explicit, embody only the general principles of government, and provide the broad outlines of government subject to interpretation, especially through the court's power of judicial review. Constitutions should not be detailed and specific but broad and flexible. Furthermore, constitutions should provide broad grants of power to specific agencies and hold government officials accountable for their actions. Last, formal amendments to the constitution should be infrequent, deliberate, and significant.

The U.S. Constitution meets these ideals. There are only 4,300 words in the original document. It broadly outlines the basic principles of government and has been amended only twenty-seven times. All but eight of these amendments involved questions of civil liberty, voting, and electoral questions. Very few of these amendments have altered the basic structure of the federal government. The document is flexible enough to allow for change without altering the basic document.

Few state constitutions can meet the standards of brevity and few amendments. This is especially true of the Texas Constitution. Table 2.1 details information about all fifty state constitutions. Several conclusions are obvious from examining this table. First, most states have had several constitutions. Only nineteen states are still operating under their first constitution, and most of these are newer states in the western part of the United States. Maine and Massachusetts are the only states of the "original thirteen," still operating under their first constitutions. Because of the Civil War and its aftermath, former Confederate states have had multiple constitutions.

Second, most state constitutions are very lengthy documents; Alabama's is the longest with 310,328 words, including the amendments. The mean word count for state constitutions is 19,300, compared with only 4,300 for the U.S. Constitution.[10] Some

TABLE 2.1

Comparisons of State Constitutions, January 2007

State	Number of Constitutions	Date of Current Constitution	Approximate Word Length	Number of Amendments	
				Submitted	Approved
Alabama	6	Nov. 28, 1901	340,136(a)(b)(c)	1,088	794
Alaska	1	Jan. 3, 1959	15,988(b)	41	29
Arizona	1	Feb. 14, 1912	28,876	254	141
Arkansas	5	Oct. 30, 1874	59,500(b)	190	92(d)
California	2	July 4, 1879	54,645	870	514
Colorado	1	Aug. 1, 1876	74,522(b)	315	150
Connecticut	4	Dec. 30, 1965	17,256(b)	30	29
Delaware	4	June 10, 1897	19,000	(e)	138
Florida	6	Jan. 7, 1969	51,456(b)	141	110
Georgia	10	July 1, 1983	39,526(b)	86(g)	66(g)
Hawaii	1(h)	Aug. 21, 1959	20,774(b)	128	108
Idaho	1	July 3, 1890	24,232(b)	206	119
Illinois	4	July 1, 1971	16,510(b)	17	11
Indiana	2	Nov. 1, 1851	10,379(b)	78	46
Iowa	2	Sept. 3, 1857	12,616(b)	57	52(i)
Kansas	1	Jan. 29, 1861	12,296(b)	123	93(i)
Kentucky	4	Sept. 28, 1891	23,911(b)	75	41
Louisiana	11	Jan. 1, 1975	54,112(b)	210	150
Maine	1	March 15, 1820	16,276(b)	203	171(i)
Maryland	4	Oct. 5, 1867	46,600(b)	257	221(k)
Massachusetts	1	Oct. 25, 1780	36,700(l)	148	120
Michigan	4	Jan. 1, 1964	34,659(b)	66	28
Minnesota	1	May 11, 1858	11,547(b)	214	119
Mississippi	4	Nov. 1, 1890	24,323(b)	158	123
Missouri	4	March 30, 1945	42,600(b)	170	109
Montana	2	July 1, 1973	13,145(b)	54	30
Nebraska	2	Oct. 12, 1875	20,048	344(m)	224(m)
Nevada	1	Oct. 31, 1864	31,377(b)	226	134(i)
New Hampshire	2	June 2, 1784	9,200	287(n)	145
New Jersey	3	Jan. 1, 1948	22,956(b)	74	41
New Mexico	1	Jan. 6, 1912	27,200	284	155
New York	4	Jan. 1, 1895	51,700	291	216
North Carolina	3	July 1, 1971	16,532(b)	42	34
North Dakota	1	Nov. 2, 1889	19,130(b)	262	149(o)
Ohio	2	Sept. 1, 1851	48,521(b)	275	163
Oklahoma	1	Nov. 16, 1907	74,075(b)	340(p)	175(p)
Oregon	1	Feb. 14, 1859	54,083(b)	477(q)	238(q)
Pennsylvania	5	1968(r)	27,711(b)	36(r)	30(r)
Rhode Island	3	Dec. 4, 1986	10,908(b)	11(s)	10(s)
South Carolina	7	Jan. 1, 1896	22,300	679(t)	492(t)
South Dakota	1	Nov. 2, 1889	27,675(b)	223	213
Tennessee	3	Feb. 23, 1870	13,300	61	38
Texas	5(u)	Feb. 15, 1876	90,000	614(v)	439
Utah	1	Jan. 4, 1896	11,000	158	107
Vermont	3	July 9, 1793	10,286(b)	211	53
Virginia	6	July 1, 1971	21,319(b)	51	43
Washington	1	Nov. 11, 1889	33,564(b)	170	97
West Virginia	2	April 9, 1872	26,000	121	71
Wisconsin	1	May 29, 1848	14,392(b)	193	144(i)
Wyoming	1	July 10, 1890	31,800	123	97

*In Delaware the legislature amends the state constitution without voter approval. Data for January 1, 2007.

Source: *Book of the States 2007* (Lexington, Ky.: Council of State Governments, 2007), Vol. 38, table 1.1, p. 9.

writers have pointed out that state constitutions have to be longer than the U.S. document because of the nature of state responsibility. While this is true, it can also be argued that most state documents are of excessive length for other reasons that will be discussed later.

Third, most state constitutions have been amended more often than the U.S. Constitution; the mean is about 117 times.[11] Alabama is again the leader with 776. Last, state constitutions have a limited life span when compared with the U.S. Constitution. The average life span for a state constitution is ninety-five years.[12]

If we compare the Texas Constitution to the "average" state constitution, we find that it is longer than most, at 93,000-plus words, and has more amendments. Texas currently has 441 amendments.[13] Only five states have drafted more constitutions. One can easily conclude that most state constitutions, including the one used in Texas, do not meet the criteria outlined previously for an ideal constitution. Most are lengthy, detailed documents that require frequent alteration. Most state constitutions might be more accurately described as statutory or legislative acts rather than constitutional law. This is especially true of the document that governs Texas.

As can be seen in figure 2.1, states of the old Confederacy have multiple constitutions. Most of the states operating on their first constitution entered the Union in the twentieth century (Oklahoma, New Mexico, Arizona, Alaska, and Hawaii) or are states in the western part of the country. Two New England states still operate under their original documents.

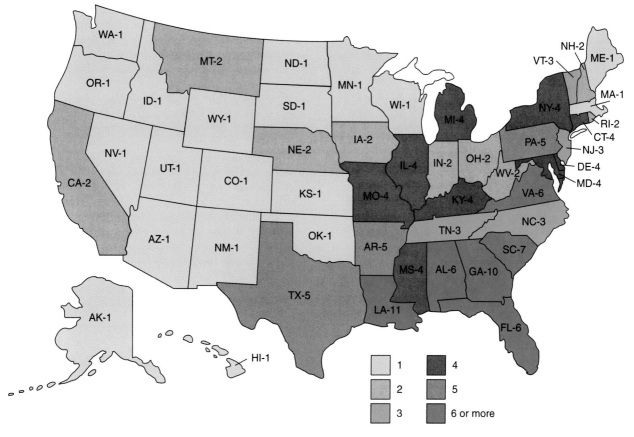

FIGURE 2.1 *Number of Constitutions Per State.*

SOURCE: Data from *The Book of the States 2007.* (Lexington, Ky.: Council of State Governments, 2007), 9.

HIGHLIGHT

Concepts from the Bill of Rights in the Texas Constitution

Article 1 of the Texas Constitution grants basic rights to citizens, as the following examples illustrate.

Texas is a free and independent State, subject only to the Constitution of the United States, and the maintenance of our free institutions and the perpetuity of the Union depends upon the preservation of the right of local self-government, unimpaired to all the States. (Section 1)

All political power is inherent in the people, and all free governments are founded on their authority, and instituted for their benefit. The faith of the people of Texas stands pledged to the preservation of a republican [representative] form of government, and, subject to this limitation only, they have at all times the inalienable right to alter, reform or abolish their government in such manner as they may think expedient. (Section 2)

Equality under the law shall not be denied or abridged because of sex, race, color, creed or national origin. (Section 3a)

All men have a natural and indefeasible right to worship Almighty God according to the dictates of their own conscience. No man shall be compelled to attend, erect or support any place of worship, or to maintain any ministry against his consent. . . . and no preference shall ever be given by law to any religious society or mode of worship. (Section 6)

No money shall be appropriated or drawn from the Treasury for the benefit of any sect, or religious society, theological or religious seminary; nor shall property belonging to the State be appropriated for any such purposes. (Section 7)

Every person shall be at liberty to speak, write or publish his opinions on any subject, being responsible for the abuse of that privilege; and no law shall ever be passed curtailing the liberty of speech or of the press . . . in all indictment for libels, the jury shall have the right to determine the law and the facts, under the direction of the court, as in other cases. (Section 8)

The people shall be secure in their persons, houses, papers and possessions, from unreasonable seizures or searches. (Section 9)

In all criminal prosecutions the accused shall have a speedy trial by an impartial jury. (Section 10)

All prisoners shall be bailable by sufficient sureties, unless for capital offenses. (Section 11)

The writ of habeas corpus is a writ of right, and shall never be suspended. (Section 12)

Excessive bail shall not be required, nor excessive fines imposed, nor cruel or unusual punishment inflicted. (Section 13)

No person, for the same offense, shall be twice put in jeopardy of life or liberty . . . after a verdict of not guilty in a court of [law]. (Section 14)

The right to trial by jury shall remain inviolate. (Section 15)

No bill of attainder, ex post facto law, retroactive law, or any law impairing the obligations of contracts, shall be made. (Section 16)

No person shall ever be imprisoned for debt. (Section 18)

No citizen of this state shall be deprived of life, liberty, property, privileges or immunities, or in any manner disfranchised, except by the due course of the law of the land. (Section 19)

No citizen shall be outlawed. No person shall be transported out of the State for any offense committed within the same. (Section 20)

No conviction shall work corruption of blood, or forfeiture of estate, and the estates of those who destroy their own lives shall descend or vest as in case of natural death. (Section 21)

Treason against the State shall consist only in levying war against it. (Section 22)

Every citizen shall have the right to keep and bear arms in the lawful defense of himself or the State; but the legislature shall have power, by law, to regulate the wearing of arms, with a view to prevent crime. (Section 23)

The military shall at all times be subordinate to the civil authority. (Section 24)

No soldier shall in time of peace be quartered in the house of any citizen without consent of the owner, nor in time of war but in a manner prescribed by law. (Section 25)

Perpetuities and monopolies are contrary to the genius of free government, and shall never be allowed, nor shall the law of primogeniture or entailments ever be in force in this state. (Section 26)

The citizens shall have the right, in a peaceable manner, to assemble together for their common good; and apply to those invested with the powers of government for redress of grievances or other purposes, by petition, address or remonstrance. (Section 27)

No power of suspending laws in this State shall be exercised except by the Legislature. (Section 28)

Food for Thought

What rights granted by the Texas Constitution are absent from the U.S. Constitution?
What rights granted by the U.S. Constitution are absent from the Texas Constitution?

There are several other generalizations that can be made about state constitutions. First, most create weak executives and strong legislatures. This will be discussed later in the text. Second, all state constitutions contain articles on taxation and finance that limit how funds can be spent. Often **taxes are earmarked** for specific purposes (a common example is the gasoline tax for state highways). Third, all but a few constitutions prohibit deficit expenditures unless approved by voters in the form of a bond election. Finally, most state constitutions contain large amounts of trivia. For example, the original Texas Constitution contained a detailed list of items protected by the homestead protection provisions from forced sale for payment of debts. The list included the number of chickens, ducks, cows, pigs, dogs, and horses exempt from forced sale for payment of debt.

earmarked taxes
Tax money dedicated to a specific expenditure. Gasoline tax goes to highways.

✦ Amending and Revising State Constitutions

All state constitutions provide procedures for amending and revising the document. Except in the state of Delaware, there are two steps involved in changing constitutions: proposing amendments and citizen approval. In Texas two-thirds of each house of the legislature must propose amendments, and a majority of the voters who vote on the amendment must approve.

Some states provide a variety of methods for proposing or recommending changes to the constitution. All state constitutions allow the legislature to propose changes. Most states require an extraordinary majority vote of both houses of the legislature to propose an amendment. Only eleven states require only a majority, and most states require a two-thirds vote of the state legislature.[14]

A second method of proposing amendments to constitutions is by voter **initiative.** Initiative requires the collection of a prescribed number of signatures on a petition within a set time. Seventeen states allow initiative. Most states with initiative are western states that entered the Union in the late nineteenth century or early twentieth century when initiative was a popular idea. Only four states with initiative are east of the Mississippi River. Texas does not have initiative. The Texas Republican party pushed the idea of initiative for many years, but in 1996 it was dropped from the party platform.

initiative
A process that allows citizens to propose changes to the state constitution through the use of petitions signed by registered voters. Texas does not have these procedures at the state level.

Most states, including Texas, allow the legislature to submit to the voters the question of calling a **constitutional convention** to propose amendments. This method is normally used for general revision and not for single amendments. Fourteen states have some provision for automatically submitting the question of a general convention to the voters periodically. If the voters approve, a convention is elected, assembles, and proposes amendments for voter approval.

constitutional convention
An assembly of citizens who may propose changes to state constitutions for voter approval.

Constitutional commissions are most often created by acts of the legislature, although other methods are provided. These commissions usually submit a report to the legislature recommending changes. If the legislature approves, the proposed amendments are submitted to the voters. In Florida, the commission can bypass the legislature and go directly to the voters. Texas last used a commission in 1973 when the legislature created a thirty-seven-member commission.[15] This commission submitted recommendations to the Texas legislature, which acted as a constitutional convention.

Except for Delaware, where the state legislature can unilaterally amend the constitution, voters must approve amendments to the constitution in an election. Most states require a majority of those voting on the amendment to approve. Some states require a majority of the voters voting for some office (usually the governor) to approve. New Hampshire requires a two-thirds vote approval on all amendments. Texas requires that a majority of those voting on the amendment approve.

↪ PATTERNS OF CONSTITUTIONAL CHANGE

If we examine the amendment processes discussed previously, several patterns of state constitutional change can be observed. The first pattern involves the frequency of change. State constitutions are amended more frequently than the U.S. Constitution. One reason is that state constitutions deal with a wider range of functions. About 63 percent of the state amendments deal with issues not covered in the U.S. Constitution. A good example of this is education. Even if we remove issues not covered in the U.S. Constitution, the rate of amendment is still 3.5 times the national rate.[16] Change is also related to length. Longer state constitutions are more likely to be amended.[17]

The second pattern involves the method used to amend. As indicated, most amendments (90 percent) are proposed by state legislatures. States that require large legislative majorities for initiation have fewer amendments proposed and approved. Most amendments proposed by legislatures also receive voter approval. About 63 percent of all amendments proposed since 1970 have been approved by the voters.[18]

In the seventeen states that allow voters to initiate amendments, two patterns emerge: More amendments are proposed and the voter approval success rate for initiative-generated amendments is about half the rate for those proposed by state legislatures (32 percent versus 64 percent).[19] This tells us that the initiative process does not screen out amendments that lack broad public support. Proposal by legislature does. Amendments that gain support from super majorities are more likely to be politically acceptable. The legislature serves as a screening process to rule out unacceptable amendments.

↪ AMENDING THE TEXAS CONSTITUTION

All amendments to the Texas Constitution have been proposed by a two-thirds vote of each house of the legislature. From 1975 to 2007, the legislature has proposed 266 amendments for voter approval. Of these, the voters have approved 224 and rejected 42 (84 percent approved).[20]

Most amendments appear on the ballot in November of odd-numbered years when no statewide offices are up for election. Since 1960, the Texas legislature has proposed 355 amendments to the constitution. Of these, 274 were voted on in odd-numbered years and 97 were approved in even-numbered years. Voter turnout for odd-year elections is lower than for even-year elections. (See table 2.2.) In odd-year elections, less than 10 percent of the voting-age population participates.[21] This means that as few as 5 percent (plus one voter) could approve an amendment to the constitution. In 2005 there was a slight increase due to the anti–gay marriage amendment that was on the ballot.

Voter turnout rates are further complicated, statewide, by the fact that many city and school board elections are held in Harris County (Houston) on the same date. The Harris County vote could be significant if turnout statewide is very low. A strongly contested race for mayor of Houston could inflate the turnout rate in that city and affect statewide election results. The Harris County vote often constituted about 30 percent of the total statewide votes cast on these amendments.

ballot wording
Description of a proposed amendment as it appears on the ballot. Can be noninstructive and misleading to voters.

Ballot wording can also contribute to voter confusion and to voter support for amendments. The state legislature dictates the ballot wording of all amendments. Sometimes this wording can be misleading or noninstructive unless the voter has studied the issue before the election. This example from the 1978 election is illustrative:

> For or against the constitutional amendment providing for tax relief for residential homesteads, elderly persons, disabled persons, and agricultural land; for personal property exceptions; truth in taxation procedures, including citizen involvement; for a

TABLE 2.2

Voter Turnout in Odd-Year Constitutional Amendment Elections

Year	Percent of Voting-Age Population Voting
2007	8.49
2005	13.8 (Gay marriage amendment)
2003	9.30
2001	5.60
1999	6.69
1997	5.32
1997	8.45 (Special election)
1995	5.55
1993	8.25
1991	16.6 (School tax reform)
1989	9.33
1987	18.6 (School tax reform)
1985	8.24
1983	6.19
1981	8.07

Source: Texas Secretary of State (*www.sos.state.tx.us/elections/historical/70-92.shtml*).

redefinition [*sic*] of the tax base; for limitations on state spending; and for fair property tax administration.[22]

Most voters probably found this wording irresistible. Could any voter not favor tax exemptions for the elderly, the handicapped, homeowners, and farmers? Does any citizen oppose fair tax administration or citizen involvement? The amendment passed by an overwhelming majority. Another example of ballot wording bias occurred in an amendment exempting personal property in Texas ports—the "freeport" amendment, which failed in 1987. The ballot read: "rendering to the exemption from ad valorem taxation, certain tangible personal property temporarily located within the states." In 1989 the ballot read: "The constitutional amendment promoting economic growth, job creation and fair tax treatment for Texans who export goods." The amendment passed by a large majority. Ballot wording is apparently an important factor in the passage or rejection of amendments.

The number of amendments and the subject matter of most amendments are not of interest to most voters. For example, in 1993 the voters were asked to approve sixteen amendments to the constitution. The subjects of most of these amendments were financial: to authorize the issuance of bonds for economic development, pollution control, veterans' land, higher education, prisons, pensions, and agricultural development. In addition, one prohibited the establishment of an income tax without voter approval and one concerned delinquent taxes. Two separate amendments (Propositions 6 and 8) abolished the office of land surveyor in Jefferson and McLennan Counties, and another amendment (no. 15) allowed voters in any counties to abolish the office of land surveyor. One amendment cleared up Spanish land-grant titles in two counties. Another allowed the legislature to set qualifications for county sheriffs, and another allowed corporations additional means of raising capital. Except for the income tax prohibition, there was little in the amendments that was of interest to the average voter. This election is typical of most constitutional amendment elections. The trivial subject matter also contributes to low voter interest and turnout. People most affected by an amendment are likely to

HIGHLIGHT

Proposed New Constitution, Considered by Texas Legislature in 1999 Session

Summary of changes proposed by Senator Ratliff and Representative Junell in the 1999 session of the Texas legislature.

Article 1. Bill of Rights—No changes except for some minor spelling changes

Article 2. Powers of Government

Expressly reserves to the state all governmental power not denied by state or federal constitution

Article 3. Legislative Branch

Six-year staggered terms for senators; four-year staggered terms for house members

Term limits—members limited to nine regular sessions in house and nine regular sessions in senate, not including service before effective date of new constitution

Compensation to be set by appointed salary commission; lieutenant governor to get same salary as governor; speaker to get 90 percent of salary of governor; speaker prohibited from other full-time, salaried employment

Veto sessions—legislature may convene in special 15-day veto session to consider override of vetoes from previous regular or special session

Pre-session organizational assembly—legislature may meet to elect officers, adopt rules, and otherwise organize before convening in regular session

Legislative membership permitted on multi-member intergovernmental bodies that include executive officers

Legislators prohibited from representing clients before state agencies

Restrictions on eligibility of other officers for election to legislature eliminated

Article 4. Executive Branch

Creates governor's executive department, consisting of cabinet and other executive agencies not expressly made independent of governor; lieutenant governor, comptroller, and attorney general remain independent elective offices

Cabinet members appointed by governor with advice and consent of senate and serve at pleasure of governor; cabinet consists of departments of state, interior, public safety and criminal justice, health and human services, education, agriculture, economic development, energy, and transportation

Governor authorized to intervene in litigation in which state is a party

Governor authorized to reorganize executive branch by reassigning functions or consolidating or abolishing agencies, officers, and governing bodies, subject to legislative disapproval of plan

Power to grant pardons, reprieves, and commutations of sentence granted to governor

Compensation of constitutional executive officers set by salary commission

Existing state agencies remain in effect until altered by statute or by governor's reorganization plan; commissioners of agriculture and general land office continue as elected offices until current office holders do not run for reelection

Article 5. Judicial Branch

Supreme Court and Court of Criminal Appeals merged into single Supreme Court of 15 justices, with civil and criminal divisions of seven justices each and single chief justice

Current justices of both courts continue serving on new unified Supreme Court, subject to retention election at end of each term; governor appoints initial chief justice

Justices of Supreme Court and judges of appeals courts and district courts appointed by governor, subject to nonpartisan retention

---

understand it and to vote. Most voters stay home because there is little else to bring them out to the polls on election day.

Finally, voter ignorance of the issues is also a factor. Even though the issues are widely discussed in newspapers and brochures provided by the League of Women Voters, many people do not take advantage of this information.

Thus, odd-year elections, confusing or noninstructive ballot wording, issues that interest few voters, and voter ignorance all contribute to low voter turnout. A very small number of voters, stimulated by personal interests and supported by an active interest group, can amend the constitution without a majority of the voters becoming involved. Many voters are not even aware that an election is being held.

H I G H L I G H T (*c o n t i n u e d*)

election without opponent at end of each term; legislature authorized to establish nominating committees and to restrict governor's appointments to committee nominees

Article 6. Voter Qualifications and Elections

Unnecessarily detailed voter residence and registration provisions removed, left to governance by statute

Secret ballot required in all elections

Even-numbered year general election required

Article 7. Education

Defines school equity standard to current court standard (substantially equal access to similar revenues per pupil at similar tax rates), but allows 5 percent of the students to be enrolled in districts in which financial resources are not equalized

Clarifies authority of legislature to provide for establishing, financing, consolidating, and abolishing school districts and community college districts

Permanent university fund, available university fund, and related bonding authority restricted, for the purpose of developing limited number of world-class research universities, to the benefit of The University of Texas at Austin, Texas A&M University at College Station, and Prairie View A&M University

For all other universities, the current higher education assistance fund becomes the higher education capital fund, with annual contribution increased to $250 million

Article 8. Finance

Prohibits state ad valorem taxes except for support of free public schools

Authorizes legislature to grant ad valorem tax exemptions or other tax relief; maintains current constitutionally mandated ad valorem tax exemptions

Retains current prohibition against state personal income tax unless approved by voters; eliminates current dedication of income tax revenues to education and school tax reduction

Approximately twenty-five detailed provisions on specific bond issues (currently in Article 3) made unnecessary by single provision on voter approval of state debts; existing bonding authority and obligations on bonds are preserved unimpaired

Provides that all state money from any source, other than trust funds established by law, may be spent only as appropriated

Article 9. Local Government

General authority of legislature to provide for special purpose districts, allowing omission of numerous special provisions related to named districts

Required county officers subject to change approved by the voters of the county (as opposed to constitutional amendments on a county-by-county basis)

Population requirements for municipal home rule subject to legislation instead of constitutional standard of 5,000 inhabitants

All local government general obligation debt subject to voter approval

Article 10. General Provisions

Official oath of office collapsed to single, simple statement

Salary commission, appointed by the governor, is established to recommend compensation for elected and appointed executive and judicial officers and to set compensation for legislators

Marriage defined for purposes of community property to include only heterosexual marriage

Provisions on homestead equity loans simplified, left to statutory regulation

Limitations on length of terms of office eliminated

Several other observations can be made regarding the amendment processes in Texas. First, most amendments pass and face little opposition. Texans have approved 457 amendments and rejected 173.[23] Most are supported by an organized interest group willing to spend money, gain support, and get the amendment passed. Second, interest groups attempt to get their interests protected in the constitution. A vested interest, protected in the constitution, is more difficult to alter than one protected by state law alone. Rights that are protected only by state law can be changed easily in the next session of the legislature. The process of constitutional change requires a two-thirds vote of the legislature plus electoral approval. An old Texas saying goes, "Neither man nor property is safe as long as the legislature is in session."

Permanent University Fund (PUF)

An example of special interests being protected within the state constitution.

A good example of such a protection in the constitution is the **Permanent University Fund (PUF)**. The University of Texas and Texas A&M University are the only state schools benefiting from this fund, which has a value of approximately $10.333[24] billion. Other state universities have long felt that they deserved a share of this protected fund. Texas A&M and the University of Texas wanted to protect their funds and formed a coalition with non-PUF schools to support an amendment that created the Higher Education Assistance Fund (HEAF). This fund provides money to non-PUF universities. In the end, higher education funding for all state universities became protected in the state constitution.

✦ CONCLUSIONS ON THE TEXAS CONSTITUTION

Many legal scholars have pointed out the need for a general revision of the current Texas Constitution, which was written in 1876 and has been amended many times over the years. In the 1970s, a serious effort at total revision was unsuccessful. A commission of legal experts, acting as a constitutional commission, made recommendations to the state legislature for major changes. The state legislature, acting as a constitutional convention in 1974, deadlocked and adjourned without making any recommendations for change. The next regular session of the Texas legislature, in 1975, proposed eight separate amendments to the voters. In November 1975 the voters rejected all amendments by a two-to-one margin.

In 1999, two prominent members of the Texas legislature introduced a bill calling for general revision of the Texas Constitution. Then Senator Bill Ratliff, Republican from East Texas, and Representative Robert Junell, Democrat from San Angelo, were the chairs of budget-writing committees in the senate and house in that session. Ratliff served as lieutenant governor of the state from 2000 to 2003. Their bill called for some substantial changes in the current constitution. A summary of these proposed changes is noted in the Highlight box. This proposal reduces the size of the current constitution, which has 93,000 words contained in 376 sections, to some 19,000 words in 150 sections. This proposal died in committees in both houses.

Lt. Governor William Hobby addressing the constitutional convention, 1974.

The Texas house did create the House Select Committee on Constitutional Revision, chaired by Representative Joe Driver. This committee has held hearings in various locations in the state and made suggestions for changes that could be characterized as elimination of dead wood and updating of wording. The committee did not see the need for general revision of the document or the calling of a constitutional convention or commission.

The piecemeal process of amending the constitution every two years will likely continue. Several reasons are generally cited for this. First, there is a lack of support for reform by significant political forces in the state. Strong political leadership from someone like the governor would be necessary. Former governor George W. Bush did not indicate any interest in supporting the effort. Given his status and support in the state and nation, Bush could have led such an effort at general revision, and it would have been the hallmark of his tenure as governor. Obviously the temptation of becoming president of the United States was far more attractive. Supporting controversial issues such as revision of the constitution had little appeal or payoff. No other statewide leader currently has the status of former Governor Bush. Governor Perry, who owes his election to President Bush, lacks the status to lead such an effort. Supporting revision is not something Perry is likely to do, given the prospects of controversy and the small likelihood of political payoff.

Second, the political culture of the state and the basic conservative nature of state politics do not support broad-scale change. The current constitution supports the traditionalistic/individualistic political culture of the state. The document serves select groups of people and protects their interests and privileges, and these groups have the resources to maintain those protections. Senator Ratliff's and Rep. Junell's proposal in the 1999 legislature avoided many of the major controversies by leaving intact important interests that are well protected by the constitution; however, not all were protected.

Third, strong opposition from powerful lobby groups whose interests are currently protected by the document would make change difficult, if not impossible. In his opening address to the constitutional convention assembled in 1974, the vice chairman of the convention, Lt. Governor William Hobby, made the following observation:

> The special interests of today will be replaced by new and different special interests tomorrow, and any attempt to draft a constitution to serve such interests would be futile and also dishonorable.[25]

This convention adjourned without approving a new rewritten constitution to be submitted to the voters. The special interests in the state had prevailed. The entire effort was, to use Lt. Governor Hobby's words, "futile and also dishonorable."

Fourth, one could cite a general lack of interest and support for change among the citizens of the state. Constitutional revision is simply not a subject that excites the average citizen. The average Texan probably does not see the need for revision. Some proud Texans would take offense at the suggestion that the state document is flawed. The document drafted at the end of Reconstruction in the 1870s will probably continue to serve Texans for many years. The prospects for general revisions do not seem great. Evidence of this can be found in the 1999 election. In that year, the voters rejected three amendments that might be considered mildly progressive. Two of these amendments would have provided that the Adjutant General of the National Guard and the Commissioner of Health and Human Services were to serve at the pleasure of the governor. Another would have created a Judicial Compensation Commission. Their procedures are the standard in most state constitutions today.

✦ THE AMERICAN FEDERAL SYSTEM OF GOVERNMENT

Texas and the other forty-nine states operate within what is called a ***federal* system of government.** Broadly, this system provided for a sharing of powers between the national, called the federal, government and the fifty state governments. This system provides for a balancing of power and responsibilities between the national government and state governments. While the United States is not unique among nations for having a federal system, most nations of the world have what is called a ***unitary* form of government.**

Under a unitary government, power is centralized in a national government and regional and local governments operate within powers granted by the national government. For example, in England (United Kingdom) the central government, through Parliament, governs the nation. Regional governments are subservient to the national government. In the United States, state governments have some powers granted to them by the constitution, and they can act independently of the national government within those areas.

Under a ***confederate* system of government**, most of the power rests with the regional and local governments and the national government has only limited powers.

federal system of government
The division of powers between a national government and regional governments.

unitary form of government
A system of government where all functions of government are controlled by the central/national government.

confederate system of government
A system that divides power between a national government and regional governments with the regional governments having most of the power.

Under the Confederate States of America, the national government found it impossible to compel state governments to contribute troops or supplies to the war effort. This lack of authority hampered the war effort during the American Civil War. Each state acted independently of the others and the national government.

In many respects a federal system falls in between the unitary and confederate systems of government. Power is divided between the national or central government and between geographic units of government. In the U.S. system, these geographic units are called states, and in Canada they are called provinces. The national government has powers and duties in assigned areas, and the regional governments have powers in assigned areas. In some cases, these powers may overlap, such as with police functions, and in other areas both governments may possess these powers. For example, both the federal and state governments have the power to tax and spend money.

✦ CONSTITUTIONAL DISTRIBUTION OF POWERS

Table 2.3 shows how the U.S. Constitution distributes power between the national and state governments. Within the Constitution powers are both granted and denied. In some cases powers are granted exclusively to the national government and in other cases exclusively to the states. In other cases powers are granted to both the national and the state governments. The same can be said for those powers denied. Some are denied to the national government, others denied to the states, and some are denied to both.

TABLE 2.3

U.S. Constitutional Distribution of Powers

Powers Granted by the Constitution to National and State Governments

National Government Only	Both State and National Governments	State Governments Only
Conduct foreign relations	Levy taxes, borrow and spend money	Create local governments
Declare war	Create courts	Regulate intrastate commerce
Provide an army and navy	Make and enforce laws	Regulate health, safety, and welfare of citizens (police powers)
Coin money	Take private property for public purposes with just compensation	Regulate and conduct elections
Regulate interstate and foreign commerce		Ratify amendments to the national constitution
Establish federal courts		Exercise all powers not given to national government or prohibited to states (Tenth Amendment)
Make all laws necessary and proper to carry out foregoing powers (Elastic Clause)		

Powers Specifically Denied to Both National and State Governments

National Government Only	Both State and National Governments	State Governments Only
Change state boundaries	Grant titles of nobility	Tax imports or exports
Tax items exported from a state	Suspend habeas corpus	Make treaties or alliances
Violate rights granted in Bill of Rights	Deny citizens right to vote because of race or sex	Declare war
	Deny life, liberty, or property without due process of law	Violate federal laws
		Impair obligations of contracts
		Coin money

Note: There are other powers granted and denied to national and state governments. These are intended as examples and not as a complete list.

Key Developments in American Federalism

Table 2.3 presents an oversimplification of the division of powers between the national and state governments. In reality, it is much more complicated and the meaning of each power has been subject to interpretation by the federal courts. If we examine four areas of the Constitution and the courts' interpretations, we gain a much better understanding of the practice of American Federalism. These four areas are: necessary and proper vs. Tenth Amendment; Interstate Commerce Clause; Equal Protection and Due Process Clause of the Fourteenth Amendment; power to tax and spend to promote general welfare.

"Necessary and Proper" and the Tenth Amendment

Article 1, Section 8, paragraph 18 of the Constitution states that Congress shall have the power "To make all Laws which shall be necessary and proper for carrying into Execution the foregoing Powers, and all other Powers vested by this Constitution in the Government of the United States, or in any Department or Officer thereof." This seems to grant considerable power to the national government. However, the **Tenth Amendment** states; "The powers not delegated to the United States by the Constitution, nor prohibited by it to the States, are reserved to the States respectively, or to the people." This seems to grant additional powers to the states. The meanings of these two sections of the Constitution were to come into conflict early in the history of the Republic.

> **Tenth Amendment**
> Amendment of the Federal Constitution that delegates or reserves some powers to the state governments or to the people.

In 1790 Congress created a national bank under the advice of Alexander Hamilton, who was serving as Secretary of the Treasury. While Article 8 of the Constitution does not grant Congress the right to create a national bank, it does grant it the power to borrow money, regulate commerce, and coin money. Hamilton felt that one could imply that Congress has the power to establish a bank into which money borrowed and coined could be deposited and commerce regulated. Thomas Jefferson objected to the creation of a national bank, fearing it could lead to centralization of power in the central government. The argument basically came down to the meaning of *necessary* and *proper*. Jefferson felt "necessary" means "indispensable," whereas Hamilton felt "necessary" means any manner that is deemed appropriate by Congress.

In 1819 the question of the meaning of the **Necessary and Proper Clause** reached the Supreme Court in the case of *McCulloch v. Maryland* (4 Wheaton 316 [1819]). The state of Maryland decided to tax the national bank located in Baltimore, Maryland. The Court accepted the Hamilton interpretation of the clause, and Justice Marshall, writing for the Court, stated, "Let the end be legitimate, let it be within the scope of the Constitution, and all means which are appropriate, which are plainly adopted to that end, which are not prohibited but consistent with the letter and spirit of the Constitution are constitutional." This provides a very broad interpretation to the meaning of this clause, and it came to be called the "Elastic Clause" of the Constitution because it allowed Congress to decide the means to carry out ends, thus "stretching" its powers to meet its needs.

> **Necessary and Proper Clause**
> Statement in Article 1, Section 8, paragraph 18, that says Congress can pass any law necessary and proper to carry out other powers. Sometimes called the *Elastic Clause*.

In addition, the *McCulloch* case also contributed the ideas of national supremacy. The Maryland law, taxing the bank, was found to be in conflict with the federal law establishing the bank. Article 6 of the Constitution says that federal law shall be the "supreme Law of the Land." State laws in conflict with national law are thus unconstitutional, and federal law would prevail over state laws. Without this interpretation any state could choose to ignore national policy and go its own way. The supremacy clause provided for the creation of national policy to which states must comply.

Interstate Commerce Clause

Another troubling area, especially under the first U.S. Constitution, called the Articles of Confederation, was the question of interstate commerce. Under the Articles of

Confederation, any state could erect interstate trade barriers and tariffs on goods moving through the state. This proved chaotic and was a harm to the commerce of the new nation. Everyone realized the need for a national control of interstate commerce. The problem is defining what constitutes interstate commerce and distinguishing it from intrastate commerce, which states can control.

During the nineteenth century and most of the twentieth the Supreme Court placed a very narrow interpretation on interstate commerce and applied it only to goods that were transported across state lines, leaving most regulation of commerce to the states. In the 1930s, under the Great Depression, the courts came under fire for their narrow view; due to political pressure and changes in court membership, the meaning of interstate commerce came to be anything that had a substantial effect on national commerce. During the 1960s the **Interstate Commerce Clause** was used to prohibit hotels and restaurants from being segregated by race. In Georgia, a man named Lester Maddox owned one fried-chicken restaurant and refused to serve African Americans. He felt he was not engaged in interstate commerce since he owned only one facility in one state. The court interpretation was that the chickens he served were shipped across state lines and therefore he was engaged in interstate commerce. Later, Maddox was elected governor of Georgia based on his segregationist stand.

There are many areas of seeming contradiction when it comes to interstate commerce. Some industries are regulated and others are not. The conclusion is that interstate commerce is whatever the courts say it is.

Another question is, When can a state prohibit the shipment of goods into a state? For example, in the past many states prohibited cattle from Texas to be shipped into the state because they were often infected with a tick fever. In another case, California prohibited citrus fruit from being imported because of infected crops in other states. Texas once prohibited California oranges from coming into Texas because of a fruit fly infection. The issues in all such cases revolve around the legitimacy of the trade barrier. If the prohibition on the importation of an item is truly to protect health, morals, and safety and not a barrier imposed to restrict trade, it will be allowed. For example, if the reason for the barriers is to protect the health of cattle or oranges, then states may erect such barriers. The courts will decide when it is done for the legitimate purposes of protection and when it is a restraint on interstate trade.

Equal Protection and Due Process of Law Clause of the Fourteenth Amendment

The Constitution provides for the protection of civil liberties and individual rights. Initially, these applied only to the national government. For example, the First Amendment states, "Congress shall make no laws respecting an establishment of religion . . ." It says Congress—not Congress and the states. In the aftermath of the Civil War Congress passed and the states approved the Fourteenth Amendment. "No State shall make or enforce any law which shall abridge the privileges or immunities of citizens of the United States; nor shall any State deprive any person of life, liberty or property, without due process of law, or deny to any person within its jurisdiction the equal protection of the law." **The Equal Protection and Due Process of Law Clause** basically means that people must be treated equally and in accordance with established rules and procedures.

After World War I the federal courts gradually began to apply the basic rights provided in the Constitution to the states. There were three primary areas where states were required to provide protection for citizens: civil liberties, criminal proceedings, and election laws.

Civil liberties include such things as freedom of speech and religion. States may no longer require prayer in public schools or allow for segregated schools. Criminal

Interstate Commerce Clause
Article in U.S. Constitution that gives Congress the exclusive power to regulate commerce between the states. Congress and the courts determine what is interstate commerce.

Equal Protection and Due Process of Law Clause
Clause in the Fourteenth Amendment of the U.S. Constitution that requires states to treat all citizens equally.

procedures include such things as protection against self-incrimination (so-called Miranda warnings) and the right to legal council in criminal procedures. Election laws overturned restrictive voter registration laws and white primaries. States were also forced to apportion legislative districts equally. These issues are covered in more detail in later chapters.

This gradual expansion of basic rights expanded the role of the national government into areas that had traditionally been reserved to the states. While state power may have been reduced, individual rights and liberties were expanded. That is the balance provided by a federal system.

Power to Tax and Spend to Promote the General Welfare of Citizens

Article 1, Section 8, grants Congress the right to tax and spend to **promote general welfare.** The national government lacks the power to provide many basic services to citizens. Congress cannot, for example, operate schools and hospitals, build roads, or do many things state governments can. These are sometimes called intrastate police powers—protection of health, morals, and safety of citizens. These powers are reserved to the states. The national government has only interstate police powers; however, the national government may provide money to state and local governments to provide these basic services.

promote general welfare
Clause in the U.S. Constitution that allows Congress to provide money to state governments to carry out functions that are not part of the federal government's powers. An example would be education.

It is in this area that the national government has had great impact on state and local authority. Congress can provide money to state and local governments and set standards for how the money can be spent. Congress supplies money to state governments to build and maintain roads and highways. When states accept this money they must agree to some standard. Most college students are aware of these standards applied to highway funds. States must agree to set a drinking age of twenty-one years if they accept federal money.

At the time Congress passed this requirement most (thirty states) already had twenty-one years of age as the drinking age, four had twenty years, thirteen had nineteen years of age, and only three had eighteen years of age. However, many citizens felt that this was an unfair exercise of national authority and an intrusion into an area reserved to the states. Similar requirements applied to the 55-mile-per-hour speed limit in the 1970s, and some states originally refused to comply or underenforced the rule.

The attitude of many state and local officials is that the national government should send money and shut up. They feel that the rules are often burdensome, inflexible, and unnecessary. There are probably cases where this is true; however, the positive side of these requirements is that they have led to improved uniformity in standards. For example, if you drive on an interstate highway anywhere in the United States (including Hawaii) there is a uniformity of highway signs and rules. Also, national requirements have led to improvements in accounting standards. State and local governments that accept federal money must comply with generally accepted accounting principles (GAAPs).

Some writers make the argument that the national government has eroded state power through the use of federal grants. In some cases the argument advanced leads one to believe that the national government is some sort of uncontrollable Leviathan preying upon the poor defenseless states. Keep in mind that all members of Congress, who make the decisions of how much money state governments receive, are all elected from states. Congress is not an independent force but consists of officials elected from states. Those who criticize the role of the federal government in providing money to states should remember that all such programs are passed by a majority vote of Congress, with the approval of the president.

In reaction to the criticism of federal encroachments into state powers, Congress has moved from grants for specific, categorical purposes to grants that are much broader in scope, generally called block grants. This allows Congress to set general rules for how money can be spent and at the same time allows state and local officials to decide specific details of how the money will be spent. Over the past fifty years states have been given much more control over how federal money is spent.

The Evolution of American Federalism

The real strength of the American federal system is flexibility. The relationship between the national government and state governments has altered and changed with time and there is no reason to expect that this will not continue. Several different models are used to describe this changing relationship over the past 230 years.

During most of the nineteenth and early twentieth centuries a system called *dual federalism* operated. Under this model, there were rather specific areas of influence. The national government had primary delegated powers as defined in the Constitution and the state governments provided most basic services to citizens. There was little financial assistance from the national government to states. Some have compared this to a layer cake with clearly defined areas of influence. While this is called dual federalism, for much of the nineteenth century states were dominant. After the Civil War, the idea of states' rights over national power began to decline.

The second model used to describe federal–state relations is often called *cooperative federalism*. This relationship began in the 1930s with the Great Depression. The federal government began to supply more money to state and local governments to provide assistance to citizens. There was a cooperative relationship between the national and state governments to provide services to citizens.

During the 1960s some saw a changed relationship with what came to be called *creative federalism*. President Lyndon Johnson sought to create a Great Society through massive expenditure of money to end poverty and lift all citizens in society. Under President Nixon the system was referred to as *new federalism*. It involved giving state governments more discretion in program administration and so-called revenue sharing. President Reagan sought to give the states more power in spending grant money while at the same time reducing the amount of money available to state and local governments. Some viewed this as a return of both power and responsibilities to the states.

Under President Clinton, with emphasis from the Republicans in Congress, federal–state relations were called *devolution of power*. This basically means that states are given even greater authority on both program construction and administration.

Thus, in the area of expenditures of money, the evolution has been from one where the national government specified programs and provided money to support them to one where state and local governments are given greater power and authority to determine how federal programs are administrated in their states. While federal grants to states declined as a percent of federal expenditures during the Reagan administration, they grew under both Presidents Bush and Clinton. About 24 percent of state expenditures are from the federal government. In Chapter 10 we examine this in more detail.

Relations between States in the Federal System

Full Faith and Credit
Clause in Article 4 that requires states to recognize the laws and judicial acts of other states, such as marriage and divorce.

It is also important to understand the relations that exist between states and between states and individuals. Article 4, Section 1, of the Constitution states, "**Full Faith and Credit** shall be given in each state to the public Acts, Records and Judicial Proceedings of every other state." This basically means that if you are married in one state, your marriage must be recognized by the other states. If your last will and testament is probated in a Texas court, other states must recognize that court action.

This is an obvious requirement since without it chaos could reign. However, this is not as simple as it seems. There are two good examples in the last fifty years where this clause in the Constitution was tested. The first is divorce. In the 1950s it was difficult in most states to get a divorce. The state of Nevada was an exception. It would grant a divorce very easily. At first some states refused to accept what were often called "quickie divorce mill" decisions. Eventually, all states had to recognize these divorces. Second, in the 1980s some states refused to enforce child custody and support payments following divorce. There were cases where one parent in a divorce would move to another state and refuse to abide by the child custody/payment agreement. Eventually, federal courts forced all states to enforce these court decrees from other states.

Section 2 of Article 4 provides for what is called the **Privileges and Immunities of Citizenship.** This means that in some cases the state may treat its citizens differently than citizens of other states. There are many examples where this happens. One area is out-of-state tuition. Differential rates can be charged for citizens of Texas and citizens of other states. This also applies to driver's licenses, hunting licenses, law licenses, and professional licenses.

Basically, Article 4, Section 1, says there are some areas where a state must treat citizens of other states the same as they treat their own citizens, and Section 2 says there are other areas where residents and nonresidents can be treated differently.

Privileges and Immunities of Citizenship
Clause in Article 4 that allows states to treat residents and non-residents differently. An example is out-of-state tuition.

The Enduring Nature of American Federalism

As was pointed out earlier, one of the real strengths of the American federal system is its flexibility and ability to change with the times. This is obvious if you examine the national Constitution and observe how little the document has been altered in the last 200 years. The document has been amended only twenty-seven times. (See table 2.1.) Also, most amendments concern civil liberties, and only a few have been structural in nature. Table 2.4 details the subject matter of amendments to the national Constitution.

TABLE 2.4

Amendments to the Federal Constitution

Civil Liberties and Voting Rights		Structural Amendments	
Number	Subject Matter	Number	Subject Matter
1–8	Various civil liberties	10	Reserved powers
9	Other liberties that may exist	11	Sovereign immunity
13	End to slavery	12	Electoral College voting
14	Equal protection, due process of law	20	When the president takes office—lame duck amendment
15	Race and voting	22	Two terms for president
16	Income tax	25	Presidential disability
17	Direct election of senators	27	Congressional pay
19	Women's right to vote		
23	D.C. vote for president		
24	End poll tax as requirement for voting		
26	18-year-old right to vote		
18 & 21	Prohibition and repeal of prohibition on sale of alcohol		

Few of the structural amendments have altered federal–state relations. The Tenth and Eleventh Amendments are often pointed to as examples. The Sixteenth Amendment gave the national government great financial resources and led to greater national influence over state spending decisions and policies.

Many of the civil and voting rights amendments have had a greater impact on federal–state relations. The Fourteenth Amendment applied many of the first eight amendments to the states. Many of the other amendments were aimed at ending violations of civil and voting rights practiced by the states (e.g., women's right to vote, poll tax).

The overall point is that the American federal system has lasted for over 200 years with few changes. Admittedly some changes were profound; however, most changes are evolutional in nature and are not major structural changes. American federalism is a flexible system that will allow for change to meet future needs and challenges.

INTERNET RESOURCES

Secretary of State's Office: *www.sos.state.tx.us/*
A copy of the Texas Constitution can be found on this page, as well as votes in all elections and recent votes on constitutional amendments.
Center for State Constitutional Studies: *www-camlaw.rutgers.edu/statecon/*
General information on state constitutional revisions among the states.

There are a number of state organizations that favor constitutional revision in Texas.
Web site for the State Bar of Texas *www.texasbar.com,* and the League of Women Voters *www.lwv.org.*

KEY TERMS

ballot wording (p. 28)
bill of rights (p. 22)
confederate system of government (p. 33)
constitutional convention (p. 27)
constitutions are a contract (p. 21)
constitutions are a limitation on the power of government (p. 21)
earmarked taxes (p. 27)
Equal Protection and Due Process of Law Clause (p. 36)

federal system of government (p. 33)
Full Faith and Credit (p. 38)
initiative (p. 27)
Interstate Commerce Clause (p. 36)
Necessary and Proper Clause (p. 35)
Permanent University Fund (PUF) (p. 32)
political culture drives institutions (p. 21)

popular sovereignty (p. 21)
Privileges and Immunities of Citizenship (p. 39)
promote general welfare (p. 37)
separation of powers (p. 22)
supremacy clause (p. 23)
Tenth Amendment (p. 35)
Texas Constitution (p. 17)
unitary form of government (p. 33)

NOTES

1. Fehrendbach, *Lone Star,* 146–47.
2. Ibid., 206.
3. Ibid., 222–23.
4. Ibid., 411–14.
5. Ibid., 434–35.
6. Ibid., 436.
7. Ibid.
8. Donald S. Lutz, "Toward a Theory of Constitutional Amendment," *American Political Science Review* 88 (June 1994): 355–70.
9. *Texas Constitution,* art. 1, sec. 3a.
10. Lutz, "Toward a Theory," 359.
11. Ibid.
12. Ibid.

13. *Book of the States 2003* (Lexington, Ky.: Council of State Governments, 2003), Vol. 35, Table 1.1, p. 10.

14. Lutz, "Toward a Theory."

15. *Texas Constitution,* art. 117, sec. 2.

16. Lutz, "Toward a Theory," 359.

17. Ibid.

18. Ibid., 360.

19. Ibid.

20. These figures are as of the general election in November 2007.

21. Number of amendments and dates of elections from Secretary of State, *Vote on Proposed Amendments to Texas Constitution, 1875–November 1993* (Austin: State of Texas, 1993), 12–29. Data 1995–2003. Secretary of State Web page *www.sos.state.tx.us*

22. Constitutional amendments ballot general election, 7 November 1978, tax relief amendment, H.J.R. 1.

23. *Book of the States 2005* (Lexington, Ky.: Council of State Governments, 2003), Vol. 37, table 1.1, p. 10.

24. www.utimco.org/Funds/Endowment/PUF/puffaq.pdf

25. *Houston Chronicle,* 8 January 1974.

PARTICIPATION IN TEXAS POLITICS

Aristotle, an early Greek philosopher, said that we are political animals. By this Aristotle meant that we are, by our very nature, predisposed to participate in politics. Some would say that Aristotle was an optimist. Most U.S. citizens do not choose to participate in state politics. Before discussing the reasons for this, let us review what opportunities are available for participation.

✦ POLITICAL PARTICIPATION

political participation
All forms of involvement citizens can have that are related to governance.

The term **political participation** refers to taking part in activities that are related to governance. Table 3.1 lists some of these activities and the percentages of people who participate in them. As can be seen from the table, most people do not take an active part in politics, even in national elections. Voting at the national level is lower than in most other industrialized nations. Participation in state politics is lower than at the national level and still lower at the local levels. Texas ranks below all but a few states in voter participation in both national and state elections. (See table 3.2.)

Besides thinking about participation as involvement in specific activities, one can also think about participation in terms of levels and kinds of activities. Sidney Verba and Norman H. Nie, in their book *Participation in America,*[1] divide the population into several groups based upon the level and kind of political activities they participate in (see figure 3.1):

Inactives, who take no part in politics
Voting specialists, who confine their efforts to voting in elections
Parochial participants, who become active in politics when the issue has a direct effect on them

TABLE 3.1

Political Participation by American Citizens

Run for public office	<1%
Become active in political parties and campaigns	4–5%
Contribute money to campaigns	10%
Wear a button or display a bumper sticker	15%
Write or call a public official	17–20%
Belong to a political organization	30–33%
Talk to others about politics	30–35%
Do not participate	30–45%
Vote	30–55%

Note: The data in this table are average levels of participation over several years. For example, on the activity "Vote," this is a composite for voting in several elections.

Source: Survey Research Center, Inter-University Consortium for Political Research, *Federal Election Studies* (1952–2000) (Ann Arbor: University of Michigan).

TABLE 3.2

Texas Rank as a Percentage of Voting-Age Population Voting in National Elections, 1976 to 2006

Year	Texas Rank*	National Turnout[†]	Texas Turnout[‡]
Presidential Election Years			
1976	44	53	47
1980	44	52	44
1984	45	53	47
1988	46	50	45
1992	46	55	49
1996	47	52	41
2000	47	50	43
2004	47	58.3	46.1
Congressional/Statewide Office Elections			
1978	46	35	24
1982	46	38	26
1986	45	33	25
1990	42	33	27
1994	45	36	31
1998	47	38	24
2002	46	38	26
2006	49	41.8	26.4

*Texas ranking compared to the 49 other states.

[†]Average turnout for all 50 states as a percentage of voting-age population voting in the election.

[‡]Percentage of voting-age population voting in Texas elections.

Sources: Statistical Abstracts of the United States, 1976, 1978, 1980, 1982, 1984, 1985, 1991, 1993, 1995, 1998, 2004, and 2006 (Washington, D.C.: U.S. Government Printing Office).

Voters cast ballots in primary election.

voter turnout
The percentage of the voting-age population that votes.

registered voters
Citizens who have formally gone through the process of getting their names on the voter registration list.

voting-age population
All citizens who meet the formal requirements to register to vote. In Texas you must be eighteen years of age and a resident of the state for thirty days before the election.

Campaigners, who like the activity and the controversial and competitive nature of political campaigns

Communalists, who, while being active voters, avoid the combat and controversy of partisan campaigns and are attracted to other kinds of nonpartisan, noncontroversial community activity

Complete activists, who get involved in all levels and kinds of activity, including voting, campaigning, lobbying officials, and participating in community affairs

The Verba and Nie portrait of the American population helps us order our thinking about both the types of participation and the intensity of involvement that citizens can assume in the political process.

→ Voter Turnout in Texas

There are two ways **voter turnout** can be expressed. One measure is the percentage of **registered voters** voting. A second measure, the one most often used by political scientists, is the percentage of the voting-age population voting. (See figure 3.2.) **Voting-age population** is defined as those eligible to vote—persons who are at least eighteen years of age and citizens of the United States. Voting-age population is the preferred measure because it discounts variations in state voting requirements and elections among the states that might affect voter turnout.

For example, North Dakota has no voter registration list. Voters show up on election day and prove they live in the voting precinct and they are allowed to vote. Seven other states allow same-day voter registration (Idaho, New Hampshire, Maine, Minnesota, Wisconsin, Wyoming, and Hawaii). These differences make it difficult to compare registered voters' turnout. For example, North Dakota would always have 100 percent of the registered voters voting.

Others point out that the VAP is distorted by large numbers of noncitizens living in the state and does not take into account those citizens who have lost their right to vote because of criminal records. Obviously, both measures have their shortcomings.

Most, but not all, states make it very easy to register to vote. Some states have no prior voter registration, allowing "same-day" registration. Voting-age population is the best measure because it compares all states on the same basis.

The secretary of state of Texas often releases figures expressed as a percentage of registered voters voting. These figures are always much higher than figures that show the percentage of voting-age population voting. (See table 3.3.) Even though Texas makes it very easy to register to vote, Texans are not big voters. As can be seen in table 3.2, Texas ranks very low among all states in terms of voter turnout. During elections held in November of odd-numbered years, voting levels decline even more, often below 10 percent of the voting-age population. In March party primary elections, participation might fall below 10 percent. In local elections for city council and school board, which are most frequently held in May, voting can decline to below 5 percent of the voting-age population.

→ Explaining Voter Turnout

How can we explain the low levels of voting among Texans? Many factors are involved. The political culture discourages participation; there is a legacy of restricted access to the ballot for many groups; and other social, economic, and political factors play a role.

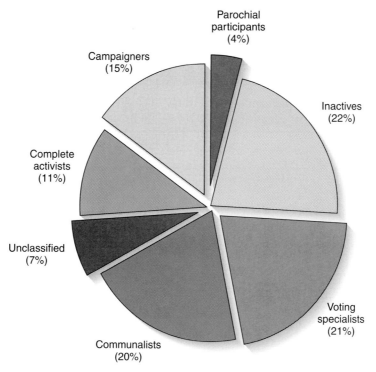

FIGURE 3.1 *Types of Political Activists, according to Verba and Nie.*

SOURCE: Sidney Verba and Norman Nie, *Participation in America* (Chicago: University of Chicago Press, 1987), 79.

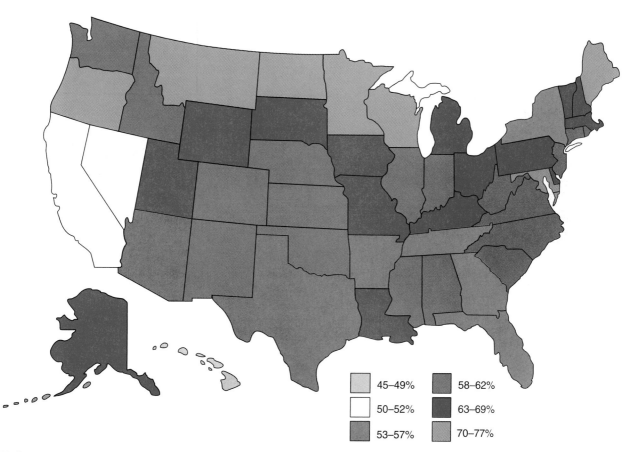

FIGURE 3.2 *Percentage of Eligible Voters Voting in 2004 Presidential Election.*

TABLE 3.3

Comparison of Percentage of Registered and Eligible Voters Voting in Texas Elections from 1970–2002

Year	Percent Registered Who Voted	Percent Voting-Age Population Who Voted
Congressional Election Years		
1970	53.9	31.1
1974	30.9	20.0
1978	41.7	25.2
1982	49.7	30.0
1986	47.2	29.0
1990	50.5	31.0
1994	50.8	33.6
1998	32.4	26.5
2002	34.2	36.7
2006	33.6	26.4
Presidential Election Years		
1972	89.6	44.8
1976	64.8	46.0
1980	68.4	45.5
1984	68.3	47.5
1988	66.2	44.3
1992	72.9	47.6
1996	53.2	40.9
2000	51.8	43.3
2004	56.8	46.1

Source: Texas Secretary of States (*www.sos.state.tx.us/elections/historical/1970–2006.shtml*). Go to election division.

Legal Restrictions Today

Like other southern states, Texas has a history of restrictive voter registration laws. In the past these laws made it difficult to qualify to vote and limited avenues of political participation. Due largely to actions by the federal government, most legal restrictions to voter registration have been removed. Recently Congress passed a bill that allows persons to register to vote when they renew their driver's license. This is called the Motor Voter Registration. Texas now has this in place.

Restrictions to registration vary greatly among the states. Eight states have allowed **same-day voter registration:** Idaho, Hawaii, Maine, Minnesota, New Hampshire, North Dakota, Wisconsin, and Wyoming. Maine, Minnesota, and New Hampshire have moralistic political cultures, and Minnesota has an individualistic/moralistic political culture. The moralistic political culture encourages voter involvement and participation. An example of how same-day voter registration may help outsider candidates is that Jesse Ventura won the governor race in Minnesota in 1998 in large part because of this provision in state law. Most of the 600,000 same-day voter registrants voted for Ventura. He won with 37 percent of the same-day registrants vote. In the other states a voter must register before election day. The time varies from ten to thirty days before the elections.

Texas now allows anyone eighteen years of age to vote if they have registered at least thirty days before an election. Texas and forty other states also allow registration by mail

same-day voter registration
Voters are allowed to register on election day. No preregistration before the election is required.

ORIGINAL   CERTIFICATE OF EXEMPTION FROM POLL TAX

STATE OF TEXAS, COUNTY OF WICHITA

1962

and through January 1963

This 1961 exemption certificate to be used in

PRECINCT NO ___24___ Date ___4 - 19___ 196_2_ **N°** **6732**

MR ___John Smith___

	YEARS
Age--------------	20
Resided in State _ _ _	20
Resided in County_ _.	10
Resided in City_ _ _ _	10

Address ___2609 Laurence___

Will be or ~~was~~ ___21___ years old on the _4_ day of ___June___ 196_2_ Male ~~Female~~ White ~~Colored~~

Occupation _____ Native born _____ Naturalized _____

Was born in ___Texas___ Reason for Exemption ___Minor___

I, the undersigned authority, do hereby certify that the within named party personally appeared before me, and being duly sworn, says that the above is correct and that ___he___ is a qualified voter under the constitution and laws of Texas.

By ___McCard___ , Deputy

Party Affiliation ___Democratic Party___

BILL CARNES
Assessor and Collector of Taxes, Wichita Co., Tex.

for all citizens. The other eight states restrict mail registration to citizens in the military, students living out of state, and persons in nursing homes.[2] North Dakota has no voter registration.

The Legacy of Restricted Ballot Access in Texas

It is very easy to register and vote in Texas today, but this has not always been the case. The state's history of restricting access to voting is very much in keeping with its traditionalistic political culture. Although the past restrictions have been removed from law, they still have an effect today. Political behavior does not change quickly. The following are a few examples of the many restrictions common in southern political cultures.

In 1902 the Texas legislature adopted, with voter approval, the payment of a **poll tax** as a requirement for voting. This law was aimed primarily at the Populist movement, which had organized low-income white farmers into a political coalition that threatened the establishment within the Democratic party.[3] This tax ($1.75) was a large amount of money for poor farmers in their predominantly barter economy in the early 1900s.* The poll tax also restricted ballot access of African Americans, as well as Hispanics, who were disproportionately poor; there were also other barriers to their voting, which are discussed later.

The poll tax had to be paid each year between 1 October and 31 January before a person could vote in the primary election, which was not held until September, nine months later. The poll tax was in effect in Texas for about sixty years. In 1964 the poll tax was eliminated as a requirement for voting in federal elections by the passage of the Twenty-fourth Amendment to the U.S. Constitution; however, Texas kept the poll tax as a requirement for voting in state elections.[4] In 1966 the poll tax as a requirement for voting was abolished by a decision of the U.S. Supreme Court.[5]

poll tax
Citizens were required to pay a tax each year between November and January to be eligible to vote the following November. Used from 1902 until 1972 in Texas.

---

*The state tax was $1.50. County could add 25 cents, and most county governments did. See Article 7, Section 3, of the Texas Constitution, 1902.

H I G H L I G H T

The Jaybird Democratic Association in Fort Bend County, Texas

There was an attempt in Texas to get around the U.S. Supreme Court's 1944 ruling that political parties were not private organizations or clubs. In Fort Bend County an organization known as the Jaybird Democratic Association conducted unofficial preprimary primary elections several weeks before the regular primary and nominated candidates.

The nominees from the "Jaybird Primary" were then placed on the regular Democratic party primary ballot and eventually on the general election ballot, generally without opposition. This organization contended that their actions did not violate the court decisions since they were a "voluntary club" and not a political party. In 1953, the U.S. Supreme Court, based on an appeal from a local group of African Americans, ruled the preprimary primary illegal and stopped the practice (*John Terry et al., Petitioners v. A.J. Adams et al.,* 345 U.S. 461).

The poll tax had the intended effect of reducing qualified voters. In 1964–65, 2.4 million Texans paid the tax. In 1968, the first election cycle after the poll tax was abolished, voter registration rose to over 4 million, an increase of about 41 percent.[6]

Even after the 1966 elimination of the poll tax as a voter requirement, Texas retained a very restrictive system of voter registration. Its annual registration system required voters to register between 1 October and 31 January each year. Registration had to be done at the courthouse, as had been required with the poll tax. In most counties, even today, the county tax collector is the voter registrar. For minorities, the trip to the courthouse could be an intimidating experience, and many would avoid it.

annual registration
A system that requires citizens to reregister every year.

Following a court decision in 1971 that prohibited **annual registration** systems,[7] the Texas legislature passed a very progressive voter registration law that eliminated annual registrations. The new law put in place a permanent registration system. Registration is open until thirty days before any election. Citizens may mail in a postage-paid voter registration form, saving a trip to the courthouse. Voters receive a new voter registration card every year; the Post Office is instructed not to forward it. If the card cannot be delivered to the addressee at the address on the card, it is returned to the voter registrar and the voter's name is removed from the list. Voters must reregister at their new address.

permanent registration
A system that keeps citizens on the voter registration list if they continue to vote at prescribed intervals.

In 1972, the first year that Texas used a **permanent registration** system, voter registration increased by almost 1.4 million.[8] Easy voter registration procedures increase the number of registered voters. All states now use some form of permanent registration.[9]

white primary
Party primary that excluded African Americans from participating in the Democratic party primary from 1923 to 1945.

Another past practice used by many southern states, including Texas, to eliminate participation by African Americans was the **white primary.** Beginning in 1923 and continuing until 1945, the Texas legislature passed bills prohibiting African Americans from participating in the Democratic party primary election. The U.S. Supreme Court declared these legislative acts unconstitutional.[10] In 1932, the state Democratic party passed rules that prohibited African Americans from participating in any activity of the party, including voting in the Democratic party primary. This action led to another U.S. Supreme Court ruling.[11] The issue before the court was whether or not a political party was an agent of government or a private organization. The Supreme Court ruled in 1935 that political parties were private organizations and could decide who could participate in primary elections. This effectively prevented African Americans from participating in the Democratic party primary. Because there was no opposition by Republicans at this time in the general election, the primary became the "general election." Thus, from 1932 until 1945, African Americans in Texas were denied the right to vote by the rules of the Democratic party and not by state law.

In 1944 the U.S. Supreme Court outlawed all white primaries in southern states in the case *Smith v. Allwright*.[12] This ruling overturned earlier rulings that political parties were private organizations. The Supreme Court ruled that political parties were agents of the state and could not exclude people from participating in primary elections because of race.

Thus, federal court actions finally ended the practice of the white primary after it had been used for two decades to deny the vote to African Americans. It was not until the end of World War II that African Americans in Texas were allowed to vote in the Democratic party primary election. Before that, African Americans had effectively been disenfranchised since there was no opposition from Republicans.

Property ownership was also used to restrict the right of people to vote in Texas, as was common in many states. These restrictions mostly applied to local elections, especially bond elections. The reason for restricting voting by property ownership was that local governments are financed primarily with property taxes, and supposedly renters did not pay property tax. However, renters might pay property tax, because landlords, when market conditions are favorable to them, do shift property taxes to renters as higher rents. Property ownership requirements were eliminated in the 1970s when permanent registration became effective in Texas. There was no way to effectively enforce the property ownership requirement.

Women's access to voting was also restricted in Texas until 1920, when the Nineteenth Amendment to the U.S. Constitution was approved. By 1914 eleven states had granted women the right to vote.[13] In 1915 the Texas legislature considered granting women the right to vote but the measure failed. However, in 1918 women were given the right to participate in primary elections, and in 1919 Texas became the first southern state to approve the Nineteenth Amendment.[14] Texas was not a leader in granting women the right to vote.

The history of Texas shows a definite pattern of limiting political participation to a few—primarily white men of means. This pattern is clearly in keeping with the traditionalistic political culture of the state. The poll tax restricted access for the poor (including poor white men), women did not get the vote until the 1920s, and African Americans were prevented from voting in state elections until the late 1940s. Property ownership limited voting at the local level until the 1970s. Annual registrations held long before the elections also restricted access to voting in elections until the 1970s. Intervention by the federal government forced Texas to eliminate these restrictive practices.

All these restrictions combined to produce the state's tradition of discouraging participation. The elimination of these restrictions and the present day's easy access to voter registration have increased the number of registered voters in Texas; however, this has not translated into significant increases in the level of participation. As we saw in table 3.2, Texas today still ranks near the bottom on voter turnout in elections. In time, the residual effect of restrictive practices may decline; given additional factors, participation levels might rise.[15]

The increasing presence of minority candidates in elections is also a factor in increasing voter participation by minorities. In the 2002 election the Democratic candidates for governor and U.S. senator were minorities; this was a factor in increasing turnout by African Americans and Hispanics.

Social and Economic Factors

Variation in participation is also strongly affected by **socioeconomic factors,** such as educational level, family income, and minority status. The high-income, well-educated are more likely to vote than are lower-income, less-well-educated. People of higher

socioeconomic factors
Factors, such as income, education, race, and ethnicity, that affect voter turnout.

socioeconomic status are likely to be more aware of elections and to perceive themselves as having a higher stake in the outcomes of elections; therefore they are more likely to vote. They are also more likely to contribute financially to political campaigns and become actively involved in elections and party activity.

Age is another factor. Young voters are less likely to vote and become involved in politics. They often have other interests, and most do not perceive themselves as having an important stake in political outcomes.

Race is also a factor in voter turnout. African Americans and Hispanics vote less than whites. Large minority populations in Texas may help explain the lower levels of voter participation among Texans, compared to other states. Voting by Hispanics is lower for a variety of reasons. Hispanics are disproportionately younger than Anglos in Texas, and many are not citizens. One estimate is that Hispanics made up about 11 percent of Texas voters in 1992.[16] Another estimate, made in 1996, placed the percentage at 19.3 percent of the voting-age population.[17] In 1998 Governor Bush received about 40 percent of the Hispanic vote and about 20 percent of the African American vote; however, voter turnout in 1998 was the lowest in twenty years. (See table 3.3.) Much of this vote was due to the personal appeal of Governor Bush. In addition, when voter turnout is lower, the high-income voters participate more than low-income voters do. High-income voters, regardless of ethnic background, tend to favor Republicans. The 1998 vote did not represent a shift in minority votes to the Republican party. There is no evidence that Hispanic voters shifted to Bush in the 2000 presidential election. More will be stated on this in chapter 5.

African Americans made up 11.4 percent of the Texas population in 2007. No estimates are available on the percentage of the African American population voting. As with Hispanics, voter turnout among African Americans is lower in part because of lower-income and educational levels and because of a high percentage of young people in these population groups.[18] See table 1.1 for population estimates for minorities in Texas.

Felony Conviction and Voting

Texas is one of fourteen states that prohibit persons convicted for a felony from voting. However in Texas, after finishing all the sentence and probation, a person may register to vote. According to U.S. Election Project, there are 482,216 adults (28.4 percent of the adult population) in Texas who could not vote.[19] This is twice the national average, and 20 percent were African Americans.

Party Competition

States can be ranked based on interparty competition. (See Chapter 5, table 5.3, for the relative strength of the parties over the years.) Although party competition in Texas has increased in recent years, the state has a long history of being a one-party state. Studies have shown that party competition is an important factor in voter turnout. In states where there are two strong competitive political parties, voter turnout is much higher. Competition increases voter interest in the election due to campaign activities and because of a perception by voters that their vote counts.

party competition
The principle that states with two active and competitive parties have higher voter turnout than states, like Texas, with weak or noncompetitive parties.

The lack of **party competition** in Texas for over 100 years partially accounts for the state's lower voter turnout. Party competition also increases grassroots political organizations that stimulate participation and turn people out to vote.[20] Texans elected Republicans to all statewide office in 2002, 2004, and 2006. It remains to be seen if this domination of state politics will be permanent.

Regional Variations

Region is also a factor in voter turnout. In fact, some writers have suggested that region is the most reliable factor in predicting voter turnout. This is supported by an examination of voter turnout in the states of the Old South, where voter participation is the lowest. Region alone, however, does not explain individual voting behavior. The states of the Old South have a history of repressed voting activity for the reasons discussed earlier— the poll tax, white primaries, annual registrations, and lack of party competition. Also, income and educational levels in this region have historically been lower than in the rest of the country. These factors combined with traditionalistic/individualistic political cultures historically reduced political participation.

In recent years voter turnout in southern states has increased,[21] in part due to the elimination of many of the past restrictions. Income and educational levels have also increased, as has immigration from other regions of the country by people from other political cultures.

Other Factors Affecting Voter Turnout

A few other things can affect voter turnout in some elections. One factor is the time of the election. Voter turnout is higher in November general elections than in odd-year elections when we do not elect a president or other state-wide or national offices. Turnout for primary elections is lower still than for general elections. Also, local elections for city councils and school boards are generally not held in conjunction with general elections; the common time for these in Texas is in May. Turnout in local elections is always lower than in other elections. There are several reasons for this: These elections are less visible and receive less attention by the media; voters do not perceive these elections as being important; and many of these races are not contested. In 1995 the Texas legislature changed state law to allow cities and school boards to cancel elections if all races are uncontested. The governing body certifies the uncontested candidates as "winners." Chapter 11 has more information on local elections.

Voters participating in an election.

The day of the week can also affect voter turnout. Tuesday is the most common day for elections in the United States. Local city and school board elections are often held on Saturday. Saturday might seem a better day than Tuesday, because many people are off work and have time to vote. However, Saturday is also a day to do other things, and people might forget to vote or might choose to use the day for recreation.

Also, in the United States, elections are held on a single day, with the polls typically being open for twelve hours. Many European countries hold elections over an entire weekend. Longer election periods might increase voter turnout.

✦ Conclusions

Political participation is affected by many factors. Some states, mostly southern and including Texas, have a legacy of restricted access to the ballot and discouraging voter participation. Even with the removal of these restrictions, participation does not immediately increase. It can take generations to change political behavior. Social and economic factors also play a role in participation. Race and ethnicity affect turnout and help explain lower turnouts in Texas. The lack of party competition also played a role in reducing voter turnout in Texas. With increased party competition, this may change. All these factors, combined with the individualistic/traditionalistic political culture of Texas, help explain the low levels of participation in the political processes of the Lone Star State.

Internet Resources

Secretary of State: *www.sos.state.tx.us/*
This Web site has information on elections going back for twenty years. Both primary and general election data are available.

For information on elections from 1789 to 2000, see *nationalatlas.gov/printable.html.*
Maps on the popular and Electoral College vote by state are available. Good resource.

The League of Women Voters has useful information on voter turnout: *www.lwv.org*
It also has links to other useful Web pages.

Key Terms

annual registration (p. 48)
party competition (p. 50)
permanent registration (p. 48)
political participation (p. 42)

poll tax (p. 47)
registered voters (p. 44)
same-day voter registration (p. 46)
socioeconomic factors (p. 49)

voter turnout (p. 44)
voting-age population (p. 44)
white primary (p. 48)

Notes

1. Sidney Verba and Norman H. Nie, *Participation in America* (Chicago: University of Chicago Press, 1987).
2. *Book of the States* (Lexington, Ky.: Council of State Governments, 2007), 293–94, table 6.6.
3. Calvert and DeLeon, *History of Texas,* 212.
4. Ibid., 387.
5. *United States v. Texas,* 384 U.S. 155 (1966).
6. *Texas Almanac and State Industrial Guide, 1970–1971* (Dallas: A.H. Belo, 1969), 529.
7. *Beare v. Smith,* 321 F. Supp. 1100.
8. *Texas Almanac and State Industrial Guide, 1974–1975* (Dallas: A.H. Belo, 1973), 529.
9. *Book of the States,* 30:23, 5.6.

10. *Nixon v. Herndon et al.,* 273 U.S. 536 (1927);
    Nixon v. Condon et al., 286 U.S. 73 (1932).

11. *Grovey v. Townsend,* 295 U.S. 45 (1935).

12. *Smith v. Allwright,* 321 U.S. 649 (1944). Also, in
    United States v. Classic, 313 U.S. 299 (1941), the U.S.
    Supreme Court ruled that a primary in a one-party
    state (Louisiana) was an election within the
    meaning of the U.S. Constitution.

13. George McKenna, *The Drama of Democracy:
    American Government and Politics,* 2d ed. (Guilford,
    Conn.: Dushkin, 1994), 129.

14. Wilbourn E. Benton, *Texas Politics: Constraints
    and Opportunities,* 5th ed. (Chicago: Nelson-Hall,
    1984), 65.

15. Steven J. Rosentone and Raymond E. Wolfinger,
    "The Effect of Registration Laws on Voter Turnout,"
    American Political Science Review 72 (March 1978):
    22–45.

16. Population Estimates and Projections Program,
    Texas State Data Center, Department of Rural
    Sociology, Texas A&M University System, *Projections
    of the Population of Texas and Counties in Texas
    by Age, Sex, Race/Ethnicity for 1990 to 2030,*
    February 1994.

17. Robert R. Brischetto, unpublished report, Southwest
    Voter Research Institute, San Antonio, 1993.
    Estimate for 1996, Southwest Voter Research
    Institute, *Southwest Voter Research Notes.* Vol. X,
    no. 1, p. 3.

18. C. Richard Hoffstedder, "Inter-Party Competition
    and Electoral Turnout: The Case of Indiana,"
    American Journal of Political Science 17 (May 1973):
    351–66.

19. www.elections.gmu.edu/Voter_Turnout_2006.htm

20. Norman R. Luttbeg, "Differential Voting Turnout
    Decline in the American States," *Social Science
    Quarterly* 65 (March 1984): 60–73.

21. Ibid.

CHAPTER 4

❦

INTEREST GROUPS
IN TEXAS POLITICS

As we saw in Chapter 3, voter participation in Texas is extremely low. This lack of citizen involvement in elections increases the importance and influence of interest groups in Texas politics. Being an active member of an interest group is another form of political participation and a way to increase one's influence on government. Early observers of American politics realized the importance of these political associations. In 1787, James Madison, writing under the name Publius in *Federalist No. 10,* pointed out that interest groups or factions would play a significant role in American politics. Madison felt that the diversity of economic and social interests would be so great, and so many factions would form, that no one group could dominate. Madison's observation regarding the diversity of interests applies to most, but not all, states. Alexis de Tocqueville, writing in 1835, observed the formation of interest groups in American politics and their importance in increasing individual influence.[1] De Tocqueville's observation to some degree is a confirmation of Madison's predictions.

Frequently it is not the individual, or the more broadly defined "public opinion," that influences government officials, but the opinions of these attentive publics, organized in interest groups, often have the ear of public officials. Involvement in interest groups is a more influential form of participation than the simple act of voting.

An interest group is an organization of individuals sharing common goals that tries to influence governmental decisions. These groups are sometimes called "lobby groups," although lobbying is a specific activity where groups try to influence legislation. Sometimes the term **political action committee (PAC)** is applied to interest groups. PACs are organizations that collect and distribute money to candidates and as such are a more specialized kind of interest group. Often broad-based interest groups have PACs associated with them.

Interest groups play an important role in a democratic society. They can have both positive and negative effects on political processes. Public attention is often focused on the negative influences; however, interest groups and their activities are protected by the First Amendment to the U.S. Constitution, which provides for the right of the people "peaceably to assemble, and to petition the Government for a redress of grievances."

political action committee (PAC)
Spin-offs of interest groups that collect money for campaign contributions and other activity.

✦ INTEREST GROUP TYPOLOGY

Interest groups are formed for any reason and may represent any interest. Some groups are permanent organizations with full-time, well-financed professional staffs. Many of these groups have both national and state organizations. The National Rifle Association, the U.S. Chamber of Commerce, Mothers Against Drunk Driving, and the National Education Association are all examples of such groups. Others are temporary organizations that fade out of existence once their issue is resolved. Groups advocating property tax reform, insurance reform, and amendments to state constitutions are examples of temporary groups. Some groups represent a single person or a private company.

Interest groups can be divided into three broad categories. (See table 4.1.) **Membership organizations** are private groups and have individual citizens as members. An example of a membership group is the National Rifle Association, which has an active membership of gun owners and hunters. **Nonmembership organizations** represent individuals, single corporations, businesses, law firms, or freelance lobbies, and do not

membership organizations
Interest groups that have individual citizens as members, such as the National Rifle Association.

nonmembership organizations
Interest groups that represent corporations and businesses and do not have broad-based citizen support.

Mothers Against Drunk Driving (MADD) organize public support. MADD is one example of an interest group active at both the state and the national level.

TABLE 4.1	

Interest Group Typology

Type	Examples
Membership Organizations	
Business/Agriculture	
Peak business organizations	State Chamber of Commerce
	State Federation of Businesses
Trade associations	Oil and Gas Producers Association
	Good Roads Association
Agricultural trade groups	Commodity groups
	Texas Farm Bureau
Retail trade associations	Texas Apartment Association
	Texas Automobile Association
Professional Associations	
Private sector organizations	Texas Medical Association
	Texas Trial Lawyers Association
Public sector organizations	Texas State Teachers Association
Organized Labor Unions	Texas AFL-CIO
Noneconomic Membership Organizations	
Racial and ethnic groups	NAACP
	League of United Latin American Citizens
Religious groups	Christian Coalition, Interfaith Alliance
Public interest groups	MADD, American Civil Liberties Union
Nonmembership Organizations	
Groups that represent individuals or single businesses	Lone Star Gas, Texaco, Republic Bank
Government Organizations	
State and local interest groups (SLIGs)	Texas Municipal League, Texas Association of Police Chiefs

Source: Charles Wiggins, professor of political science at Texas A&M University, class handout, 1999.

government organizations
Interest groups that represent state and local governments. Called SLIGs for state and local interest groups.

have broad-based citizen support. **Government organizations** represent local government (city, county, school board, special districts) and state and federal agencies. Membership in these organizations ranges from local elected officials (such as mayors and council members) to government employees (police officers, firefighters, and federal and state employees).[2]

Membership Organizations

peak business organizations
Interest groups that represent statewide business organizations, such as a state Chamber of Commerce.

Peak business associations are interest groups that represent statewide interests, such as the state Chamber of Commerce, the Texas Association of Manufacturers, and the National Federation of Independent Business Owners. These groups try to promote the interests of their members and present a united front against policies that do not promote a "good business climate" in the state. They are often the most active at the state level and are generally well financed.

Trade associations differ from peak business associations in that they represent more specific business interests. In Texas, examples of these groups abound. Two trade associations that are often classified as among the more powerful are the Mid-Continent Oil and Gas Association, representing oil and gas producers, and the Good Roads Association, which represents highway contractors. Some groups represent more specific economic interests.

trade associations
Interest groups that represent more specific business interests.

Agriculture is an important part of the Texas economy. There are three types of agricultural groups. First are those that represent general farm interests. The Texas Farm Bureau represents large agricultural producers in the state. The Texas Farmers Union represents family farms and ranches. Second are organizations that represent commodity groups, such as cotton growers, cattle raisers, chicken raisers, and mohair producers. The third type of agriculture interest group represents suppliers of services to agriculture producers. Such groups represent cotton ginners, seed and fertilizer producers, and manufacturers and sellers of farm equipment.

Examples of retail trade groups are the Texas Apartment Association, the Texas Automobile Dealers Association, the Texas Restaurant Association, and the Association of Licensed Beverage Distributors. The primary goal of these groups is to protect their trades from state regulation deemed undesirable by the groups and to support regulation favorable to the groups' interests.

Professional associations differ from trade associations in two ways: (1) there is generally a professional license issued by the state, and (2) the state controls their scope of practice. They represent such professions as physicians (the Texas Medical Association) and attorneys (the Texas Trial Lawyers Association, which represents some attorneys). There are also organizations representing the interests of architects, landscape architects, engineers, surveyors, plumbers, accountants, librarians, barbers, hairdressers, cosmetologists, funeral directors, dentists, nurses, chiropractors, optometrists, pharmacists, podiatrists, clinical psychologists, veterinarians, and many other professional groups.

professional associations
State and local employee organizations that generally require a license and lack the right to collective bargaining.

In Texas, public employees are not granted the right of **collective bargaining** as they are in many states. Collective bargaining is a process that forces the government to enter into negotiations with an organization representing government workers. Both sides must enter into the negotiations and reach an agreement. State law in Texas does not grant this right to state or local employees.

collective bargaining
The right of union members to force governments to enter into negotiations.

Because of this lack of collective bargaining in Texas, public sector employee organizations are professional associations rather than labor unions. In other states, such groups are classified as public sector labor unions.

The League of United Latin American Citizens is concerned with advancing civil rights and gaining economic and political power.

The Texas State Teachers Association (TSTA) is the largest professional group in the state. Affiliated with the National Education Association, TSTA is generally considered the more liberal teachers' group. TSTA is well organized and sometimes presents a united front. At other times TSTA members have been known to fight among themselves. The Association of Texas Professional Educators is a more conservative organization that represents some teachers in the state. It was formed to counter the TSTA and has strong associations with the Texas Republican party.

The Texas High School Coaches Association is an example of a specialized "educational" association, of which there are several. In a state where football is a Friday-night tradition, this organization has some political clout. In recent years they formed a PAC to fight the new "no pass, no play" rule that required students to pass classes or be barred from playing in athletic events. This became known as the Flunk PAC.[3]

In Texas, private sector labor unions are not powerful and represent only a small fraction of the workers. Strong labor unions are an anathema to the traditionalistic/individualistic political culture of Texas. In many industrialized states, organized labor unions are important and powerful interest groups, although their influence has been declining in recent years. Except in a few counties on the Texas Gulf Coast, where organized labor represents petrochemical workers and longshoremen, organized labor in Texas is very weak. In 1996, only 6.6 percent of the total Texas workforce belonged to labor unions.[4] As in most of the South, strong antiunion feelings are very much a part of the political culture. Texas is one of twenty states with "right-to-work" laws. These laws prohibit union shops where all workers, based on a majority vote of the workers, are forced to join the union within ninety days of employment to retain their jobs.

African Americans and Hispanics are the two most active ethnic groups in the state. Hispanics are represented by a variety of groups that are sometimes at odds with each other. The **League of United Latin American Citizens (LULAC)** is the largest such group in the state. Other such organizations include Mexican American Democrats (MAD), the Mexican American Legal Defense and Education Fund (MALDEF), and the Political Association of Spanish-Speaking Organizations (PASSO). The National Association for the Advancement of Colored People (NAACP) and the Congress of Racial Equality (CORE) represent African Americans in Texas.

These groups are primarily concerned with advancing civil rights, ending discrimination, improving government services, and gaining political power. While they do not always share common interests, gaining economic and political equality is an interest they do share.

Texas has a history of active religious groups. As in the rest of the Old South, Protestant churches fought to eliminate the sale of alcoholic beverages in the state. Even today, large sections of the state are "dry," meaning that alcohol is not sold there. In areas where alcohol can be sold, only beer and wine can be sold on Sunday, and only after 12 noon.

In the past twenty-five years the Catholic Church has become active in state politics. This activity, primarily among Hispanic Catholics, is driven by concerns about economic advancement, local services, and the abortion issue. In San Antonio the Catholic Church was a driving force for the creation of Communities Organized for Public Service (COPS). This organization successfully challenged the Good Government League, which had dominated city elections for decades.[5] In the Rio Grande Valley, the Catholic Church was a driving force in the formation of the Interfaith Alliance. In the El Paso area the Inter-religious Sponsoring Organization was created to advance Hispanic interests.

In recent years there has been increased activity by fundamentalist religious groups on the national level. This has also happened in Texas. Organizations such as the Christian Coalition attempt to promote antiabortion campaigns, abstinence-based sex education, home schooling, a school voucher system, prayer in school, and, of course, "family values." These groups have had some success at electing local school boards and now control the Texas State Board of Education, which governs some aspects of school policy statewide.

They have also had success in gaining control of the Republican party State Executive Committee in Texas. In 1994, fundamentalist groups took control of the

League of United Latin American Citizens (LULAC)
Largest organization representing Latinos in Texas.

HIGHLIGHT

Some political action committees have interesting nick-names for their organizations. For example, the beer lobby is known as Six Pack, the chiropractors are known as Back Pac, lawyers are Lift Pac. The high school coaches are affectionately known as Flunk Pack for the opposition to no-pass, no-play rules. The funeral directors were once called Morti Pac, and the pharmacists, Pill Pac.

The contractors are known as Cat Pack, and the air conditioners as Pac Pac. Truckers are Trans Pac, and automobile dealers are Auto Pac.

Republican state party convention and elected a state party chair favorable to their causes. This group retained control of the Republican party in 1996 and maintained control until today.

Public interest groups represent causes or ideas rather than economic, professional, or governmental interests. Many of these Texas organizations have national counterparts—for instance, Mothers Against Drunk Driving (MADD), the National Organization for Women (NOW), the National Right to Life Association, the Sierra Club, the American Civil Liberties Union (ACLU), Common Cause, the League of Women Voters, and Public Citizen. These groups usually limit their support or opposition to a narrow range of issues.

Nonmembership Organizations

Nonmembership organizations, which do not have active members and generally represent a single company, organization, corporation, or individual, form the largest category of interest groups. Even a cursory glance at the list of organizations registered with the Texas Ethics Commission in Austin reveals that there are hundreds of these groups. For example, Chili's Grill and Bar in Dallas, El Chico Corporation, and H. Ross Perot are all registered as interest groups with the Ethics Commission. Many law firms are also available as "hired guns" to represent a variety of interests in the state.

Government Organizations

Government organizations are separated in this typology from membership groups, though some of these organizations have active members. The membership of these **state and local interest groups** (SLIGs) consists of government employees and officials. These groups represent the organization and not the interests of individual members.

state and local interest groups (SLIGs)
Interest groups that represent state and local governments, such as Texas Association of Counties.

Local government officials also organize groups to protect and advance their interests. Examples of these groups are the Texas Municipal League, the Texas Association of Police Chiefs, the Combined Law Enforcement Association of Texas, the Texas Association of Fire Fighters, the City Attorneys Association, the Texas Association of County Officials, and the Texas School Board Association. These groups have in common the goals of protecting local government interests from actions of the state legislature, the governor, and state agencies.

This is only a partial list of interest groups in Texas. Interest groups found in Texas are comparable to those found in other states. The number and kind of interest groups will vary according to several factors discussed later in this chapter. Table 4.2 summarizes data on interest groups, according to the most recent study on this issue.

TABLE 4.2

Interest Groups in the Texas Legislature, by Type

Type	Percentage of Groups	Percentage of Lobbyists	Number of Groups	Number of Lobbyists
Business	64.9	63.0	517	969
Finance/insurance	17.0	11.4	135	176
Energy/chemicals	8.2	9.0	65	139
Building/construction	2.2	2.7	18	41
Transportation	4.8	6.0	38	93
Utilities/telecommunications	4.9	7.7	39	119
Real estate	0.9	1.8	7	27
Alcohol related	1.5	1.1	12	17
Aerospace/steel/high-tech	2.0	2.3	16	35
General	0.6	0.5	5	8
Misc. commercial	20.2	18.0	161	276
Misc. manufacturing	2.6	2.5	21	38
Professional	7.0	9.8	56	151
Attorneys	1.6	2.7	13	42
Health related	2.9	4.7	23	71
Architects/engineers/CPAs	0.8	1.4	6	22
Miscellaneous	1.8	1.0	14	16
Employee	5.3	6.2	42	95
Private sector	2.0	1.4	16	21
Public sector				
Education	1.4	3.3	11	51
Local government	1.4	1.0	11	15
Miscellaneous	0.5	0.5	4	8
Agriculture/ranch/forestry	2.5	2.2	20	34
Noneconomic	16.0	13.7	127	210
General	2.1	3.4	17	52
Specific issue				
Nationality/ethnicity	0.1	0.1	1	1
Education	3.0	2.2	24	34
Taxation	0.3	0.3	2	4
Morality, gambling, abortion	0.5	0.4	4	7
Conservation/natural resources	1.4	1.2	11	19
Miscellaneous	8.6	6.1	68	93
Local governments/Special Districts	4.3	5.1	34	79
Total	**100.0**	**100.0**	**796**	**1,538**

Note: Not all groups that register as interest groups also register as lobbyists.

Source: Keith E. Hamm and Charles W. Wiggins, "The Transformation from Personnel to Information Lobbying" in *Interest Group Politics in the Southern States,* ed. Ronald J. Hrebenar and Clive S. Thomas (Tuscaloosa: University of Alabama Press, 1992), 160–61.

→ THE REGULATION OF INTEREST GROUPS

Most states have laws that regulate two kinds of activities of interest groups: lobbying and making financial contributions to political campaigns. Lobby regulations generally consist of requiring organizations that have regular contacts with legislators to register

---

HIGHLIGHT

Lobbying Texas Style

Sometime after Franklin Roosevelt died and before Swatch watches, Lubbock elected a state senator who proceeded to Austin, where he holed up in the Driskill Ho-tell with another senator-elect; they's drinkin wiskey and "interviewin" secretaries. Comes a knock-knock-knock on the door and there's the lobbyist for the chiropractors; he offers 'em each $200 to vote for the chiropractor bill. Guy from Lubbock takes the money. Damn ol' bill comes up first week of the session. Guy from

Lubbock votes against it. Hacks off the chiropractor lobbyist something serious.

"You take my money and you vote against me!" he says.

Guy from Lubbock says, "Yeah, but the doctors offered me $400 to vote against you."*

Such activity would not be common in Texas today. New rules make it illegal to accept campaign contributions thirty days before the legislative session begins.

*Molly Ivins, *Molly Ivins Can't Say That, Can She?* (New York: Random House, 1991), 91.

---

and provide reports on their activities. Often this requirement is weak, and the reports might not reflect the true activities of such organizations.

Texas first required the registration of interest groups in 1907. This statute prohibited "efforts to influence legislation 'by means other than appeal to reason' and provided that persons guilty of lobbying were subject to fines and imprisonment."[6] The act was never enforced. In 1957 a new law was passed that required lobbyists to register and disclose information about their activities; however, the law had many loopholes and was ineffective. In 1973 a new law was passed that called for more stringent reporting. The act was again amended in 1983. Under current law three kinds of persons must register as lobbyists: individuals who lobby as professionals; "individuals who receive more than $200.00 in one calendar quarter as pay for lobbying"; and individuals who spend more than $200 for gifts, awards, or entertainment to influence legislation.[7] Each year about fifteen hundred groups and persons register. (See table 4.2.) Government officials who lobby for state agencies and universities are exempt from registration. Also, some lawyers do not register because they claim they are representing clients and are not lobbying. Thus, the total number of persons who actually lobby the legislature is much higher.

The ethics of interest group activity will vary from state to state, dictated by the political culture of the state. What is viewed as acceptable in a traditionalistic/individualistic state like Texas may be considered corrupt in a state with a moralistic political culture. The late Molly Ivins, a well-known Texas newspaper writer and observer of Texas politics, once said that in the Texas legislature, "what passes for ethics is if you're bought, by God, you stay bought."[8] While this is very much an overstatement on Ms. Ivins's part, there was a time in the past when this may have described the lobby activity in Texas.

→ TECHNIQUES USED BY INTEREST GROUPS

Interest groups use a variety of techniques to influence public policy. The type of technique depends upon the type of group and the resources available to that group.

Lobbying

Perhaps the best known and most common technique is **lobbying** the state legislature. This is why interest groups are often called "lobby groups." The term *lobbying* refers to

lobbying
The practice of attempting to influence the legislature, originally by catching members in the lobby of the capitol.

the practice of waiting in the lobby of the legislative chamber. Commonly, in the past, legislators did not have offices; their office was the desk on the floor of the chamber. Only members of the legislature were allowed on the floor, and they met other people "in the lobby." Today the term *lobbying* covers many more activities.

In Texas the legislature meets every two years for 140 days, and the most intense lobby activity is concentrated during the regular session. All legislatures, however, including the one in Texas, perform some activities between regular sessions, and interest groups will attempt to influence interim committees and other activities of the legislature.

Lobby efforts that are specifically aimed at influencing the members of the state legislature during legislative sessions include the following kinds of activities:

1. Contacting members of the legislature before the session begins
2. Getting members of the legislature to file a bill favorable to the group
3. Testifying before a committee, informing legislators of the effect a bill will have on their district
4. Keeping group members informed about legislative activities
5. Asking members of the group to contact legislators (letter-writing campaigns)
6. Issuing press releases and buying newspaper and television ads
7. Presenting written material to members of the legislature[9]

HIGHLIGHT

Money Spent for Lobby Activity in 2007 Session of the Texas Legislature

Each year the lobby spends a lot of money during the legislative session to have its issue presented to the members. Here are the major costs incurred in the 2007 session of the legislature by the major lobby groups.

Interest Group	Max. Value of Contracts	Min. Value of Contracts	No. of Contracts	Percentage of Max. Value
Agriculture	$6,995,000	$3,230,072	179	2%
Communications	$19,130,003	$9,400,143	400	6%
Computers/Electronics	$12,890,003	$6,310,134	313	4%
Construction	$9,985,000	$4,630,091	242	3%
Energy/Natural Resources	$41,710,008	$20,790,311	910	14%
Finance	$21,540,000	$10,275,279	538	7%
Health	$38,035,001	$17,970,371	911	13%
Ideological/Single Issue	$44,495,004	$20,035,596	1,244	15%
Insurance	$18,390,004	$8,565,309	536	6%
Labor	$5,745,000	$2,690,042	137	2%
Lawyers & Lobbyists	$16,355,016	$9,380,153	334	5%
Misc. Business	$34,833,001	$16,398,372	870	12%
Other	$3,235,000	$1,440,036	91	1%
Real Estate	$16,930,002	$8,770,123	336	6%
Transportation	$11,849,001	$5,039,182	348	4%
Unknown	$2,005,000	$810,033	66	1%
Total	**$304,122,043**	**$145,735,247**	**7,455**	**100%**

Source: Texans for Public Justice, *Austin's Oldest Profession: Texas' Top Lobby Clients & Those Who Serve Them,* July 2007 (www.tpj.org).

Lobbying does not stop when the legislature adjourns. Most legislation requires a signature by the governor. Persuading the governor to either sign or veto a bill is an important part of lobbying activity.

If the governor signs a bill, it will require an administrative agency to enforce it. Administrative discretion in enforcement of a law can also be the object of lobbying. Interest groups devote great efforts to influencing how agencies interpret and enforce laws. Enforcement can be made easier by the appointment of people to governing boards and commissions who favor the interest group. Thus, lobbying involves many activities and goes far beyond simply waiting in the lobby of the legislative chamber for a chance to talk with legislators.

Lobbyists can be classified into five types. (1) Contract lobbyists are hired to represent a client. Most represent more than one client. It is estimated that this group constitutes about 15 to 25 percent of all lobbyists. (2) In-house lobbyists are employees of businesses or associations and lobby as part of their job. They constitute 40 to 50 percent of all lobbyists. (3) Governmental lobbyists and legislative liaisons work for a governmental organization and lobby as part of their job. They might not be required to formally register as lobbyists. One estimate is that they constitute about 25 to 35 percent of all lobbyists. (4) Citizen or volunteer lobbyists are nonpaid volunteers representing citizen groups and organizations. A good example is volunteers for Mothers Against Drunk Driving. This type constitutes about 10 to 20 percent of all lobbyists. (5) Finally there are private individuals. Sometimes called "hobbyists," these individualists act on their own behalf and do not officially represent any organizations. They usually have a pet project or issue. They constitute less than 5 percent of all lobbyists.[10]

Lobbying tactics have changed in recent years. In the past the process was described primarily as "booze, bribes, and broads." There is much less of that today, but entertaining members of the legislature is still very much a part of the process. "As for making women 'available' to interested male lawmakers, a veteran lobbyist reported in 1981 that 'I got hit up for the first time this session by a member wanting me to get him a woman. I told him I have trouble enough getting my own dates.' "[11]

Interest groups today are more likely to rely on other tactics, outlined next, such as electioneering, public relations, and mobilization of support. Lobbyists emphasize information and public relations over the old tactics.

HIGHLIGHT

Texas is now one of the top states in terms of money spent by lobbies. According to the Texans for Public Justice (*www.TPJ.org*), Texas now ranks second among the states in the amount of money spent by lobbies.

Top Lobby States in 2005

2005 Rank	State	2005 Lobby Spending	No. of Lobbyists	No. of Clients
1	California	$227,940,496	1,162	2,639
2	Texas	$173,594,357	1,703	2,644
3	New York	$149,000,000	4,264	2,656
4	Pennsylvania	$124,813,732	468	1,261
5	Massachusetts	$70,955,161	578	1,057

Source: Preliminary *Center for Public Integrity* data and TPJ. Org, *Austin's Oldest Profession.*

Electioneering

Interest groups devote considerable time and effort to trying to influence the outcome of elections. Their most important resource is money, usually funneled to candidates through PACs. At the national level, only about 20 percent of interest groups have organized PACs. Some interest groups prefer to give money to other groups, who in turn funnel the money to campaigns.

Most states require some formal registration of PACs. In Texas a PAC created by corporations or labor unions must be formed exclusively to support or oppose a ballot issue and may not be created to support or oppose a candidate for office. "However, employees, members or families of corporation employees, unions and associations may form a PAC and make individual donations."[12] PACs must register with the **Texas Ethics Commission,** designate a treasurer, and file periodic reports. These reports must give the names of persons donating more than $50 to campaigns. PACs are also prohibited from making a contribution to members of the legislature during the period beginning thirty days before the start of a regular session and ending thirty days after the regular 140-day session. In Texas, except for voluntary limits in judicial campaigns, there is no limit in state law as to how much an individual or PAC may contribute to a candidate. Listed in the Highlight box is the amount of money contributed by the major PACs in Texas broken down by major category.

The process of **electioneering** is much broader than making a monetary contribution to a campaign. It begins with candidate recruitment. Interest groups work to recruit candidates for office many months before the election. They encourage individuals who will be sympathetic to their cause to seek nominations in party primaries. This encouragement takes the form of promises of support and money in the election. Some interest groups might encourage both Democratic and Republican candidates to seek nomination in their parties. This covers their bets. If either candidate wins, they win.

After the primary election, interest groups often give money to candidates in the general election. They might give money to both Democratic and Republican candidates, hoping to have access and influence regardless of who wins the general election. Some writers have observed that PAC money has undermined party loyalty and weakened

Texas Ethics Commission
State agency responsible for enforcing requirements for interest groups and candidates for public office to report information on money collected and activities.

electioneering
Various activities engaged in by interest groups to try and influence the outcome of elections.

HIGHLIGHT

PAC Spending from 1996 to 2004

The total amount of money spent by general purpose PACs in the 2002 spending cycle was double the amount they spent in 1996. PAC spending went from $43 million to $85 million. There was a decrease in the number of PACs and the amount of money from 2002 to 2004.

Election Cycle	Number of Active PACs	PAC Spending	Spending Increase from Previous Cycle	Spending Increase (%)
1996	911	$43,082,546	NA	NA
1998	893	51,543,820	$8,461,274	20
2000	865	53,996,975	2,453,155	05
2002	964	85,320,226	31,323,251	58
2004	850	68,904,524	(−16,415,702)	(19)

Source: Texans for Public Justice (*www.tpj.org/reports/txpacs02total.html*).

political parties in this country. Candidates no longer owe their loyalty to the party that helped elect them but to interest groups. Political action committees buy access in

> an intricate, symbiotic relationship involving trust, information exchange, pressure and obligations. The inescapable fact is that resources, and especially money, are at least three-fourths of the battle in building and maintaining good relations and in securing the other essential elements that lead to access and influence.[13]

Interest groups might also become directly involved in campaigns. As can be seen in the Highlight box on page 64, the amount of spending on campaigns has doubled between 1996 and 2002. In the 2004 cycle, spending decreased by $16 million on 19 percent. There is little doubt it will continue to increase. This can involve running television and newspaper ads explaining the record of officials or the virtues of a nonincumbent, or working in voter registration drives and get-out-the-vote campaigns. Interest groups might also aid candidates by helping to write speeches and organize rallies, and by staging political events such as fund-raisers. Some groups keep track of legislators' voting records and circulate "good guy/bad guy score cards" to members of the organization, instructing members to vote for or against candidates.

Public Education and Public Relations: Grassroots Lobbying

Interest groups also attempt to influence public policy through public relations activities. These efforts attempt to portray the organization in the best possible light by creating a favorable public image of the group. Obviously, much of this information can be very self-serving and can be called propaganda. Not all such information is wrong, but some filtering of the information by public officials is necessary. Competing interest groups can often counter the information provided by another interest group. In a mass media society, with much public scrutiny, an interest group's credibility can be compromised if the group often provides inaccurate or misleading information.

Additionally, interest groups often provide research information to members of the legislature. This information can also be self-serving, but the information provided is often accurate and can be an important source for state legislators. The Texas legislature has only limited, part-time staff. An interest group that provides good, high-quality research and information can have an impact on public policy. Over the years several business-sponsored groups in Texas have developed a reputation for producing quality research and information to the Texas legislature.[14]

Besides efforts to present a favorable opinion of themselves to the public, interest groups also try to curry favor with public officials. Inviting public officials to address organizational meetings is also a technique to advance the group's standing in the eyes of public officials. Giving awards to public officials at such gatherings, thanking them for their service to the public, is also a common technique.

✦ RESOURCES AND STRENGTHS OF INTEREST GROUPS

There are many resources available to interest groups. Some groups spend large amounts of money; others have very little money. Resources depend on the kind of group, the number of members in the group, and who the members are. For example, the Texas State Teachers Association (TSTA) has strength because it has so many members (hence voters). The Texas Municipal League (TML) represents Texas city officials. It has very little money and fewer members than the TSTA, but it has **influential members** who are mayors and council members. The TML has lists of representatives and senators keyed with local officials. The TML contacts local officials and asks them to contact

influential members
Interest groups having members that can influence members of the legislature, such as the Texas Municipal League with mayors and council members.

representatives and senators regarding legislation. Local elected officials can easily contact their local representatives, and those representatives will listen to them, even if they might not always agree with them.

The status and number of members of the group are important determinants of power. Obviously the presidents of large banks and corporations in Dallas can command the ear of most of the senators and representatives from the Dallas area. Groups with many members can also be important. A barrage of telephone calls and messages to legislators can influence legislative actions.

The total number of interest groups representing a particular interest may not be an indication of strength. For example, in recent years the number of groups representing business interests has greatly increased. The number of groups representing local government's interests has grown very little. One could take this as a sign that business groups have increased in influence because their numbers have increased. Numbers do not necessarily indicate increased influence. They probably indicate an increase in the diversity of economic interests in Texas over the last twenty-five years. Except for special districts, the number of local governments has not grown in the past forty years. Some writers look at numbers and attribute this to increased strength. It is a mistake to do this. Other factors, discussed next, are more important than numbers.

Leadership and Organization

Leadership quality and organizational ability can also be important factors in the power of interest groups. Many interest groups hire former legislators to help them. Some groups are decentralized, with a loose-knit membership, making mobilization difficult. Other groups, like the Texas Municipal League, are highly organized, monitor legislation being considered, and can easily contact selected members to influence bills while they are still in committee. Even before the legislative session begins, the TML has a legislative committee that recommends positions on legislation likely to be considered. At an annual meeting, the TML membership adopts stands on key items. This action gives the leadership a firm basis on which to act, and constant contact with all members is not necessary. Key members are contacted only when quick action is required.

Geographic Distribution

Some groups can have more influence than others because they have representatives in all geographic areas of the state and can command the attention of many more legislators. The Texas Municipal League has city officials in every senator's and representative's district. Legislators will listen to citizens from their district but might not listen to citizens from other legislative districts. Legislators will listen to local elected officials. They may not always agree but they will listen.

geographic distribution
Some interest groups have representatives in all regions of the state.

Thus, having members that are geographically distributed across the state is very important. Obviously, some groups cannot have **geographic distribution.** Commercial shrimp fishers are limited to the Gulf Coast region of Texas. Texas bankers and lawyers, on the other hand, are everywhere in the state.

Money

Money is always an important resource for any organization. Interest groups that can afford to hire a full-time staff and travel to meet with legislators obviously have more influence than those that must depend upon volunteers and part-time staffs. Money will also help the group to develop its public image.

HIGHLIGHT

Grassroots or Astroturf?

Astroturf is a political term for phony grassroots organizations supported with corporate money. In one of the more bizarre developments in the history of modern politics, astroturf has become such a profitable (estimated $1 billion a year) and sophisticated business that public relations firms are now warring with one another about

who provides astroturf and who provides "real" grassroots organizations. "Real" in the context of the PR industry does not mean real; it means PR campaigns that are harder to spot as astroturf. In other words, "real" means a better grade of phony.

Source: Molly Ivins, "Getting to the Grass Roots of the Problem," *Bryan-College Station Eagle,* 13 July 1995, A4. Reprinted by permission of Pom, Inc.

As indicated earlier, some groups have no membership but represent individuals, corporations, or businesses. With enough money, you do not need members to have an impact on government policy. Some of these groups do a very good job of mobilizing nonmember citizens to their cause. For example, through the use of television ads, newspaper ads, and "talk radio," one such group, the Coalition of Health Insurance Choice (CHIC), managed to mobilize opposition to President Clinton's health care proposal. One writer has referred to such nonmembership groups, which lack a grassroots organization, as "**astroturf** organizations."

astroturf

A political term for an interest group that appears to have many grassroots members but in fact does not have any active members.

✦ THE VARYING STRENGTH OF INTEREST GROUPS

The strength and influence of interest groups vary among the states. Most writers explain this variation based on four factors: economic diversity, party strength, professionalism of the legislature, and government fragmentation.[15] Political culture is also a factor.

Economic Diversity

States differ in their economic diversity. States that are highly industrialized and have a great variety of industries will have a multitude of interest groups. Because of the diversity and complexity of the state's economy, no single industry or group can dominate. The many interests cancel each other out, as Madison predicted they would in *Federalist No. 10*. In other states a single or a few industries dominate the economy.

In the past, the Texas economy was dominated by a few industries: cotton, cattle, banking, and oil. Today, the Texas economy is more diversified and the number of interest groups has grown accordingly. It is much more difficult for one or a few interests to dominate state politics. Still, some states today are dominated by a single industry. In Alaska, oil is still dominant. Coal mining dominates Wyoming's economy and provides much of the state's revenues. Copper mining once dominated the state of Montana, and lumbering is still the dominant industry in Oregon.

Political Party Competition

The strength of the political parties in the state can influence the strength of the interest groups. States with two strong competitive parties that recruit and support candidates for office can offset the influence of interest groups. Members of the legislature in competitive party states might owe their election to the political party and be less influenced by interest groups. In Texas, a history of weak party structure has contributed to the power of interest groups.

Professionalism of the State Legislature

In Chapter 7, we define a professional legislature as one that has a full-time staff, is well-paid, serves full-time, and has good research and advisory services. Full-time, well-paid legislators with a professional staff are less dependent upon information supplied by interest groups, and the exchange of information between the lobbyist and the legislator is reduced. The Texas legislature has improved the quality of the staff in recent years; most members have full-time staff members in Austin and in local offices. In addition, committee staff has increased. The Texas legislature now provides more money than any other state for staff salaries. The Texas Legislative Council also provides excellent staff assistance in research and information. A professional staff reduces the dependency of the legislature on interest groups.

Fragmented Government Structure

fragmented government structure
A government structure where power is dispersed to many state agencies with no central control.

As indicated previously, interest groups spend much of their effort trying to influence the administration of state laws. The degree to which interest groups succeed depends upon the structure of the state government. If the government is centralized under a governor who appoints and removes most of the heads of departments, interest groups will find it necessary to lobby the governor directly and the agencies indirectly. Texas has a **fragmented government structure.** The governor of Texas makes few significant appointments of agency heads. Each interest group tries to gain access to and influence the state agency. Often these agencies are created to regulate the industry that the interest group represents. For example, the Texas Railroad Commission, originally created to regulate railroads, also regulates the oil industry in Texas. Historically the oil industry lobby groups have dominated the three members who serve on the Railroad Commission and the decisions of that commission.[16] In 1971 the *Texas Almanac* contained a full-page ad paid for by the Texas Independent Producers and Royalty Owners Association and the American Association of Oil Well Drilling Contractors, thanking the Railroad Commission. The ad read: "Since 1891, The Texas Railroad Commission Has Served the Oil Industry." There was some public outcry over this ad, and the ad in the 1974 edition of the *Texas Almanac* was changed to read: "Since 1891 The Texas Railroad Commission Has Served Our State."[17]

Similar relationships exist between many state agencies and interest groups. Until the Texas Sunset Commission was created in 1977 to review most state agencies every twelve years, the members of most state licensing boards (such as the Texas State Bar, State Board of Medical Examiners, State Board of Morticians) were professionals in that field. Members of the profession still dominate these boards. These licensing boards were created to "protect the public interest," but they often spend most of their time protecting the profession by limiting the number of persons who can be licensed and by making rules favorable to the group. For example, in Texas a person cannot be cremated until they have been dead for seventy-two hours. However, if they are not buried within twenty-four hours the body must be embalmed. Supposedly, the reason for embalming before cremation is to protect the public from the spread of diseases. Others have suggested the procedure is unnecessary and demonstrates the degree to which interest groups control rule making and influence how much money the group makes.

capture
The situation in which a state agency or board falls under the heavy influence of its constituency interest groups.

When the relationship between the state agency and the interest group becomes very close, it is referred to as **capture.** The interest group has "captured" the agency. However, capture of the agency by the interest group is probably more the exception than the rule. Often there are competing interest groups that vie for influence with the agency and reduce the likelihood of capture by a single interest group. The creation of

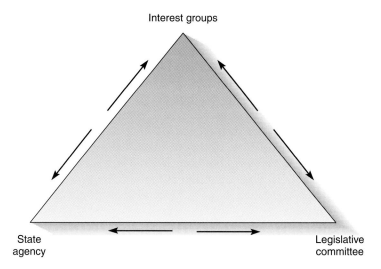

FIGURE 4.1 *There is often a close relationship between the state agency created to regulate an industry, the legislative oversight committee, and interest groups. This relationship is sometimes called the "Iron Triangle."*

the Public Utility Commission is a good example of this. (See Highlight box below.) Political scientists often refer to the "Iron Triangle" to describe the policy-making process. (See figure 4.1.) In this model, the interest group, the state agency, and the legislative committee (with oversight of the agency) share in the process of making policy.

Sharing does not mean that interest groups do not exert influence. In Texas the fragmented nature of the state government, the many independent boards and commissions, and the separately elected state agency heads all increase the strength of interest groups and their influence on state government.

H I G H L I G H T

The Texas Public Utility Commission

In 1975 the Texas legislature passed the Public Utilities Regulatory Act and created the Public Utility Commission (PUC). This act created three classes of electrical public utilities: investor-owned or private electrical companies, rural electrical cooperatives (RECs), and municipally owned systems. Each class of utility was subject to varying degrees of regulation by the PUC. Municipal groups were under the least amount of regulation, and some municipal officials felt the act did not apply to city electrical systems. Gradually the PUC began to extend regulatory control over the municipal systems, and by 1978–79 issued orders requiring municipal certification of areas served by these systems.

The electrical cooperatives had an active interest group that extended back to the late 1930s when Congress created the Rural Electrification Administration. The investor-owned systems were represented by a longstanding organization that had originally fought the creation of the PUC. With the energy crisis of the 1970s, the investor-owned group sought statewide regulation of rates.

Until 1980 the municipally owned electrical systems in Texas had no statewide organization. When the PUC gradually began to exert control over the municipal systems, the Texas Public Power Association was created to represent this group. Three interest groups, representing each type of electrical distributor, now attempt to exert influence over the PUC. However, no one group is dominant. Citizen "watchdog" groups have also formed to monitor the PUC.

✛ THE CLASSIFICATION OF INTEREST GROUP PATTERNS

Clive S. Thomas and Ronald J. Hrebenar have classified interest group patterns in the fifty states. (See table 4.3.) Five states are listed as being dominated by interest groups. It should be noted that, except for Nevada and Montana, all of these states are southern states with predominantly traditionalistic cultures and some individualistic cultures. Twenty-six states, including Texas, have dominant/complementary interest group patterns. In these states such groups are dominant but must negotiate with state agencies and the legislature. In sixteen states, the relationship is classified as complementary—interest groups, state agencies, and legislative committees complement each other. Lastly, in three states interest groups are generally subordinate to state agencies and the legislature. In no state are interest groups entirely dominated by the state government.

TABLE 4.3

Classification of States Based on the Overall Impact of Interest Groups in 2006–2007

Dominant (4)	Dominant/ complementary (26)	Complementary (15)	Complementary/ subordinate (5)	Subordinate (0)
Alabama	Alaska	Colorado	Kentucky	
Florida	Arizona	Connecticut	Michigan	
Hawaii	Arkansas	Indiana	Minnesota	
Nevada	California	Maine	South Dakota	
	Delaware	Massachusetts	Vermont	
	Georgia	Montana		
	Idaho	New Hampshire		
	Illinois	New Jersey		
	Iowa	New York		
	Kansas	North Carolina		
	Louisiana	North Dakota		
	Maryland	Pennsylvania		
	Mississippi	Rhode Island		
	Missouri	Washington		
	Nebraska	Wisconsin		
	New Mexico			
	Ohio			
	Oklahoma			
	Oregon			
	South Carolina			
	Tennessee			
	Texas			
	Utah			
	Virginia			
	West Virginia			
	Wyoming			

Source: Anthony Nownes, Clive S. Thomas and Ronald J. Hrebenar, "Interest Groups in the States" in *Politics in the American States: A Comparative Analysis,* 9th edition, edited by Virginia Gray and Russell L. Hanson. Copyright © 2008 Congressional Quarterly Press, Washington, D.C. Reprinted by permission. Table 4.3, 121.

✦ CONCLUSIONS

Even though they are often criticized, interest groups play a very important role in state politics. The First Amendment to the U.S. Constitution protects free speech and association, and interest groups are a necessary part of the political process. Efforts by government to control interest groups are, and should be, limited. Interest groups are a necessary part of a democratic society. Knowing the tactics used to influence government is a necessary part of understanding how politics works in state government.

There is little doubt that the influence of interest groups, especially PACs, will continue to increase in the years ahead. In some campaigns, PAC money has replaced the political party as a nominating and electing agent. There is no doubt that this money influences legislation. In a mass media age, little can be done to curb the influence of these groups.

Given the low levels of voter turnout in Texas, one can only suspect that interest groups will continue to dominate Texas state politics. The traditionalistic/individualistic political culture also supports such domination. A reorganization of state agencies into a centrally controlled administration seems unlikely. The present decentralized state administrative structure assists interest groups in their control of state agencies, and this will persist for many years to come.

INTERNET RESOURCES

Texas Ethics Commission: *www.ethics.state.tx.us/*
   This page has information on campaign contributions and interest group registrations.
Texans for Public Justice: *www.tpj.org/*
   This organization is an advocacy group that compiles information on many aspects of Texas state government, including listings of lobbyist and campaign contributions by PACs, money to judicial candidates, and many items on state government.
Many interest groups have Web sites that present information to the public regarding their positions. One such group is the National Rifle Association: *www.nraila.org/*

You can find data on political contributions at the state and national level at *www.opensecrets.org/*
   You can enter your zip code and find local contributors to campaigns at the national level.
You may review the Encyclopedia of Associations at *library.dialog.com* and visit Associations Unlimited through the Harvard Business School Library/ Bloomberg Center at *http://library.hsb.edu/guides/retail/ associations.html*

KEY TERMS

astroturf (p. 67)
capture (p. 68)
collective bargaining (p. 57)
electioneering (p. 64)
fragmented government structure (p. 68)
geographic distribution (p. 66)
government organizations (p. 56)

influential members (p. 65)
League of United Latin American Citizens (LULAC) (p. 58)
lobbying (p. 61)
membership organizations (p. 55)
nonmembership organizations (p. 55)
peak business organizations (p. 56)

political action committee (PAC) (p. 55)
professional associations (p. 57)
state and local interest groups (SLIGs) (p. 59)
Texas Ethics Commission (p. 64)
trade associations (p. 57)

NOTES

1. Alexis de Tocqueville, *Democracy in America,* trans. George Lawrence, ed. J.P. Mayer (Garden City, N.J.: Anchor Books, 1969), 190–91.

2. Adapted from a typology developed by Charles Wiggins, Professor of Political Science, Texas A&M University, College Station, 1999 (unpublished class handout).

3. "Flunk-PAC," *Washington Post, National Weekly Edition,* 30 December 1985, 22.

4. *Statistical Abstract of the U.S. 1997,* p. 441. Table 690.

5. Robert Lineberry, *Equity and Urban Policy: The Distribution of Urban Services* (Newbury Park, Calif.: Sage, 1977).

6. Keith E. Hamm and Charles W. Wiggins, "The Transformation from Personnel to Information Lobbying," in *Interest Group Politics in the Southern States,* ed. Ronald J. Hrebenar and Clive S. Thomas (Tuscaloosa: University of Alabama Press, 1992), 152.

7. Hamm and Wiggins, "Transformation," 157.

8. Molly Ivins, *Molly Ivins Can't Say That, Can She?* (New York: Random House, 1991), 58.

9. Adapted from Ronald Hrebenar, Melanee Cherry, and Kathanne Green, "Utah: Church and Corporate Power in the Nation's Most Conservative State," in *Interest Group Politics in the American West,* ed. Ronald Hrebnar and Clive Thomas (Salt Lake City: University of Utah Press, 1987), 117.

10. Clive S. Thomas and Ronald J. Hrebenar, "Interest Groups in State Politics," in *Politics in the American States,* ed. Virginia Gray, Herbert Jacob, and Robert Albritton, 5th ed. (Glenview, Ill.: Scott Foresman/ Little, Brown, 1990), 150–51.

11. Hamm and Wiggins, "Transformation," 170.

12. Ibid., 157.

13. Thomas and Hrebenar, "Interest Groups in State Politics," 154.

14. The Texas Research League recently changed its name to the Texas Taxpayers and Research Association. It is headquartered in Austin.

15. Thomas R. Dye, *Politics in States and Communities,* 7th ed. (Englewood Cliffs, N.J.: Prentice Hall, 1991), 112–13.

16. David F. Prindel, *Petroleum Politics and the Texas Railroad Commission* (Austin: University of Texas Press, 1981).

17. Richard H. Kraemer and Charldean Newell, *Texas Politics,* 2d ed. (St. Paul: West, 1984), 79. Also see *The Texas Almanac and State Industrial Guide, 1970–71* (Dallas: A.H. Belo, 1970), 425; and *The Texas Almanac and State Industrial Guide, 1974–75* (Dallas: A.H. Belo, 1974), 19.

CHAPTER 5

POLITICAL PARTIES IN TEXAS

For the average citizen, the concept of a political party might not have much meaning. Many people do not identify themselves with either the Democratic or the Republican party, but categorize themselves as independents. For some people, party identification and the activities of political parties are things to avoid; however, the strength and organization of political parties play a very important role in a democracy, contributing to its health.

Political parties can be defined as electoral organizations seeking to control government. The primary functions of political parties are these: recruiting candidates, nominating candidates, mobilizing voters, contesting elections, coordinating policy across independent units of government, and providing accountability.[1]

While these functions are common to some state political party organizations, for many reasons they do not apply to all state party organizations. Some states have highly organized and developed party organizations that perform all of these functions. In other states, one party might be well organized and perform all these functions, while the other party is less well developed.

Parties often fall short on the sixth function—providing accountability. Under this function, the electorate holds parties responsible for their politics and actions. In states where one party is dominant, however, making that party accountable is difficult.

In other states the difference between Democrats and Republicans might not be great. To win elections, political parties must appeal to the middle of the road and avoid taking extreme positions.[2] This often means that there is no clear policy difference between the parties. Also, voters do not always select candidates based upon their stands on issues. They might vote based on images portrayed in the campaign. Once officeholders are elected, there is no effective mechanism to bind them to the party's position. In addition, forces independent of the party often decide who gets elected. Parties cannot control party nominations in primary elections. PACs are an independent force beyond party control; they go directly to the candidates and bypass the party. The role of mass media also undercuts the effectiveness of political parties. Campaigns are often media events controlled by groups independent of the political party.

Thus, the idea of holding a party accountable does not apply very well to many state party systems. Each state party system is unique. Some states might come close to meeting the responsible party ideal, but most do not. In Texas, neither party has a strong party organization or a strong grassroots organization. Candidates can act quite independently of either party.

The 1996 Democratic primary election to nominate a candidate to face Senator Phil Gramm provides a good example of this. Two Texas congressmen, Jim Chapman and John Bryant, vied for this nomination. John Bryant was forced into a runoff primary election against a political unknown—Victor Morales, a schoolteacher from the Dallas area. Congressman Bryant had the support of most party officials in Texas in the runoff primary election; however, Morales won with 51 percent of the vote. Parties do not always control the nomination processes and cannot bind officials to policies once they are elected, and so they often escape being held accountable.

→ FIFTY STATE PARTY SYSTEMS

In the United States we do not have strong national parties but fifty state party systems. The lack of elected national officials contributes to this. President and vice president are the only elected national offices. All others are state offices. The only time we see anything that resembles a national party organization is every four years when the Democrats and Republicans hold a convention to nominate their candidate for president. Both parties hold odd-year national conventions, but these receive little notice from the news media and the average citizen is unaware of them.

Most laws that govern the election of candidates and the activities of political parties are state, not national, laws. Voters elect members to the U.S. Congress at the state level. Technically, even voting for president is a state function, since members of the Electoral College are elected by state. The lack of national offices is a factor that weakens national parties and shifts emphasis to the state parties. Another factor is that each of the fifty state party organizations can act independently of the others and of the national party organization.

There is often a clear distinction between officials elected to state offices and those elected to congressional offices. For example, in Texas we elect two U.S. senators and thirty-two U.S. representatives. These members of Congress spend most of their time in Washington, focusing on national policy, not state policy. Texans also elect thirty-one state senators and 150 representatives to the state legislature. The members of the state legislature have a state focus. Occasionally the two groups of legislators (U.S. Congress and state legislature) might come together on common ground; most often they have different interests, agendas, and priorities. Thus, although state-elected officials might carry common party labels—*Democratic* and *Republican*—there is little interaction between state and national party officials. The national and state party organizations often act independently of each other.

Years ago, V. O. Key, Jr., observed this about state party systems:

> The institutions developed to perform functions in each state differ markedly from the national parties. It is an error to assume that the political parties of each state are but miniatures of the national party system. In a few states that condition is approached, but . . . each state has its own pattern of action and often it deviates markedly from the forms of organization commonly thought of as constituting party systems.[3]

Professor Key's observation is as valid today as it was in the 1950s. State party systems vary widely, and often the only common link is the name *Democrat* or *Republican*.

✦ CHANGES IN POLITICAL PARTIES

In the nineteenth and early twentieth century, state parties were controlled by party bosses in many states. These party bosses controlled government jobs, which they were allotted to the party faithful. The party boss also often controlled the nominating process by controlling the party caucus or convention, discussed later in this chapter.

After World War II the control and role of parties began to change, and today there are fewer patronage jobs to dispense to the party faithful. Today, parties are more oriented toward candidates and getting candidates elected to office. They collect money, recruit candidates, give money to candidates, register voters, and provide other supports to local party organizations. Both parties often have full-time, professional staffs that maintain offices in various locations on a year-round basis.

✦ PARTY STRENGTH

States can be classified according to the strength of party organization within the state. In Texas and other southern states, the Democratic party dominated state politics from Reconstruction in the 1870s until the 1960s. Few Republicans placed their names on the ballot.

Most studies of competition between the parties, including the ones used to construct the information provided in figure 5.1, rely upon several measures: (1) the percentage of votes won by each party in races for governor and state legislature; (2) the length of time each party controls the legislature and office of governor; and (3) the frequency with which parties divide control of the governorship and the legislature. These studies do not rely on voting for the office of president of the United States. For reasons discussed next, the vote for presidential candidates is not a good measure of party strength within a state.

The Republican party in Texas has been gaining strength for the past twenty-five years. It now controls both houses of the Texas legislature, and it has captured the governor's office six times in the last seven elections (1978, 1986, 1994, 1998, 2002, and 2004). Republicans hold all statewide elected offices. These victories have changed the classification for Texas from a modified one-party Democratic state to a modified one-party Republican state.

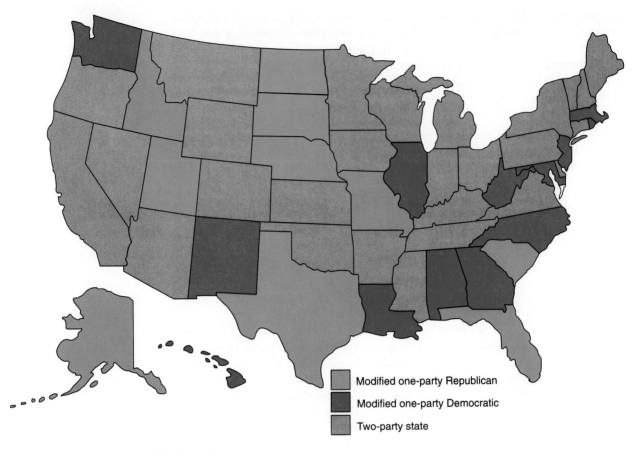

FIGURE 5.1   *Party Competition in the States.*

*SOURCE:*Thomas M. Holbrook and Raymond J. La Raja "Parties and Elections" in *Politics in the American States: A Comparative Analysis,* 9th edition, edited by Virginia Gray and Russell L. Hanson. Copyright © 2008 Congressional Quarterly Press, Washington, D.C. Table 3.4, p. 84. Reprinted by permission.

Table 5.1 shows party competition from 2003–2006. These data have been updated since 1946 in six separate studies. Since 1946 state party competitive patterns have changed. Three patterns are obvious. (See table 5.2.) First, one-party Democratic states have disappeared and are now classified as either modified one-party Democratic, two-party competitive, or modified one-party Republican states. Second, modified one-party Republican states have increased slightly in the past five years. Third, the number of two-party competitive states has decreased from thirty-one to twenty-six in 2006. From 1946 to 1994, a total of thirteen states remained two-party competitive states. Most of these changes in party competitive patterns are explained by changes in southern states where one-party Democratic states have become two-party competitive or modified one-party Republican states. In most other parts of the country, changes in party competitiveness have been less dramatic.

→ PARTY IDEOLOGY

party ideology
Basic belief system that guides the party.

The party labels *Democratic* and *Republican* do not necessarily indicate ideology. **Party ideology** is the basic belief system that guides the party. The Democratic party in one state can be quite different ideologically from the Democratic party in another state. For

TABLE 5.1

Index of Party Competitiveness in the Fifty States, 2003–2006

Modified One-Party Democratic

Massachusetts	0.724	Louisiana	0.808
West Virginia	0.730	Hawaii	0.828
Arkansas	0.758	North Carolina	0.835
New Mexico	0.765	Illinois	0.844
Rhode Island	0.773	Alabama	0.845
Maryland	0.785	Washington	0.847
New Jersey	0.808		

Two-Party Competition

Tennessee	0.859	Pennsylvania	0.998
Vermont	0.882	Delaware	0.978
Maine	0.889	Montana	0.973
Oklahoma	0.905	Nevada	0.972
Colorado	0.908	Michigan	0.971
California	0.910	Wisconsin	0.961
New York	0.917	New Hampshire	0.961
Connecticut	0.919	Indiana	0.950
Oregon	0.921	Arizona	0.919
Mississippi	0.935	Virginia	0.911
Iowa	0.968	Wyoming	0.887
Minnesota	0.971	Kansas	0.880
Kentucky	0.986	Ohio	0.860

Modified One-Party Republican

Missouri	0.841	Nebraska	0.745
Georgia	0.839	South Dakota	0.743
South Carolina	0.823	North Dakota	0.739
Texas	0.812	Utah	0.734
Florida	0.802	Idaho	0.717
Alaska	0.798		
Fifty-state average	0.863		

Note: The number shows the degree of interparty competitiveness. The range of the index is from zero (total Republican success) to 1 (total Democratic success). There are no one-party Republican or one-party Democratic states.

Source: Thomas M. Holbrook and Raymond J. La Raja "Parties and Elections" in *Politics in the American States: A Comparative Analysis,* 9th edition, edited by Virginia Gray and Russell L. Hanson. Copyright © 2008 Congressional Quarterly Press, Washington, D.C. Table 3.4, p. 84. Reprinted by permission.

many years in Texas, the Democratic party has had very strong conservative leanings. The Democratic party in Massachusetts, the home of Senator Edward Kennedy, has a liberal orientation. The conservatism of Texas Democrats shows in voter support for presidential candidates. Since the end of World War II, Texans have most often supported Republican candidates. Texas supported Dwight Eisenhower in 1952 and 1956, Richard Nixon in 1972, Ronald Reagan in 1980 and 1984, George Bush in 1988 and 1992, Bob Dole in 1996, and George W. Bush in 2000 and 2004. In the past twelve presidential elections, Texas has voted Democratic only four times; in two of these cases a native-son

TABLE 5.2

Patterns of Party Competition in the Fifty States, 1946 to 2003

Years	One-Party Democratic	Modified Democratic	Two-Party	Modified Republican	One-Party Republican
1946–63	8	9	25	8	0*
1956–70	7	13	23	7	0
1974–80	8	19	22	1	0
1981–88	1	21	22	6	0
1989–94	0	13	31	6	0
1995–98	0	9	28	12	0
1999–2003	0	9	31	10	0
2003–2006	0	13	26	11	0

*Data on Alaska and Hawaii not included for years 1946–53; included for 1953–63. Nebraska has nonpartisan legislative elections, so data are for governor only. There are some problems with the accuracy of this party index when used to measure competitiveness over long periods of time. The accuracy decreases with time. For a full discussion of this, see Harvey J. Tucker, "Interparty Competition in American States: One More Time," *American Politics Quarterly* 10 (January 1982): 93–116.

Sources: Data for 1946–63: Austin Ranney, "Parties in State Politics," *Politics in the American States*, ed. Herbert Jacob and Kenneth Vines (Boston: Little, Brown, 1965), 65. Data for 1956–70: Jacob and Vines, 2d ed. Data for 1974–80: John F. Bibby, Cornelius P. Cotter, James L. Gibson, and Robert J. Huchshorn, "Parties in State Politics," *Politics in the American States*, 3d ed., ed. Virginia Gray, Herbert Jacob, and Kenneth Vines (Boston: Little, Brown, 1983), 99. Data for 1981–88: *Politics in the American States*, 5th ed., ed. Virginia Gray, Herbert Jacob, and Robert B. Albritton (Boston: Little, Brown, 1990), 85–122. Data for 1989–94: John F. Bibby and Thomas M. Holbrook, "Parties and Elections," *Politics in the American States*, 6th ed., ed. Virginia Gray and Herbert Jacob (Washington, D.C.: Congressional Quarterly Press, 1996), 105. Data for 1999–2003: John F. Bibby and Thomas M. Holbrook, "Parties and Elections," *Politics in the American States: A Comparative Analysis*, 8th ed., ed. Virginia Gray and Russell L. Hanson (Washington, D.C.: Congressional Quarterly Press, 2004), 88. Data for 2003–2006: Thomas M. Holbrook and Raymond J. La Raja, "Parties and Elections," *Politics in the American States: A Comparative Analysis*, 9th ed., ed. Virginia Gray and Russell L. Hanson (Washington, D.C.: Congressional Quarterly Press, 2008), 84.

policy-relevant states
States in which political parties have measurably different policy orientations. The party in power supports policies different from those of the other party.

Democrat was on the ballot. Texans voted Democratic in 1960 and 1964 for Lyndon Johnson, and for Hubert Humphrey, vice president under Johnson, in 1968. Texans supported Jimmy Carter in 1976, in part because he was a southerner and in part due to the backwash from the Watergate scandal. This strong support for Republican presidential candidates results from ideological differences between the more conservative Texas Democratic party and the more liberal national Democratic party organization.

An examination of policy relevance will reveal more important distinctions than party labels. Policy relevance is defined as change in policy when control of the state government shifts from one party to another. If the "out" party captures either the office of governor or one or both houses of state government and policies change (e.g., Republicans decrease welfare spending), the state is classified as a policy-relevant state. A study found that most states are not **policy-relevant states**.[4] In this study, of the twenty-five states classified as two-party competitive states, twenty had policy-relevant political parties and five did not. In the ten states with modified competitive party systems, five were policy-relevant party states. Nineteen states were classified as noncompetitive party states, and only one of these had a policy-relevant party system.

Texas is ranked in this study as a noncompetitive, non-policy-relevant state. In recent years, a change in the person holding the office of governor has not resulted in any policy changes. The policies under Democrat Dolph Briscoe did not change when Republican Bill Clements was elected governor in 1976, nor did policies change much when Democrat Mark White replaced Bill Clements in 1982, or when Clements in turn replaced White in 1986. When Ann Richards was elected governor as a Democrat in 1990, replacing Bill Clements, only a few policy changes occurred. George W. Bush, a

Republican, defeated Ann Richards in 1994 and was reelected in 1998. In 2001, Rick Perry continued the conservative policies of the past. A close examination of the actions from 1995 to 2007 sessions of the Texas legislature shows little change from the conservative policies of the past. The traditionalistic/individualistic political culture of the state preserves the status quo and protects elite interests, regardless of the party of the governor or the majority party in the legislature. Bipartisan cooperation, so evident during the three Bush sessions of the legislature, was made easier because of philosophical agreements between the governor and the leadership of the house and senate. Texas has gone from a one-party Democratic controlled state to one dominated by the Republicans with no change in philosophy or policy. In the 2003 session of the legislature, bipartisan cooperation disappeared and has continued into the 2007 session.

Political buttons are a popular way for voters to declare their loyalty to a particular candidate.

✦ Democratic and Republican Party Strength in Texas

Texas has moved from being a one-party Democratic state to being a one-party Republican state, and this movement is reflected in public opinion polls. (See table 5.3.) In public opinion polls in 1952, only about 6 percent of Texans identified themselves as Republican. In the mid-1970s this number had increased to about 14 percent. In 1994 the number of individuals identifying themselves as Republican increased to 29 percent. More importantly, in the same period, Democratic party support decreased from 66 percent in 1952 to about 30 percent in 1994. Democrats and Republicans were equal at approximately 30 percent, and independents stood at about 30 percent until 2002. In 2005, independents have declined to 29 percent, Republicans have increased to 39 percent of the populous, and Democrats have declined to 55 percent. The question is, why did this change occur, and who supports each party today? To understand this, we need to examine the traditional areas of support for the Democratic and Republican parties in Texas. This will help to explain how Texas has become a two-party state.

✦ The One-Party Era in Texas

From the end of Reconstruction in 1874 until the 1960s, Texas was a **one-party Democratic state.** When Reconstruction ended, the switch from Republican control to Democratic control was almost immediate and absolute. From 1874 until 1961 no Republican was elected to statewide office, and only a few were elected to other offices. In 1928 the state did vote Republican, casting its Electoral College votes for Herbert Hoover. President Hoover's opponent was Al Smith, a Roman Catholic, and the vote was more anti-Catholic and anti-New Yorker than pro-Republican.

    This anti-Republicanism can be traced to the Civil War and Reconstruction. V. O. Key, Jr., observed that following the Civil War and the experiences of Reconstruction, southerners felt a very strong resentment toward the rest of the nation. This resentment bonded the South together as a unit, and they voted against all Republicans.[5]

one-party Democratic state
Control of most state offices from governor to local offices held by the Democratic party.

TABLE 5.3

Party Realignment in Texas, 1952 to 2005
Percentage of Population Identifying as Democrat, Republican, and Independent

Year	Democratic (%)	Republican (%)	Independent (%)
1952	66	6	28
1972	57	14	29
1983	39	23	38
1985	34	33	33
1994	30	29	41
1996	31	31	38
1998	33	33	34
2002	33	33	34
2005	25	39	29

Sources: Data for 1952–85 from James A. Dyer, Arnold Vedlitz, and David B. Hill, "New Voters, Switchers, and Political Party Realignment in Texas" in *The Western Political Quarterly* 41:156, March 1988. Data for 1994 from *The Texas Poll,* 1994, Harte-Hanks Communications. Figures for 1996 and 1998 from Texas Poll data, Scripps Howard Inc., University of Texas at Austin. Figures for 2002 and 2005: Texas Poll data, Scripps Howard Inc. In all cases data on independents include those identified as other party and as don't know.

Although this experience explains the initial one-party dominance in post-Reconstruction Texas, other factors prevented a challenge by the Republican party and allowed the Democratic party to dominate. Several second-party movements developed during the last three decades of the nineteenth century, and the conservative Democrats who controlled the party effectively destroyed all opposition.

In 1877 the Greenback party (initially, Greenback Clubs) formed in the South and West in reaction to declining farm prices. In Texas the Greenbackers were recruited from the more radical farmers. They demanded currency expansion ("greenbacks") to drive up agricultural prices, an income tax, the secret ballot, direct election of U.S. senators, better schools, and reduced railroad freight rates. In the governor's race in 1880, the Greenback party's candidate received about 12 percent of the vote. By 1884 the organization had faded out of existence. Also formed at this time was the Texas Farmers' Alliance, which became known as the Grange. This organization also represented small farmers and made an uneasy alliance with African Americans, who were the primary supporters of the Republican party.[6]

The large landowners and businesses of Texas controlled the state Democratic party and successfully destroyed these party movements. Gibson and Robinson point out:

> To protect their political power, the established agricultural leaders moved to divide the lower social groups by directing the discontent of the lower-income whites against the African Americans. The rural Bourbon elites, who manifested traditionalistic political values and wanted to consolidate power in the hands of the privileged few, also created an alliance with the mercantile, banking and emerging industrial leaders, who reflected individualistic views of a limited government that served to protect their interests. The two dominant forces consolidated political power and control and merged the politics of race with the politics of economics.[7]

This alliance between landowners and merchants allowed the Democratic party to dominate state politics from the late 1880s until the 1960s. There was no effective challenge to their dominance, except for a brief period during the Great Depression of the

1930s when the more liberal faction of the party had success in electing some state officials.

From the end of Reconstruction until at least the 1950s, Republicans were held in disrespect and the subject of joke and insult. Calling someone a Republican was an insult. Some termed the Republican party the "party of Yankee aggression." While living in Austin in the 1890s, the famous writer O. Henry once said, "We have only two or three laws [in Texas], such as against murder before witnesses and being caught stealing horses and voting Republican."

→ PARTY REALIGNMENT IN TEXAS

From 1940 to 1960, political conflicts and competition were confined to the Democratic party. As James R. Soukup, Clifton McCleskey, and Harry Holloway noted in 1964:

> Until recently, only Democratic Party nominees had an opportunity to capture state offices, and, therefore, ambitious men representing all shades of opinion tried to squeeze in under the same Democratic roof. The old guard Republicans failed not only to win elections, but even to provide mild criticism. Consequently, public officials saw little need for openly declaring themselves; in fact, they often felt that taking a stand would alienate rather than impress prospective voters. The resulting confusion of the general public reinforced the frequently observed American tendency to vote according to personalities rather than principles—thus making it difficult for political organizers to mobilize votes on the basis of well-defined politics.[8]

Writing about Texas political parties in 1949, V. O. Key, Jr., observed: "In Texas the vague outlines of a politics are emerging in which irrelevancies are pushed into the background and the people divided broadly along liberal and conservative lines." This division, according to Professor Key, is due to "personal insecurity of men suddenly made rich who are fearful lest they lose their wealth. . . . The Lone Star State is concerned about money and how to make it, about oil and sulphur and gas, about cattle and dust storms and irrigation, about cotton and banking and Mexicans."[9]

In Texas until the late 1960s, politics revolved almost exclusively around personality and economic issues. Race issues, which dominated many southern states, were less important in Texas.[10] The period from 1940 to 1960 might even be characterized as an era of nonpartisan politics, with domination by the conservative business community. Factional issues within the party, between liberals and conservatives, were driven by economics. Business people, oilmen, wealthy farmers, and cattle ranchers formed the backbone of the conservative element.

> The liberal element in Texas was also based on economic consideration. Liberalism in Texas encouraged welfare spending by means of deficit spending if necessary; promoted equal treatment for Negroes, Latin Americans, and other minorities; increased government regulation of business in accordance with the preceding aims, the expansion of the national government powers; trade union organization; and taxes on business—especially on large, interstate corporations—rather than on sales or individuals. Furthermore, liberals in Texas at this time made loyalty to the national Democratic Party a part of their creed.[11]

People voted Democratic partially out of habit and because of a lack of competition from the Republicans. Party primary elections replaced November general elections because there was no competition from Republicans. On the few occasions when Republicans mounted a challenge to Democrats in the November general election, most Texans still voted a straight ticket. The old saying "I would vote for a yellow dog before I'd vote for a Republican" summarizes the attitude of many voters. Yellow dogs ranked above Republicans.

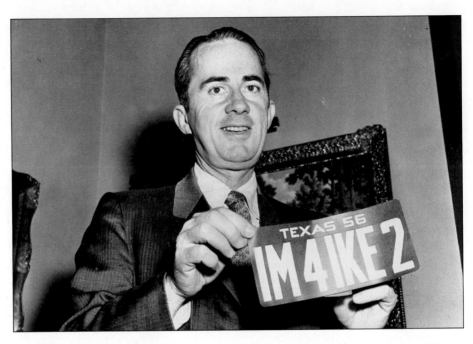

Democratic Governor Allan Shivers led a group of Democrats, the "Shivercrats," who endorsed Republican candidate Dwight D. Eisenhower.

The Beginning of Change

Yellow Dog Democrats
People who voted straight ticket for Democrats—would vote for a yellow dog if it ran as a Democrat.

In the 1952 and 1956 presidential elections, many **Yellow Dog Democrats** broke with tradition and voted for Eisenhower. The leader of this movement was the Democratic governor, Allan Shivers, the leader of the conservative faction of the party. This faction chose to dissociate themselves from the New Deal/Fair Deal element of the national Democratic party and with any candidate it might pose.

In the fall of 1952, at the state Democratic party convention, Governor Shivers succeeded in getting the state delegates to endorse the Republican candidate for president—Dwight D. Eisenhower. The Republican state party convention also nominated Shivers and most statewide Democratic candidates as the Republican party's nominees. Thus, Shivers and most statewide office seekers were candidates for both political parties in 1952. This group became known as the **Shivercrats.** The liberal faction of the Democratic party became known as the "Loyalists" and associated with the national Democratic party.[12]

Shivercrats
Democrats who followed Governor Allen Shiver's example and voted for Eisenhower in 1952 and 1956.

This action, and a similar action in 1956, began the Texas tradition of supporting Republican presidential candidates while retaining Democratic party dominance over state offices. Presidential politics in 1952 broke the tradition of voting a **straight ticket,** at least for the top of the ticket.

straight ticket party voting
Casting all your votes for candidates of one party.

The Election of John Tower

In 1960 Lyndon Johnson, the senior senator from Texas, ran as the Democratic candidate for the U.S. Senate and as the vice presidential candidate with John F. Kennedy. Johnson's presence on the Democratic ticket temporarily stayed the movement toward the Republican party. In a special election in 1961, John Tower was elected U.S. senator to fill the seat formerly held by Lyndon Johnson and became the first Republican statewide officeholder since the 1870s. Tower's win was helped by a special election that attracted seventy-one candidates. Tower received 41 percent of the vote in the first election and managed a slight majority in the runoff election.

The selection of Senator John Tower as the first statewide Republican officeholder since the end of Reconstruction was originally heralded as the beginning of a new era of two-party politics in the state. In the 1962 elections, Republicans managed to field candidates for many statewide, congressional, and local races. There were, for a variety of reasons, few successes. Some of these candidates were very weak and some proved an embarrassment for the Republicans. Tower won reelection in 1966, 1972, and 1978, but it would be seventeen years before another Republican (Bill Clements in 1978) won statewide office.

The Election of Bill Clements

Republicans had some success in electing legislators and local officeholders. The election of Bill Clements as governor in 1978 marked the real beginning of two-party politics in Texas. Governor Clements used his power to make appointments to boards, commissions, and judgeships (see Chapter 8) and to recruit people who would publicly declare their Republicanism. Some referred to these new converts as "closet Republicans" that had finally gone public. These appointments helped build the Republican party in Texas, the start of **party realignment in Texas.**

party realignment in Texas
The change from a state dominated by one political party to a two-party system operating today.

Governor George W. Bush, giving his inaugural address in 1995.

The loss of the governorship by Clements in 1982 to Democrat Mark White was a blow to the Republicans because the party also had little success in gaining other statewide offices. In that year the Democrats elected Ann Richards as state treasurer, Jim Hightower as agriculture commissioner, Gary Mauro as land commissioner, and Jim Mattox as attorney general. In 1986 Republican fortunes improved when Bill Clements returned to the governor's office. He defeated Mark White in what many termed a "revenge match."

The "Conversion" and Election of Phil Gramm

In 1983, John Tower announced that he would not seek reelection to the U.S. Senate in 1984. Phil Gramm, the Democratic representative from the sixth Congressional District, used Tower's retirement to advance from the U.S. House to the Senate. Gramm had been first elected as a Democrat in 1976. By early 1981 Gramm had gained some national prominence by helping President Reagan "cut the federal budget."[13] Gramm, who served as a member of the House Budget Committee, was accused of leaking Democratic strategy to the White House budget office. David Stockman, budget director under Ronald Reagan, confirmed that he had.[14] Because of his disloyalty to the party and because of house rules, Gramm was not reappointed to another term on the Budget Committee.

In a smart political move, Gramm used this loss of his committee seat as an excuse to convert to the Republican party. In 1983 Gramm resigned his seat in the U.S. House. Outgoing Republican Governor Clements called a special election, which was held thirty days after Gramm's resignation. Since no other candidate could possibly put together a successful campaign in so short a time, Gramm easily won reelection to Congress as a Republican. In 1984, "fully baptized" as a Republican, Gramm won election as U.S. senator, pulled along on the coattails of President Ronald Reagan. The Republican party retained the seat in the U.S. Senate. Gramm easily won reelection in 1990 and 1996 but chose not to run for reelection in 2002, thus ending a long political career in Texas politics.

The Move toward Parity with the Democrats, 1988–1994

In 1988 the Republicans made significant gains, aided by Bill Clements's return in 1987 to the governor's mansion and George Bush's election to the presidency. The party won four statewide offices. Three Republicans won election to the Texas Supreme Court, and Kent Hance was elected to the Texas Railroad Commission.

In 1990 Republicans captured the offices of state treasurer and agricultural commissioner and another seat on the state supreme court. The big setback for the Republicans in 1990 was the loss of the governor's office. Bill Clements did not seek reelection. Clayton Williams, a political newcomer, used his considerable wealth to win the Republican nomination. His campaign for governor was something of a disaster, and he managed to lose to Democrat Ann Richards. This loss by Williams enabled George W. Bush to be elected in 1994. Since Clayton Williams would probably have served two terms, George W. Bush could not have been elected governor until 1998 and this would not have provided him with enough experience to make a race for president in 2000.

In 1992 Democrat Lloyd Bentsen, after serving as U.S. senator from Texas for twenty years, resigned to become secretary of the treasury under President Clinton. His resignation allowed Republicans to capture their second seat in the U.S. Senate with the election of Kay Bailey Hutchison. In 1996 Phil Gramm was elected to a third term as U.S. senator from Texas.

In 1994 the Republicans captured all three seats on the Railroad Commission and a majority of the seats on the state supreme court, and they retained control of the agriculture commissioner's office. In addition, Republicans captured three additional seats on the state board of education, for a total of eight seats. More important, George W. Bush was elected governor. When the dust cleared, Republicans controlled a total of twenty-three statewide offices. These wins, coupled with additional seats in the Texas house and senate, substantially changed Texas party structure. Texas moved into the two-party era.

Governor Bush and the Republican Dominance, 1995–2001

In 1994 the son of former President George Bush ran for governor of Texas and beat the Democratic incumbent Ann Richards. Governor George W. Bush, to a large degree, won because of family name recognition rather than political experience. Governor Bush had no statewide electoral experience before running for governor. In 1976 he ran for Congress in his "hometown" of Midland. He lost to Kent Hance, who later changed parties and won a seat on the Texas Railroad Commission as a Republican. During the 1995 and 1997 sessions of the Texas legislature, Governor Bush developed a reputation as a bipartisan leader. This was in part due to the rather noncontroversial nature of his programs and good economic times in the state. The legislature was not faced with the need to raise taxes, but with the decision about what to do with a surplus.

In 1998 Governor Bush again won election with 67 percent of the popular vote in a low voter turnout election, which always favors Republicans because Republicans are likely to be from higher income groups, and higher income people are more likely to vote than lower income people. While Bush touted this as a huge victory, only 18 percent of the qualified voters voted for him. It was a landslide victory of sorts.

The popularity of Bush also helped down-ballot candidates win election for all statewide executive offices and many judicial offices. For the first time in over 120 years Texas elected Republicans to all but one statewide elected office.

It is not clear at this time if this Republican sweep of all but one statewide office is a trend toward a one-party Republican state or a unique event. The extreme popularity of Governor Bush and his family, coupled with the lowest turnout (24 percent) since 1978 (the year Bill Clements was first elected), contributed to this Republican sweep of offices.

With the election of Governor George W. Bush as president, some have speculated that his absence from state politics may make it easier for Democrats to regain some offices. Lt. Governor Ratliff called Governor Bush the Grizzly Bear of Texas politics. He remarked that with the Grizzly gone to Washington, things were going to be different in Texas. The absence of George W. Bush, coupled with the increase in minority populations in the state, may mark the beginning of a new era in which the Republicans face more competition from the Democrats.

In December of 2000, Rick Perry, lieutenant governor under George W. Bush, succeeded Bush as governor. While Perry had served as lieutenant governor with some success, he has had limited success in filling the void left by Bush's departure. He had little impact on the legislative agenda in 2001; his budget message and programs were generally ignored by the legislature in the 2001 and 2003 sessions, and in a special session in the summer of 2004.

✦ REPUBLICAN DOMINANCE IN 2002-2004

In the 2002 election the Republican party captured all statewide elected offices, controlled the Texas senate, and for the first time in 125 years, controlled the Texas house. It is evident in the 2002 election of straight ticket party voting across the board in most elections. The exceptions were legislative races where Democrats were able to hold on to some county-level offices and to retain sixty-two state house seats, twelve Texas senate seats, and seventeen of thirty-two congressional districts.

TABLE 5.4

Voting by Demographic Neighborhoods in Harris County in 2002

Type of Neighborhood	% Voted	% Perry	% Sanchez	% Others
Mexican American	27.6	10.4	88.5	1.1
Low-income Anglo/Hispanic	23.8	30.1	68.5	1.4
Low-income African American	29.5	5.0	94.3	0.7
Middle-income African American	43.1	8.8	90.5	0.7
Middle-income Anglo	39.2	73.5	24.6	1.9
Upper-income Anglo	55.0	72.3	25.9	1.8

Type of Neighborhood	% Voted	% Kirk	% Cornyn	% Others
Mexican American	25.6	85.3	12.8	1.9
Low-income Anglo/Hispanic	22.3	66.7	31.8	1.5
Low-income African American	29.3	97.5	1.9	0.5
Middle-income African American	42.8	95.5	4.1	0.4
Middle-income Anglo	38.9	27.6	71.2	1.2
Upper-income Anglo	54.8	30.1	69.1	0.8

Note: Voting precincts in Harris County were broken down by income, race, and ethnic background to determine voting patterns. Upper-income black and Asian Americans were not included in the survey because registered voters in those categories do not live in concentrated areas in large enough numbers to constitute a voting block. More than 75 percent of the Hispanic registered voters in Harris County are Mexican Americans and are predominantly lower to middle income.

Source: Houston Chronicle, Thursday, November 14, 2002, page 32A. Data collected by Richard Murray, University of Houston.

Republicans will continue to be the dominant party in Texas for some time. As Texas becomes a majority-minority state it remains to be seen if these new participants (Hispanics, African Americans, and Asians) will continue to show strong support for Democratic candidates. If they do, the dominance of the Republican party will be reduced in the next thirty years. While Republicans claim to have made strong inroads into the Hispanic community, most Hispanics still show strong support for Democratic candidates. Table 5.4 shows that in the 2002 election in Harris County, Hispanics gave strong support to Democratic candidates in statewide races. This is also true of black voters. Table 5.4 clearly shows the low levels of voter turnout in both Hispanic and black neighborhoods. One could question if Harris County is representative of the state as a whole. We do know that the Harris County vote for constitutional amendments (see table 2.3) does mirror the statewide vote.

As can be seen in table 5.4, Hispanics and blacks do not vote in large numbers, and until they do, the likelihood of Democratic candidates getting elected is slim. Low voter turnout among minority groups was evident in the 1998 and 2002 elections. Until Hispanic and black voting increases, Texas is likely to remain a dominant Republican party state.

✦ THE STRENGTH OF THE REPUBLICAN PARTY

Statewide success has been recent for the Republicans, but there are areas of the state where Republicans have enjoyed support for many years. As we saw in Chapter 1, German immigrants to Texas accounted for much of the Republican vote in Texas from the end of Reconstruction until the 1960s. Republicans also traditionally received votes from the Panhandle region of the state, which was settled by immigrants from the Midwest who brought their Republican loyalties with them. These two areas provided the traditional Republican support in the state.

In the 1950s and 1960s, Republicans began to gain strength in the suburban areas of Dallas and Houston, in oil-producing counties in East Texas, and in the Midland-Odessa area of West Texas. Voters in oil-producing areas supported Republican candidates largely because of national Republican party policies that favored the oil industry. The suburban areas of Houston and Dallas contained many immigrants from other states with Republican loyalties.

Republican support is found today in the traditional areas and among young professionals and new immigrants to the state who have settled in the suburbs of Dallas/Fort Worth, Houston, and San Antonio. These new residents are not socialized into voting a straight Democratic ticket as older native Texans were. Republicans also draw disproportionally from among young voters. (See table 5.5.)

The profile of the average Republican supporter in Texas would include the following: young, high income, well educated, Anglo, professional, living in the suburbs of a large metropolitan area. In addition, Republican voters are likely to be newcomers to the state. One study concluded that about one-fourth of Texas Republicans are new arrivals in the state.[15]

By contrast, the Democratic party draws support from older residents, native Texans, the lower-income groups, the less educated, and minority groups, especially Mexican Americans in South Texas and African Americans in urban areas and East Texas. There is also some variation among religious groups, with Catholics, especially Catholic Mexican Americans, showing strong support for the Democratic party and Protestant fundamentalists showing more support for the Republican party. A careful examination of table 5.5 will help in understanding these differences between Republicans and Democrats.

There is some concern among Texans that party realignment will produce race-based political parties. The Republican party's appeals to whites, especially appeals that have racial overtones, could drive most Mexican Americans and African Americans into the Democratic party. In Chapter 7 we examine this question in more detail, and we see how race is a central force in legislative elections.

In the 1998 election, Governor Bush seemed to realize that it is necessary for Republicans to appeal to minority voters if they are to remain the dominant party. He especially made appeals to the Mexican American voters, and this effort may have paid off. He received about 40 percent of the Mexican American votes. However, this was not a significant change in how Mexican Americans vote. It was more a vote for Bush; to some degree the percent Bush received was magnified by low voter turnout.

Party realignment in Texas is in part the result of regional and national trends. There is more support nationally for Republicans, and this has an impact on Texas. Texas voters, like voters elsewhere in the Old South, have switched from the Democratic to the Republican party. Immigration to Texas from other states has also helped the growth of the Republican party.

In addition to electing statewide officeholders, the Republicans have made inroads into controlling locally elected offices, especially at the county level. While Democrats still control about 75 percent of the state's 254 counties, this is also changing. Some county officials are converting to the Republican party, and the party is having some success at electing local officials. In 1994 Republicans controlled 900 local

TABLE 5.5

Party Identification among Texans by Socioeconomic Factors, 2005

Total %	Republican, 39%	Democrat, 25%	Independent, 23%	Other, 10%
Age				
18–29	41	25	22	7
30–39	43	23	19	13
40–49	43	21	18	15
50–59	39	24	26	9
60 and older	36	30	26	7
Race/Ethnicity				
Hispanic	26	34	29	8
Anglo	47	21	22	9
Black	8	58	17	12
Gender				
Male	40	20	27	10
Female	29	30	18	10
Region				
East	39	23	26	9
West	43	25	27	5
South	34	31	22	11
North	42	24	22	9
Gulf	47	28	18	7
Central	33	27	30	8
Income				
Less than $10,000	27	42	22	7
$10,001–$20,000	27	38	19	12
$20,001–$30,000	33	34	26	7
$30,001–$40,000	33	27	25	14
$40,001–$50,000	40	22	23	11
$50,001–$60,000	41	32	16	9
$60,001 and above	52	16	21	9
Education				
Some high school	29	40	20	8
High school grad	34	30	22	9
Some college	43	25	16	14
College grad	45	18	29	7
Graduate school	40	22	26	11

Source: Texans poll, Scripps Howard News Service. Reprinted by permission.

offices, an increase from 814 in 1992 and 717 in 1990. (See table 5.6.) By 2002, this number had increased to approximately 1,327, and 1,391 by 2004.

Control of local offices is beginning to occur even in the East Texas Piney Woods region of the state, most noted for straight ticket voting. Although Democrats control a majority of the county judges, the area is beginning to vote for Republican candidates. George W. Bush carried twenty of the thirty East Texas counties in the 1994 governor's race.[16] Five of these counties (Bowie, Hardin, Harrison, Shelby, and Titus) had never

TABLE 5.6

Total Offices Held by Republicans, by Year, 1974 to 2006

Year	U.S. Senate	Other Statewide	U.S. House	Texas Senate	Texas House	County Office	State Board of Education*
1974	1	0	2	3	16	53	
1976	1	0	2	3	19	67	
1978	1	1	4	4	22	87	
1980	1	1	5	7	35	166	
1982	1	0	5	5	36	270	
1984	1	0	10	6	52	377	
1986	1	1	10	6	56	504	
1988	1	5	8	8	57	608	5
1990	1	6	8	8	57	717	5
1992	1	7	9	13	58	814	5
1994	2	13	11	14	61	900	8
1996	2	13	11	17	68	950	8
1998	2	18	11	16	71	973	9
2000	2	18	11	16	71	1,231	9
2002	2	27	15	19	88	1,327[†]	10
2004	2	27	22	19	87	1,390	10
2006	1	27	22	20	81	1,410	10

*State Board of Education was not elected until 1988.

[†]County offices are estimates by the author.

Sources: Houston Chronicle, 13 November 1994, 16A. Copyright © 1994 Houston Chronicle Publishing Company. Reprinted with permission. All rights reserved. Figures for 1996 and 1998 from own sources. Data for 1996–2000 generated by the author. Data for 2002, 2004, and 2006 from the secretary of state's Web page.

before voted for a Republican governor.[17] In 1998 Governor Bush carried all of these East Texas counties. In fact, Bush failed to carry only 15 of the 254 counties in the state. All but one of these 15 counties (Foard County) were in South Texas along the Rio Grande river where Mexican Americans have traditionally voted Democratic.

In 2000 and 2002, Republicans dominated most races in East Texas. The exceptions are house, senate, and congressional races where some Democrats were elected. The era of the Yellow Dog Democrat may be at an end. In part, it has been replaced by straight ticket voting Republicans. One sage referred to them as **Yellow Pup Republicans.**

Yellow Pup Republican
Younger voters who tend to vote straight ticket for Republican candidates.

✦ THE DEATH OF THE YELLOW DOG DEMOCRAT?

In 1995 the then state agricultural commissioner, Rick Perry (the current Republican governor) pronounced, "Yellow Dog Democrats are dead."[18] Some Democrats disagree. Ed Martin, executive director of the Texas Democratic party at that time, said, "Anybody who thinks Yellow Dogs are dead may be looking for tooth marks." Martin attributes much of the success of the Republicans in East Texas to hot-button issues: "They focus on hot-button issues, get Texans to look the other way while picking their pockets. The old saw is that Republicans have successfully used **guns, gays, and God** as polarizing wedges to define themselves. We have nothing equally emotional to define ourselves."[19]

Since Yellow Dog Democrats are more likely to be older, native Texans, the Yellow Dogs are dying off. The Republicans have had great success at getting voters to

guns, gays, and God
Wedge issues used by Republicans to get Democratic voters to vote for Republican candidates.

cast a straight Republican ticket. In Harris County in 1994, sixteen contested Democratic incumbents for district and county judges were replaced by straight ticket voting for Republican judges. Only one incumbent Democrat was reelected. In 1998 the remaining Democratic judges who were up for election lost their seats. In 1998 only one Democratic party judge remained in office in Harris County—Judge Katie Kennedy, who was not up for reelection until the year 2000. In 2000 Judge Kennedy did not seek reelection and was replaced by a Republican. In the 2002 election, straight ticket voting was evident, especially in the statewide judicial races, all of which were won by Republicans by similar vote counts.

In the 1998 and 2000 elections there was less emphasis on straight ticket voting by the Republican party; however, the clean sweep by the Republicans may well spell the end to the Yellow Dog Democrat. In the 2002 election, Republicans managed to win many additional seats in the Yellow Dog stronghold of East Texas. According to Dick Murray, a political scientist at the University of Houston, in past elections, Democrats managed to get about 35 percent of the white vote. In 2002, Ron Kirk, the Democratic candidate for senator (who is black) managed to get only 31 percent of the white vote, and gubernatorial candidate Tony Sanchez got only 27 percent of the white vote. Murray estimates that for every Hispanic voter the Democrats gain, they lose one white one.[20]

If the Republican efforts to encourage straight ticket voting are successful, especially with younger Texans, perhaps Yellow Dogs are not so much dead as changed from Yellow Dog Democrats to Yellow Pup Republicans. In the final analysis, this might not mean much in terms of a change in state policy. The traditionalistic/individualistic political culture has not changed and will not change any time soon. Texas is experiencing party realignment while maintaining continuity of political ideology.[21] The change can be described as a change in party label rather than change in ideology or policy.

party de-alignment
View that holds that a growing number of voters and candidates do not identify with either major political party but are independents.

Ross Perot's campaigns are an excellent example of an independent candidate's efforts to affect a presidential race.

→ PARTY DE-ALIGNMENT

An alternate view of party realignment is **party de-alignment**. This view holds that the growing number of voters who do not identify with either party, but instead call themselves independent, is an indication of the low esteem for political parties and politics in general among American voters.[22] Many citizens do not see any difference in the two major parties and do not identify with either major party. In addition, candidates can operate independently of any party and capture a nomination without party support. With enough money, candidates can gain the party nomination. In recent years, Clayton Williams, Kay Bailey Hutchison, and Richard Fisher have all gained nomination using media-driven campaigns with limited support from party officials. More recently, Victor Morales gained the Democratic party nomination for the U.S. Senate without support from party officials. Steve Forbes made inroads in the Republican primaries using mass media campaign techniques in 1996. Similarly, in 2002 Democrat Tony Sanchez used mass media to gain recognition in the governor's race, although he had

support of the state party organization. In addition, the media play a larger role in screening candidates. The net effect of party de-alignment is that parties play a less important role today in state politics. Parties no longer perform traditional functions, because other institutions (such as interest groups, professional campaign managers, and the media) have assumed these functions. For parties to regain their prominence, they must begin to again perform these functions. Thus, the changing nature of parties in Texas is not unique to the state but part of a much larger national change in the role played by political parties.

✧ THIRD-PARTY MOVEMENTS IN TEXAS

Although this chapter has concentrated on the two major political parties in the state, it should be noted that from time to time third-party movements develop in Texas. Some of these third parties are national; others have been state-based organizations. There have been several third-party efforts in Texas since the end of World War II. George Wallace used the American Independent party to run for president in 1968 and managed to gain 18 percent of the Texas vote.[23] In the 1970s the **Raza Unida** (United Race) party ran candidates for several state and local offices, especially in South Texas. Ramsey Muniz managed to gain 7.2 percent of the vote for governor in 1972. The Libertarian party has also run candidates for state offices in Texas for many years. Seldom do their candidates manage to gain more than a small percentage of the votes. The most successful was Jeff Daiell, who received 4 percent of the vote for governor in 1990. In the 2002 election, the Libertarian party lost its status as a minor party by failing to gain 2 percent of the vote in statewide races. Party status is determined by the state election code, which is discussed subsequently.

Raza Unida
Minor party (United Race) supporting election of Mexican Americans in Texas in the 1970s.

Ross Perot's run as an independent candidate for president in 1992 is yet another example. Even though Perot received about 22 percent of the statewide vote, he did not affect the outcome. President George H. Bush won Texas's thirty-two electoral votes. In 1996, Ross Perot began but abandoned his effort to have his Reform party placed on the ballot. In Texas he ran as an independent in 1996 and had little impact on the outcome.

In 1996 the Natural Law party gained enough signatures to have its name placed on the ballot. This organization promotes the idea of transcendental meditation as a way to reduce crime and strongly supports environmental protection, clean energy, and health issues. The party's presidential candidate was Dr. John Hagelin of Maharishi University of Management in Fairfield, Iowa. The party planned to run candidates for congressional and state offices.[24] In 1998, in part due to a change in state law, the Libertarian party appeared on the ballot and fielded candidates for many statewide and local offices. The Libertarian party also fielded candidates for many offices in the 2000, 2004, and 2006 elections. None was successful.

Finally, in the 2000 presidential election, Green party candidate Ralph Nader ran for president. He received only 137,000 votes in an election where about 7 million votes were cast.

To date, third parties have not had much impact on Texas politics. The rules governing elections in Texas, as in many other states, do not make it easy for third parties to gain access to the ballot. Even if third parties do gain access to the ballot, they still face an uphill battle to gain the financial resources necessary to run a successful high-dollar media campaign. Often the best a minor party can hope to do is to have its ideas picked up by a major party. Ross Perot is credited with focusing on the need to balance the federal budget in his 1992 campaign. Few other good examples of third-party movements that have had an impact on state or national policy can be found in the last three decades of the twentieth century.

✦ Party Organization in Texas

Political parties in all states have formal organizations. Their organizational structure is partly determined by state law, but parties have some discretion in deciding specific arrangements. Additionally, rules established by the national Democratic and Republican party organizations might dictate state party actions in selected areas, such as the number of delegates to the national convention and how they are selected.

In Texas, the Texas Election Code decides many aspects of party activity, especially the conduct of primary elections. Earlier we discussed the white primaries in Texas, which excluded African Americans from voting in Democratic party primary elections and which were eventually outlawed by the U.S. Supreme Court. This is a good example of party activity being restricted by national or state laws. Thus parties are not free agents or private organizations, but quasi-public agents.

We will be discussing the party organization in Texas, but this is very similar to that used in the other forty-nine states. There are two broad categories of party organization in all states: the permanent party organization and the temporary party organization. While there are variations among the states, party organization is basically the same for the Democratic and Republican parties.

Permanent Party Organization

permanent party organization
Series of elected officials on a political party that keep the party organization alive between elections.

The **permanent party organization** consists of elected party officers. At the lowest level is the precinct chair. Each county in Texas is divided into voting precincts or polling places. Each voting precinct contains about two thousand voters, although in rural areas there may be as few as a hundred voters in a precinct. Statewide there are about nine thousand voting precincts. When voters register, they are assigned to a precinct-based polling place near their home. Polling places are normally located in public buildings (schools, city halls, churches) but may be located in private homes when no public building is available.

The precinct chair is elected for a two-year term during the party's primary election, which is normally held in March of even-numbered years. Any registered voter may file for precinct chair, and his or her name will be placed on the ballot. Occasionally these races are contested, but more often the precinct chair is reelected without opposition. Write-in votes are allowed with no pre-election filing notice required. It is not uncommon for a person to win election by writing in his or her name. In 1976 Paul Van Riper, a professor of political science at Texas A&M, was elected precinct chair in Brazos County with one write-in vote, his own. In 1978 his name appeared on the ballot, and he was reelected with three votes.

precinct chair
Party official elected in each voting precinct to organize and support the party.

Ideally, the role of the **precinct chair** is to organize the precinct, identify party supporters, make sure they are registered to vote, turn out voters on election day, and generally promote and develop the interests of the party at this level. In the one-party Democratic era in Texas, few precinct chairs performed these duties; generally their only duty was to serve as election judge during primary and general elections. As Texas develops into a two-party state, the role of the precinct chair may change from election judge to party organizer at the grassroots level. In some counties this already has occurred, but neither party is well organized at the grassroots level.

county chair
Party officials elected in each county to organize and support the party.

The next office in the party hierarchy is **county chair.** This position is also filled during the primary election, and the person elected serves a two-year term. Any registered voter may file for the office. In large urban counties this office is usually contested. The role of the county chair is similar to that of the precinct chair, but at the county level. Informally, the county chair's duties consist of representing the party in the county, serving as the official spokesperson for the party, maintaining a party headquarters (in some counties), and serving as a fund-raiser. Formally, the county chair is responsible for receiving formal filings from persons seeking to have their names placed on the party's primary election ballot, conducting the primary election, filling election judge positions, and officially counting the ballots in the primary election.

In large urban counties, the county chair is often a full-time paid employee whose job is to organize the party at the county level. This involves voter registration, fund-raising, candidate recruitment and education, and aiding in the election of candidates in the general election.

The **county executive committee** is the next level in the permanent party organization. It is composed of all precinct chairs and the county chair. The degree of organization of this committee varies greatly from county to county. In some counties the executive committee is an active organization that works to promote the party's interests. In many counties, especially in rural areas, this committee is more a paper organization that fulfills the formal duties of canvassing the election returns and filling vacancies in party offices when they occur. Occasionally, the committee might be called upon to fill a vacancy on the general election ballot if a nominee has died or has become ineligible to run between the time of the primary and the general election.

county executive committee
Committee made up of county chair and all precinct chairs in the county. Serves as the official organization for the party in each county.

Many large metropolitan counties use, instead of the county executive committee, a district executive committee for some functions. This is an organizational convenience because these counties have such large county committees. District committees are organized around the state senatorial districts. In Harris, Dallas, Tarrant, and Bexar Counties, there are several senate districts. (See Chapter 7, figure 7.3, for a map of these districts.)

The next level of permanent party organization is the **state executive committee.** From each of Texas's thirty-one senatorial districts, each party, by tradition, elects one man and one woman to serve on the state executive committee. Their election usually occurs during the state convention, which traditionally is held in June of even-numbered election years. Delegates to this convention caucus by senatorial district and elect their representative to the state executive committee; the state convention, as a whole, ratifies these choices.

state executive committee
Committee made up of one man and one woman elected from each state senatorial district that functions as the governing body of the party.

Being selected to serve on the state executive committee is considered an honor, usually reserved for those who have strong political ties and who have supported the party for many years. Occasionally a maverick group will surface and take control of the party, electing their people, who might not be the longtime party faithful. The Texas Republican party experienced this from 1994 to 2002, when the Christian Right took control of the party; it has maintained that control for the last decade.

The state convention also elects a state party chair and vice chair; one must be a woman. Traditionally in the Democratic party, the state chair and vice chair were chosen by the governor or gubernatorial candidate, and the state chair office was often filled by the governor's campaign manager. With the rise of the Republican party and the election of three GOP governors, the state chair is not the automatic choice of the governor; however, the party candidate for governor still has influence in deciding who the state party chair will be. Governor Bush found himself in the position of being somewhat uncomfortable with the leadership of the Republican party in Texas and with the state party platform, especially in 1998 and 2000. As was indicated earlier, then Governor Bush did not attend the Republican state convention in 2000.

At the state level, the functions of the state chair and the state executive committee are very similar to those of the county chair and county executive committee. They have similar informal duties of organizing the party and formal duties of conducting primary elections. Both parties in Texas have permanent, full-time, paid professional staffs that

SARGENT © 1994 Austin American-Statesman. Reprinted with permission of Universal Press Syndicate. All rights reserved.

do most of the work at the state level. The state chair and executive committee are policy-making positions. Their main function should be to provide leadership for the party.

Temporary Party Organization

temporary party organization
Series of meetings or conventions that occur every two years at the precinct, county, and state level.

The **temporary party organization,** for both parties, consists of a series of conventions (caucuses) held in even-numbered years. The precinct convention is held on the same day as the party primary, usually the second Tuesday in March. Any voter who has voted in that party's primary is eligible to attend the precinct convention. The polls usually close at 7:00 P.M., and the precinct convention begins at 7:30 to 7:45 P.M. The precinct chair acts as temporary chair of the convention, checking to see that attendees have voted in that party's primary election, calling the meeting to order, and directing the election of permanent officers. Usually the precinct chair is elected permanent chair of the convention, and his or her temporary appointees for vice chair and secretary are usually selected as permanent officers. Sometimes, especially during presidential election years, control of the convention's officers becomes an issue. In non–presidential election years, attendance is usually very low, and control of the convention is generally not an issue.

After officers are elected, the most important function of the convention is the selection of delegates to the county convention (or the district convention, in large metropolitan counties). This convention is held two weeks after the precinct convention. The number of delegates a precinct sends to the county convention is based on party support in that precinct; the higher the party support, the larger the number of delegates. For years, Democrats have awarded one county convention seat for every twenty-five votes cast for the party's candidate for governor in the last election. During presidential election years, many people are interested in attending the county convention, and the seats can be hotly contested. In odd years, finding enough volunteers to attend the county convention is often difficult. Precinct conventions may also adopt resolutions in hopes of having them included in the party platform.

The county convention (or district convention) is a replay of the precinct convention. Selection of delegates to the state convention is its most important function. Again, the number of delegates a county sends to the state convention depends on the county's support for the party's gubernatorial candidate in the last election.

Democratic Party Convention in 2008

In most election years few people attend the precinct conventions. In 2008, the situation was quite different. Hillary Clinton and Barack Obama were in a very tight race for delegates. The precinct conventions were attended by thousands of people statewide. Most caucus chairs were overwhelmed by the crowds of participants. Sign-in sheets, used to show candidate support, were in short supply. In a few cases, campaign signs were used to sign up attendees.

News reports described the meetings as attended by rowdy mobs. Often the size of the room was inadequate to hold the large crowd. In a few cases, police were called in to quell the attendees. Many meetings lasted until late in the evening. Most attendees had never attended a precinct meeting before and were unaware of why they were there and what the meeting would accomplish. The news reports had described the activity as a chance to vote twice, and many showed up thinking they were going to vote again.

The county and district conventions held two weeks after the precinct meetings were equally well attended and almost as disorganized. Many attendees were first timers and did not know the rules. Some were suspicious that those running the convention were somehow not playing fairly. Often these meetings ran from noon to late in the evening. Many attendees left the meeting before it ended. Some suggested that the whole process proved the old saying by Will Rogers, "I am not a member of any organized political party. I am a Democrat."

The state convention is normally held in June of even-numbered years. Normally the convention is held in a major city and moved around to different cities for political reasons. At the state convention during presidential election years, the most important event is the selection of delegates to the national convention that nominates the party's candidate for president. In the past three presidential elections, Texas has used a presidential preference primary, held in March. The primary decides the presidential preference of most, but not all, of the delegates from Texas at the national convention. Without presidential preference primary elections, all delegate preferences would be decided at the state convention.

In addition to the state party officers chosen at these state conventions, during presidential election years these conventions also elect the representatives (electors) who will serve in the Electoral College if their party candidate wins the popular vote in Texas. By tradition, Texas Democrat delegates caucus by senatorial districts at the state convention and choose their elector. Republicans caucus by U.S. congressional districts. These decisions are ratified by the convention as a whole.[25] Those chosen to serve in the Electoral College are generally longtime party supporters. The electors of the party winning the popular vote meet in Austin, in the Senate Chamber, at 2 P.M. on the first Monday after the second Wednesday in December following their election and cast their vote.[26]

Both parties hold national conventions every four years. These conventions attract national media attention and are usually covered from gavel to gavel. They are perhaps the best-known American party institution. Although the main purpose of these conventions is to nominate a candidate for president, they also elect the Democratic or

Republican national executive committee. This body acts as a policy-making group for the national party, as the state executive committee does for the state. Service is considered a great honor, usually reserved for the longtime party faithful.

✢ Caucus and Primary Delegate Selection Systems

presidential preference primary
Elections held every four years by political parties to determine the preferences of voters for presidential candidates.

Iowa caucuses
Precinct conventions held every four years to select delegates to county and state conventions. Presidential preference of these delegates is also determined at these meetings.

For the past eight presidential elections, Texas has used a primary system to determine the preferences of most, but not all, of the state delegates to the national convention. In states without **presidential preference primaries,** such as Iowa, precinct conventions (also called caucuses) take on greater significance. Delegates selected at the precinct level go to the county level and eventually to the state and national conventions. A well-organized group, such as the Moral Majority, can take control of these caucuses. In 1988 Pat Robertson used his organization and worked with local churches to win more delegates than any other candidate in the Iowa caucuses. Pat Buchanan also benefited from these organizations in the 1996 **Iowa caucuses.** Churches are used as a rallying point before the evening caucus. Potluck dinners, child-care services, and church buses that help deliver voters to precinct conventions produce a turnout that exceeds the candidate's actual support among the voting population. By contrast, Steve Forbes's media campaign in Iowa had little effect in either 1996 or 2000.

Thus, a caucus system can be an effective way to win delegates to conventions. However, it requires an organization of active volunteers to produce results. Win enough delegates to enough precinct conventions, and you can take over the county. Win enough counties, and you control the state. Control the state, and you select the delegates to the national convention. Control enough states, and you might win the nomination for president.

If Texas were to change from a preference primary to a caucus system, different campaign organization and strategies would be required. Preference primaries are mass media events that require big money and professional organizations. Caucus systems require grassroots organizations and dedicated volunteers. At the 1996, 1998, and 2000 Republican state conventions, some Christian organizations called for an end to preference primaries and a return to a caucus system of selecting delegates to the national convention. Obviously the caucus system is in their best interest and would allow them to control most of the delegates to the national convention. If the Texas caucus were held early enough in the election process, it might affect the direction of the Republican presidential race or, at least, give the winner some early exposure.

✢ Conclusions

In the past, the state executive committees of both parties were likely to be part-time organizations with limited staff. Today, both parties have a permanent headquarters, a full-time paid professional staff, and financial resources to help party development. They are actively engaged in organizing and building the party through voter identification and registration, candidate recruitment, candidate education, get-out-the-vote drives, and supporting candidates during the general election.

The average citizen has little awareness of party organization at the state and local levels. Control of this element of American politics is left to the few active elite of the party; however, it is not very difficult to become a part of this group. Any citizen, with a little time, can become active in precinct, county, and state party activities. Most of these are not paid positions. Individuals must be willing to contribute their time and money to serving the party.

Texas is emerging as a two-party state. Party organization at the local level is still not well developed. In an era of candidate-centered politics, the role of the political party has changed. Both the Democratic party and the Republican party in Texas are redefining the role of the state party organization in state politics. State party organizations must continue to develop their services to help candidates and develop local party organizations if they are to remain major forces in state politics.

INTERNET RESOURCES

Democratic party: *www.txdemocrats.org/*
Republican party: *www.texasgop.org/*
Many county party organizations have Web pages. A general search for Democratic or Republican party will find these pages.
College students can find the College Republicans at Texas at *http://utdirect.utexas.edu/dsorg/detail.wb?code=00522*

College students can find the College Democrats at Texas at *http://www.geocities.com/CapitolHill/Lobby/7013/*
An organization promoting other election systems is the Center for Voting and Democracy at *www.fairvote.org/* This organization has a slight Republican lean.

KEY TERMS

county chair (p. 92)
county executive committee (p. 93)
guns, gays, and God (p. 89)
Iowa caucuses (p. 96)
one-party Democratic state (p. 80)
party de-alignment (p. 90)
party ideology (p. 76)
party realignment in Texas (p. 83)

permanent party organization (p. 92)
policy-relevant states (p. 78)
precinct chair (p. 92)
presidential preference primary (p. 96)
Raza Unida (p. 91)
Shivercrats (p. 82)

state executive committee (p. 93)
straight ticket party voting (p. 82)
temporary party organization (p. 94)
Yellow Dog Democrats (p. 82)
Yellow Pup Republican (p. 89)

NOTES

1. Peverill Squire, James M. Lindsay, Cary R. Covington, and Eric R.A.N. Smith, *Dynamics of Democracy* (Madison, Wis.: Brown & Benchmark, 1995), 212–14.
2. Ibid., 217.
3. V.O. Key, Jr., *Politics and Pressure Groups,* 4th ed. (New York: Thomas Y. Crowell, 1958), 331.
4. Thomas R. Dye, "Party and Policy in the States," *Journal of Politics* 46 (November 1984): 1097–116.
5. V.O. Key, Jr., *Southern Politics in State and Nation* (New York: Knopf, 1949), 7.
6. Calvert and DeLeon, *History of Texas,* 201–7.
7. L. Tucker Gibson, Jr., and Clay Robinson, *Government and Politics in the Lone Star State: Theory and Practice,* 2d ed. (Englewood Cliffs, N.J.: Prentice Hall, 1995), 163.
8. Soukup, McCleskey, and Holloway, *Party and Factional Division,* 6.

9. Key, *Southern Politics,* 225.
10. Soukup, McCleskey, and Holloway, *Party and Factional Division,* 8.
11. Ibid., 11.
12. Douglas O. Weeks, *Texas Presidential Politics in 1952* (Austin: University of Texas, Institute of Public Affairs, 1953), 3–4.
13. The budget actually increased during this time period.
14. David A. Stockman, *The Triumph of Politics: How the Reagan Revolution Failed* (New York: Harper & Row, 1986).
15. James A. Dyer, Arnold Vedlitz, and David B. Hill, "New Voters, Switchers, and Political Party Realignment in Texas," *Western Political Quarterly* 41 (March 1988): 164.
16. Secretary of State, "Election Returns, 1994," Texas Secretary of State home page (*www.sos.state.tx.us*).

17. R.G. Ratcliffe, "Political Landscape of Texas Receives Makeover," *Houston Chronicle,* 13 November 1994, 16A.
18. Allan Turner, "Snapping Back: GOP Nipping on Heels of Yellow Dog Democrats," *Houston Chronicle,* 5 March 1995, 1D.
19. Ibid.
20. John Williams, "Yellow Dogs Lose Bite in East Texas," *Houston Chronicle,* 18 November 2002, pp. 17A and 24A.
21. James A. Dyer, Jan E. Leighley, and Arnold Vedlitz, "Party Identification and Public Opinion: Establishing a Competitive Two Party System," in *Texas Reader,* ed. Tony Champagne and Ted Harpham (New York: Norton, 1997), 113–28.
22. Walter D. Burnham, *The Current Crisis in American Politics* (Oxford: Oxford University Press, 1982).
23. James E. Anderson, Richard W. Murray, and Edward L. Farley, *Texas Politics: An Introduction* (New York: Harper & Row, 1989), 70.
24. Alan Bernstein, "Natural Law Party Plans to Put Dozens on Ballot," *Houston Chronicle,* 30 May 1996, 22A.
25. Interview with Neeley Lewis, Democratic party chair for Brazos County, Texas, 30 May 1996.
26. Benton, *Texas Politics,* 80–81.

CHAPTER 6
❦

ELECTIONS AND CAMPAIGNS IN TEXAS

Elections are the heart of any democratic system and perform a number of important functions that make government work. Elections bestow legitimacy upon government. Without elections, all actions of governments are questionable. Elections also provide for an orderly transition of power from one group to another. One of the great stabilizing forces in the American system of government has been this orderly transfer of power. Elections also allow citizens to express their opinions about public policy choices. By voting in elections, citizens tell government officials what they want the government to do. As indicated in Chapter 3, many citizens do not participate in elections. Nonetheless, elections are still the most essential element of any democracy.

In this chapter we will examine a number of institutional factors—such as election cycles, the timing of elections, ballot access, and campaigns—that influence the conduct of elections.

Elections occur at regular intervals as determined by state and federal laws. All states conduct elections on two-year cycles. The date established by federal law for electing members of the U.S. Congress and the president is the first Tuesday after the first Monday in November of even-numbered years. States must elect members of Congress and vote for the president on this date. Most states also use this November date to elect governors, state officials, state legislators, and some local offices.

Texas holds **general elections** every two years. During nonpresidential years, voters elect candidates to statewide offices: governor, lieutenant governor, attorney general, land commissioner, agricultural commissioner, comptroller, some members of the Texas Railroad Commission and the Texas State Board of Education, and some members of

general elections
Regular elections held every two years to elect state officeholders.

It is extremely difficult to get enough signatures for a petition to meet state election law requirements for minor or third parties. In 2006, however, both Kinky Friedman and Carole Strayhorn got their 45,000+ to run for governor.

the two supreme courts in the state.[1] Before 1976, all nonjudicial officeholders served two-year terms. In 1977 the state constitution was amended, and four-year terms were first used in 1978.

Every two years, voters also elect all 150 members of the Texas house of representatives (for two-year terms), one-half of the members of the Texas senate (for four-year terms), many judges to various courts, and local county officials.

→ Ballot Form

ballot form
The forms used by voters to cast their ballot. Each county, with approval of the secretary of state, determines the form of the ballot.

Each county in Texas decides the **ballot form** and method of casting ballots. The method used to cast votes must be approved by the secretary of state's office. Some systems are precleared by the secretary of state's office, and counties can choose any of these systems. In the 2006 election, all 254 counties in Texas used electronic voting systems. These systems were purchased with federal funds provided by the Help America Vote Act. The secretary of state must approve all electronic voting systems before counties can purchase them. Three systems are currently approved by the secretary of state's office. The Premier Election System (formerly called Diebold) is used by six counties in Texas, the Electronic Systems Software (ESS) is used by 148 counties, and the Hart e-slate systems are used by 100 counties.

Counties in Texas once used paper ballots using a party column format, where candidates are listed by party and by office. The party that holds the governor's office was the first party column on the ballot. Being first on the ballot is an advantage—voters often chose the first name when all candidates are unfamiliar to them.

party column format
Paper ballot form where candidates are listed by party and by office.

The **party column ballot** also encourages straight ticket voting and was advocated strongly by the Democratic party for many years. In recent years, straight ticket voting has worked to the advantage of the Republicans in some elections, especially judicial offices.

office block
Ballot form where candidates are listed by office with party affiliation listed by their name. Most often used with computer ballots.

Most computer ballots are **office block.** (See figure 6.1.) This ballot form lists the office (e.g., president), followed by the candidates by party (e.g., Republican: George W. Bush;

SAMPLE BALLOT- *(BOLETA DE MUESTRA)*
GENERAL ELECTION-SPECIAL ELECTION
(ELECCION GENERAL-ELECCION ESPECIAL)

(Condado de) BRAZOS COUNTY, TEXAS
NOVEMBER 5, 2002 - *(5 de noviembre de 2002)*

INSTRUCTION NOTE: You may cast a straight-party vote (this is cast a vote for all the nominees of one party). If you cast a straight-party vote for all the nominees of one party and also cast a vote for an opponent of one of that party's nominees, your vote for the opponent will be counted as well as your vote for all the other candidates of the party for which the straight-party vote was cast.
(NOTA DE INSTRUCCION: Usted todrá votar por todos los candidatos de un solo partido politico ("straight ticket") . Si usted votar por uno de los partidos politicos y también votar por el contrincante de uno de los candidatos de dicho partido politico se contará su voto por el contrincante tanto como su voto por el contrincante tanto como su voto por todos los demás candidatos del

STRAIGHT-PARTY VOTE
(Para votar por todos candidatos)

REPUBLICAN PARTY	6
DEMOCRATIC PARTY	7
LIBERTARIAN PARTY	8
GREEN PARTY	9
INDEPENDANT	10

United States Senator
(Senador de los Estados Unidos)

JOHN CORNYN	REP	13
RON KIRK	DEM	14
SCOTT LANIER JAMESON	LIB	15
ROY H. WILLIAMS	GRN	16

United States Representative, District 31
(Representante de los Estados Unidos, Distrito Núm.31)

JOHN R. CARTER	REP	22
DAVID BAGLEY	DEM	23
CLARK SIMMONS	LIB	24
JOHN S. PETERSEN	GRN	25
R. C. CRAWFORD	IND	26

Governor
(Gobernador)

RICK PERRY	REP	29
TONY SANCHEZ	DEM	30
JEFF DAIELL	LIB	31
RAHUL MAHAJAN	GRN	32

Lieutenant Governor
(Gobernador Teniente)

DAVID DEWHURST	REP	35
JOHN SHARP	DEM	36

Commissioner of Agriculture
(Comisionado de Agricultura)

SUSAN COMBS	REP	60
TOM RAMSAY	DEM	61
VINCENT J. MAY	LIB	62
JANE WOODWARD ELIOSEFF	GRN	63

Railroad Commissioner
(Comisionado de Ferrocarriles)

MICHAEL L. WILLIAMS	REP	66
SHERRY BOYLES	DEM	67
NAZIRITE R. FLORES PEREZ	LIB	68
CHARLES L. MAUCH	GRN	69

Chief Justice, Supreme Court
(Juez Presidente, Corte Suprema)

TOM PHILLIPS	REP	72
RICHARD G. BAKER	DEM	73
EUGENE J. FLYNN	LIB	74

Justice, Supreme Court, Place 1
(Juez, Corte Suprema, Lugar Núm. 1)

MIKE SCHNEIDER	REP	79
LINDA YANEZ	DEM	80
QUANAH PARKER	LIB	81

Justice, Supreme Court, Place 2
Juez, Corte Suprema, Lugar Núm.2)

DALE WAINWRIGHT	REP	84
JIM PARSONS	DEM	85
BRAD ROCKWELL	GRN	86

Justice, Supreme Court, Place 3 - Unexpired Term
Juez, Corte Suprema, Lugar Núm.3Term no Comp.)

WALLACE B. JEFFERSON	REP	89
WILLIAM E. MOODY	DEM	90

Justice, Supreme Court, Place 4 - Unexpired Term
Juez, Corte Suprema, Lugar Núm.4 Term no Comp.)

STEVEN WAYNE SMITH	REP	93
MARGARET MIRABAL	DEM	94

Judge, Court of Criminal Appeals, Place 1
(Juez, Corte de Apelaciones Criminales, Lugar Núm.1)

TOM PRICE	REP	99
JOHN W. BULL	DEM	100
STEPHAN KINSELLA	LIB	101
ROBERT C. (ROB) OWEN	GRN	102

Judge, Court of Criminal Appeals, Place 2
(Juez, Corte de Apelaciones Criminales, Lugar Núm.2)

FIGURE 6.1 *A Sample Texas General Election Ballot, Formatted by Office Block.*

Democrat: John F. Kerry; Libertarian: Michael Badnarik). The ballot for each county in Texas is available before each election at *www.sos.state.tx.us.*

The office block format is often advocated as a way of discouraging straight ticket voting; however, Texas law allows computer-readable ballots to enable voters to vote a straight ticket. By marking a single place on the ballot, the voter can vote for all candidates for that party. The voter can then override this by voting in individual races. For example, a voter could vote a straight Republican ticket, but override this and vote for the Democratic candidate for selected offices.

✦ Ballot Access to the November General Election

To appear on the November general election ballot, candidates must meet criteria established by state law. These criteria prevent the lists of candidates from being unreasonably long. The Texas Election Code specifies three ways for names to be on the ballot.

Independent and Third-Party Candidates

independent candidate
A person whose name appears on the ballot without a political party designation.

To run as an independent, a candidate must file a petition with a specified number of signatures. For statewide office, signatures equal to 1 percent of the votes cast for governor in the last general election are required. For example, in the 2002 governor's race, a total of 4.5 million votes were cast. An **independent candidate** for statewide office in 2006 would have to collect 45,000 signatures. For multicounty offices, such as state representative, signatures equal to 5 percent of the votes cast for that office in the last election are needed. On the average, 30,000 to 40,000 votes are cast in house races.[2] For county offices, signatures equal to 5 percent of votes cast for those offices are needed. This might seem like a large number of signatures, but the process is intended to weed out people who do not have a serious chance of getting elected. Few candidates file for statewide office as independents. However, it is not uncommon to have independents for house and senate races. In 1996, thirteen people filed by petition as Libertarians and two filed as independents for the 150 Texas house seats. In 1998, only three people filed as independents for these house seats.[3] In 2000, the Libertarian party had candidates in 22 of 150 house seats and one senate seat. In 2002, the Libertarian party fielded 12 candidates for the state senate and 29 for the state house. Even if these candidates declare a party, such as Libertarian, they may still be considered independents under the state election code.

Getting signatures on a petition is not easy. Each signer must be a registered voter and must not have participated in the primary elections of other parties in that electoral cycle. For example, persons who voted in either the Democratic or the Republican party primary in 1996 were not eligible to sign a petition to have Ross Perot's Reform party placed on the 1996 ballot. If you vote in the primary of either the Democratic or Republican party, you may not sign the nominating petition of an independent candidate or a minor party candidate. Signing the petition is considered the same as voting. This provision of state law makes it all the more difficult for independents to get signatures and get on the ballot.

The 2006 governor's race in Texas was an exception to this. Both Carole Keeton Strayhorn, the then Comptroller, and Kinky Friedman, a country-western singer and mystery writer, qualified for positions on the ballot as independents. Friedman and Strayhorn suffered the same fate as most independent and third-party candidates: they pulled enough votes away from the Democratic candidate to upset the election outcome.

HIGHLIGHT

Judge Upholds "Sore Loser" Law

A federal judge . . . upheld Texas' sore loser law that bans commentator Pat Buchanan from appearing on the general election ballot as a presidential candidate because he already ran unsuccessfully in the Republican Primary.

U.S. District Judge James Nowlin rejected arguments from the U.S. Taxpayers Party that the law violates the U.S. Constitution. He said the law merely guarantees that internal party fights will not be carried over to the general election.

"Once you select a team in (an election cycle) that season you've got to stay on that team," Nowlin said. "Professional sports would be a lot better off if they followed a similar rule."

U.S. Taxpayers Party lawyers said they will appeal the ruling to the 5th U.S. Circuit . . . and continue a petition drive to get the party listed on the Texas ballot in the November general election. . . . The party has until May 28 [1996] to gather the signatures of 43,962 registered voters to get on the ballot this fall.

The Taxpayers Party lawyers Herb Titus and Bill Malone had argued that the Texas sore loser law is invalid because only the U.S. Constitution determines who is eligible to be a presidential candidate. "Texas has exceeded its authority under the Constitution," Titus said. Titus said that the current case [Buchanan] is different from the 1974 Supreme Court

case that ruled sore loser laws were valid in U.S. Senate and House races. He said the difference in a presidential race is that no single state primary determines who will be a national party's nominee. "A person who loses a party's presidential primary in Texas could be a party's presidential nominee," Titus said.

Malone said the sore loser law was enacted in Texas in 1963 after several Democrats who lost primaries in the Dallas area switched parties in 1962 and won election as Republicans. He said at the time Texas was a one-party Democratic state. "The intent was clearly to perpetuate a political monopoly," Malone said.

Nowlin, a Republican appointee to the court, said that was an "interesting history lesson" but irrelevant to the case and "was obviously intended to appeal to my biases."

Assistant Attorney General Christopher Johnsen argued that the state has a valid interest in controlling the primary process and factionalism to avoid possible voter confusion. Johnsen said the Taxpayers Party easily could have had Buchanan as its presidential nominee in Texas if they had "joined forces a little earlier," before Buchanan ran as a Republican.

Source: From R.G. Ratcliff, "Judge Upholds 'Sore Loser' Law, Blocks Buchanan From Ballot," in *Houston Chronicle,* 25 April 1996, pages 1A and 29A. Copyright © 1996 Houston Chronicle Publishing Company. Reprinted with permission. All rights reserved.

Governor Perry won with a plurality of 38.1 percent while Friedman had just 12.6 percent and Strayhorn 18 percent. Chris Bell, the Democratic candidate, did better than expected with 30 percent. The role of these write-in candidates was to help reelect an unpopular governor who, after six years in office, managed to get less than 40 percent of the votes.

Candidates who were defeated in the primary election may not file as independents in the general election for that year. This is the **"sore loser" law.**

Write-in candidates are sometimes confused with people who file and are listed on the ballot as independents. The process of filing as a write-in candidate is a separate procedure. To be "official" **write-in candidates,** individuals must file their intention before the election. This is true for all elections, including local, city, and school board elections. If a person does not file before the election, votes for that person are not counted. For some state offices a filing fee may be required to have your name listed on the ballot as a write-in candidate. The amount varies from $3,000 for statewide office to as little as $300 for local justices of the peace. People sometimes write in things like "Mickey Mouse" and "None of the above." These are recorded but not counted. In 1990, nineteen write-in candidates filed for governor. Bubbles Cash, a retired Dallas stripper, led the pack with 3,287 out of a total of 11,700 write-in votes.[4]

Party Caucus

The state election code defines a *minor party* (sometimes called a **third party**) as any political organization that receives between 5 and 19 percent of the total votes cast for

"sore loser" law
Law in Texas that prevents a person who lost the primary vote from running as an independent or minor party candidate.

write-in candidate
A person whose name does not appear on the ballot. Voters must write in that person's name, and the person must have filed a formal notice that he or she was a write-in candidate before the election.

third party
A party other than the Democratic or Republican party. To be a third party in Texas, the organization must have received between 5 and 19 percent of the vote in the last election.

party caucus

A meeting of members of a political party that is used by minor political parties in Texas to nominate candidates.

any statewide office in the last general election. In the last thirty years, there have been three minor parties: the Raza Unida party in South Texas in the 1970s,[5] the Socialist Workers party in 1988, and the Libertarian party in the 1990s. Parties that achieve minor-party status must nominate their candidates in a **party caucus** or convention and are exempt from the petition requirement discussed previously.

In 1998 and 2000 only the Libertarian party held the status as a minor political party. In 1998 it fielded twenty-two candidates in the thirty U.S. House races, all statewide offices, and a few state house races. None was elected. Nearly the same pattern prevailed with the Libertarian party in the 2000 election. It fielded candidates for most statewide and congressional offices but elected no one. In the 2002 election, it received less than 1 percent of the statewide vote and lost its status as a minor party.

Primary Election

The Texas Election Code defines a *major party* as any organization receiving 20 percent or more of the total votes cast for governor in the last election. Obviously, only the Democratic and Republican parties hold this status today. By law, these party organizations must nominate their candidates in **primary elections.**

primary election

An election used by major political parties in Texas to nominate candidates for the November general election.

open primary system

A nominating election that is open to all registered voters regardless of party affiliation.

closed primary

A nominating election that is closed to all voters except those who have registered as a member of that political party.

semiclosed primary

A nominating election that is open to all registered voters, but voters are required to declare party affiliation when they vote in the primary election.

Texas has an **open primary system.** Some states have "closed primary" elections. There are several important variations on open and closed primaries, and these deserve discussion. (See table 6.1.)

Closed primaries are currently used in thirteen states. This system requires voters to declare their party affiliation when they register to vote. They may vote only in the primary of their party registration. Most of these states have a time limit after which a voter may not change party affiliation before the election.

Semiclosed primaries allow voters to register or change their party registration on election day. Registration as a member of a party is required on election day.

In a semiopen primary, the voter may choose to vote in the primary of either party on election day. Voters are considered "declared" for the party in whose primary they vote. This is the system used in Texas. If you vote in the Republican party primary, you are in effect declaring that you are a member of that party. You may not participate in any activity of any other party for the remainder of that election year. For example, if you vote in the Republican primary, you may not attend the precinct convention of the Democratic party. This also limits the voter in other ways.

Open primaries allow the voter to vote in any primary without a party declaration. The voter can vote as a Democrat and attend the Republican precinct convention or participate in any activity of the opposite party.

HIGHLIGHT

Party Switching Proves Costly

Jim Kuboviak, the Democratic county attorney in Brazos County, had no opponent in the primary election or the general election in 1988. Since he was assured of renomination by his party, he did not vote in the Democratic party's primary election but instead voted in the Republican primary. By voting in the GOP primary, he officially declared his party affiliation to be Republican and was ineligible to be the

Democratic party candidate for county attorney. His name was removed from the ballot. The Democratic county executive committee could have named a replacement but chose to leave the ballot position vacant. Since no Republican had filed in that party's primary, the Republicans could not name a candidate. Jim "Killer" Kuboviak won reelection in a write-in campaign as an independent. His main concern was that no one could remember how to spell his name. He produced buttons to assist the voters in the spelling of his name.

TABLE 6.1

Primary Systems Used in State Elections

Closed Primary: Party Registration Required before Election Day

Alaska	Maine	New York
Connecticut	Nebraska	Oklahoma
Delaware	Nevada	Pennsylvania
Florida	New Jersey	South Dakota
Kentucky	New Mexico	

Semiclosed Primary: Voters May Register or Change Registration on Election Day

Arizona	Massachusetts	Utah
Colorado	New Hampshire	West Virginia
Iowa	North Carolina	Wyoming
Kansas	Oregon	
Maryland	Rhode Island	

Semiopen Primary: Voters Required to Request Party Ballot

Alabama	Mississippi	Virginia
Arkansas	Ohio	
Georgia	South Carolina	
Illinois	Tennessee	
Indiana	Texas	

Open Primary: Voters May Vote in Any Party Primary

California	Missouri
Hawaii	Montana
Idaho	North Dakota
Michigan	Vermont
Minnesota	Wisconsin

Nonpartisan: Voters May Switch Parties between Races

Louisiana	Washington

Blanket

Formerly used in Alaska, California, and Washington. Declared unconstitutional by the U.S. Supreme Court in 2000.

Source: John R. Bibby and Thomas M. Holbrook, "Parties and Elections," in *Politics in the American States: A Comparative Analysis,* 9th ed., edited by Virginia Gray and Russell L. Hanson. (Washington, D.C.: Congressional Quarterly Press, 2008). Reprinted by permission.

In the past, three states, Alaska, California, and Washington, used a **blanket primary.** This system allowed voters to switch parties between offices. A voter might vote in the Republican primary for the races for governor and U.S. House, and in the Democratic primary for the U.S. Senate race. These have been ruled unconstitutional by the U.S. Supreme Court. Alaska currently uses a closed primary with voter registration by party, while California has adopted an open primary system. Washington has adopted Louisiana's system of a nonpartisan primary for all statewide and U.S. House and Senate races. Under this system, all candidates are listed on the ballot by office. The voter can choose one candidate per office. If no person receives a majority, the top two candidates face each other in a runoff.

blanket primary

A nominating election in which voters could switch parties between elections.

→ POLITICAL DIFFERENCES BETWEEN OPEN AND CLOSED PRIMARY SYSTEMS

The primary system used in a state may affect the party system in the state. Advocates of the closed primary system say that it encourages party identification and loyalty, and therefore helps build stronger party systems. Open primary systems, they say, allow participation by independents with no loyalty to the party, which weakens party organization. There is no strong evidence that this is the case.

Open primaries do allow crossover voting. This occurs when voters leave their party and vote in the other party's primary. Occasionally voters in one party might vote in the other party's primary in hopes of nominating a candidate from the other party whose philosophy is similar to their own. For example, Republicans have been accused of voting in the Democratic primary in Texas to ensure that a conservative will be nominated. This occurred in the 1970 U.S. Senate race when Republicans voted for the more conservative Lloyd Bentsen over the liberal Ralph Yarborough. Many voting precincts carried by Bentsen in the Democratic primary voted for Republican George H. W. Bush in the general election.

From 1996 to 2002, more Texans have voted in the Republican primaries than in the Democratic primaries. Republicans claimed that this was evidence that their party was the majority party. Democrats suggest that these differences in turnout are explained by the low levels of opposition in the Democratic primaries. For instance, President Clinton did not have any opposition in his primary election, while Bob Dole and Pat Buchanan were still actively seeking the Republican nomination; some Democratic party leaders claim that many traditional Democratic party voters, therefore, crossed over and voted in the Republican primary in an attempt to affect whom the Republican nominee would be. In the 2000 primary season there were few reasons to vote in the Democratic primary except in the few cases where local house or senate races were contested in the primary.

As it turned out, the Democrats' explanation may be the more accurate. In the 2002 primary election, 400,000 more people voted in the Democratic party primary than in the Republican party primary. The difference is due almost entirely to the lack of contested races in the Republican primary and the highly contested races for U.S. Senate and governor in the Democratic primary. Governor Perry had no opponents and John Cornyn had little opposition for the U.S. Senate seat.

Party raiding and crossover voting are difficult to orchestrate. Once such an effort becomes public, it can be countered by the other party and may work to stimulate voter participation in the opposite direction. Such practices can have an effect in individual races, as in the 1970 U.S. Senate race and again in 1976 when conservative Democrats voted for Ronald Reagan in the special Republican presidential primary. Reagan won the Republican primary against President Gerald Ford, who lost the general election to Jimmy Carter in November 1976. Except for one case in a runoff primary, mentioned here, the 1980s and 90s provided few examples of this kind of party raiding or crossover voting. The candidates and issues have simply been absent.

→ RUNOFF PRIMARY ELECTIONS

runoff primary
Election that is required if no person receives a majority in the primary election. Primarily used in southern and border states.

Runoff primaries are held in eleven southern and border states, plus South Dakota. A **runoff primary** is required if no candidate receives a majority in the first primary. Until recently in the South, winning the Democratic party primary was the same as winning the general election, and the runoff primary became a fixture, supposedly as a way of requiring the winner to have "majority" support. In reality, voter turnout in the runoff primary is almost always lower than in the first primary, sometimes substantially lower. The "majority" winner often is selected by a small percentage of the electorate, those who bother to participate in the runoff primary.

Racial and ethnic minority candidates have challenged the runoff primary system in these eleven states. They charge that because voter turnout decreases in the runoff and minorities are less likely to vote in runoff elections, the system is racially biased. The only evidence available suggests that this might not be the case. A study in Georgia examined 215 runoff elections between 1965 and 1982 and found no support for racial bias in runoff primary elections.[6]

Crossover and raiding might occur in the runoff primary. The Texas Election Code specifies that voters who voted in the primary election of one party may not participate in the runoff primary of the other party. Occasionally in the past decade there have been charges that this has happened, as in a 1992 Democratic primary congressional race in Houston. The Houston congressional district had been drawn to "ensure" that a Mexican American could be elected, but the primary was won by an Anglo, Gene Green. His opponent, Ben T. Reyes, charged that Republicans had "raided" and voted for Green. There was some evidence that this had happened, but it had not changed the results of the election. The current system of record keeping and the difficulty of checking voter lists make it almost impossible to prevent such raiding or crossover voting from occurring in runoff primaries. A reform might be to require voters to sign a statement saying they had not voted in the opposition party's primary election.

Occasionally runoff primary elections get voter attention. In 2002 Ron Kirk, former mayor of Dallas, and Victor Morales were locked in a bitter runoff primary. This contest generated 620,517 votes, more than the total vote in the Republican primary election that same year (614,716). Turnout is obviously related to a number of factors, among them the degree of competition in the election.

✦ THE ADMINISTRATION AND FINANCE OF PRIMARY ELECTIONS

In the past, primary elections were considered functions of private organizations and the state did not regulate them. As we discussed in Chapter 3, courts have ruled that political parties are not private organizations and their functions are subject to control by state law. The Texas Election Code governs primary elections. It specifies the time (currently the second Tuesday in March) and method of conducting primary elections. Runoff elections are held in April.

In the past the cost of conducting primary elections was borne entirely by political parties. Persons wanting to file for an office in the primary election had to pay a **filing fee.** In 1970, court cases forced Texas to alter its filing fee system. Before that the cost of filing for county offices had increased substantially. The cost of filing for a countywide race in Dallas County was $9,000 in 1970. In 1972 the state of Texas assumed part of the cost of financing primary elections. There are still filing fees, but they are lower. Currently the cost for filing for a statewide office is $4,000. For countywide races the fee is $500. Anyone who cannot pay the filing fee can get a place on the primary ballot by filing a petition. For statewide office, about 45,000 signatures are required; for district or local office, signatures equal to 3 percent of the votes cast for that office in the last election are required.

filing fee
A fee or payment required to get a candidate's name on the primary or general election ballot.

Some candidates file a petition as a campaign tactic to show they have broad support. Occasionally, petitioners also pay the filing fee just to play it safe and prevent a challenge to the validity of the petition.

Technically, primary elections are administered by the local party county chair and executive committee and by the state party officials at the state level; however, the Texas Election Code and the secretary of state oversee the administration of elections to ensure that the rules are followed, and the party really has only limited discretion in the conduct of these elections.

✦ THE FEDERAL VOTING RIGHTS ACT

Voting Rights Act
A federal law that allows the U.S. Justice Department to oversee the operation of voter registration and elections at the state level.

In 1965 under the leadership of President Lyndon Johnson, the U.S. Congress passed the Voting Rights Act. This act has had extensive effects upon the state of Texas and the conduct of elections. The original 1965 act has been amended by Congress and was extended to Texas in 1975. Currently in Texas a person must register to vote at least thirty days before an election. The **Voting Rights Act** requires pre-clearance, by the U.S. Justice Department, of all changes in election procedures—including such things as ballot form, the time and place of an election, and the method of electing legislators.[7]

The Voting Rights Act allows the federal government to oversee the operation of elections at the state level. The greatest impact has been felt in southern states, where racial and ethnic minorities were formerly barred from participating in elections. Lawsuits filed under the Voting Rights Act forced many local governments to alter their method of electing city council and school board members—from at-large to single-member district elections. (See Chapter 11 for discussion of council elections.)

The Voting Rights Act also required Texas to use a bilingual ballot for all elections in counties that contain more than 20 percent of Spanish-speaking residents. Ballots are printed in both English and Spanish for all elections—federal, state, and local.

✦ ABSENTEE AND EARLY VOTING

absentee voting
A process that allows a person to vote early, before the regular election. Applies to all elections in Texas. Also called *early voting*.

All states allow some form of **absentee voting.** This practice began as a way to allow members of the U.S. armed services who were stationed in other states or overseas to vote. In all but a few states it has been extended to other individuals. In most states, persons who will be out of the county on election day may file for absentee voting.

In Texas before 1979, to vote absentee, voters had to sign an affidavit saying they would be out of the county and unable to vote on election day. They could also file for an absentee ballot to be sent to them if they were living out-of-state or confined to a hospital or nursing home. In 1979 the state legislature changed the rules to allow anyone to vote absentee without restrictions. In Texas this is called "early voting." Early voting now begins seventeen days before an election and closes four days before the election. During that period, polls are open from 7 A.M. to 7 P.M. Voters simply go to an early voting polling place and present their voter registration cards; then they are allowed to vote.

Some people are critical of early voting. They fear that those who take advantage of the process would be middle- and upper-class voters, who are likely to vote Republican and for conservative candidates. There is some evidence to support this, since Republican candidates usually carry the absentee vote. Voter participation in early voting has increased since the process was begun and will probably continue to do so. In the 2006 general election, 39 percent of the votes cast were early votes. In the 2006 primary election, 35 percent of the votes cast in the Republican primary were early votes, and in the Democratic primary that same year 36 percent of the votes were cast in early balloting.

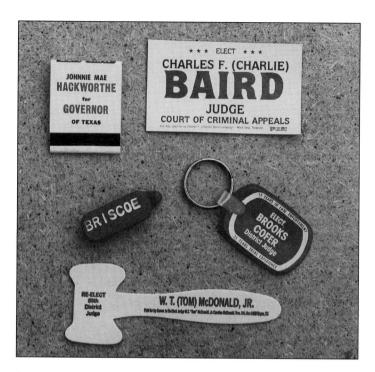

"Keepers" are items given to voters in hopes that the voter will remember a candidate's name when it's time to vote.

In the November 2006 election, 39 percent of the votes were cast during early voting (1.6 million of 4.3 million votes). In the race for governor, Republican Rick Perry received 40 percent of the vote in absentee voting (702,322).

→ CAMPAIGNS

Campaign activity in Texas has changed considerably in the past two or three decades. These changes are not unique to Texas but are part of a national trend. Norman Brown, in his book on Texas politics, describes the form of political campaigning in the state as "local affairs."[8] Candidates would travel from county seat to county seat and give "stump" speeches to political rallies arranged by local supporters. Brown devotes special attention to the campaigns of Governors Jim and Miriam Ferguson ("Pa" and "Ma" Ferguson). Jim Ferguson, when campaigning for himself and later for his wife, would travel from county to county, telling each group what they wanted to hear—often saying different things in different counties. Brown contends that Ferguson and other candidates could do this because of the lack of a statewide press to report on these inconsistencies in such political speeches.

In modern-day Texas, the media play a significant role in political campaigns. Reporters often follow candidates for statewide office as they travel the vast expanses of Texas. Political rallies are still held but are most often used to gain media attention and convey the candidate's message to a larger audience. Candidates hope these events will attract media attention and convey a favorable image of them to the public.

Heavy media coverage can have its disadvantages for the candidates. For instance, in 1990 Clayton Williams, the Republican candidate for governor, held a media event on one of his West Texas ranches. He and "the boys" were to round up cattle for branding in a display designed to portray Williams as a hardworking rancher. Unfortunately for Williams, rain spoiled the event and it had to be postponed. Resigned to the rain delay, Williams told the reporters, "It's like rape. When it's inevitable, relax and enjoy it." The state press had a field day with this remark, and it probably hurt Williams's chances with many voters. The fact that his opponent was a woman (Ann Richards) helped to magnify the significance of the statement.

Similarly in 1994, George W. Bush was the Republican candidate for governor running against incumbent Ann Richards. In Texas the opening day of dove season is in September, and the event marks the beginning of the fall hunting season. Both Bush and Richards participated in opening day hunts in an attempt to appeal to the strong hunting and gun element in the state. Unfortunately for Bush, by mistake he shot a killdeer rather than a dove. Pictures of Bush holding the dead bird appeared in most state papers and on television. He was fined for shooting a migratory bird. A Texas Democratic group in Austin produced bumper stickers reading: "Guns don't kill killdeer. People do." In 1998 Governor Bush did not have a media event for the opening day of dove season. He was so far ahead in the polls that even opening the issue could result in nothing but a painful reminder.

Most campaign events are not as disastrous as the cattle-branding and dove-hunting incidents. Some gain attention and free media coverage for the candidate; however, free media attention is never enough. Candidates must purchase time on television and radio and space in newspapers. In a state as large as Texas, this can be quite costly. Candidates try to make the most of the expensive time they purchase by conveying simple messages. This has led to the **sound bite commercial,** a 30-second message that, it is hoped, will be remembered by the voters. This is not unique to Texas but occurs nationwide.

These sound bites can be classified into at least five types. The **feel good spot** lacks substance or issues, and is designed to make the public feel good about the candidate or the party. In 1984 Ronald Reagan told us it was "morning in America." The commercial featured scenes of a "middle America" town filled with happy people. In 1988 President Bush told us he saw "a thousand points of light." Others promise "fresh, bold leadership" or claim to have "common sense and uncommon courage." Still others, including Clayton Williams, say, "Share my vision." In 1998 Governor Bush ran a number of TV spots that asked voters to support his effort to have every child read and become a productive member of society.

Sainthood spots try to depict the candidate as having saintly qualities:[9] "Senator Smith is a Christian family man, Eagle Scout, Little League coach, Sunday school teacher, involved, concerned, committed, community leader who fights the people's fights. Let's keep him working for us."

Good ol' boy (or "good ol' girl") spots are testimonials from other citizens on the candidate. In a staged "person on the street" interview, the citizen says something like, "Senator Smith is the most effective leader this state has seen since Sam Houston. He's so effective it's frightening. He is committed to his job, and we need him to fight the coming battles with the liberals." In Texas, cattle and horses in the background provide a down-to-earth backdrop for ranchers' good ol' boy testimonials.

NOOTS ("No one's opposed to this") commercials are also common. In these ads, candidates take courageous stands on issues everyone supports: sound fiscal management, planned orderly growth, good schools, open government, getting tough on crime, no new taxes, and so on.

Basher spots are the last type. In these, candidates play on voters' emotions by painting their opponent in a very unfavorable light. If your opponent is a lawyer, you can point out that he or she defends criminals. You can also pull the gay card by pointing out

sound bite commercial
A short, usually 30-second TV political advertisement that conveys a simple message about the candidate or the opponent.

feel good spots
Short political messages, often devoid of meaning, aimed at conveying a message that makes the voters have good feelings about the candidate.

sainthood spots
Political advertisements that portray the candidate as a virtuous person.

NOOTS
No one opposed to this; political advertisements that contain messages that few citizens oppose.

basher spots
Political advertisements that portray an opponent in a very negative way.

that your opponent has received money from gay rights organizations. Governor Rick Perry, running for secretary of agriculture in 1990, defeated Democratic incumbent Jim Hightower. In one of his commercials, Perry claimed that Hightower had once visited the home of Jane Fonda. Fonda is often used as a symbol for the radical war protesters of the 1960s because of her visit to Hanoi during the Vietnam War. When pressed for details on the visit, Perry said that Hightower had visited Los Angeles, and that Los Angeles was the home of Jane Fonda.

Basher spots have developed into a fine art. Newt Gingrich, former speaker of the U.S. House, extended the art when he used his GOPAC political action committee to help "train local Republican candidates." In 1990, GOPAC mailed a glossary of 131 words to over four thousand state Republican candidates. This glossary included a list of "optimistic positive governing words" that Republican candidates should use to describe themselves and a list of "contrasting negative words" they should use to describe their opponents. Republicans are described as having common sense and Democrats as big spending liberals.

These types of advertisements are used because most often they work to the advantage of the candidate. Occasionally, basher spots can backfire on the candidate. These ads plant in the voter's mind a simple message that they carry into the voting booth. Most citizens do not spend much time studying issues or candidates' backgrounds. They are often entirely dependent upon advertisements for information. While the news media (which receives most of the money spent in campaigns) often denounce such ads, they do not refuse to run them.

✦ Political Consultants

The use of professional campaign consultants is common in almost all races. Most candidates find it necessary to have such professionals help run their campaigns. If their opponents use professionals, candidates might be disadvantaged by not having one. Professional campaign consultants use many techniques. They take public opinion polls to measure voter reaction to issues so the candidate knows what stands to take. They run **focus groups** where a panel of "average citizens" is asked to react to issues or words. Consultants also help the candidate in the design of written and visual advertisements and generally "package" the candidate to the voters. In 2002, David Dewhurst filmed a TV spot for his consulting firm praising its effectiveness in making him look professional.

focus groups
Panel of "average citizens" who are used by political consultants to bounce off ideas and words for later use in campaigns.

✦ Money in Campaigns

Using media advertisement, professional consultants, and a full-time paid campaign staff increases the cost of running for state office. The cost can run into the millions even for a race for the Texas House of Representatives.

The amount of money spent in campaigns is increasing each selection cycle. Most of this money comes from political action committees.

Table 6.2 shows the increase in the total amount of money contributed by PACs from 1966 to 2006. The amount has more than doubled in the time period.

Statewide races can be quite costly, and costs have continued to increase. Most of the money is coming from PACs, who obviously want something from government for their contributions. A few candidates, such as Tony Sanchez in 2002, are able to self-finance their campaigns. In that year Sanchez self-financed $27 million (89% of total) and received campaign contributions totaling $3.5 million.[10] In that same election year, Governor Rick Perry raised $31,402,362 from political action committees.[11]

TABLE 6.2

Total PAC Money in State Campaigns from 1996 to 2006

Sector	1996 Cycle	1998 Cycle	2000 Cycle	2002 Cycle	2004 Cycle	2006 Cycle	'04–'06 Growth
Business	$27,314,623	$31,516,817	$34,416,627	$48,000,676	$46,088,137	$57,034,732	+24%
Ideology	$13,713,797	$17,719,192	$16,870,715	$33,466,788	$17,789,167	$37,003,210	+108%
Labor	$1,886,325	$2,259,742	$2,707,704	$3,776,290	$4,512,391	$5,116,613	+13%
Unknown	$167,801	$48,068	$1,929	$76,473	$514,829	$13,099	
Totals	**$43,082,546**	**$51,543,820**	**$53,996,975**	**$85,320,226**	**$68,904,524**	**$99,167,654**	**+44%**

Source: Texas PACs: 2006 Election Cycle Spending. *www.tpj.org.*

TABLE 6.3

War Chests by Elected Officials in 2006

Office	Major Candidates	Amount Raised In 2006 Cycle	No. of Winners	Amount Raised By Winners
House	309	$59,579,810	150	$42,009,324
Senate*	48	$27,477,218	16	$14,686,447
Governor	7	$42,493,800	1	$21,091,448
Lieutenant Governor	3	$10,912,099	1	$10,837,273
Comptroller	2	$4,532,012	1	$4,476,390
Attorney General	2	$7,064,317	1	$6,855,483
Agricultural Commissioner	2	$2,284,820	1	$2,203,298
Railroad Commissioner	3	$2,167,938	1	$2,165,588
Land Commissioner	2	$1,056,149	1	$1,051,743
Totals	**378**	**$157,568,163**	**173**	**$105,376,994**

*Includes 15 senators who raised money but did not face reelection in 2006.

Source: Texans for Public Justice, "Money in PoliTex: A Guide to 2006 Texas Elections." *www.tpj.org/reports/politex2006/index06.html.*

Table 6.3 shows the amount of money major office holders and candidates had in their so called war chests. It includes 15 senatorial candidates that did not face reelection in 2006. All elected officials hope to keep part of the money they raise in a war chest, which can have the effect of forcing likely opponents to think twice before running against them. Also, candidates without opponents for many years, such as a Speaker of the House, may contribute part of their war chests to House candidates in hope of getting or keeping their support.

Money supplied by PACs obviously has an impact on elected officials. At the least, PAC money buys the group access to the official. At the worst, PAC money buys the vote of the elected official. Distinguishing between the two is almost impossible. Most states, including Texas, have passed laws designed to regulate campaign finances. Many other states have passed laws limiting the amount of money that could be spent on campaigns, but these laws have been invalidated by the U.S. Supreme Court. (See Chapter 4 on interest groups.)

Candidates sometimes loan themselves money that they can later repay with what are sometimes called "late train" contributions. Special interest groups seldom will retire

the debt of losers. The law limits the amount of money that a candidate can collect to retire personal campaign debts for each election (primary, runoff, general) to $500,000 in
personal loans. In 2002, several candidates far exceeded this amount in personal loans.
The leaders were gubernatorial candidate Tony Sanchez with $22,262,662 in personal
loans and lieutenant governor elect David Dewhurst with $7,413,887 in outstanding
debt.[12]

Today the regulation of campaign finances in Texas is limited to requiring all
candidates and PACs to file reports with the Texas State Ethics Commission. All contributions of over $50 must be reported with the name of the contributor. An expenditure
report must also be filed. These reports must be filed before and after the election. The
idea behind the reporting scheme is to make public the sources of the funds received by
candidates and how the candidates spend their funds. Sometimes these reports are examined closely by the news media and are given significant media coverage, but this is
not common. The best source for Texas funds is tpj.org. Citizens mostly are left to find
out such information on their own, which is difficult for the average citizen. While Texas
has no limit on the amount of money candidates can spend for statewide races, many
states do. Figure 6.2 shows this for the states. Compare this map with figure 1.3, on political culture, in Chapter 1.

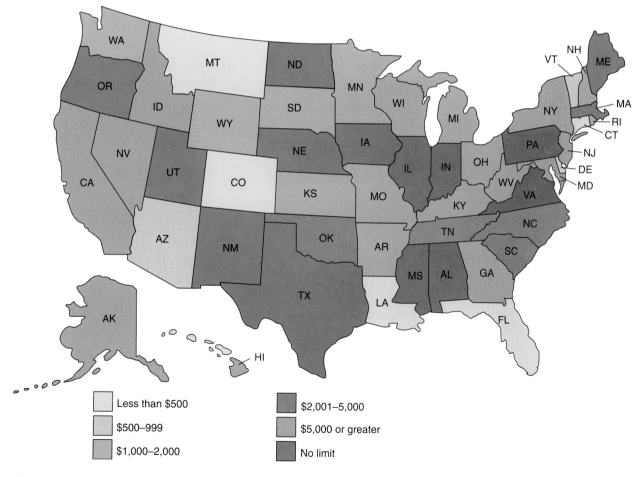

Legend:
- Less than $500
- $500–999
- $1,000–2,000
- $2,001–5,000
- $5,000 or greater
- No limit

FIGURE 6.2   *Limitations on Campaign Contributions in Statewide Races.*

SOURCE: National Conference on State Legislation. (*www.ncsl.org/programs/legman/about/contriblimits.htm*)

✦ Conclusions

Elections and campaigns are essential to any democracy. The rules governing the conduct of elections have an impact on who gets elected and on the policies enacted by government. For reasons discussed in Chapter 3, active involvement in politics in Texas is limited to a small number of citizens. The electoral process is dominated by the Anglo population, which controls a disproportionate share of state offices. Most citizens choose not to participate in elections or the activities of political parties. As in other states, campaigns in Texas have become media affairs dominated by political consultants, sound bite ads, and money.

The big unknown in Texas politics is the role of the Hispanic voter. Thus far, voting among Hispanics has remained quite low. In 2002, many thought that the presence of a Hispanic at the top of the ticket (Tony Sanchez) would bring out the Hispanic vote. This did not happen, and Hispanic voters stayed away in droves. An effort to register more minority votes was not successful. The vote received by Sanchez by Anglo voters was much lower than that normally received by Democratic candidates. If Hispanic voters begin to vote, it is not certain that they will remain strong Democratic party voters.

Internet Resources

Texas Ethics Commission: *www.ethics.state.tx.us/*
This site has information on campaign contributions reported by candidates for office as well as interest groups.

Secretary of State: *www.sos.state.tx.us/*
This page has information on election laws and voter turnout.

Texans for Public Justice: *www.tpj.org*
This site has information on campaign spending and lobbying.

Key Terms

absentee voting (p. 108)
ballot form (p. 100)
basher spots (p. 110)
blanket primary (p. 105)
closed primary (p. 104)
feel good spots (p. 110)
filing fee (p. 107)
focus groups (p. 111)

general elections (p. 99)
independent candidate (p. 102)
NOOTS (p. 110)
office block (p. 100)
open primary system (p. 104)
party caucus (p. 104)
party column format (p. 100)
primary election (p. 104)

runoff primary (p. 106)
sainthood spots (p. 110)
semiclosed primary (p. 104)
"sore loser" law (p. 103)
sound bite commercial (p. 110)
third party (p. 103)
Voting Rights Act (p. 108)
write-in candidate (p. 103)

Notes

1. The office of treasurer was also a statewide elected office. In 1996 the voters abolished this office by constitutional amendment. The functions of this office have been taken over by the state comptroller and other state agencies.
2. Texas Secretary of State home page (*www.sos.state.tx.us*).
3. Ibid.
4. James A. Anderson, Richard W. Murray, and Edward L. Farley, *Texas Politics: An Introduction*, 6th ed. (New York: HarperCollins, 1992), 34.
5. The Raza Unida party did not receive enough votes to qualify as a minor party but challenged this in court. The federal court sustained the challenge, and they were allowed to operate as a minor party.

6. Ann O. Bowman and Richard C. Kearney, *State and Local Government* (Boston: Houghton Mifflin, 1990), 158–59. Also see Charles S. Bullock III and Loch K. Johnson, *Runoff Elections in the United States* (Chapel Hill: University of North Carolina Press, 1992).

7. A court case in 1971 ended the early registration procedures in Texas (*Beare v. Smith,* 31 F. Supp. 1100).

8. Norman D. Brown, *Hood, Bonnet and Little Brown Jug: Texas Politics, 1921–1928* (College Station: Texas A&M University Press, 1984).

9. Bowman and Kearney, *State and Local Government,* 166. The "feel good" and "sainthood" classifications were adopted from this source.

10. Texans for Public Justice, "Tony Sanchez's War Chest: Who Gives to a $600 Million Dollar Man?" *www.tpj.org/docs2002/10reports/sanchez/page3.html*

11. Texans for Public Justice, "Governor Perry's War Chest: Who Said Yes to Governor No?" *www.tpj .org/docs/2002/10/reports/perry/page3.html*

12. Lobby Watch, "Texas Loan Stars Incurred $48 Million in Political Debts" (*www.tpj.org/lobby_Watch/ latetrain.html*).

CHAPTER 7

THE TEXAS LEGISLATURE

There is an old saying regarding the Texas legislature: "Neither man nor property is safe while the legislature is in session." This statement suggests the importance of the Texas legislature in state politics and the fear people have of government. While the office of governor is important, as are courts and state agencies, the legislature is the most important agency. There are many things that cannot happen without legislative actions. Money cannot be spent, taxes cannot be levied, state laws cannot be enacted or changed, and finally, in most states, the constitution cannot be amended without the approval of the legislature. Simply put, without actions by the legislature, most state governments would soon come to a halt. In recent years, the federal government has shifted more responsibility to state governments, and this has resulted in state legislatures becoming more important as policy-making bodies.

The Texas Constitution makes the legislature the most important decision-making body in the state. The framers of the 1876 constitution distrusted government generally, but they especially were leery of executive authority and gave more power to the legislature than to the executive.

This does not mean that the office of governor is insignificant in state politics. Governors play an important role. However, what power the governor of Texas possesses is derived primarily from informal and not formal sources. (See chapter 8.)

✦ THE SIZE OF THE TEXAS LEGISLATURE

The Texas legislature consists of two houses. The Texas senate has 31 members elected for four-year overlapping terms; half the membership is elected every two years. The Texas house of representatives now consists of 150 members elected for two-year terms. The first house, elected following the adoption of the 1876 constitution, consisted of 93 members. After 1880 a new house seat was added for every 50,000 inhabitants until the membership reached 150 members.[1]

State legislatures vary in size. Nevada has the smallest senate, with 21 members, and Minnesota has the largest, with 67 senators. Lower house membership ranges from 41 in Delaware to 400 in New Hampshire. The New Hampshire house is unusually large; the next largest house is Pennsylvania's, at 203.[2] The median size for state senates is 40; for the lower houses it is 100.

The size of legislatures raises several issues. Large bodies might promote the representation of diverse interests within the state; however, statewide interests might go unrepresented. One can also point out that large legislatures can become inefficient at decision making or, in part because of the inefficiency, become dominated by a few members. There is no doubt that decision-making dynamics depend on the size of the legislative body. The Texas senate, with 31 members, is generally regarded as more sedate and genteel in its proceedings. Historically, few people have dominated it, and senators act more independently. While the lieutenant governor is powerful, his or her power comes from the senate rules. The house, on the other hand, is generally more "disputatious" in its proceedings, and historically the speaker of the house dominates.

✦ METHODS OF ELECTION

Members of legislative bodies most often are elected from **single-member districts.** Under this system, each legislative district has one member in the legislative body. In Texas there are 31 senatorial districts and 150 house districts. The voters living in these districts elect one house and one senate member to represent the district. This system allows for geographical representation—all areas of the state get to choose representatives to the state legislature. In 2002 each house member in Texas represented about 139,000 citizens and each state senator represented about 673,000 citizens. Figures 7.1 and 7.2 show the details of single-member election districts in the major metropolitan areas of the state. Figures 7.3 and 7.4 show the senate and house districts for the entire state.

Some states use multimember districts for some legislative elections. Twelve percent of all lower-house districts are multimember districts, but only 3 percent of senate seats are elected from multimember districts.[3] While multimember election methods vary widely, the most common method is to elect two or three members per district. Voters get one vote for each seat in the multimember district, and more than one state representative represents each voter. Table 7.1 shows the various multimember district systems used in other states.

single-member district
District having one member elected to the legislature.

House chamber in the state capitol.

Senate chamber in the state capitol.

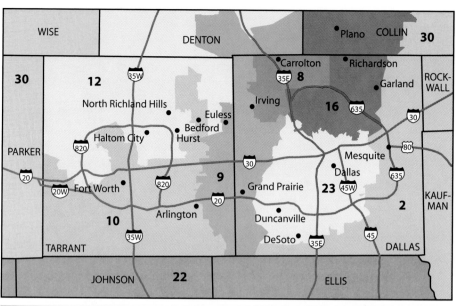

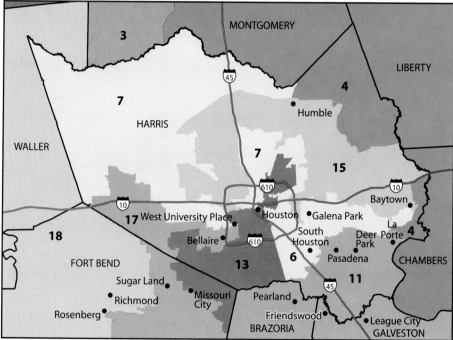

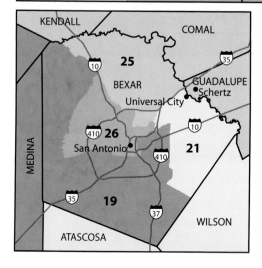

FIGURE 7.1 *Texas Senate Districts: 2002–2011 Elections.*

SOURCE: Data from Texas Legislative Council.

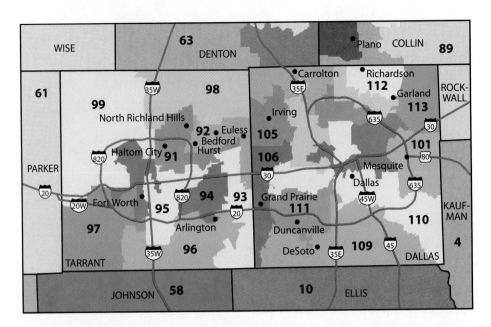

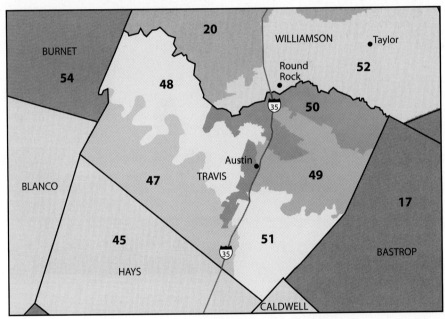

FIGURE 7.2   *Texas House of Representative Districts: 2002–2011 Elections.*

SOURCE: Data from Texas Legislative Council.

multimember districts

District having more than one member elected to the legislature.

While Texas used **multimember districts** in the past, it most recently used them in the larger urban counties during the 1970s. The Legislative Redistricting Board, which is discussed later in this chapter, drew up this plan after the plan drawn by the Texas legislature was invalidated by federal court action. This board created eleven multimember districts with a total of sixty state representatives. The other ninety state representatives were elected from single-member districts. For example, Dallas County had eighteen representatives elected by ballot place (Place 1 through Place 18). Candidates filed for a ballot place, and voters cast one vote in each of the eighteen legislative races.

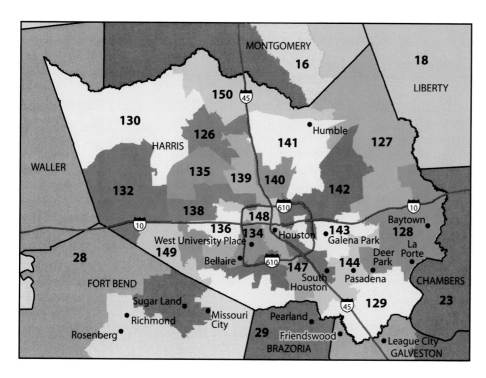

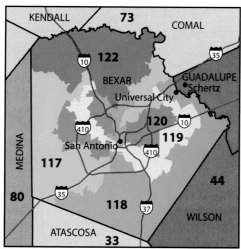

FIGURE 7.2   (*continued*)

    In 1971 the courts invalidated the Legislative Redistricting Board's multimember
plan. Minority groups contested the plan, pointing out that the system allowed for a
majority to elect all the representatives and for minorities to be frozen out. Some writers
have called this the "Matthew effect" after the words of Matthew 13:12: "For whoever has
to him more will be given, and he will have abundance; but whoever does not have, even
what he has will be taken away from him."[4] In a single-member district system, a party
or a candidate need win only a majority of the vote in a district to win one seat. In
countywide districts, a majority of the voters in the county can control all the seats.
Under a single-member district system, districts can be drawn to the advantage of ethnic
and political minorities within the county. This issue will be discussed later.

TABLE 7.1

Multimember State Legislative Districts

State	Legislative Body	Number of Multimember	Largest Number Seats in a District
Arizona	House	30 of 30	2
Arkansas	House	3 of 96	2
Idaho	House	35 of 35	2
Maryland	House	44 of 63	3
Nevada	Senate	5 of 16	2
New Hampshire	House	99 of 193	11
New Jersey	House	40 of 40	2
North Carolina	Senate	8 of 42	2
North Dakota	House	49 of 49	2
South Dakota	House	35 of 35	2
Vermont	Senate	10 of 13	6
	House	41 of 109	2
Washington	House	40 of 40	2
West Virginia	House	23 of 56	7
	Senate	17 of 17	2

Source: National Council of State Legislatures (*www.ncsl.org*).

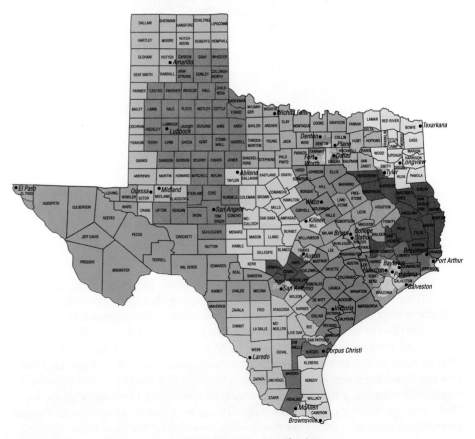

FIGURE 7.3   *Texas State Senate Districts: 2002–2011 Elections.*

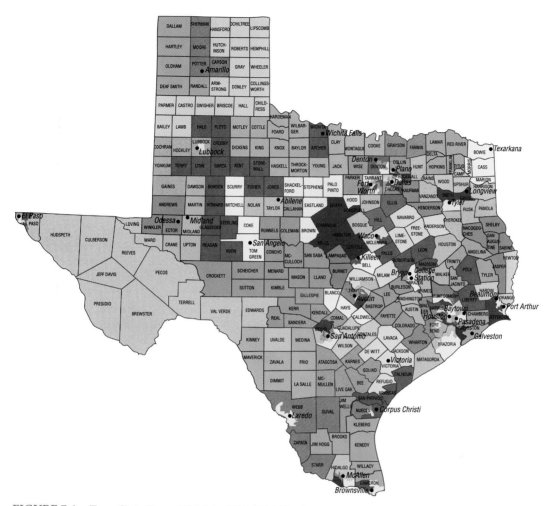

FIGURE 7.4 *Texas State House Districts: 2002–2011 Elections.*

Thus, multimember districts promote majority representation or domination, and single-member districts can promote geographical representation. Depending upon how district lines are drawn, they can also promote racial and ethnic minority representation.

→ REAPPORTIONMENT AND REDISTRICTING ISSUES

The U.S. Constitution requires that Congress reapportion the seats in the U.S. House of Representatives among the states following each federal census (every ten years). The Texas Constitution likewise requires the state legislature to reapportion the seats following each federal census.[5] Two terms are usually used to describe this process: **reapportionment and redistricting.** The term *reapportionment* refers to the process of allocating representatives to districts; *redistricting* is the drawing of district lines. The terms are generally interchangeable and will be used interchangeably in this text.

Apportioning seats in any legislative body is a highly political process. Each interest within the state tries to gain as much as possible from the process. Existing powers, such as the majority party in the legislature, will try to protect their advantages. Incumbent legislators will try to ensure their reelection. The primary issues raised by

reapportionment and redistricting

Drawing of new legislative districts normally after each new census of population—every 10 years.

reapportionment are equity of representation, minority representation, and gerrymandering (drawing district boundary lines for political advantage).

Equity of Representation

equity of representation
Each member of a legislative represents about the same number of people.

The issue of **equity of representation** is not new; it is perhaps as old as legislative bodies. Thomas Jefferson noted the problem in the Virginia legislature in the eighteenth century.[6] During most of the nineteenth century, legislative apportionment most often resulted in equity. Each representative represented an equal number of citizens. Some states had provisions that limited the number of seats a single county could have. In the early twentieth century, population shifted from rural to urban areas, and gradually the rural areas were overrepresented in many state legislatures. In the 1960s only two states (Wisconsin and Massachusetts) had rural/urban representation in the legislature that equaled population distributions in the state.[7]

From 1876 until the 1920s, the Texas legislature made an effort to reapportion the seats after each census. This process was made easier by the addition of one seat for each increase of 50,000 in the population. From 1880 until 1920 a total of 57 seats were added to the legislature to bring the total to 150 members. However, in 1930 and 1940, the legislature failed to reapportion legislative seats, and no new seats were added. Thus, in 1951 the Texas legislative seats had not changed since 1921,[8] but major population shifts from rural to urban areas had occurred. This was especially true during and immediately after World War II. These shifts in population created a serious disparity in representation between rural and urban areas of the state. Most urban counties were vastly underrepresented.

Legislative Redistricting Board (LRB)
State board composed of elected officials that can draw new legislative districts for the house and senate if the legislature fails to act.

In an attempt to resolve the inequality of representation in the state, the Texas Constitution was amended in 1948 to create the **Legislative Redistricting Board (LRB).** This board was given the authority to redistrict the seats in the house and senate if the legislature failed to act. The LRB is made up of the lieutenant governor, the speaker of the house, the attorney general, the comptroller of public accounts, and the commissioner of the general land office.[9]

The creation of the LRB and the threat of action forced the legislature to act in 1951. Representation shifted from rural to urban areas, but large urban counties were still underrepresented in 1952. This underrepresentation was due in part to a 1936 amendment to the Texas Constitution that limited the number of representatives any county could have to seven until the population reached 700,000 and then the county could have one additional representative for each 100,000 population.[10] For example, in 1952, had apportionment been based on population alone, each state representative would have represented about 50,000 people. This means that Dallas County would have increased from seven to twelve representatives, Harris County from eight to sixteen, and Bexar County (San Antonio) from seven to ten. The constitution also prohibited any county from having more than one senator, no matter how large the county's population.

Baker v. Carr
Court case that required state legislative districts to contain about the same number of citizens.

Reynolds v. Sims
Court case that required state legislative districts to contain about the same number of citizens.

In 1962, in the case *Baker v. Carr,* the U.S. Supreme Court decided that these inequalities in the apportionment of legislative districts denied voters "equal protection of the law" and said that "as nearly as practicable, one man's vote would be equal to another's."[11] Two years later in *Reynolds v. Sims,* the court ruled that both houses of state legislatures had to be apportioned based on population. The court rejected the analogy to the U.S. Senate, which is based on geographic units, and said, "Legislators represent people, not trees or acres. Legislators are elected by voters, not farms or cities or economic interests."[12] These two cases forced all states to redistrict based on population and led to the "one person, one vote" rule. Over time, the general rule on reapportionment became that legislative districts could vary no more than 5 percent, plus or minus, from the mean population for districts. In Texas, in 2002 the deviation from the mean for house districts was 2.65 percent and for the senate it was 2.60 percent.

In 1965, a federal district court ruled that the provisions in the Texas Constitution that limited a county to seven house seats and one senate seat were unconstitutional.[13] This forced the apportionment of both houses of the Texas legislature to be on the basis of population. The political consequences of these court decisions shifted power from rural to urban areas. A discussion of the impact of these decisions on the makeup of today's Texas legislature follows later in this chapter.

By the 1970s the issue of equity of representation had not been settled and it is no longer an issue. With advancements in computers it is quite easy to draw districts with approximately the same number of people. Other issues, just as contentious, have replaced the equity issue.

Minority Representation

The second issue raised by redistricting is **minority representation.** Not only should legislative districts be approximately equal in population, they should also allow for minority representation. This issue was first raised in Texas in the 1970s when Texas used multimember districts in some large urban counties. This was discussed earlier. Multimember districts were invalidated by court actions.[14]

minority representation
Requirement that in drawing legislative districts racial and ethnic minorities should be given seats where they can elect representatives.

The 1981 session of the legislature produced a redistricting plan that advanced minority representation in both houses. However, Bill Clements, the Republican governor, vetoed the senate plan, and the Texas Supreme Court invalidated the house plan. This forced the Legislative Redistricting Board to draw new districts. The new plan was challenged in federal courts and by the U.S. Justice Department, which ruled that the plan violated the federal Voting Rights Act because it did not achieve maximum minority representation. African Americans and Mexican Americans felt that the plan diluted their voting strength. A new plan, drawn up by federal courts, maximized minority representation by creating districts that contained a majority of ethnic minorities—"majority–minority" districts.

Similar battles took place in the 1990s. Minorities gained many seats as did Republicans, who managed to take control of the Texas senate for the first time in over 100 years. In the 2001 session of the legislature, minorities did not gain significantly. Later in this chapter the effects of this redistricting are discussed in detail.

Political and Racial Gerrymandering

Political party gerrymandering is the drawing of legislative districts to achieve the political advantage of one political party over another. The term also has been applied to the practice of creating minority districts—racial gerrymandering. The practice dates to the early days of the Republic. In 1812 Governor Elbridge Gerry of Massachusetts drew a legislative district shaped somewhat like a salamander. A political cartoonist for the *Boston Globe* dressed up the outlines of the district with eyes, wings, and claws and dubbed it a "Gerrymander." (See figure 7.5.)

political party gerrymandering
Drawing legislative districts to the advantage of a political party.

With the rise of the Republican party, political gerrymandering in Texas has intensified. Until 2003, Republicans repeatedly charged that the Democrats have reduced the number of potential Republican districts, especially in suburban areas. In the 1980s, the Republicans forged alliances with minority groups. Republicans support the creation of **racially gerrymandered majority–minority districts,** and minority groups support the Republican efforts. As we shall see subsequently, the creation of majority–minority districts aids the Republicans as well as minorities.

racially gerrymandered majority–minority districts
Legislative districts that are drawn to the advantage of a minority group.

FIGURE 7.5 *The Original Gerrymander in Massachusetts, 1812.*

A legal challenge to overturn the practice of creating majority–minority districts has been reviewed by the U.S. Supreme Court.[15] This challenge was aimed at U.S. congressional districts, rather than state house and senate districts, but it will eventually affect these.

In ruling against three Texas U.S. congressional districts, the Court gave several reasons. Writing for the majority, Justice O'Connor stated that these districts were "formed in utter disregard for traditional redistricting criteria" (compactness) and that the shapes of the districts "are ultimately unexplainable on grounds other than the racial quotas established for these districts," resulting in "unconstitutional racial gerrymandering." Justice O'Connor also stated in her opinion that "districts can be oddly shaped but not bizarrely so."[16] While such a vague legal "standard" does not provide clear guidance, the Court is saying there is a limit to the use of race as a criterion for drawing legislative district lines.

In April 2001 the U.S. Supreme Court, in *Hunt v. Cromartie* (No. 562US 541-[2001]), placed further limitation on the use of racial gerrymandering in drawing legislative districts. The Court said that while race can be a factor, it couldn't be the primary factor in determining the makeup of legislative districts. Partisan makeup can be a primary factor, but race cannot.

This is an obvious departure from the past practice of packing minorities into safe districts. It is clear that this new court ruling reduced the practice of racial gerrymandering. While political party and race often coincide, it is now possible to pack minority Democrats into districts so long as your intent is not race.

The fine art of gerrymandering has been with us since the development of political parties and will remain a part of the political landscape for years to come. Only the limits of political gerrymandering remain in question.

→ IMPACT OF REDISTRICTING

What impact has redistricting had on the Texas legislature and, more generally, on Texas politics? Equity of representation has been achieved. Each member of the house and senate represents about the same number of people. Representation has shifted from

View the Current Legislative District Plans and Your Home Districts

You can view maps on the Texas Legislative Council Web page at *www.tlc.state.tx.us/research/redist/redist.htm.* Using the RedViewer page you can retrieve maps of all legislative district plans that were proposed by many interest groups as well as the current map. If you use the zoom feature you can view your home district. If you don't know your state representative or senator you can find them by using the zip code finder on the main Web page for the Texas Legislative Council (*www.tlc.state.tx.us*). You can also view maps of congressional districts at this site. Texas gained two new congressional seats in 2002 for a total of thirty-two members of Congress. State senators and members of Congress now represent about the same number of citizens. Compare your senatorial and congressional districts and see how different they are.

rural to urban areas, especially to suburban areas in the major metropolitan centers. Initially, redistricting increased turnover in the state legislatures. Turnover increased from around 30 percent in the 1960s to 40 percent in the 1970s; however, it had declined to about 20 percent in the 1990s. There was less than 20 percent turnover in the Texas legislature in the 2002 election cycle despite the drawing of new districts.

Redistricting has also had an impact on minority representation in the Texas legislature. Redistricting efforts in the 1990s increased the number of majority-minority districts. This concentration of minority populations in districts has also had the effect of increasing the number of legislative districts that are majority Anglo and that vote Republican.

✦ REDISTRICTING IN 2001

In the 2001 session of the legislature several issues surfaced and none are really new. Both parties hoped to gain seats through the redistricting process. Texas gained two additional U.S. congressional seats, for a total of thirty-two, and the fight between Democrats and Republicans over these added to the controversy in the legislature.

With both parties almost evenly divided between the Texas house and senate, even the shift of a few seats could change party control in either house. As the session wore on the battle over redistricting intensified. Republican party activists were more vocal in their criticism of the plans presented by the house and senate Redistricting Committees than the Democrats. The GOP chair, Susan Weddington, was especially critical of the house plan. She referred to the plan as a "...thinly veiled attempt to protect the careers of Speaker Pete Laney and incumbent politicians." Weddington said, "The Republican Party supports a fair redistricting plan that puts the interests of the people of Texas ahead of protecting incumbent politicians."[17] The chair of the Redistricting Committee, Republican Delbert Jones of Lubbock, denied that this was the intention of the committee. Other house Republicans were pressured by their party and threatened with primary opponents if they did not support the GOP position on redistricting.

Some Republican attacks were also aimed at house committee chairs who are Republicans. The charge was that these committee chairs were supporting a plan that would keep current house speaker Pete Laney in power so they could keep their committee chairs in the next session should Laney be reelected. If a Republican replaced Laney in the next session, these Republican chairs would lose their positions.

The battle over redistricting even extended into the question of abortions. "The Texas Right to Life Committee called on its members to lobby against the (House) plan that the committee described as 'anti-life.' The pro-abortion Democrats and Republicans are lobbying for the Laney plan, which doesn't represent us—it's clearly anti-life."[18]

Some house minority members felt that they should gain more seats in the house. The Mexican American Legal Defense and Education Fund and the League of United Latin American Citizens complained that the house committee recommendations did not take into account the growth in minority populations. Part of this dissatisfaction stems from the fact that the fastest growing areas of the state from 1990 to 2000 were in the predominantly white/Anglo suburbs of Houston, San Antonio, and Dallas. While the inner cities of Houston and Dallas gained population they did not increase as significantly as the surrounding suburban areas. In 1990 each house member represented about 109,000 people. In 2002, each house member represented about 139,000. For the senate the numbers go from 550,000 in 1990 to 673,000 in 2002. While many Democratic districts are overpopulated, Republican districts in the suburbs tend to be more overpopulated. Harris County lost one of the twenty-five representatives it had in 1990. The 2000 population of Harris County was 3,400,578. Divide this by 25, and you get 136,023, which is a deviation of 2.15 percent below the "ideal district" of 139,000. While this is within the margin of acceptability, the Republican-controlled Legislative Redistricting Board gave the seat to the more Republican-leaning suburban area of Fort Bend County (see subsequent discussion). While Dallas and Fort Worth did not lose seats, the suburban areas gained seats. The suburbs in the Austin (Travis County) area also gained seats.

There is one other important difference in reapportionment in the 2001 session of the legislature. As indicated earlier, in the 1980s and 1990s the federal Voting Rights Act required state legislatures to consider racial makeup of districts. In April 2001 the U.S. Supreme Court in *Hunt v. Cromartie* ruled that race can be a factor, but not the predominant factor, in drawing legislative districts. In the same case the Court again allowed the use of political party affiliation as a factor in drawing district lines (political gerrymandering). As indicated previously, minority groups tend to vote Democratic, and it may be possible to achieve the same results by using party rather than race in drawing district lines.

The Texas house and senate adjourned without approving new redistricting plans. The senate rules require two-thirds (twenty-one members) approval before a bill can be considered on the senate floor. The plan voted out of the committee did not receive enough support for floor consideration, so it died. The senate also failed to consider the house-approved plan. As a result of this inaction by the senate, the Legislative Redistricting Board, consisting of the lieutenant governor, speaker of the house, comptroller, land commissioner, and attorney general, had to establish new districts for the Texas house and senate. Only one member of this board is a Democrat—Speaker Laney, who was effectively frozen out of the discussion. Lt. Governor Ratliff objected to the proceeding. The remaining three members, Attorney General Cornyn, Land Commissioner Dewhurst, and Comptroller Rylander, proceeded to draw districts that greatly favor Republicans.

Due to these redistricting efforts by the Legislative Redistricting Board, Republicans gained sixteen house seats and three senate seats for the 2003 and 2005 sessions. The Republicans held eighty-eight house and nineteen senate seats.

⤳ Re-redistricting in 2003

Redistricting normally takes place every decade following the new federal census. In the 2003 session Republicans controlled both houses of the Texas legislature for the first time in 130 years and used their new control to redistrict the state's thirty-two congressional districts. This mid-decade redistricting or re-redistricting is unprecedented.

As indicated earlier, in the 2001 session of the legislature Republicans in the senate refused to approve any redistricting plans. The house and senate districts were drawn by the Republican-controlled Legislative Redistricting Board. This board drew districts that greatly favored Republicans in both house and senate elections. This board cannot redistrict congressional districts, and Governor Perry refused to call a special session in 2001 to consider the issue. Instead he stated that the matter was best left to the courts.

The congressional district map used in the 2002 election cycle was drawn by a special three-judge federal court. While this may have favored Republicans in a majority of the districts, Democrats managed to win election in seventeen of the thirty-two districts, leaving the Republicans with fifteen districts. There were five districts that heavily favored Republicans but were won by Democrats. With these unexpected results, U.S. House Majority Leader Tom DeLay, a Republican from Sugarland, Texas, forwarded a plan to the Texas legislature in the 2003 session to redraw the 2001 court-ordered congressional district map.

The Texas house, under the direction of newly elected Speaker Tom Craddick(R), took up the cause and a new congressional district map was reported out of committee. The Texas senate, under the direction of newly elected Lt. Governor David Dewhurst, did not debate the issue during the regular session due to the senate's two-thirds rule, which required that twenty-one members of the Senate agree to allow a bill to be considered by the whole senate. Senate Democrats, with twelve members, refused to consider any bills.

The Texas house rules state that a quorum is two-thirds of the whole membership, or one hundred members. A quorum must be present before the house can act. During the last week of the regular session in 2003, fifty-two Democrats left the state and took up residence in the Holiday Inn in Ardmore, Oklahoma. This boycott by the Democrats effectively prevented the house from acting, and the re-redistricting bill failed to pass. This boycott infuriated most of the state and national Republican leadership. Texas Rangers were sent to try and get the renegades back to Austin but all efforts failed.

Despite much statewide opposition to continuing the re-redistricting battle, on June 19, 2003, Governor Rick Perry called a special session of the legislature, to begin June 30, to reconsider the re-redistricting proposal. Clay Robison, an editorial writer for the *Houston Chronicle,* expressed the sentiment of much of the state press and the degree of acrimony developing in the state at that time.

> Gov. Rick Perry's insistence that the Legislature waste your tax dollars to redraw Texas' congressional districts leads to two possible conclusions about the governor, and neither is flattering. One is that he has a stubborn, partisan streak made meaner by his pique over the Democratic walkout that killed the unnecessary redistricting effort last month. The other is that he is a tail-wagging lap dog, eager to play "go fetch" for the right wing of his party, U.S. House Majority Leader Tom DeLay and, now, President Bush.

Despite many misgivings, on July 8, 2003, the Texas house quickly passed a new congressional map by a highly partisan vote of 83 to 62. In this first special session Lt. Governor Dewhurst left in place the two-thirds rule required to consider a bill on the senate floor.

While the Democrats held twelve seats they could block the house-passed bill from being considered by the senate; however, several Democrats at first withheld their support for blocking the legislation. Some minority Democratic senators were offered passage of legislation favorable to their districts. Others were offered "safe" congressional seats in exchange for favoring re-redistricting. On July 15, 2003, Senator Bill Ratliff, a Republican from Mount Pleasant, joined ten Democrats in blocking the re-redistricting bill.

Great pressure was applied to Lt. Governor Dewhurst to drop the two-thirds rule; however, many senators, both Democratic and Republican, opposed the change. Newspapers across the state urged Dewhurst to hold the line and not change the rules. Statewide polls showed Governor Perry losing support over the redistricting issue.

On July 28, 2003, eleven Texas senators fled to Albuquerque, New Mexico. Two things prompted this action. First, they anticipated that the governor was going to adjourn the first special session early and call a second special session immediately thereafter (which he did). The rumor was that the senate sergeant-at-arms had been ordered to lock the senators in the senate chamber as soon as the session was called to prevent them from busting a quorum. Second, Lt. Governor Dewhurst had stated he would suspend the two-thirds rule for future sessions.

While the Texas governor and lt. governor were livid at the actions of these Democratic senators, the Democratic governor and lt. governor of New Mexico were delighted and welcomed the eleven to the state. Republicans and Democrats held dueling press conferences, each accusing the other of wrongdoing. The governor at one point blamed the absent senators for preventing consideration of a bill to fund child healthcare Medicaid benefits. Perry had earlier vetoed part of the state budget that would have allowed this funding.

A few hours after the second special session began and a quorum was present, the house passed the same redistricting bill passed in the first special session. The quick passage of the bill led some Democrats to question the fairness of the process since no debate or discussion was allowed.

The Republican senators in Austin attempted to force the return of the eleven Democrats by imposing fines. In the end the fines amounted to $57,000 for each of the stray senators. The Republicans also took away the parking spaces of the boycotting senators. Some have questioned the legality of this action since a quorum was not present and technically the senate could not take action. The fines were later removed on the condition that there would be no more boycotts until the end of the term in January 2005.

The eleven Democratic senators stayed in New Mexico until the thirty-day special session expired on August 26, 2003. They did not immediately return to the state because they were afraid that they would be arrested and taken to Austin for a third special session call. On September 3, 2003, the stalemate was broken when Senator John Whitmire, Democrat from Houston, broke the boycott and returned to the state.

On September 10, 2003, Governor Perry called a third special session of the legislature to consider redistricting. Some were surprised that a third session was called since a state poll by Montgomery and Associates, an independent research firm, found that most Texans were opposed to redistricting. In fact, only 47.9 percent of self-identified Republicans supported redistricting. The poll also showed the governor with a negative rating on job performance.

The house and senate quickly passed different redistricting bills, which went to a conference committee. These differences quickly led to infighting among the Republicans, with the main issue being congressional districts in West Texas. House Speaker Tom Craddick wanted a district dominated by his hometown of Midland but Senator Robert Duncan, Republican from Lubbock, wanted to keep Midland in a district with Lubbock.

The fight over the West Texas districts became so intense that Governor Perry and U.S. Congressman Tom DeLay became involved. Eventually Congressman DeLay was seen marching between house and senate chambers in the capitol. He claimed he was there as a diplomat, but most felt he was there as an enforcer. In the end, an entirely new map, unseen before DeLay's arrival, was produced by the conference committee and accepted by both houses in mid-October 2003. (See figure 7.6.)

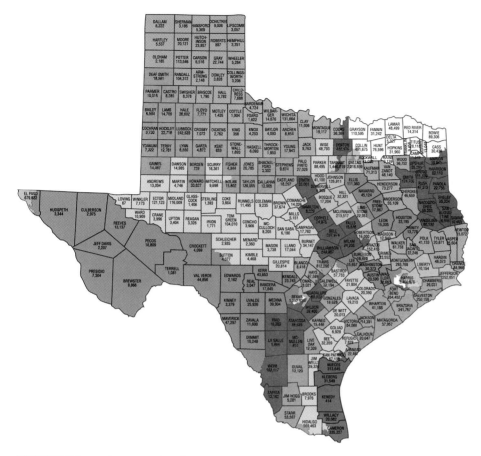

FIGURE 7.6 *U.S. Congressional Districts: 2004 Elections.*

Although many predicted that the DeLay redistricting map would be found in violation of the federal Voting Rights Act because it split minority voters rather than concentrating them into majority–minority districts, they were wrong. U.S. Attorney General Ashcroft issued a one-sentence letter saying that he did not object to the new map. At the time, Democratic Texas house members claimed that the professional staff of the U.S. Justice Department objected to the map and they asked that the report be made public but it was not released. When it was later released, they were proved right.

A three-judge special court consisting of two Republicans and one Democrat approved the map, voting along party lines. The logic that prevailed in essence sets aside the Voting Rights Act by allowing minority voters to be divided into many congressional districts so long as the intention is to divide Democrats and not to divide minority voters. Partisan gerrymandering is considered legal. Since most minorities vote for Democrats, they can be split into many districts so long as the gerrymandering is partisan in intent. This established a new standard for redistricting. The U.S. Supreme Court later forced the change in four of these districts because they had diluted the voting strength of minorities.

Governor Perry, Congressman Tom DeLay, and the Republicans were successful in their redistricting efforts. In the 2004 election, the Republicans gained five Congressional seats and now control the Texas delegation to Congress 21 to 11. Democrats entered the decade with a 17 to 15 majority. All targeted Democrats were either defeated or chose not to run. Only Congressman Chet Edwards won reelection in District 17.

In July of 2006, the U.S. Supreme Court heard an appeal to the DeLay redistricting. They ruled that nothing in the Constitution prohibited redistricting at mid-decade. However, they did order the redrawing of three Congressional districts due to concerns over minority representation.

It is interesting to note that on the national level, Republicans increased their control of the U.S. House of Representatives by six seats. Five of these came from the redistricting effort in Texas. Without this redistricting, the Republicans might not have retained control of the House of Representatives in the 109th Congress. This may prompt midterm redistricting in other states and add a new dimension to the redistricting game. It may very well be that rather than voters picking Congress members, Congress members pick the voters they need to get elected.

✦ QUALIFICATIONS FOR LEGISLATORS

Setting aside for a moment the politics of state legislatures, let us examine the formal and informal qualifications for membership. Formal qualifications include age, citizenship, state residency, district residency, and qualified voter status. Among the states, the lowest minimum age for house membership is 18 years and the upper minimum age is 25. Most states require U.S. citizenship, residency in the state from one to five years, and district residency for a year or less.

A Texas house member must be a U.S. citizen, a registered voter, at least 21 years of age, and must have lived in the state for two years and in the district for one year. To be a Texas state senator, a person must be 26 years of age and reside in the district for one year preceding their election and have resided in the state for five years before the election.

Formal requirements are minimal and keep few citizens from serving. More important are informal qualifications that limit many people's ability to serve. These include income, education, occupation, ethnicity, and gender. On these dimensions, state legislators tend not to represent the general population. Nationwide, legislators tend to be male, well-educated, and professionals (often lawyers).

"birthright" characteristics
Social and economic characteristics of legislators that match these characteristics of their district. Representatives are of the people on social and economic traits but above the people on income and education.

Other dimensions, sometimes called **"birthright" characteristics,** include such things as race, ethnicity, religion, and national background. On these dimensions, representatives tend to represent their district.[19] If the legislative district is predominantly Mexican American, the representative will likely be Mexican American; the same is true for African American districts. Even though legislators generally represent their constituents on these characteristics, legislators are usually better educated and from selected occupational groups.

Thus, legislators are *of the people* in terms of ethnicity but *above the people* in terms of income, education, and occupation. An African American legislator is generally better educated than his or her constituents and drawn from a selected occupational group. For example, in the 2001 session of the Texas house, nine of the fourteen African Americans were attorneys and sixteen of the thirty-one Mexican Americans were attorneys. All had a higher level of education than their constituents.[20] The same is also true for Anglo legislators. In 2006 a total of 1,681 women or 22.8 percent of all state legislators nationwide were women. This is an increase of only 2 percent since 1993. In 1969 only 301 women (4 percent of all legislators nationwide) served in state legislatures.[21] While the first women to serve in a state legislature were elected in 1894 to the Colorado house of representatives, few women served until the early 1970s. The number of women increased steadily until 2000 but has remained at about that level (22 percent). (See figure 7.7.) In Texas, the number of women legislators has increased from the one woman in each chamber in 1971 to thirty-six in 2003. (See table 7.2.) Four are senators and thirty-three are state representatives.

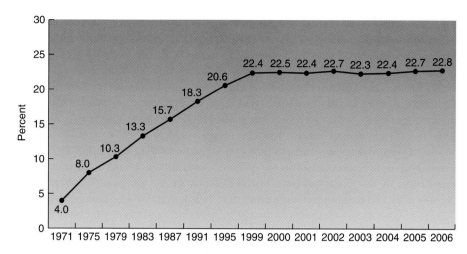

FIGURE 7.7   *Women in State Legislatures.*

SOURCE: Center for American Women and Politics, Eagleton Institute of Politics, Rutgers University (*www.cawp.rutgers.edu*).

T A B L E   7 . 2

Background of Members of the Texas Legislature 2007

	House	Senate
Sex		
Male	117	27
Female	33	4
Race		
Anglo	105	22
Hispanic	30	7
African American	14	2
Asian	1	
Longevity		
Incumbent	125	26
Freshman	23	5
Party		
Democratic	68	11
Republican	81	20

Source: Texas legislature Web page.

The numbers of Hispanics and African Americans have also increased in legislatures across the nation, in part due to reapportionment. Both ethnic groups are underrepresented in the Texas legislature when compared with their numbers in the population. In 2007, Hispanics made up 30 percent of the population of Texas and held 20 percent of the house seats and 22.5 percent of the senate seats. African Americans made up 13.4 percent of the Texas population and held 9.3 percent of the seats in the legislature.

Even with the changes in apportionment, minorities and women are still underrepresented in state legislatures. Most legislators are upwardly mobile white males. Most are from old, established, often very wealthy families. The legislature is a good place to begin a political career. Having family and money helps launch that career. In addition, some professions, especially law, allow a person time to devote to legislative duties. As we shall see later, most states do not pay their legislators well, and having other sources of income is essential. Also, unlike the U.S. Congress, most state legislatures are part-time bodies, meeting for a set number of days annually or biennially. A survey by the National Conference of State Legislatures shows that most legislators do not consider themselves full-time legislators, although the number who do has been increasing nationwide. In Texas only about seven members identify themselves as full-time.

The percentage of attorneys in the Texas legislature (33.6 percent in 2007) is much higher than the average legislature (16.5 percent). In addition, Texas has fewer legislators who identify themselves as full-time. Texas legislators are not well paid ($7,200 per year), and this might contribute to their feeling that their legislative jobs are only part-time. There is a higher than average percentage of businessmen and women in the Texas legislature, and a lower than average percentage of schoolteachers. In some states, state employees can serve in the state legislature and keep their jobs as teachers. This is prohibited in Texas. A Texas state employee may not hold an elective and appointive office and receive pay for both.

→ Getting Elected

Now that we know something about who gets elected to state legislatures, let us turn our attention to what it takes to get elected. In chapter 6 we saw that running for office can be costly. Although most candidates for the state legislature face little or no opposition in either the primary or general election, there are exceptions. Even when candidates do not face opposition, they are likely to collect large amounts of money from various groups, especially from PACs.

In the 2006 races for the legislature, house winners collected an average of $208,000 and senate winners collected an average of $917,000. The range for the house was from $11,500 to $1,973,830 for Speaker Craddick. In the senate the range was $31,989 to $2,102,633.

Most money comes from contributors who live outside the senator's or representative's district. In the house, only seven members received 50 percent or more of their **money from within the district.** On average only 19 percent of the money received by house members comes from within the district. In the senate, three members received 50 percent or more from residents living in their district and on average 22 percent of a senator's money came from residents living in the district. Races in both the house and senate are financed by PACs and large contributors living outside their districts.

money from within the district
Campaign money that is collected from citizens living in the representative's district.

Competition for House and Senate Seats

As has been noted, in the one-party Democratic era in Texas (1870s to 1970s) most of the competition for all offices was in the Democratic party primary. Today, competition is more likely to be in the general election. In the 2006 election, a total of 70 of 150 house seats had Democratic and Republican party candidates. In the 2004 election only 25 seats were competitive. Table 7.3 shows the level of competition in 2004 and 2006 elections.

In the last eight years there has been an increase in the level of competition in the Republican party primary elections. Some of this competition is related to House Speaker Craddick, who has been known to seek opponents for those members who oppose his agenda and may threaten his continuation as speaker. Even with this increase in competition, most incumbents still service election challenges.

TABLE 7.3

Competition in House and Senate Elections in 2004 and 2006

	Opponents in Primary Elections			
	Democrats		Republicans	
	2004	2006	2004	2006
House	22	17	23	38
Senate	3	2	1	5
	Opponents in the General Election			
	2004		2006	
House	25		70	
Senate	3		7	

Note: Only half of the Senate (16 of 15) members are up for election every two years. In the House, all 150 members are up for election every two years.

Source: Secretary of State Web page. Calculated by the author.

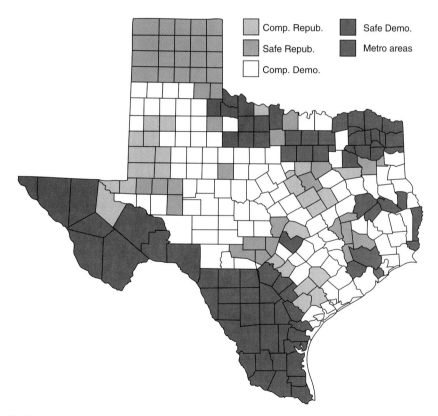

FIGURE 7.8   *Texas House of Representatives Party Competition in 2002–2010.*

This lack of competition in Texas legislative races is the result of several factors, but the major reason is the degree to which districts are politically and racially gerrymandered, creating safe election districts for both parties. This can be seen by comparing two characteristics of Texas legislative districts in 2004: the strength of party voting in the district and the percentage of minority population in the district. As figures 7.8 and 7.9

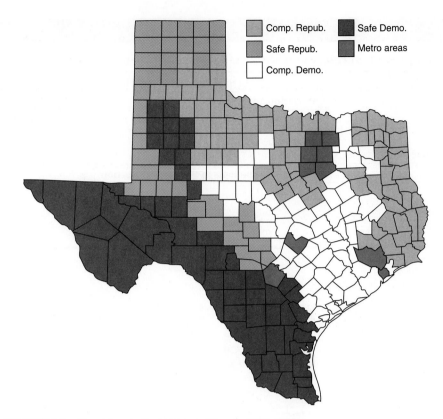

FIGURE 7.9   *Texas Senate Party Competition in 2002–2010.*

safe Democratic and safe Republican districts

Noncompetitive districts that can only be won by the party with 55 percent or more of the votes in the district.

clearly show, house and senate seats are clustered into **safe Democratic and safe Republican districts** with only a few competitive seats.

Party voting is a measure of the strength of a political party in the legislative district based on voter support for the party's candidates in previous elections. This is also a measure of party competition. Studies of party competition in the U.S. House and Senate seats define *noncompetitive* as any district in which either party receives 55 percent or more of the votes. Thus a district in which party vote is between 44 and 54 percent is considered competitive.[22] The measure used here to gauge party competitiveness is the combined vote received by either party for all offices/candidates in the district in the 2000 general election. This is the composite party vote. Thus, a house or senate district in which the Republican party candidates for statewide office collectively received 55 percent or more of the votes is considered a safe Republican district. Table 7.4 shows the number of competitive and noncompetitive seats in the Texas house and senate.

The second variable is racial composition of the district. This is simply the percentages of minority and nonminority population of the district. If we compare these two characteristics (party competition and minority population in the district) using some simple statistics, we can see that most Texas house and senate seats fall into two categories—noncompetitive Republican Anglo districts and noncompetitive Democratic minority districts. (See figures 7.10 and 7.11.) The creation of minority–majority districts results in the creation of safe Republican districts. Since minority support for Democratic candidates is always very high, concentrating minorities in districts also concentrates Democratic party support in these districts. Many remaining districts are

TABLE 7.4

Competitive and Noncompetitive Seats in the Texas House and Senate, 2002–2010

	Safe Democratic	Safe Republican	Competitive
House	58 (39%)	55 (37%)	37 (24%)
Senate	11 (35%)	11 (35%)	9 (30%)

Note: Safe seats are those in which the combined party vote for all offices in the district was 55 percent or greater.

Note: While this map shows the district based on 2000 Census and voting data, since 2000 both the demographics and the voting patterns have changed and some districts have become more competitive, especially for Democrats in South Texas and inner-city districts.

Source: Calculated from data on the home page of the Texas Secretary of State (*www.sos.state.tx.us*).

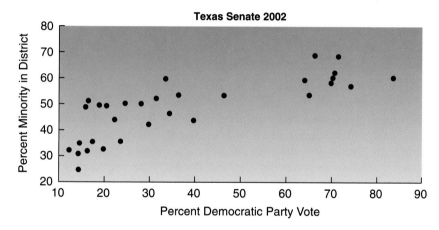

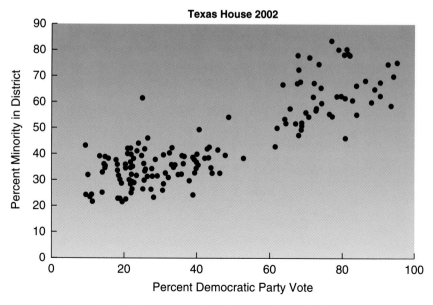

FIGURES 7.10 AND 7.11   These scatterplots show the relationship between minorities and party votes. Each dot on the graph represents a legislative district. In the lower left are the high-Anglo, high-Republican voting districts, and in the upper right are the high-minority, high-Democratic voting districts. As the percentage of minorities increases, the percentage of support for the Democratic party increases.

noncompetitive Republican districts. Other studies have found the same is true for U.S. congressional districts.[23]

Thus, one reason for the low competition in Texas legislative races is racial and political gerrymandering. Competition in such districts is most likely to occur at the primary level and when there is no incumbent. Competition in the general elections is less likely. Safe Democratic districts exist primarily in two places: South Texas, where there are concentrations of Mexican Americans, and East Texas, the traditional stronghold of Democrats. Republicans are strong in the Panhandle and the German Hill Country. Metropolitan areas of the state also contain both safe Democratic and safe Republican districts—Democrats in the inner city and Republicans in the suburbs.

Each election year only about one-third of the house members face opposition in the general election. Most members who seek reelection are reelected. Even fewer face opposition in the primary elections. Unless legislators are in a competitive district, they can generally stay as long as they like. Most voluntarily retire after a few years of service.

✦ TURNOVER IN STATE LEGISLATURES

turnover
The number of new members of the legislature each session.

One could conclude from the lack of competition for Texas legislative seats that there would be low turnover of the membership. This is not the case. **Turnover** refers to the number of new members of the legislature each session. Turnover is high in all state legislatures, and normally it is higher for the lower house than for the upper chamber.[24] In elections from 1992 to 1998, turnover in state houses ranged from a low of 2 percent in Alabama to a high of 58 percent in Alaska. However, the average is about 30 percent. Senate turnover ranged from 4 percent in Maryland to 70 percent in Arizona. The median change from 1992 to 2002 for the lower house was 25 percent, and for the upper house it was about 20 percent.[25]

Table 7.5 lists the number of years of service for members of the Texas legislature. In 2001 almost 48.5 percent of the house and 57 percent of the senate had served less than five years. Over time, turnover rates in Texas are very high. In 2001 the turnover rate was one of the smallest with only four new house members and one new senator. Turnover is not due mainly to electoral defeat; most members voluntarily retire from service. Retirement is prompted by poor pay, the lack of professional staff assistance, redistricting,

TABLE 7.5

Years of Service of Members of the 2005 Legislature

	House		Senate	
	Number	Percent	Number	Percent
30 or more	3	2.00%	0	0.00%
20 or more	5	3.33%	3	2.00%
16–18 years	15	10.00%	4	2.67%
10–14 years	35	23.33%	4	2.67%
6–8 years	24	16.00%	4	2.67%
2–4 years	38	25.33%	4	2.67%
First term	30	20.00%	12	8.00%
	150		31	

Sources: Texas House of Representatives (*www.house.state.tx.us/members*); The Texas Senate (*www.senate.state.tx.us*).

the requirements of the job, the demands upon one's family, fund-raising demands, and the rigors of seeking reelection.[26] Some use the office as a stepping-stone to higher office and leave to become members of Congress or take statewide office.

Why is turnover significant in state legislatures? It can be argued that high turnover contributes to the amateurish nature of state legislatures and reduces their effectiveness. In recent years this has been especially significant in those states where term limits have kicked in. If 20 to 25 percent of the members are new each session, these new members are learning the rules and finding their way. This allows a few "old timers" to control the legislative process. Even in Texas, with only nine new members in the house, a few "old timers" still control the process, as we shall see later in this chapter.

→ Term Limits

Though turnover in state legislatures nationwide is quite high, in recent years voters have supported formal **term limits** for state legislators. From 1990 to 1996, twenty-one states approved term limits for both house and senate seats. Fourteen of these states have imposed these limits with constitutional amendments and seven by statutes.[27] These limits were approved despite the fact that self-limiting of terms was working for many years. For example, "nationally, 72 percent of the house members and 75 percent of the senators who served in 1979 had left their respective chamber by 1989."[28] The Texas legislature has self-imposed term limits.

term limits
Limitation on the number of times a person can be elected to the same office in state legislatures.

→ Sessions

The Texas legislature meets in biennial sessions (every two years) of 140 days in odd-numbered years, beginning in January. Texas is one of only six states that still meet in **biennial sessions.** Arkansas, Montana, Nevada, North Dakota, and Oregon are the others. In recent years, the trend has been toward annual sessions. At the end of World War II, only four states held annual sessions. There were twenty meeting annually by 1966 and forty-two by 1974.[29]

Voters in Texas rejected a move to annual sessions in 1969 and again in 1972. In keeping with the traditionalistic/individualistic political culture of the state, there is some concern that the more often the legislature meets, the more damage it can do. One political wag once remarked that there was a typographical error in the original Texas Constitution, and that the founders had intended the legislature to meet for two days every 140 years.

biennial session
Legislature meets every two years.

At the end of the 140-day session, the Texas legislature must adjourn (*sine die*) and cannot call special or longer sessions. In recent years, many state governments have placed limits on the number of days a legislature can stay in session. Thirteen states do not place a limit on the length of legislative sessions.[30] Another important factor is the ability of the legislature to call itself into special session (called **extraordinary session**). In Texas and fifteen other states, the legislature cannot call itself into special session. The lack of ability to call special sessions makes the limit on the regular session even more meaningful. The legislature must finish its work in the prescribed time and leave.

sine die
Legislature must adjourn at end of regular session and cannot continue to meet.

extraordinary session
Legislative session called by the legislature, rather than the governor. Not used in Texas.

In Texas only the governor may call **special sessions,** of not more than thirty days each. There is no limit on the number of special sessions the governor may call. Also, in Texas, the governor decides the subject matter of the session, thus limiting the range of topics the legislature can consider. This gives the governor tremendous power to set the agenda of the legislature during special sessions and a bargaining chip to get the legislature to do what the governor wants.

special session
Session called by the governor to consider legislation proposed by the governor only.

The lack of ability of the Texas legislature to call itself into special session also gives the governor stronger veto powers. If the governor vetoes a bill and the legislature has adjourned, the veto stands. This in part helps to explain why so few vetoes of the governor are overridden.

States like Texas, that limit the number of days of regular sessions, are often forced to resort to special sessions. Budgetary problems, reapportionment issues, school finance, and prison funding have forced the Texas legislature to have many special sessions in the past decades. Many critics of the Texas biennial sessions point to the frequency of special sessions as evidence that the state needs to go to annual sessions. Budgeting for two years is extremely difficult. As we will see in Chapter 10, the tax structure in Texas is closely tied to economic conditions in the state. Predicting state revenues for two-year periods is extremely difficult.

→ SALARIES

Some citizens feel that because the legislature meets for only 140 days every two years, it is part-time and members should be paid accordingly. The pay reflects this attitude. Texas pays the 181 members of the legislature $7,200 a year plus an additional $124 per day for the first 120 days the legislature is in session. In years when the legislature meets, the total compensation is the $7,200 in salary plus the $14,880 in per diem pay for a total of $22,080. The Texas Ethics Commission recommends the per diem rate. In recent years they have used the per diem rate set by the federal government for travel. Since most legislators must have a second home in Austin while the session is going on, the per diem pay is not high. Housing costs in Austin are among the highest in the state. In years when the legislature is not in session, legislators receive their $7,200 in salary and may receive some additional per diem pay for off-session committee work.

HIGHLIGHT

Pay for State Legislatures

Texas currently pays members of the state legislature $600 per month. Among the fifteen large states, Texas has the lowest pay. Only eleven states pay more than $30,000 per year. Many states pay less than Texas, some as little as $5 per day. Some, like our neighbor to the west, New Mexico, pay only a per diem and no salary. Texas legislators currently receive $124 per day when in session or doing some interim committee work.

On two occasions in the last half of the twentieth century, voters in Texas rejected an amendment that would have let the legislature set its own salary by statute. This attitude is very much in keeping with the political culture of the state.

Should members of the legislature be paid a living wage salary?
No: Citizens should be willing to serve their state without being drawn to the job by pay. Serving in a citizen legislature is in keeping with our founders' view of public service. One serves in the legislature and makes policy that is in the best interest of all citizens. A living wage pay would encourage members to become full-time legislators. They might broaden their view of their role from one of a citizen legislature to one of professional legislatures seeking to serve themselves rather than the public's interest. Members currently receive a salary and per day compensation that equals over $15,000 per year. This is not bad pay for a part-time job.

Yes: Low pay greatly limits the number of citizens who can serve in the legislature to a few wealthy citizens or those members who can afford to be away from their jobs for long periods of time. Lawyers who serve in the legislature can have any cases delayed as long as the legislature is in session. Some lawyer members are hired by those wanting to delay cases. Other members may be hired as consultants by companies seeking favors in the legislature. The average citizen, especially the working poor, is not represented in the legislature. If you examine the financial disclosure statements filed by members of the house and senate, you will discover a plethora of millionaires. If the Texas legislature is to become a representative body as envisioned by the founders, the pay should be a living wage.

The salary of the Texas legislature has not been increased in the past thirty years. Several attempts to change the state constitutional limit have been rejected by the voters. Low pay contributes to the small number of legislators who consider themselves full-time. (See table 7.6.) The current pay in Texas qualifies legislators who have no other income for food stamps and other federal assistance. Obviously, most legislators have other sources of income. Many are attorneys or successful businessmen and women. Lack of compensation is very much in keeping with the traditionalistic political culture of the state, according to which only the elite should serve in the legislature. Also, note in table 7.6, other southern states (Florida, Georgia, and North Carolina) also have low salaries.

Most citizens are excluded from being legislators because they would not be able to devote the large amount of time to legislative work and still earn a living. Service in the Texas legislature is possible only for the independently wealthy, "political consultants," and people who can find a person or group to support them while they are in the legislature. In Texas, attorney-legislators who have cases in courts while the legislature is in session can have their cases delayed until the legislature adjourns. Some attorney-legislators receive cases from people who want to delay court action. Unlike many other states, Texas does not have a financial disclosure law that forces members to disclose their sources of income. This leaves the sources of members' income an open question. Some might receive income as "consultants" to businesses with interests in current legislation. One can question the objectivity of members under these circumstances.

Pay in other states varies greatly. The states with the lowest salaries are New Mexico (no pay), New Hampshire ($100 per year), Alabama ($10 per day for 105 days of session), and Rhode Island ($5 per day for 60 days of session). In New Mexico there is no pay but a per diem expense based on federal policy ($140 per day). At the high end is California at $99,000 per year and eleven other states that pay salaries of more than $30,000 per year.[31] (See table 7.6.) Per diem expenses also vary greatly among the states (see *www.ncsl.org/*). Texas, at $124 per diem, is at the high end. Four states pay no expenses, and some provide a fixed amount for the year. Most states also provide additional expenses and income to people in leadership positions such as committee chairs and presiding officers. Most states, including Texas, provide money to legislators for office and staff expenses although there is great variation among the states. This will be discussed later.

TABLE 7.6

Legislative Salaries in the Ten Most Populous States

State	Annual Salary 2006
California	$110,886
Texas	7,200
New York	79,500
Florida	29,916
Pennsylvania	69,647
Illinois	57,619
Ohio	56,261
Michigan	79,650
North Carolina	14,951
Georgia	16,524

Sources: Council of State Governments, *The Book of the States 2006* (Lexington, Ky.: Council of State Governments, 2006), Vol. 38, 84–86, table 3.9.

At least forty-one states give members of the legislature retirement benefits. In Texas, legislators' retirement pay is tied to the retirement pay of state district judges, which is tied to the judges' salary. The Texas legislature sets the salary of district judges. Most sessions result in pay raises for district judges. This produces an increase in retirement pay for legislators.

Texas appears to have the most generous retirement benefits. Legislators may retire at 60 years of age with eight years of service and at 55 years of age with twelve years of service. Compensation ranges from $4,800 to $5,700 per month depending on years of service and age of retirement. This high retirement may prompt some members to retire after getting the minimum time in. They can count on cost-of-living pay raises as the legislature increases the salaries of district judges. Most sessions of the legislature will see the compensation of district judges increase, thus increasing the retirement benefits of the legislature. Some increase can also come from cost-of-living adjustments given to all state retirees. In short, as an active member of the legislature you are worth only $600 per month. Retire and you can get a pay increase of $5,100 per month.

✦ Procedures of the Legislature

All legislatures have formal rules of procedure that govern their operations. These rules prescribe how bills are passed into law and make the process of passing laws more orderly and fair. These rules also make it difficult to pass laws. A bill must clear many hurdles before it becomes a law. Rules that make it difficult to pass bills have two results: they prevent bills from becoming law without careful review, and they preserve the status quo. In the traditionalistic/individualistic political culture of Texas, these rules protect the ruling elite and enable them to control the legislative process. Thus, it is more important to understand the impact of rules on legislation than to have a detailed understanding of the actual rules. This will be the basic approach used here to explain how laws are made in Texas.

✦ Leadership Positions in the Texas Legislature

In any legislative body, those holding formal leadership positions possess considerable power to decide the outcome of legislation. In the Texas legislature, power is very much concentrated in the hands of two individuals: the speaker of the house and the lieutenant governor. These two individuals control the output of legislation.

Speaker of the House

speaker of the house
Member of the Texas house, elected by the house members, who serves as presiding officer and generally controls the passage of legislation.

The members of the house elect the speaker of the Texas house of representatives by majority vote. The election of the **speaker of the house** is the first formal act of the members. The secretary of state presides over the election. Only occasionally is the outcome of this election in doubt. Who the speaker will be is generally known far in advance of the beginning of the session, and this individual spends considerable time lining up supporters before the session begins. In all but a few cases the person elected is a long-time member of the house and has support from current members. When a third of the members are new the person elected speaker may also have to gain support from some of these new members. It is illegal for candidates for speaker to formally promise members something in exchange for their vote, but key players in the election of the speaker often receive choice committee assignments.

It should be noted that for many years the Texas house of representatives operated on a bipartisan basis. In the 2003 thru 2007 sessions, much of this bipartisanship disappeared when the Republicans held a majority of the seats in the house and Rep. Tom Craddick became speaker. In the 2001 session of the legislature Democrats controlled the house and Democrat Pete Laney was speaker. Bipartisanship was much more apparent in committee assignments and the overall tone of the session. In the 2003 session, partisanship was the order of the day, the tone set by Speaker Craddick. Rep. Dawnna Dukes (Democrat from Houston) stated that the Republicans did not feel the need to compromise on issues since they controlled a majority of the seats.

Retiring Speaker Laney served in the Texas house since 1969 and chaired several important committees. Incumbent speakers are almost always reelected. A new speaker is chosen only after the death, retirement, or resignation of a sitting speaker. Traditionally, speakers served for two terms and retired or moved to higher offices. From 1951 to 1975 no speaker served more than two terms. In 1975 Billy Clayton broke with this tradition and served for four terms. Gib Lewis, who succeeded Clayton, served for five terms as did Laney.[32]

Tom Craddick was elected speaker for the 2003 session. He is the first Republican speaker since reconstruction. After serving two terms as Speaker, Craddick's fourth term is in doubt. In the 2008 election, the Republicans held onto a one seat majority (76/75). There is possibility of a tie since one seat will be subject to a recount, or could change due to 280 provisional ballots yet to be counted. With the House in a virtual tie, there must be compromise over leadership. Many are calling for Speaker Craddick not to run for re-election and allow a compromise candidate to seek the position.

Many feel that speaker of the house is the most powerful position in Texas government. There is no doubt that the speaker is extremely powerful. Generally, speakers have the power to direct and decide what legislation passes the house. The speaker gains power from the formal rules adopted by the house at the beginning of each session. These rules allow the speaker to do the following:

1. *Appoint the chairs of all committees.*
2. *Appoint most of the members of each standing committee.* About half of these committee seats are assigned based on a limited seniority system. In reality, the backers of the speaker often use their seniority to choose a committee assignment, thus freeing up an appointment for the speaker.
3. *Appoint members of the calendar and procedural committees, conference committees, and other special and interim committees.*
4. *Serve as presiding officer over all sessions.* This power allows the speaker to recognize members on the floor who wish to speak, generally interpret house rules, decide when a vote will be taken, and decide the outcome of voice votes.
5. *Refer all bills to committees.* As a rule, bills go to subject matter committees. However, the speaker has discretion in deciding what committee will receive a bill. Billy Clayton used the State Affairs Committee as his "dead bill committee." Bills assigned to this committee usually had little chance of passing. Also, the speaker can assign a bill to a favorable committee to enhance its chances of passing.

These rules give the speaker control over the house agenda. The speaker decides the chairs of standing committees, selects a majority of the members of all committees, and refers bills to committees. The selected chairs are members of the "speaker's team." Few bills pass the house without the speaker's approval. For example, in the 2005 session of the legislature, House Bill 1348 which would have limited campaign contributions from corporations and labor unions was being cosponsored by two-thirds of the

Rep. Tom Craddick—speaker of the Texas house of representatives, 2007.

lieutenant governor
Presiding officer of the Texas senate. Elected by the voters of the state.

members of the house, both Democrats and Republicans. The bill was not given a hearing by the Elections Committee due to the influence of the speaker.

Speaker Craddick Challenged

In the 2007 session of the legislature an attempt was made to remove Tom Craddick as speaker before the end of the session due in large degree to his partisanship and actions that many felt were arbitrary. Several attempts were made to advance a motion to vacate the chair, but the speaker refused to recognize anyone wanting to make that motion. When the speaker was overruled by the two parliamentarians, Speaker Craddick forced them to resign and brought in two former house members and colleagues to act as parliamentarians who upheld the speaker's decision to not recognize any member wanting to make a motion to vacate the chair.

This action to remove the speaker in part failed because the members failed to agree on a replacement for Craddick. Mr. Craddick has indicated his intention to run for another term. His success in seeking a fourth term will depend upon the outcome of the 2008 house races. If the Democrats gain additional seats and some of the Republican Craddick–supporters lose their seat, Mr. Craddick may not get a fourth term.

Lieutenant Governor

Unlike the speaker of the house, the voters elect the **lieutenant governor** for a four-year term in the general election. The lieutenant governor does not owe his or her election to the legislative body, is not formally a senator, and cannot vote except in cases of a tie. One might assume that the office was not a powerful legislative office. In most states this is true; however, the lieutenant governor in Texas possesses powers very similar to those of the speaker. Lieutenant governors can do the following:

1. *Appoint the chairs of all senate committees.*
2. *Select all members of all senate committees.* No formal seniority rule applies in the senate.
3. *Appoint members of the conference committees.*
4. *Serve as presiding officer and interpret rules.*
5. *Refer all bills to committees.*

On the surface, it appears that the lieutenant governor is more powerful than the speaker. Lieutenant governors do not owe their election to the senate, and they have all powers possessed by the speaker. The reality is different. The powers of the lieutenant governor are assigned by the formal rules of the senate, which are adopted at the beginning of each session. What the senate gives, it can take away. Lieutenant governors must play a delicate balancing role of working with powerful members of the senate and often compromising in the assignment of chairs of committees and committee membership. The same is true for all other powers. Thus, the lieutenant governor must forge an alliance with key senators to effectively utilize these powers.[33]

From 1876 to 1999, the Democrats controlled the lieutenant governor's office. They controlled the senate from 1876 to 1997. Until recently, party control was not a factor. It is often suggested that if the lieutenant governor and the senate are ever of opposite parties, the powers of the lieutenant governor could be diminished. Such concerns have been voiced in the past few years, and given the pattern in other states, this seems quite likely. Having such a powerful lieutenant governor is unusual among the states. There are only five other states (Alabama, Georgia, Mississippi, South Carolina, and Vermont) where the lieutenant governor can appoint committee members and assign bills to committees. In Arkansas, the lieutenant governor can assign bills to committees but does not appoint committees.[34]

In most states the lieutenant governor is not a powerful leader. Eight states do not have lieutenant governors (Arizona, Maine, New Hampshire, New Jersey, Oregon, Tennessee, West Virginia, and Wyoming).[35] In the twenty-six states where their only legislative duty is to serve as the presiding officer, most lieutenant governors attend a senate session only when their vote is needed to break a tie.[36] Most lieutenant governors are figureheads who stand in when the governor is out of state. In states where the lieutenant governor is a figurehead, or when there is no lieutenant governor, the senate elects one of its members to be the presiding officer, called the pro tempore, president of the senate, or speaker of the senate.[37]

Thus, the office of lieutenant governor in Texas is quite different from the office in most other states. This has not always been true in Texas. J. William Davis, in his book *There Shall Also Be a Lieutenant Governor,* traces the concentration of power in this office to the actions of Allen Shivers and Ben Ramsey during the 1940s and 1950s. Apparently, over a period of several years the office gained power in the senate.[38]

Lt. Governor David Dewhurst

The 1999 session was the first since Reconstruction where Republicans held the majority of the senators and the lieutenant governor's office. Then Lt. Governor Rick Perry retained the powers usually given to lieutenant governors. Retaining those powers will depend upon a lieutenant governor's ability to compromise and get along with the thirty-one members of the senate. Acting Lt. Governor Ratliff retained these powers. This is not surprising since he is a member of the senate and was elected by that body to be lieutenant governor. Republican senators ensured that Lt. Governor Dewhurst kept these powers. It is not in the interests of the Republicans, with nineteen seats, to break with the lieutenant governor. It takes twenty-one votes to bring a bill up for debate on the floor of the senate.

The speaker and the lieutenant governor also have other, extra legislative powers. They appoint members of other state boards or they serve as members of such boards. For example, they appoint the members of the Legislative Budget Board, which writes the state budget, and they serve as the chair and vice chair of this board. These are important powers because these boards make policy. The Legislative Budget Board writes the state budget, which is a policy statement in monetary terms. The budget decides what agencies and programs will be funded and in what amounts.

✦ COMMITTEES IN THE HOUSE AND SENATE

Most of the work of the legislature is done in **standing committees** established by house and senate rules. Besides the standing committees, there are also subcommittees of the standing committees, **conference committees** to work out differences in bills passed by the two houses, temporary committees to study special problems, and **interim committees** to study issues between sessions of the state legislature.

Of these, the standing committees are the most important. There are fourteen standing committees in the senate and forty-one in the house. These are listed in table 7.7.

standing committees
Committees of the house and senate that consider legislation during sessions.

conference committees
Joint committees of the house and senate that work out differences in bills passed in each chamber.

interim committees
Temporary committees of the legislature that study issues between regular sessions and make recommendations on legislation.

TABLE 7.7

Standing Committees of the Texas House and Senate, 2007 Session

Senate Committees	House Committees
Administration	Agriculture and Livestock
Business & Commerce	Appropriations
S/C on Emerging Technologies	Border and International Affairs
& Economic Dev.	Business and Industry
Committee of the Whole Senate	Calendars
Criminal Justice	Civil Practices
Education	Corrections
S/C on Higher Education	County Affairs
Finance	Criminal Jurisprudence
Government Organization	Culture, Recreation & Tourism
Health & Human Services	Defense Affairs and State-Federal Relations
Intergovernmental Relations	Economic Development
S/C on Flooding & Evacuations	Elections
International Relations & Trade	Energy Resources
Jurisprudence	Environmental Regulations
Natural Resources	Financial Institutions
S/C on Agriculture, Rural Affairs,	General Investigating & Ethics
& Coastal Resources	Government Reform
Nominations	Higher Education
State Affairs	House Administration
Transportation & Homeland Security	Human Services
Veteran Affairs & Military Installations	Insurance
S/C on Base Realignment and Closure	Judiciary
	Juvenile Justice and Family Issues
	Land and Resource Management
	Law Enforcement
	Licensing and Administrative Procedures
	Local and Consent Calendars
	Local Government Ways & Means
	Natural Resources
	Pensions and Investments
	Public Education
	Public Health
	Redistricting
	Regulated Industries
	Rules and Resolutions
	State Affairs
	Transportation
	Urban Affairs
	Ways and Means

Source: Texas Legislature Online (*www.capitol.state.tx.us*).

Many citizens mistakenly believe that state legislators spend a lot of time "goofing off."

The chairs of these standing committees have powers similar to those of the speaker and lieutenant governor at the committee level. They decide the times and agendas for meetings of the committee. In doing so, they decide the amount of time devoted to bills and which bills get the attention of the committee. A chair that strongly dislikes a bill can often prevent the bill from passing. Even if the bill is given a hearing, the chair can decide to give that bill to a subcommittee that might kill the bill.

Thus, as in most legislative bodies, in Texas the power is concentrated in a few powerful individuals who control the agendas and actions of the legislature. Few bills can pass the legislature without the support of these individuals.

✦ FORMAL RULES: HOW A BILL BECOMES A LAW

Figure 7.12 lists the formal procedures in the Texas house and senate for passing a bill. Each bill, to become law, must clear each step. The vast majority of bills that are introduced fail to pass. Few bills of major importance are passed in any given legislative session. Most bills make only minor changes to existing law.

At each stage in the process, the bill can receive favorable or unfavorable actions. At each step a bill can die by either action or inaction. There are many ways to kill a bill, but only one way to pass a bill. To pass, a bill must clear all hurdles.

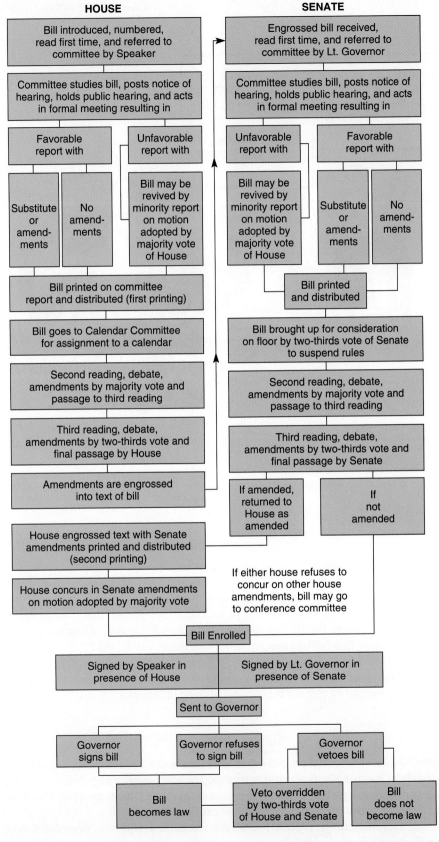

HOUSE

Bill introduced, numbered, read first time, and referred to committee by Speaker

Committee studies bill, posts notice of hearing, holds public hearing, and acts in formal meeting resulting in

Favorable report with

Unfavorable report with

Substitute or amend- ments

No amend- ments

Bill may be revived by minority report on motion adopted by majority vote of House

Bill printed on committee report and distributed (first printing)

Bill goes to Calendar Committee for assignment to a calendar

Second reading, debate, amendments by majority vote and passage to third reading

Third reading, debate, amendments by two-thirds vote and final passage by House

Amendments are engrossed into text of bill

House engrossed text with Senate amendments printed and distributed (second printing)

House concurs in Senate amendments on motion adopted by majority vote

SENATE

Engrossed bill received, read first time, and referred to committee by Lt. Governor

Committee studies bill, posts notice of hearing, holds public hearing, and acts in formal meeting resulting in

Unfavorable report with

Favorable report with

Bill may be revived by minority report on motion adopted by majority vote of House

Substitute or amend- ments

No amend- ments

Bill printed and distributed

Bill brought up for consideration on floor by two-thirds vote of Senate to suspend rules

Second reading, debate, amendments by majority vote and passage to third reading

Third reading, debate, amendments by two-thirds vote and final passage by Senate

If amended, returned to House as amended

If not amended

If either house refuses to concur on other house amendments, bill may go to conference committee

Bill Enrolled

Signed by Speaker in presence of House

Signed by Lt. Governor in presence of Senate

Sent to Governor

Governor signs bill

Governor refuses to sign bill

Governor vetoes bill

Bill becomes law

Veto overridden by two-thirds vote of House and Senate

Bill does not become law

FIGURE 7.12 *Basic Steps in the Texas Legislative Process.* This diagram displays the sequential flow of a bill from the time it is introduced in the house of representatives to final passage and transmittal to the governor. A bill introduced in the senate would follow the same procedure in reverse.

The rules of the Texas senate have a conserving force on legislation. Before the sixtieth day of the legislative session, a bill can clear the senate with a simple majority vote. Few bills pass before the sixtieth day. After the sixtieth day, before a bill can be considered on the floor of the senate, a two-thirds vote is required. Technically, after the sixtieth day, senate rules state that bills must be considered in the order they are reported out of committees. If bills are not considered in the order reported out of committees, a two-thirds vote is required. By design, bills are never considered in the order reported out of committee. If two-thirds of the senators agree to consider the bill, it can pass by a simple majority. Because of this rule, few bills clear the senate that are not supported by more than a simple majority of the senators. This rule makes the senate a conserving force in the legislative process.

In some cases, the formal rules can be used to hide actions of the legislature. It is not uncommon in legislative bodies to attach riders to appropriations bills. A **rider** can be a subject matter item (creation of a new state regulatory board) or a money item (money for a park in a legislator's district). In the Texas legislature the practice adds a new twist. Riders can be attached to appropriations and they are not known to the public or media. They are called closed riders. They are closed to public inspection and only appear after the appropriation bills have passed the house and senate and go to conference committee. In the conference committee the cloak is removed and they appear for public inspection for the first time. At this stage, which is always near the end of the session, the likelihood of change is remote. Unless there is a governor's veto, these **closed riders** become law without public comment.

A recent example of this dealt with the Bush School at Texas A&M University. In the 1999 session of the legislature, the Bush School was separated from the College of Liberal Arts and made a separate school within the university and its budget was increased by several million dollars. This was done at the request of Governor George W. Bush.

rider
Provision attached to a bill that may not be of the same subject matter as the main bill.

closed riders
Provisions attached to appropriations bills that are not made public until the conference committee meets.

✦ Major and Minor Calendars and Bills

To fully understand the legislative process, one must distinguish between major and minor bills, because state legislators treat them very differently. Two organizations, the Federal Advisory Commission on Intergovernmental Relations and the Citizens Conference on State Legislators, have both recommended that state legislatures use different calendars to distinguish between major, controversial bills and minor or local bills.[39] By using different calendars, legislatures can better manage their limited time and devote attention to important matters. Texas is one of thirty-six states that use both a local and a consent calendar in both chambers.[40]

The Texas house has two different **calendars** for minor bills—the local calendar and the consent calendar. To be assigned to these calendars, a bill must meet tests established by house rules. Local bills must not have an effect upon more than one of the 254 counties in the state. Bills for the consent calendar must be minor, noncontroversial bills. To be placed on either the local or the consent calendar, bills must meet two further criteria. First, they must receive unanimous support in the substantive house committee handling the bill. Second, the **Local and Consent Calendars Committee** must approve them. If this committee does not approve the bill, it is sent to the **Calendars Committee** (regular calendars) for assignment to another calendar. A bill may be removed from the local or consent calendar if there is objection by five members during floor debate. Also, if debate exceeds ten minutes, the bill is withdrawn and effectively killed.[41] These procedures safeguard against important bills being approved without adequate review by the whole house.

calendars
Procedures in the house used to consider different kinds of bills. Major bills and minor bills are considered under different procedures.

Local and Consent Calendars Committee
Committee handling minor and noncontroversial bills that normally apply to only one county.

Calendars Committee
Standing committee of the house that decides which bills will be considered for floor debate and to which committee they will be assigned.

Table 7.8 demonstrates the fate of bills in the seventy-ninth session of the Texas legislature. As can be seen, only about 25 percent of all bills introduced in the house and senate make it into law. Most bills (66 percent) are introduced in the house. While the senate introduces only a third as many as the house, more make it into law (27 percent in the senate and 25 percent in the house). Along the way bills are not advanced. While most make it to a committee for deliberation (60 percent in the senate and 68 percent in the house), about a third are given approval at the committee level and are considered on the floor of either chamber (46 percent in the senate and 35 percent in the house). Most bills die at the committee level, and some are dead on arrival and never see the light of day. Some bills are introduced to satisfy a constituency, and the member has no intention of working to pass the bill.

There are three calendars for major bills: the emergency calendar, the major state calendar, and the general state calendar. The Calendars Committee only has the authority to assign bills to these calendars. This power is rarely challenged. The distinction among the major calendars is not important until the final days of the legislative session, when time is limited.

There are a few similarities and differences between major and minor bills. The bills are identical in three ways:

1. They originate in either chamber.
2. They are equally as likely to be vetoed.
3. They receive final action toward the end of the legislative session.

TABLE 7.8

Bill Survival in the 79th Session of Texas Legislature, 2005

	Senate Bills	Percent	House Bills	Percent	Total Bills	Percent
Total bills introduced	1,892	100	3,592	100	5,484	100
Committee action in origination chamber	1,139	60*	2,427	68	3,629	65
Passed by committee originating chamber	986	52	1,685	47	2,671	49
Floor consideration originating chamber	875	46	1,247	35	2,122	39
Pass originating chamber	861	46	1,186	33	2,047	37
Committee action in second chamber	747	39	986	27	1,733	32
Passed committee in second chamber	716	38	963	26	1,679	31
Floor consideration second chamber	538	28	903	25	1,441	36
Pass second chamber	522	28	900	25	1,422	26
Passed both	513	27	876	24	1,389	25
Passed into law	502	27	868	24	1,370	25
Vetoed	11		8		19	

Source: Adapted from Harvey J. Tucker, "Legislation Deliberation in the Texas House and Senate." Paper presented at Annual Meeting of Midwest Political Science Association, Chicago, Illinois, April 15–18, 2004. Data in this table updated for 2005 session by Harvey Tucker.

Major and minor bills are treated differently in six ways:

1. Major bills are introduced earlier in the session than minor bills.
2. Companion bills are introduced in the other chamber more frequently for major bills than for minor bills.
3. Major bills are more evenly distributed across committees; minor bills are more concentrated in a few committees.
4. Major bills are amended more frequently than minor bills.
5. Major bills are more likely to be killed; minor bills are more likely to be passed by the legislature.
6. Final actions to kill major bills occur later in the session than final actions to kill minor bills.[42]

→ Legislative Workload and Logjams

According to much of the literature on state legislatures, most bills pass the legislature in the final days of the session. This scenario suggests that the legislature "goofs off" for most of the session and then frantically passes bills just before adjournment, producing laws that are given only "hasty consideration, of poor quality and are confused and inferior."[43]

In Texas it is true that most legislation is passed in the final two weeks of the session. In 1985 almost 80 percent of all bills passed in this time period. The question remains, Does this result in poor quality and inferior legislation? The answer is, probably not. One must understand the process of setting the agenda in the Texas legislature.

First, bills may be introduced at any time prior to the session and up until the sixtieth day of the 140-day session. After the sixtieth day, only local bills, emergency appropriations, emergency matters submitted by the governor, and bills with a four-fifths vote of the house may be introduced. Thus, for the first sixty days the agendas for both houses are being set. After the sixtieth day the legislature begins to clear these agendas. As indicated, most bills die in committees and are never assigned to a calendar. Killing a bill in committee is an action by the legislature, and it occurs at a regular rate during the session.[44] The bill is dead if it does not make it out of committee. This leaves only about a third of all bills for further consideration late in the session. As Tucker observes:

> Once the agenda has been set it is cleared at a fairly even rate. Final action on most bills passed occurs at the end of the session by design. Conflicting and complementary bills are reconciled. Bills tied directly or indirectly to the state budget are delayed until the final days of necessity. The legislature is not able to appropriate funds until the Comptroller of Public Accounts certifies the amount of revenues that will be available. The "certification estimate" is not made until the very end of the legislative session, because, among other reasons, the estimate must be informed by any actions the legislature takes that would affect state revenues.[45]

Thus, the image of the legislature as goofing off for 120 days is not accurate. The nature of the legislative process requires the passage of major legislation near the end of the session. Also, about half the bills that pass toward the end of the session are minor bills, and they are cleared late for different reasons than are major bills.

Thus, the formal rules of the house and senate are very important factors in determining how and what kind of legislation gets passed. These rules have the effect of preserving the status quo. It is very difficult to pass legislation and very easy to kill a bill. Although the Texas legislature is not remarkably different from most other legislatures in this respect, in Texas these rules protect the status quo of the traditionalistic/individualistic political culture of the state.

You Better Be Good—The Lobby Is Watching

In the upper right-hand gallery of the Texas house chamber, looking toward the speaker's podium, is a section "reserved" for the most powerful members of the lobby.

Some lobbyists are almost always there when business is being conducted on the floor. They watch members of the house, and the house members know they are being watched. Members are sometimes contacted by these lobbyists and are "encouraged" to vote right.

Members of the house call this space the "Owners' Box."

→ INFORMAL RULES

informal rules
Set of norms or values that govern legislative behavior.

In addition to the formal rules, there are also **informal rules,** or legislative norms, that all state legislators must learn if they are to be successful. Examples include the following:

Do not:

> conceal the real purpose of a bill.
> deal in personalities in floor debate.
> be a thorn in the side of the majority by refusing unanimous consent.
> speak on issues you know nothing about.
> seek publicity from the press to look good to the people back home.
> talk to the press about decisions reached in private.[46]

Each legislature will have a different set of norms and place different value on them. In Texas, dealing in personalities during floor debate was viewed as acceptable behavior by a large number of Texas legislators, whereas in the other states only a few members viewed this as acceptable behavior.[47] Legislators must learn the norms of their legislature and adhere to them, or they might find themselves isolated and ineffective. The informal rules are as important as the formal rules governing the legislature.

→ ROLE PLAYING

Members of the legislature are expected to play many roles during the legislative sessions. We have already discussed formal leadership roles. Each speaker will approach the job in different ways. Historically, most speakers have exerted very tight control over the house. This was true of Billy Clayton, speaker from 1975 to 1983. However, Gib Lewis, who followed Clayton, exerted much less control. He allowed the members of his team—namely, committee chairs—to control the process, and he himself took a much more "laid back" attitude. Pete Laney was more like Billy Clayton in that he controlled the house. The newly elected speaker, Tom Craddick of Midland, follows a role similar to that of Speakers Laney and Clayton.

There can also be great differences in the leadership styles of lieutenant governors. For instance, Bill Hobby, the son of a former governor, served as lieutenant governor for eighteen years (1972–90). Hobby, a very quiet-spoken, low-key person, seldom forced his will on the members of the senate. He preferred to work behind the scenes and forge compromises.

Hobby chose not to run for reelection in 1990, and Bob Bullock succeeded him. Bullock had served for sixteen years as the state comptroller and had developed a reputation for strong, effective leadership, but he often went out of his way to make enemies. Bullock's leadership style as lieutenant governor is almost the opposite of Hobby's. Stories have circulated of shouting matches and angry behavior, sometimes even in open sessions of the senate. The senate seemed to adjust to Bullock's style of leadership, and he managed to get much of his agenda passed. Hobby and Bullock illustrate very different ways to be effective leaders of the senate.

Rick Perry, while serving as the Texas agricultural commissioner, did not have the reputation of a compromiser; however, judging from all reports, he performed quite effectively in the 1999 session. The newly elected Lt. Governor Dewhurst was something of a political unknown, having served only four years as land commissioner prior to his election. Dewhurst's performance received mixed reviews. He was an effective leader in the regular session and was partisan in the three special sessions. Powerful Republican leaders have ensured that he will keep the broad powers normally given to lieutenant governors.

Leadership in legislative bodies can take many forms. In addition to formal leadership roles, some members develop reputations as experts in some areas of legislation and are looked to by other members as leaders in those areas. Being recognized by other members as the expert in some area of legislation obviously increases one's influence. For instance, a person who is a recognized expert on taxation issues can use this reputation to forge coalitions and pass tax legislation.

Representational Roles

Constituencies have expectations about their legislators' roles. For centuries, members of legislatures have argued about the representational role of a legislator. Who do legislators represent? Are they **delegates,** sent by the voters to represent the voters' interests, or are they **trustees,** entrusted by the voters to make decisions based on their best judgment? The delegate role is perceived as being more democratic—as doing what the people want. The trustee role can be characterized as elitist—as doing what one thinks is best.

In reality, members may play both the delegate and the trustee role, depending upon the issue before them. For example, in 1981 the Texas legislature passed a bill prohibiting the catching of redfish by commercial fishermen in some waters in the Gulf of Mexico. The bill was written and advanced by sport fishermen. Representatives from coastal communities in Texas voted as delegates—with the commercial fishermen and against the bill. Representatives from the Panhandle, however, were free to vote as trustees. In matters affecting the livelihood of Panhandle ranchers but not coastal fisheries, these representatives would reverse their voting roles. Which role representatives play is largely dependent on how the issues affect their district. The problem with this is that local interests can take the forefront, leading legislators to neglect long-term statewide or larger public interests.

delegate
Representational role of member which states that he or she represents the wishes of the voters.

trustee
Representational role of a member which states that the member will make decisions on his or her own judgment about what is best for voters.

Partisan Roles

As we saw earlier, party is not a strong factor in the Texas legislature today. Members of both parties are given committee assignments. Texas contrasts with states with a tradition of strong partisanship, where party leadership roles are important, formal leadership positions are assigned on the basis of party, and party leaders try to ensure that party members support party positions on issues.

In the past, coalitions in the Texas legislature have organized more around ideology than around party. The 1970s saw the formation of the "Dirty Thirty" coalition of liberal Democratic and conservative Republican house members to fight the conservative Democrats. This uneasy alliance of those excluded from leadership positions was short-lived.

In more recent years, conservative Republicans and Democrats organized the Texas Conservative Coalition to fight what they view as liberal ideas. Other caucuses represent Hispanics and African Americans. In 1993 the Republicans formed a caucus to promote the election of Pete Laney as speaker. In reward, they were assigned several committee chairs. Partisan factors will play a much larger role in the Texas legislature in the next decade.

In the 2001 and 2003 sessions this bipartisanship has been evident in the redistricting battles. Some of this bipartisanship may be the result of incumbents interested in protecting their seats and this has masked stronger feelings of partisan gains. With the Republicans in control of both the house and the senate in the 2003 session there was promise of bipartisan cooperation. The new speaker, Tom Craddick of Midland, promised to continue bipartisanship. Speaker Craddick did appoint fourteen (29.2 percent) Democrats to chair committees; however, there was little evidence of bipartisanship elsewhere during the session.

✦ RATING THE TEXAS LEGISLATURE

How does the Texas legislature compare to legislatures of other states? Making comparisons is always difficult. Thirty years ago, the Citizens Conference on State Legislatures developed the "FAIIR" index, based on five criteria: function factors, accountability, informed factors, independence, and representativeness.[48] Unfortunately this index has not been updated; however, there are other ratings that come to the same general conclusions. Several political scientists have developed indexes to measure the "professionalism" of state legislatures.

Most of these indexes of professionalism rely on several measures. Two important measures are the annual salary and the number of days the legislature is in session. A third measure that is often employed is the amount of money available for staff assistance. The most important of these three factors is the salary and staff assistance. Based on these criteria three types of state legislatures emerge.

Professional Legislatures are those with annual salaries in excess of $35,000, meet annually for nine to twelve months, and have annual office staff allowances.
Hybrid Legislatures are those with $32,000 or less in annual salaries, meet for fewer days each year, and have adequate staff assistance.
Citizen, Nonprofessional Legislatures are those that meet for fewer days, with little or no salary, and have very limited staff assistance.[49]

Other writers have also used the criteria of percent metropolitan as a factor in explaining professional development of state legislatures. The argument goes that large, metropolitan states will cause an increase in the number of bills introduced, because of the increased problems that come with urban growth. Increased problems cause more bills to be introduced, which requires more time of the legislature, which results in longer sessions. When sessions become longer, lasting most of the year, pay and staff assistance tend to increase.[50]

Given these criteria, how does the Texas legislature stack up when compared with other states on the professionalism ranking? Texas is a mixed bag on these criteria.

Staff Assistance

On this criterion, the state provides more money than any other state. Most members keep open offices on a full-time basis in their district, and many do in the state capital as well. The recent renovations of the state capitol building have provided each senator and house member with excellent office and committee hearing space. Texas senators receive $25,000 per month for staff salary support plus office expenses. House members each receive $8,500 per month for staff salary plus office expenses. In addition, standing committees have staff salary support during and between legislative sessions. California provides $20,000 to both house and senate members. New York provides staff support similar to Texas for its legislature. The Texas Legislative Council has a large, professional staff to assist the legislature. It has produced one of the best Web pages of any of the states and provides easy access to the citizens during and between legislative sessions. The house also has the House Research Organization, which produces very professional assistance to the legislature.

Building Facilities

With the renovations to the state capitol building some twelve years ago, the Texas legislature has excellent facilities for their staff, committee hearings, and legislative work.

Salary

As indicated, among the large urban states, Texas pays the least at $7,200 per year. The voters have failed to approve amendments to the state constitution that would have raised salaries. In most studies ranking legislators, salary was an important indicator of professionalism. Perhaps this is a factor; however, other factors such as staff assistance and building facilities are also important factors. On these Texas ranks above average.

Annual Sessions

Texas is only one of five states that does not meet in annual sessions. Also sessions are limited to 140 days, and the legislature cannot call itself into special session.

Texas is a large urban state with many problems, and many bills are introduced each session. Annual sessions have been considered by past legislatures and rejected by the voters. This is not likely to change any time soon. Texas will continue to be a low-pay, part-time legislature with a very professional staff. It is interesting to note that when voter approval is required for a constitutional amendment to raise pay and have annual sessions, the voters reject these changes. When voter approval is not required in such areas as staff and facilities, the legislature has provided these. In 1994 the National Conference of State Legislatures produced a professionalism ranking based on four factors: full-time or part-time, pay, staff size, and turnover. In this ranking, Texas was classified as a moderate professional/citizen legislature.[51]

✦ Conclusions

Thomas R. Dye comes to three conclusions on state legislatures, all of which apply very well to the Texas legislature.[52]

First, Dye observes that

state legislatures reflect socioeconomic conditions of their states. These conditions help to explain many of the differences one encounters in state legislative politics: the level of legislative activity, the degree of inter-party competition, the extent of party cohesion, the professionalism of the legislature . . . the level of interest group activity.[53]

This means that the legislature is greatly influenced by the social and economic conditions in the state, and that policies passed by the legislature reflect those conditions. This certainly applies to Texas.

Second, legislatures function as "arbiters of public policy rather than initiators" of policy change.[54] State legislatures wait for others—state agencies, local governments, interest groups, and citizens—to bring issues to them for resolution. Someone other than members of the legislature writes most bills introduced. The rules make it much easier to delay legislation than to pass it. Leadership most often comes from others outside the legislature, often the governor. With a few exceptions this applies to Texas.

Third, legislatures "function to inject into public decision making a parochial influence."[55] By this Dye means that state legislatures tend to represent local legislative interests and not statewide interests. Legislators are recruited, elected, and reelected locally. Local interests will always be dominant in determining how legislators vote on proposed legislation. Frequently no one represents statewide interests. This conclusion certainly applies to Texas. Statewide interests often get lost in the shuffle to protect and promote local interests.

INTERNET RESOURCES

Texas Legislature: *www.capitol.state.tx.us/*
This is an excellent site. You can find your state representative or senator if you know your postal zip code. You can look up bills by subject matter or by bill number, author, and sessions.

The Texas Legislative Reference Library: *www.lrl.state.tx.us*
This site has an excellent collection of information about the current and past legislatures.

National Conference of State Legislatures: *www.ncsl.org*
This site has information of state legislatures. Some past studies are available online.

Redistricting information from the Texas Legislative Council is available at *www.tlc.state.tx.us/research/redist/redist.htm* You can examine the various plans that were introduced in the past session of the legislature. This site also has information on redistricting worldwide.

KEY TERMS

Baker v. Carr (p. 124)
"birthright" characteristics (p. 132)
biennial session (p. 139)
calendars (p. 149)
Calendars Committee (p. 149)
closed riders (p. 149)
conference committees (p. 145)
delegate (p. 153)
equity of representation (p. 124)
extraordinary session (p. 139)
informal rules (p. 152)
interim committees (p. 145)
Legislative Redistricting Board (LRB) (p. 124)

lieutenant governor (p. 144)
Local and Consent Calendars Committee (p. 149)
minority representation (p. 125)
money from within the district (p. 134)
multimember districts (p. 120)
political party gerrymandering (p. 125)
racially gerrymandered majority–minority districts (p. 125)
reapportionment and redistricting (p. 123)

Reynolds v. Sims (p. 124)
rider (p. 149)
safe Democratic and safe Republican districts (p. 136)
sine die (p. 139)
single-member district (p. 117)
speaker of the house (p. 142)
special session (p. 139)
standing committees (p. 145)
term limits (p. 139)
trustee (p. 153)
turnover (p. 138)

NOTES

1. *Texas Constitution,* 1876, art. 3, sec. 2.
2. Council of State Governments, *Book of the States, 1997–98* (Lexington, Ky.: Council of State Governments, 1998), 68, table 3.3.
3. Malcolm E. Jewell and Samuel C. Patterson, *The Legislative Process in the United States* (New York: Random House, 1985), 21.
4. Samuel C. Patterson, "Legislators and Legislatures in the American States," in *Politics in the American States: A Comparative Analysis,* 6th ed., ed. Virginia Gray, Herbert Jacob, and Kenneth N. Vine (Boston: Little, Brown, 1996), 164.
5. *Texas Constitution,* art. 3, sec. 26.

6. Leroy Hardy, Alan Heslop, and Stuart Anderson, *Reapportionment Politics* (Beverly Hills, Calif.: Sage, 1981), 18.

7. Gordon E. Baker, *The Reapportionment Revolution: Representation, Political Power and the Supreme Court* (New York: Random House, 1966).

8. Wilbourn E. Benton, *Texas: Its Government and Politics,* 2d ed. (Englewood Cliffs, N.J.: Prentice Hall, 1966), 141.

9. *Texas Constitution,* art. 3, sec. 28.

10. Ibid., sec. 26a.

11. *Baker v. Carr,* 369 U.S. 186 (1962).

12. *Reynolds v. Sims,* 377 U.S. 533 (1964).

13. *Kilgarlin v. Martin,* 1965.

14. *Graves v. Barnes,* 343 F. Supp. 704 (W.D. Tex. 1972); *White v. Register,* 412 U.S. 755 (1973).

15. *Bush, Governor of Texas et al. v. Vera et al.,* No. 94-805. Case decided on 13 June 1996.

16. Ibid.

17. R.C. Ratcliffe, "Re-mapping of the Districts Draws Fire: 18 Incumbents Would Square Off," *Houston Chronicle,* 24 April 2001, p. 1.

18. R.C. Ratcliffe, "Redistricting Battle Flares as Critics Call Plan Anti-life," *Houston Chronicle,* 4 May 2001, p. A27.

19. Dye, *Politics in States and Communities,* 157.

20. Harvey Tucker and Gary Halter, *Texas Legislative Almanac 2001* (Texas A&M University Press, 2001).

21. Rich Jones, "State Legislatures," in *Book of the States, 1994–95,* 101.

22. Gary C. Jacobson, *The Politics of Congressional Elections,* 3d ed. (New York: HarperCollins, 1992).

23. Kevin A. Hill, "Does the Creation of Majority Black Districts Aid Republicans? An Analysis of the 1992 Congressional Election in Eight Southern States," *Journal of Politics* 57 (May 1995): 348–401.

24. Samuel C. Patterson, "Legislative Politics in the States," in *Politics in the American States,* 6th ed., eds. Virginia Gray and Herbert Jacob (Washington, D.C.: Congressional Quarterly Press, 1996), 179–86.

25. *Book of the States, 2004.*

26. Lawrence W. Miller, *Legislative Turnover and Political Careers: A Study of Texas Legislators, 1969–75,* Ph.D. dissertation, Texas Tech University, 1977, 43–45.

27. *Book of the States, 1994–95,* 29, table A. Also see the Web site of the National Conference of State Legislatures (*www.ncsl.org*).

28. *Book of the States, 1994–95,* 27.

29. Rich Jones, "State Legislatures," *Book of the States, 1994–95,* 99.

30. *Book of the States, 1998–99,* 64–67, table 7.2.

31. Ibid., 123, table 3.9.

32. *Presiding Officers of the Texas Legislature, 1846–2002* (Austin: Texas Legislative Council, 2002).

33. Interview with William P. Hobby, 1993, Texas A&M University, College Station.

34. *Book of the States, 1998–99,* 48, table 2.13.

35. Ibid., 33, table 2.9.

36. Ibid., 48, table 2.13.

37. In Tennessee, the speaker of the senate also holds the title of lieutenant governor.

38. J. William Davis, *There Shall Also Be a Lieutenant Governor* (Austin: University of Texas, Institute of Public Affairs, 1967).

39. Harvey Tucker, "Legislative Calendars and Workload Management in Texas," *Journal of Politics* 51 (August 1989): 632.

40. Ibid.

41. Ibid., 633.

42. Ibid., 643.

43. Harvey J. Tucker, "Legislative Workload Congestion in Texas," *Journal of Politics* 49 (1987): 557.

44. Ibid., 569.

45. Ibid., 575.

46. E. Lee Bernick and Charles W. Wiggins, "Legislative Norms in Eleven States," *Legislative Studies Quarterly* 7 (May 1983): 194–95.

47. Ibid., 194.

48. Citizens Conference on State Legislatures, *The Sometime Governments: A Critical Study of the Fifty American State Legislatures,* 2d ed. (Kansas City: Citizens Conference on State Legislatures, 1973).

49. National Conference of State Legislatures, *State Legislature* 20 (November 1994), 5.

50. Keith E. Hamm and Gary F. Moncrief, "Legislative Politics in the States," *Politics in the American States: A Comparative Analysis,* 7th ed., eds. Virginia Gray, Russell L. Hanson, and Herbert Jacob (Washington, D.C.: Congressional Quarterly Press, 1999), 145, table 5.1.

51. See Norman R. Luttbeg, *Comparing the States and Communities: Politics, Government, and Policy in the United States* (Dubuque, Iowa: Eddie Bower Publishing, 1999), 242–43.

52. Dye, *Politics in States and Communities,* 192–93.

53. Ibid., 192.

54. Ibid., 193.

55. Ibid.

CHAPTER 8

THE OFFICE OF GOVERNOR AND STATE AGENCIES IN TEXAS

The governor is the most salient political actor in state government. Whether the true power center of the state is embodied in the occupant of the office or somewhere else, the office is the focal point of state government and politics. The governor is expected to perform many tasks and is blamed for not doing others, even if the office is formally very weak. The expectation is that governors will be leaders in their state.

The power and respect accorded to governors have varied greatly over time. During the colonial period, little power or respect was afforded the office—some have argued that the American Revolution was a war against colonial governors. The experiences of southern states following Reconstruction led to a return of weak governors in the South. There is an old Texas saying: "The governor should have only enough power to sign for his paycheck." In recent times, the power and prestige of the office have increased, as evidenced by recent presidential politics. In both Democratic and Republican parties, many presidential candidates have been former governors. In the past twenty-seven years only President George H. Bush had not served as governor prior to becoming president. Today the office of governor has assumed new significance because of a change in attitude toward the role of the federal government. The Republican Congress of the 1990s promised to return power and responsibility to state governments and to allow states more flexibility in administering programs funded by the federal government. Even without the renewed significance of the office, and even though many governors have little formal power, governors are important players in state politics.

✦ ROLES

Citizens expect governors to play many roles. They should be the chief policy makers, formulating long-term goals and objectives. This requires selling the program to state legislators and coordinating with state agencies that administer the programs.

The governor is also expected to act as **chief legislator.** Governors do not formally introduce bills, but they must have the support of some significant members of the legislature who will carry their program, so they must spend considerable time and energy developing these relationships. If the governor is of one party and the other party dominates the legislature, it might be more difficult to get legislation passed. The governor might have to spend considerable resources to accomplish his or her goals.

The governor must also act as **party chief.** As the most important party official in the state, the governor should lead the party and aid its development and growth. This will involve helping legislators and other elected officials in their reelection efforts, raising money for the party, and creating a favorable image of the party in the state.

The governor also serves as the ceremonial leader of the state. The demands of **ceremonial duties** are extreme. "Where two or more are gathered together," there also is the governor expected to be. The governor will receive many invitations to speak, make presentations, and cut ribbons. Some governors become trapped in the safe, friendly environment of ceremonial duties and neglect or avoid the other duties of their office. For governors with an agenda for action, ceremony is a diversion from more important and difficult objectives.

Governors can, however, use ceremonial duties as communication opportunities to promote their programs. They must wisely choose which invitations to accept and which to delegate to others or decline. Ceremonial appearances, such as graduation speaker, provide an opportunity to generate favorable press coverage and support for one's programs. Former Governor Bush used these opportunities both to promote his state programs and as an avenue to promote his race for the presidency.

chief legislator

The expectation that a governor has an active agenda of legislation to recommend to the legislature and works to pass that agenda.

party chief

The expectation that the governor will be the head of his or her party.

ceremonial duties

The expectation that a governor attends many functions and represents the state. Some governors become so active at this role that they get caught in a "ceremonial trap" and neglect other duties.

The governor's office, an exact replica of its 1910 appearance.

Former Governor George W. Bush performing a ceremonial role at Admiral Nimitz Museum in Fredricksburg on the 50th Anniversary of the end of World War II.

W. Lee O'Daniel won elections in large measure because of his country western swing band called the "Light Crust Dough Boys," which he used to charm voters. In one of the songs was the line "Ahha! Pass the biscuits Pappy!" This led to the governor's being called W. Lee "Pass the biscuits Pappy" O'Daniel.

In recent years a new role for the governor has been added to that list—**crisis manager.** Governors are expected to react to a crisis such as a hurricane or other natural disasters or man-made disasters. How well the governor reacts to these situations may very well have an impact on the re-election chances. For example, during hurricane Katrina in Louisiana, Governor Blanco was not viewed as a strong leader, and this influenced her decision no to seek re-election in 2007.

The governor is also the chief **intergovernmental coordinator,** working with federal officials and officials in other states. The governor must also work with the state congressional delegation of U.S. senators and representatives, the president, and cabinet officials to promote the interests of the state.

Thus many roles are assigned to governors. In Texas the formal powers of the governor are very weak, and this complicates things. The governor cannot rely on formal authority but must develop and use the power and prestige of the office to persuade others to accept his or her program. This informal leadership trait, the power to persuade others, is perhaps the most important and necessary "power" the governor must develop.

crisis manager
The expectation that the governor will provide strong leadership in times of a natural or man-made disaster.

intergovernmental coordinator
The expectation that a governor coordinates activities with other state governments.

✦ QUALIFICATIONS

In most states the formal qualifications to be governor are minimal. All but six states set a minimum age requirement, and most require a candidate to be a resident of the state for five to ten years preceding election. Also, most states require governors to be U.S. citizens and qualified voters.

In Texas the formal qualifications are simple: One must be at least thirty years of age, a citizen of the United States, and a resident of the state for five years preceding election. There is no requirement to be a registered voter. In the 1930s W. Lee O'Daniel ran for governor stressing that he was not a "professional politician." To prove this, he made a point of not being a registered voter.

informal qualifications
Additional qualifications beyond the formal qualifications that men and women need to be elected governor. Holding statewide elected office is an example.

Informal qualifications are more important. Nationwide most governors have held elected office before becoming governor. An examination of the 933 people serving as governor between 1900 and 1997 reveals that the most common career path to that office is to begin in the legislature, move to statewide office, and then move to the governor's office.[1] Others who are elected governor have served as U.S. senator or representative, and a few have served in local elected offices (such as mayor). Thus having held elected office is an important informal qualification for becoming governor. Some governors gain experience as appointed administrators or as party officials. Between 1970 and 1999, only 10 percent of all people elected governor had no prior political office experience.[2]

These observations of governors generally apply very well to Texas governors. Table 8.1 lists the men and women who have served as governor in Texas since 1949 and their prior office experience. Most had served in elected office, five in statewide offices. Only two had not held elected office. The current governor, Rick Perry, followed a rather typical pattern prior to becoming governor. He served in the state legislature, as agricultural commissioner, and as lieutenant governor prior to becoming governor when George Bush resigned to assume the office of president of the United States. He was elected governor in his own right in 2002 and 2006.

Besides electoral experience, there are many other informal qualifications. Nationwide most people who have served as governors have been white, male, Protestant, well-educated, wealthy individuals. Only one African American, Douglas Wilder of Virginia, has been elected. Several Hispanics have served as governor: Tony Anaya, Jerry Abodaca, and Bill Richardson in New Mexico, Bob Martinez in Florida, and Raul Castro in Arizona.

More women have served as governor in recent years. In 1924 Wyoming elected the first woman governor, Nellie T. Ross, who served one term. She succeeded her husband who died in office. Later in 1924 Texas elected Miriam A. Ferguson governor. She was re-elected in 1932. Mrs. Ferguson was a "stand-in" for her husband, Jim Ferguson, who had been impeached, removed from office, and barred from seeking reelection. Similarly in

TABLE 8.1

Previous Office Experience of Texas Governors, 1949–2001

Governor	Terms of Office	Previous Offices
Allan Shivers	1949–57	State senate, lieutenant governor
Price Daniel	1957–63	U.S. Senate
John Connally	1963–69	U.S. secretary of the navy*
Preston Smith	1969–73	Texas house and senate, lieutenant governor
Dolph Briscoe	1973–79	Texas house
Bill Clements	1979–83	Assistant secretary of defense*
	1987–91	
Mark White	1983–87	Attorney general
Ann Richards	1991–94	County office, state treasurer
George W. Bush	1995–2001	None
Rick Perry	2001–present	State legislature, agricultural commissioner, and lieutenant governor

*Appointive offices. No electoral experience before becoming governor.
Source: James Anderson, Richard W. Murray, and Edward L. Farley, *Texas Politics: An Introduction,* 6th ed. (New York: HarperCollins, 1992), 166–188. Governors Bush and Perry from other sources.

Two governors for the price of one: "Ma and Pa" Ferguson in 1924.

1968, Lurleen Wallace was elected governor of Alabama as a stand-in governor for her husband, George Wallace, who could not be reelected because of term limits.

While Ferguson and Wallace were stand-in governors for husbands ineligible for reelection, several women besides Wyoming's Ross have been elected in their own right. Since 1974, twenty-six women have served as governor, as we see in table 8.2.[3]

The number of women serving as governor will undoubtedly increase. There are currently eleven women serving as lieutenant governors and fifty-five women serving in other statewide elected offices. As indicated previously, service in statewide office is a good stepping-stone to the governor's office.

Historically, the men who have served as governor of Texas have generally had one thing in common—wealth. A few, such as Dolph Briscoe and Bill Clements, were very wealthy. If not wealthy, most have been successful in law, business, or politics before becoming governor. Ann Richards was something of an exception to these informal qualifications. She was not wealthy or from a wealthy family, and had no business or law experience. Governor Bush is an example of past governors in terms of background, with a famous family name and family wealth. Governor Perry, while claiming the status of a sharecropper's son, came from a family with a moderate, middle-class background.

⟶ Salary

Governors receive much higher pay than state legislators. As of 2006, salaries ranged from a low of $70,000 in Maine to a high of $179,000 in New York. The Texas salary of $116,000 per year is slightly above the mean salary of $90,000 in 2004.[4] In addition, Texas also provides the governor with a home in Austin, an automobile with a driver, an airplane, and reimbursement for actual travel expenses. Texas governors also receive a budget for entertaining and maintaining the Governor's Mansion. Compared with members of the state legislature, the governor in Texas is extremely well paid. Given the demands and responsibilities of the job, the governor is not overpaid compared with executives of large corporations who receive many times this amount.

TABLE 8.2

History of Women Governors

Twenty-nine women (18D, 11R) have served as governors in 22 states. In addition, one woman has served as governor in Puerto Rico. Arizona is the first state where a woman succeeded another woman as governor and the first state to have had three women governors. Of the 29 women governors, 19 were first elected in their own right; 3 replaced their husbands, and 7 became governor by constitutional succession, 2 of whom subsequently won a full term. The record number of women serving simultaneously, set in 2004 and 2007, is 9.

Name (Party-State)	Dates Served	Special Circumstances
Nellie Tayloe Ross (D-WY)	1925–1927	Won special election to replace deceased husband.
Miriam "Ma" Ferguson (D-TX)	1925–1927, 1933–1935	Inaugurated 15 days after Ross; elected as surrogate for husband who could not succeed himself.
Lurleen Wallace (D-AL)	1967–1968	Elected as surrogate for husband who could not succeed himself.
Ella Grasso (D-CT)	1975–1980	First woman elected governor in her own right; resigned for health reasons.
Dixy Lee Ray (D-WA)	1977–1981	
Vesta Roy (R-NH)	1982–1983	Elected to state senate and chosen as senate president; served as governor for 7 days when incumbent died.
Martha Layne Collins (D-KY)	1984–1987	
Madeleine Kunin (D-VT)	1985–1991	First woman to serve three terms as governor.
Kay Orr (R-NE)	1987–1991	First Republican woman governor and first woman to defeat another woman in a gubernatorial race.
Rose Mofford (D-AZ)	1988–1991	Elected as secretary of state, succeeded governor who was impeached and convicted.
Joan Finney (D-KS)	1991–1995	First woman to defeat an incumbent governor.
Ann Richards (D-TX)	1991–1995	
Barbara Roberts (D-OR)	1991–1995	
Christine Todd Whitman (R-NJ)	1994–2001	Resigned to take presidential appointment as commissioner of the Environmental Protection Agency.
Jeanne Shaheen (D-NH)	1997–2003	
Jane Dee Hull (R-AZ)	1997–2003	Elected as secretary of state, succeeded governor who resigned; later elected to a full term.
Nancy Hollister (R-OH)	1998–1999	Elected lieutenant governor; served as governor for 11 days when predecessor took U.S. Senate seat and successor had not yet been sworn in.
Jane Swift (R-MA)	2001–2003	Elected as lieutenant governor, succeeded governor who resigned for an ambassadorial appointment.
Judy Martz (R-MT)	2001–2005	
Sila Calderon (Popular Democratic Party–PR)	2001–2005	Former mayor of San Juan, first woman governor of Puerto Rico.
Olene Walker (R-UT)	2003–2005	Elected as lieutenant governor, succeeded governor who resigned to take a federal appointment.
Ruth Ann Minner (D-DE)	2001–present	
Jennifer M. Granholm (D-MI)	2003–present	
Linda Lingle (R-Hl)	2003–present	
Janet Napolitano (D-AZ)	2003–present	First woman to succeed another woman as governor.
Kathleen Sebelius (D-KS)	2003–present	Father was governor of Ohio.
Kathleen Blanco (D-LA)	2004–2007	
M. Jodi Rell (R-CT)	2004–present	Elected as lieutenant governor, succeeded governor who resigned.
Christine Gregoire (D-WA)	2004–present	
Sarah Palin (R-AK)	2007–present	

✦ POSTGUBERNATORIAL OFFICES

For some governors, the office is a stepping-stone to other offices. Some go on to the U.S. Senate, and several have been elected president of the United States. For example, former Governor W. Lee O'Daniel served as U.S. senator from 1941 to 1949, and as everyone knows, George W. Bush became president in 2001. Postgubernatorial administrative service in the federal government is also common. Presidents often call upon former governors to head departments of government. President George H. Bush chose former Governor John Sununu of New Hampshire as his chief of staff. Bruce Babbitt, former Governor of Arizona, was chosen to be secretary of interior by President Clinton, who also appointed former Governor Richard Riley of South Carolina as secretary of education. Former Texas governor John Connally served as secretary of the treasury under President Richard Nixon. President George W. Bush selected several governors to be in his cabinet. However, for most governors (64 percent nationwide), the office is the peak of their political career and they retire to private life.[5] This is true of most Texas governors. George W. Bush was the first Texas governor since 1941 to go on to higher elected office.

✦ SUCCESSION TO OFFICE AND ACTING GOVERNOR

Most states provide for a successor if the governor dies or leaves office for any reason. Forty-three states have lieutenant governors who advance to the office if it is vacant for any reason. In the seven states without lieutenant governors, another officeholder, usually the leader of the state senate, succeeds to the governor's office. In nineteen states, the lieutenant governor and the governor are separately elected. In twenty-four states, the governor and lieutenant governor are jointly elected. They run as a "team," much as candidates for president and vice president do. In these cases, the candidate for governor picks the lieutenant governor. Former governor Paul Cellucci who resigned to become ambassador to Canada selected Jane Swift as his lieutenant governor. She became governor of Massachusetts in February 2001 when he resigned.

    When the governor leaves the state, the lieutenant governor becomes **acting governor.** This is unlike the office of vice president of the United States, who does not become acting president if the president leaves the country. Some governors have experienced problems with their lieutenant governor when they have left the state. For instance, in 1995 Jim Guy Tucker of Arkansas had problems with Senate President Pro Tem Jerry Jewell, who was acting as governor in the absence of the lieutenant governor. Jewell "granted two pardons and executive clemency to two prison inmates."[6] Also, the Arkansas lieutenant governor, Republican Mike Huckabee, "signed a proclamation for a Christian Heritage Week after Tucker declined to do so earlier."[7]

    In Texas, now governor Rick Perry may hold the record as serving the most time as acting governor when Governor George W. Bush was campaigning for president outside the state. When serving as acting governor, the lieutenant governor in Texas receives the same pay as the governor.

acting governor
When a governor leaves a state, the position held by the lieutenant governor who performs the functions of the office.

✦ REMOVAL FROM OFFICE

All states except Oregon have a procedure for removing governors by a process generally called impeachment. Technically, the lower house of the legislature adopts articles of impeachment and then a trial on these articles of impeachment is held in the senate. If the senate finds the governor guilty, he or she is removed from office. Together the two

impeachment and conviction
The process by which some elected officials, including governors, may be impeached (accused of an impeachable offence) by the lower house adopting articles of impeachment and the senate trying the official under those articles. If convicted, the official is removed from office.

steps—the adoption of articles of **impeachment and conviction** by the senate—are commonly called impeachment. Sixteen governors have had impeachment trials, and eight have been removed from office.[8]

Technically, impeachment is a judicial process, but it is also a very political process. Impeached governors have generally been guilty of some wrongdoing, but they are often removed for political reasons. For example, one of the eight impeached governors was Jim Ferguson of Texas (1915–17). Ferguson was indicted by the Texas house, technically for misuse of state funds, and was convicted and removed from office by the senate. In reality he was impeached because of his fight with the University of Texas board of regents. When the governor could not force the board of regents to terminate several professors who had been critical of the governor or force the resignation of board members, he vetoed the entire appropriations bill for the University of Texas.[9] This veto led to his removal from office.

Ferguson tried to prevent his impeachment by calling the legislature into special session. Since only the governor may decide the agenda of a special session, Governor Ferguson told the legislature it could consider any item it wanted, except impeachment. This ploy did not work, and he was removed from office. Courts later upheld Ferguson's impeachment.

A few years after the Ferguson affair in Texas, Oklahoma impeached two consecutively elected governors. These two impeachments were as political as the one in Texas. In 1921 there were several "race riots," in which many African Americans were killed. The most noted of these was in the Greenwood area of Tulsa, Oklahoma. Thirty-five square blocks of this segregated African American community were burned and destroyed and over forty people were killed. In 1922, John C. Walton was elected governor as member of the Farmer-Laborite party. Walton tried to break up the Ku Klux Klan in the state, and this led to his impeachment.

The lieutenant governor, Martin Trapp, served out the remainder of Walton's term but was unable to run for reelection because Oklahoma had a limit of one term at that time. Henry S. Johnson was elected governor in 1926 as a pro-KKK candidate and refused to use his office to quell Klan activity in the state. Johnson used the National Guard to try to prevent the legislature from meeting to consider his impeachment. The legislature was kept out of the state capitol building and had to meet in a hotel in Oklahoma City. Johnson was convicted and removed from office. He had been indicted on eighteen counts and found not guilty on all but one—"general incompetence" for which he was impeached.[10]

The impeachment of Evan Mecham in Arizona in 1988 was equally political. Mecham made a number of racist remarks and had become a source of embarrassment in the state. Technically he was impeached for misuse of state funds during his inaugural celebration.

These four impeachments illustrate the highly political nature of the process. Technically, all impeached governors had committed some malfeasance of office, yet were impeached for political reasons.

recall of the governor
The removal of the governor or an elected offical by a petition signed by the required number of registered voters and by an election in which a majority votes to remove the person from office.

Fifteen states also allow **recall of the governor.** Texas does not provide for recall of state officials. Many Texas home-rule cities do allow recall of city councils and mayors. Recall involves getting petitions signed by some number of voters, followed by an election, where, if a majority approves, the governor can be recalled or removed from office. Two governors have been recalled. Lynn J. Frazier of North Dakota was recalled in 1921, the same time when governors were being impeached in Texas and Oklahoma. In 1988 Governor Mecham of Arizona was spared a recall election when impeached by the legislature.[11] In 2003, Gray Davis of California was recalled. With so few examples of recall of governors, it is impossible to make any generalizations on the politics of recall.

✦ Formal Powers of the Governor

As indicated previously, most governors do not have great formal powers. The formal powers of the office of governor can be measured using six factors: tenure of office, appointive/administrative powers, budgetary powers, legislative authority, judicial powers, and military powers. By examining each of these factors, we can compare the formal powers of governors and, more specifically, the powers of the Texas governor.

Tenure

Tenure of office is the legal ability of governors to succeed themselves in office and the length of term. Historically, the tenure of governors has been less than that for most other statewide elected state officials, in part because of term limits.[12] Term limits for governors have been a fixture since the beginning of the Republic. Ten of the governors in the original thirteen states had one-year terms. States first moved to two-year terms, then four-year terms. In the 1960s, states borrowed from the federal Constitution the idea of limiting governors to two four-year terms.[13] Southern states were the last to move to longer terms. Many southern states once prohibited the governor from serving consecutive terms in office. Today, only Virginia retains this provision. (See figure 8.1.)

tenure of office
The ability of governors to be reelected to office.

Tenure is an important determinant of power. If governors can be continually reelected, they retain the potential to influence government until they decide to leave office. Only fourteen states do not limit how long a person can serve as governor. When prevented from being reelected by term limits, governors suffer as "lame ducks" toward the end of their terms. Long tenure also enables governors to carry out their programs. Short terms (two years) force governors to continually seek reelection and make political compromises. Only two states retain the two-year term—Vermont and New Hampshire.

Longer tenure is also an important factor in the governor's role as intergovernmental coordinator. Building up associations with officials in other states and in Washington is important and takes time. Short tenure makes it difficult for governors to gain leadership roles in this area and has the effect of shortchanging the state that imposes them.[14] The map in figure 8.1 details state term limits.

The Texas governor has the strongest tenure—four-year terms with no limit on the number of terms. Dolph Briscoe was elected to a two-year term in 1972. In that same election, Texas changed to a four-year term, which became effective in 1975. Briscoe was reelected to serve one 4-year term (1975–79). After Briscoe, Governors Clements, White, and Richards were limited to one term, although Clements did serve two nonconsecutive terms. George W. Bush was the first governor to be elected to two consecutive four-year terms. Bush served only six years because he became president in 2001.

Few Texas governors have served more than four years in office. Since 1874 nineteen Texas governors have served for four years; most of these (fifteen) were for consecutive two-year terms. Seven served for two years, four served six years, and only one (Allan Shivers, 1949–57) served for eight consecutive years—four 2-year terms.[15] Bill Clements served for eight nonconsecutive years. Thus the history of Texas governors is not one of long tenure. Serving two 2-year terms was the norm for most of the state's history. From 1874 until 1953, no person served more than four years as governor in Texas.[16]

Had Governor Bush not been elected president in 2000, he would have been the first governor to serve two consecutive four-year terms. Governor Perry is the first governor to be elected to two consecutive terms.

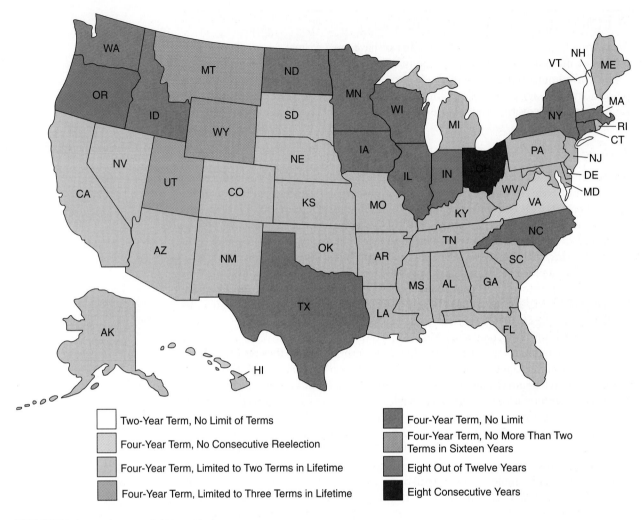

FIGURE 8.1   *Gubernatorial Term Limits.*

SOURCE: Council of State Governments, *The Book of the States 2003* (Lexington, Ky.: Council of State Governments, 2002), Vol. 34, table 4.9, pp. 199–200.

Appointive and Executive Powers

appointive power

The ability of a governor to appoint and remove important state administrators.

More important than tenure of office is the **appointive power** of the governor to make appointments and control the agencies of state government. Obviously, if the governor can appoint and remove the heads of most state agencies, he or she can better control the administration of programs.

Historically governors have not had strong appointive powers. For most of the nineteenth century the traditional method of selecting the heads of state agencies was by election. This is called **Jacksonian statehouse democracy.** President Andrew Jackson expressed ultimate faith in the ballot box for selecting administrators. Toward the end of the nineteenth century, there was a proliferation of agencies headed by appointed or elected boards and commissions. The governor was just one of many elected state officials and had little formal control over state administration.[17] Governors often share power with many other elected individuals. Such arrangements are known as plural executive structures.

Jacksonian statehouse government

A system in which most of the major department heads in state government are chosen by the voters at the ballot box.

Equally important to the appointive power is the power to remove administrators, which is discussed in a later section of this chapter. Without the power of removal, the appointive powers of the governor are greatly diminished. Beginning in the early twentieth century, the powers of the governor to appoint and remove officials were increased in some states. This expansion of executive authority has increased in the last three decades in many states.[18] This has not been the pattern for much of the South or for the office of governor in Texas. In 2001 the voters in Texas even rejected an amendment that would have made the adjutant general of the Texas National Guard subject to removal by the governor. The traditionalistic culture does not support the idea of strong executive authority even for relatively minor offices.

The ability of the Texas governor to control administrative functions through formal appointive and removal powers is exceptionally weak. The voters elect many important state administrators. Texas is thus a good example of the plural executive structure. Voters elect a lieutenant governor, an attorney general, a comptroller of public accounts, a state land commissioner, an agricultural commissioner, the Railroad Commission, and the Texas State Board of Education.[19]

The governor does appoint a few agency heads, the most significant being the secretary of state, who serves as the chief record keeper and election official for the state. The governor also appoints the executive directors of the Departments of Commerce, Health and Human Services, Housing and Community Affairs, and Insurance, the Office of State-Federal Relations, and the Fire Fighters Pension Commission. The governor appoints the head of the Texas National Guard and appoints the executive director of the Texas Education Agency from recommendations made by the elected Texas State Board of Education. The governor also appoints the chief counsels for the Public Utility Commission, the Insurance Commission, and the State Office of Administrative Hearings.

Thus, significant portions of state government are beyond the control of the governor because several agency heads are elected. In terms of numbers, most agencies are controlled by independent boards and commissions, over which the governor has little control. These independent state agencies are usually governed by three-, six-, or nine-member boards or commissions appointed by the governor for six-year, overlapping, staggered terms. Usually, one-third of the membership is appointed every two years. In total, the number of governing and policy-making positions filled by gubernatorial appointment is about 2,600.[20] If the governor stays in office for two terms (eight years), she or he will have appointed all members of these agencies and boards and might have indirect influence over them. (See table 8.3.) The governing board chooses the heads of these agencies. A good example of this is the president of a state university, who is selected by the board of regents, who are appointed by the governor. The governor often exercises influence with his or her appointees on the board of regents. In 2002, it was rumored that Governor Perry strongly supported the selection of retiring Senator Phil Gramm for president of Texas A&M University. All of Governor Perry's appointees supported Gramm.

The governor also appoints a number of persons to non-policy-making and governing boards that recommend policy and programs to the governor or other state officials. These are not included in this discussion. Many of these non-policy-making boards recommend changes in policy and programs. Others are simply window dressing and allow the governor to reward supporters. Most often these non-policy-making boards do not require senate approval.

Some gubernatorial appointments are subject to approval by a two-thirds vote of the senate. In these cases, the governor must clear his or her appointments with the state senator from the appointee's home district. This limits the discretion of the governor. This process is known as **senatorial courtesy.** If the senator from an appointee's home district disapproves of the appointment, the senate might not confirm the appointees. Senatorial courtesy does not apply to all gubernatorial appointments, especially the non-policy-making boards.

The discretion of the governor is also limited by other factors. For example, some boards require geographic representation. Members of river authority boards must live

senatorial courtesy
The courtesy of the governor clearing his or her appointments with the state senator from the appointee's home district.

TABLE 8.3

Texas Governor Appointments to Policy-Making and Governing Boards, Commissions, and Agencies

Type of Agency	Number of Agencies	Number of Appointees
General Government	31	244
Health and Human Services	31	366
Higher Education Boards of Regents	12	117
Other Education	16	149
Business Regulation	9	37
Business and Economic Development	24	176
Regional Economic Development	32	276
Licensing and Professional Examining Boards	38	461
Public Safety and Criminal Justice	22	158
Natural Resources	16	156
Employee Retirement Boards	8	53
Interstate Compact Commissions	8	24
Water and River Authorities	18	210
Judicial	18	151
Others	18	251
Totals	301	2,829

Source: Data supplied by the Texas State Governor's Appointment Secretary, Freedom of Information Request. August 2000. Categories for state agencies are by the author. List can be obtained from Governor's Appointment Secretary, State Capitol, Austin, Texas.

in the area covered by the river authority. Good examples of this are the Trinity River Authority and the Lower Colorado River Authority. Other boards require specified professional backgrounds. Membership on the Texas Municipal Retirement Board, for instance, is limited to certain types of city employees—such as firefighters, police, and city managers.[21]

Of course, there are always political limits placed on the governor's ability to appoint people. Interest groups pay close attention to the governor's appointments to these boards and commissions and try to influence the governor's choices. The governor may have to bend to demands from such groups. Chapter 4 discussed this subject in more detail.

In Texas, the appointive power of the governor, even with these formal limitations, allows the governor to indirectly influence policy. It is unlikely that a governor will select men and women to serve on these boards and commissions who do not agree with the governor on major policy issues. Ann Richards used her appointive powers to increase the number of women and minorities serving on these boards and commissions. This broad appointive power allows the governor to influence policy even after leaving office, since some of the appointees will remain on these boards and commissions. Richards's successor, George W. Bush, appointed some women and minorities, but tended mainly to appoint businessmen to these positions. Governor Perry, for the most part, appoints business leaders as well.

Thus the governor exerts indirect, not direct, control over policy by appointing people with similar policy views. This influence will continue for some time after the governor leaves office, since his or her appointee will remain in office for four to six years after the governor's term ends.

Governors appoint people they know and trust.

Appointments and Campaign Contributions

Governors have also been known to appoint people to governing boards and commissions who were supporters in their campaigns. People who were loyal supporters, especially those giving big campaign contributions, are often rewarded with appointment to prestigious state boards and commissions. University governing boards are especially desired positions. Listed in table 8.4 are the contributions given by individuals appointed to state boards and commissions by Governor Perry.

Removal Powers

The other side of the power to appoint is the power to remove persons from office. U.S. presidents may remove many of their appointees, but state governors are often very restricted by either the state constitution, statutes creating the agency, or term limits set for appointees. Some states allow the governor to remove a person only for cause. This requires the governor to make a case for wrongdoing by the individual. Of course, the governor can force the resignation of a person without formal hearings, but the political cost of such forced resignations can be quite high and beyond what the governor is willing to pay.

In Texas, the removal power of the governor is very weak. Before 1981 Texas state law was silent on the issue of removal. In 1981 the constitution was amended to allow governors to remove any person they personally appointed, with a two-thirds vote of the senate. Governors may not remove any of their predecessors' appointees. To date no

TABLE 8.4

Campaign Contributions and Appointment to Boards and Commissions by Governor Rick Perry

Appointed Office Category (% of all Appointments)	Average Appointment Price	No. of Appointments	Percent Involving Donations	Total Appointee Donations
Education (12%)	$10,616	135	35%	$1,433,093
Humanitics (4%)	8,316	45	44%	374,220
Natural Resources (12%)	6,410	133	42%	852,556
Insurance (1%)	6,167	15	20%	92,500
Finance (4%)	3,940	41	32%	161,527
Corrections/Security (9%)	2,673	100	22%	267,278
Other (7%)	2,171	79	27%	171,535
Housing (2%)	1,982	17	29%	7,000
Infrastructure/ Transportation (3%)	1,938	39	46%	77,296
Law (7%)	1,501	78	36%	117,080
Health/Human Services (14%)	958	153	16%	146,507
Economy (6%)	840	62	26%	52,070
Licensing (18%)	559	198	25%	110,712
Retirement (2%)	248	28	29%	6,950
Total	**$3,446**	**1,123**	**32%**	**$3,870,324**

Source: TPJ.org "Well appointed boards."

person has been formally removed from office using this procedure, but it does provide the governor with some leverage to force an appointee to resign. It might also be used to force a policy change wanted by the governor. It does not, however, allow the governor to control the day-to-day administration of state government.

Budgetary Powers

budgetary powers
The ability of a governor to formulate and budget, present it to the legislature, and execute or control the budget.

Along with tenure of office and appointive/executive authority, the **budgetary powers** are an important determinant of executive authority. Control over how money is spent is at the very heart of the policy-making process. Some writers define a budget as a statement of policy in monetary terms. If the governor can control budget formation and development (the preparation of the budget for submission to the legislature) and budget execution (deciding how money is spent), the governor can have a significant influence on state policy. There are four kinds of constraints that can undercut the governor's budgetary authority:

1. The extent to which the governor must share budget formation with the legislature or with other state agencies
2. The extent to which funds are earmarked for specific expenditures and the choice on how to spend money is limited by previous actions
3. The extent to which the governor shares budget execution authority with others in state government
4. The limits on the governor's use of a line-item veto for the budget

HIGHLIGHT

A Case of the Overactive Governor Veto?

New Mexico's Republican governor Gary Johnson may have set a record vetoing bills in the 1995 session of the legislature. A self-made millionaire, Governor Johnson rode into office on the antigovernment vote in November 1994. He had never held elected office before and admitted that he had little knowledge of government.

Johnson set a new state and national record by vetoing 200 of the 424 bills passed by the legislature. This passed the previous record set in 1957 by Edwin L. Mechem, who vetoed only 100 bills. While some of Governor Johnson's vetoes were aimed at reducing government expenditures and setting a conservative agenda, some seemed to defy explanation. One "harmless example was the veto of a bill making Red or Green (as in red or green chili) the official state question." Another example is a bill that required the posting of total federal and state taxes paid per gallon of gasoline. The bill had the support of gasoline distributors and retailers who were concerned that citizens did not know how much tax they paid.

Even some of the more conservative Republicans in the state were surprised at the bills that were vetoed, some of which actually reduced the cost of government. In the 1996 session of the legislature the governor faced a few setbacks by having many of his vetoes overridden.

Source: Peter Eichstaedt, "No, No, Two Hundred Times No," in *State Government: CQ's Guide to Current Issues and Activities 1996–97*: edited by Thad L. Beyle, Copyright © 1997 Congressional Quarterly Press, Washington, D.C., 120–123.

In forty states the governor is given "full" authority over budget formation and development.[22] In those states where the governor is given authority for budget formation, agencies must present their requests for expenditures to the governor's office, which combines them and presents a unified budget to the legislature. In some states, the governor is limited in how much he or she can reduce the budget requests of some state agencies. If the governor can change the requests of agencies, this gives the governor tremendous control over the final form of the budget submitted to the legislature. A common practice of state governments is to earmark revenue for specific purposes. For example, funds received through the gasoline tax are commonly earmarked for state highways. This also limits the discretion of the governor.

Budget execution authority is more involved. There is a variety of ways that governors and others control budget execution. If the governor controls the appointment of the major department heads of state government, he or she will have some discretion in how money is spent. The governor may decide not to spend all the money appropriated for a state park. Administrative discretion over how money is spent is a time-honored way to expand executive authority over the budget.

Another area where governors can often exercise control over budgets is veto authority. All but seven governors have a **line-item veto** that allows them to exercise great influence over the budgetary process.[23]

In Texas the governor's budgetary powers are exceptionally weak except in the area of the line-item veto. The governor is not constitutionally mandated to submit a budget. This power is given to the **Legislative Budget Board (LBB)**, an agency governed by the speaker of the house and the lieutenant governor. Agencies of the state must present budget requests to the LBB. The LBB produces a budget that is submitted to the legislature. Historically, governors have submitted budget messages to the legislature, often in the form of reactions to the LBB proposed budget. Someone once said that the "governor's budget" has the same effect as a letter to Santa Claus since it has little effect on the final budget form. In 2003, Governor Perry presented a budget with all zeros, claiming it was a "zero-based" budget. It was not, and many saw the move as an attempt to avoid dealing with the $10 billion shortfall.

line-item vetoes

The ability of a governor to veto part of an appropriation bill without vetoing the whole bill.

Legislative Budget Board (LBB)

State agency that is controlled by the leadership in the state legislature and that writes the state budget.

In Texas many funds are earmarked by the previous actions of the legislature. One estimate from the LBB is that 80+ percent of all funds are earmarked for specific expenditures, such as highways, teachers' retirement, parks, and schools. This will be discussed in Chapter 10.

In Texas the governor has very limited authority over budget execution. Outside of the governor's immediate office, control over the budget rests with other state agencies over which the governor has little or no control. Only in cases of fiscal crisis can the governor exercise any influence. A constitutional amendment approved in 1985 created the Budget Execution Committee, composed of the governor, the lieutenant governor, the comptroller, the speaker of the house, and chairs of the Finance and Appropriations Committees in the senate and house. The Budget Execution Committee can exercise restraints over the budget if there is a fiscal crisis such as a shortfall in projected revenue.

The one area where the Texas governor does have influence over budget decisions is the line-item veto. The governor can veto part of the appropriations bill without vetoing the entire bill. The legislature determines what a line item is. It can be a department within an agency, or the entire agency. For example, Governor Clements once vetoed the line items appropriating money to operate the systems administration offices of the University of Texas and Texas A&M University. He did not veto all money appropriated to these schools, just the funds for the operation of the systems offices. The governor might line-item veto money for a state park without having to veto the money for all state parks.

The legislature can override this veto by a two-thirds vote of each house. However, as we saw in Chapter 7, appropriations bills generally pass in the last days of the session, so the legislature has adjourned by the time the governor vetoes items. Since the legislature cannot call itself back into session ("extraordinary" sessions), overriding a line-item veto is impossible. The governor may call special sessions, but he or she controls the agenda. If the governor thought there was a chance of a veto override, this would not be included in the agenda of the special session.

Thus, the line-item veto is a very important power possessed by the Texas governor. More important than the actual veto is the threat of a veto. Historically in Texas, governors have used this threat to discipline the legislature. It is not uncommon for the governor to threaten to veto a local line item, such as an item creating a new state park in a legislator's district. This threat to veto local appropriations can be used to gain legislative support for items important to the governor but unrelated to the park. It should be noted that typically governors do not veto many bills. While there are occasional exceptions to this, as a general rule, threats are more important than the actual veto.

Nationally, the U.S. Congress granted the president of the United States a limited line-item veto. The U.S. Supreme Court declared this act unconstitutional. While many have advocated that the president needs the line-item veto to control congressional spending, a constitutional amendment will be required to grant this power. If this happens, presidents might use the threat of veto to control members of Congress and get their support for other programs.

Legislative Powers

While the line-item veto can be viewed as a budgetary power, it is also a **legislative power.** There are also other types of vetoes. All governors possess some form of veto authority, but this varies among the states. (See table 8.5.) Forty-three states have formalized **partial vetoes,**[24] where the legislature can recall a bill from the governor so that objections raised by the governor can be changed and a veto avoided.[25] Texas does not have a formal partial

legislative power
The formal power, especially the veto authority, of the governor to force the legislature to enact his or her legislation.

partial vetoes
The ability of some governors to veto part of a nonappropriations bill without vetoing the entire bill. A Texas governor does not have this power except on appropriations bills.

TABLE 8.5

Veto Authority of State Governors with Override Provisions

Type of Veto	No. of Governors
General veto and item veto: two-thirds needed to override	37
General veto and item veto: majority elected needed to override	6
General veto, no item veto: special legislative majority to override*	6
General veto, no item veto: simple majority to override	1

*Most common is 3/5 vote. Data changes slightly.

Source: Thad L. Beyle, "Governors: The Middlemen and Women in Our Political System" in *Politics in the American States,* 8th edition, ed. Virginia Gray and Russell L. Hanson. Copyright © 2004 Congressional Quarterly Press, Washington, D.C. Reprinted by permission.

veto process; however, the governor can still state objections to a bill before it is passed and thus seek to effect changes in legislation. Formalizing the process would shift some power to the office of governor and give the governor more say in the legislative process.

Requirements for overriding a governor's veto also vary widely among the states. Most states require a two-thirds vote to override, although a few allow a simple majority.[26] In Texas, the governor has very strong veto authority. The office possesses a general veto and line-item veto, with a two-thirds vote of each house required for override. Very few vetoes have been overturned. From 1876 to 1968, only 25 of 936 vetoes were overridden in the legislature. Most of these vetoes occurred before 1940. This low number of veto overrides is primarily due to late passage of bills and adjournment of the legislature. Only one veto has been overturned in recent years, and it was not a significant bill. In 1979 during his first term, Bill Clements vetoed fifty-two bills. The legislature, in an attempt to get the governor's attention, overrode the veto on a bill that limited the ability of county governments to prohibit hunters from killing female deer.[27] Since 1979 no votes have been overridden by the legislature.

There are fifteen other states besides Texas where the legislature may not call a "special" session. These are usually called *extraordinary sessions* to distinguish them from special sessions, which are called by the governor. States where the legislature cannot call extraordinary sessions add to the power of the governor to veto bills. In the last session of the Texas legislature Governor Perry set a new record by vetoing eighty-two bills. If the Texas legislature could have called an extraordinary session, there is little doubt that it would have happened and that some vetoes would have been overridden.

Thus the veto authority of the Texas governor is very significant. Getting two-thirds of each house of the legislature to override is very difficult. If the legislature has adjourned, it is impossible. For these reasons, there have been few overrides.

Some governors have a pocket veto, meaning that they can veto a bill by not signing it. The governor just "puts the bill in a pocket" and forgets about it. The Texas governor does not have a pocket veto. If the legislature is in session, the governor has ten days to sign a bill or it becomes law without his or her signature. If the legislature has adjourned, the governor has twenty days to sign a bill or it becomes law without a signature. Sometimes governors do not like a bill but do not want to veto it for some reason. Letting the bill become law without a signature can be a way of expressing displeasure short of an actual veto.

In recent years governors have used the line-item veto to eliminate more than a line item in the appropriations bill. In Arizona the GOP-controlled legislature has twice sued Democratic governor Janet Napolitano with the claim that she has misused her

Oh! Pardon Me, Governor

During "Ma" Ferguson's second term, the selling of pardons became common knowledge. The process was so open that this story was widespread:

A man steps off the elevator in the state capitol in Austin and accidentally bumps into Governor "Ma" Ferguson. "Oh! Pardon me, Governor," he says. Governor Ferguson says, "I'm sorry, you'll have to see Pa about that."

line-item veto authority. The most recent case involved the veto of a bill involving a state employee pay plan. The governor vetoed a section of the bill that exempted employees making more than $47,758 from the state merit pay plan. The Republicans contend that this is a misuse of the power.

Judicial Powers

judicial powers

The ability of a governor to issue pardons, executive clemency, and parole for citizens convicted of a crime.

Governors are also given limited **judicial powers** to grant pardons, executive clemency, and parole. Historically, governors have misused this power. This has led to the creation of some checks on the ability of governors to exercise this authority. In Texas James "Pa" Ferguson was accused of misusing this power, especially during the second term of his wife, Miriam Amanda "Ma" Ferguson (1933–35). It was charged that Jim Ferguson sold pardons and paroles to convicted felons.[28] These charges led to the creation of the state Pardons and Paroles Board. Today this eighteen-member board, appointed by the governor, recommends to the governor the action he or she can take in such matters and serves as a check on the process. Independent of board action, the governor may grant only one thirty-day stay of execution for any condemned prisoner. This board must recommend all other actions by the governor.

In the Fergusons' defense many of the pardons were given to people who were in prison because they had violated the Prohibition laws. Laws prohibiting the use of alcoholic liquors were the war on drugs several generations ago. Former Lt. Governor Hobby put it this way: "Prohibition's laws filled the prisons and ruined lives then just as marijuana laws do now. The Fergusons may have rightly concluded that the state was better served by these men being home supporting their families."[29]

Military Powers

military powers

Powers giving the governor the right to use the National Guard in times of natural disaster or civil unrest.

The **military powers** of the governor are quite limited and come into play only in times of natural disaster or civil unrest. The governor appoints the adjutant general of the National Guard and can direct the Guard to protect the lives and property of Texas citizens. The most common use of this power is during natural disasters, where the Guard is employed to help evacuate people, protect property, and supply food and water to victims.

✦ POWERS OF THE TEXAS GOVERNOR COMPARED

If we take the five indexes of power—tenure of office, appointive powers, budgetary powers, veto powers, and judicial powers—and compare the Texas governor with the other forty-nine governors, the Texas office is comparatively weak in formal powers. (See table 8.6.)[30]

The office is formally weak because of the limitations placed on administrative and budgetary powers. The office is strong on tenure and veto authority. This formal weakness in the office of governor is very much in keeping with the traditionalistic/individualistic political culture of the state. As was discussed earlier, the present constitution was written in a time when limited government was very much on the minds of the framers of the constitution. Having experienced strong executive authority during Reconstruction, these framers wanted to limit the governor's ability to act, especially in budgetary and administrative matters. They succeeded. In recent years the powers of the Texas governor have been increased somewhat, but the office is still very weak on the budgetary and administrative dimensions. Given this formal weakness, Texas governors must use all their informal powers of persuasion and their political skills if they are to be successful. Also, in recent years the voters have rejected constitutional amendments that would have expanded the governor's ability to appoint and remove agency heads. (See Chapter 2.)

TABLE 8.6

Summary of Institutional Powers of Governors by State, 2007*

Alabama	2.8
Alaska	4.1
Arizona	3.4
Arkansas	3.6
California	3.2
Colorado	3.9
Connecticut	3.6
Delaware	3.5
Florida	3.6
Georgia	3.2
Hawaii	3.4
Idaho	3.3
Illinois	3.8
Indiana	2.9
Iowa	3.8
Kansas	3.3
Kentucky	3.3
Louisiana	3.4
Maine	3.6
Maryland	4.1
Massachusetts	4.3
Michigan	3.6
Minnesota	3.6
Mississippi	2.9
Missouri	3.6
Montana	3.5
Nebraska	3.8
Nevada	3.0
New Hampshire	3.2
New Jersey	4.1

(Continued)

TABLE 8.6 (*continued*)	
New Mexico	3.7
New York	4.1
North Carolina	2.9
North Dakota	3.9
Ohio	3.6
Oklahoma	2.8
Oregon	3.5
Pennsylvania	3.8
Rhode Island	2.6
South Carolina	3.0
South Dakota	3.0
Tennessee	3.8
Texas	3.2
Utah	4.0
Vermont	2.5
Virginia	3.2
Washington	3.6
West Virginia	4.1
Wisconsin	3.5
Wyoming	3.1
Fifty-state average	**3.5**

*Scores computed using six variables: election of other statewide executives, tenure of office, governor's appointive powers, governor's budgetary powers, veto powers, and governor's control over party. Five points were given for each variable and total divided by six to get score.

Source: Thad L. Beyle, "Governors" in *Politics in the American States,* 9th edition, edited by Virginia Gray and Russell L. Hanson. Copyright © 2008 Congressional Quarterly Press, Washington, D.C. Reprinted by permission

→ INFORMAL POWERS

While the office of Texas governor is formally very weak, the office can be strong politically. The governor's primary political resource is the ability to exert influence. The governor is the most visible officeholder in the state and can command the attention of the news media, holding press conferences and announcing new decisions on policy issues. Such news conferences usually are well covered and reported by the press and other media. This enables the governor to have an impact on the direction of state government. The governor can also stage events that are newsworthy to emphasize things she or he is interested in changing.

The popularity of the governor in public opinion polls is also an important aspect of informal leadership. Governors who consistently rank high in popularity polls can use this fact to overcome opposition to their policies and reduce the likelihood of opposition, both to policies and electoral challenges. A governor who is weak in public opinion polls becomes an easy target for political opponents.

In very general ways, governors are judged on their leadership abilities. Some governors develop reputations as being indecisive, while others become known as effective, decisive leaders. The characterization attached to the governor will affect his or her ability to be effective. The press will begin to repeat the reputational description of the governor, and if this happens often enough, the reputation will become "fact." Therefore, developing a good image is very important.

Party Leadership

As indicated earlier, governors are expected to be leaders of their political party and in most states are recognized as the leader of the party. In the one-party era in Texas, the Democratic candidate for governor picked the state party chair and controlled the state party organization. Often such control was based on a personal following rather than a well-organized party structure. Governor Bill Clements, a Republican, especially during his second term made use of his election to build the party in the state. He managed enough control over the Republican party and its elected house members to thwart Democratic control of the legislature on some issues.

Today governors might influence the choice of party leadership, but they do not control the party. George W. Bush found himself in the uncomfortable position of having to work with a state party chair chosen by the Social Conservatives. Governor Bush would probably have made a different choice for party chair. He did not attend the 2000 meeting of the Republican party convention. He claimed to be very busy campaigning for president. This may have been the first time a sitting governor did not attend his/her state party convention. It indicated the degree of disagreement between the governor and the party leaders. As the two-party system matures in Texas, party leadership by the governor will have to become more of a fixture in state politics. Governor Perry has not embraced the Social Conservatives' program or the party platform and has avoided becoming closely attached or associated with this wing of the party.

The Governor's Staff

In Texas the trend in recent years has been to expand the staff of the governor's office. In 1963 when he became governor, John Connally made the first use of a professional staff of advisors. Previous governors often appointed only a handful of individuals who were loyal to them politically, but not necessarily highly professional. Other governors since Connally have added to the governor's staff. Today an organizational chart is necessary to maintain lines of authority and responsibility. Currently the governor has a staff of about two hundred.

H I G H L I G H T

Campaign Money Used to Pay Members of Governor's Staff

Michael Toomey, chief of staff to Governor Rick Perry, has a state salary of $135,000. From his political campaign fund, Perry adds an additional $113,281, for a total of $248,281. President Bush started the practice when he was governor but the amount paid from campaign funds has increased dramatically. Bush paid his chief of staff an additional amount of only $9,228.

In addition to the supplemental pay given to Toomey, other members of Perry's staff also get additional pay. The State Comptroller, Carole Keeton Strayhorn, pays her deputy comptroller Billy Hamilton an additional $72,000.

"The potential for corruption is huge. The employees frequently know their salary is coming from political contributions and may well know whose contribution was solicited to pay for their salary," said Tom "Smitty" Smith of *Public Citizen.*

The governor and other state officials justify the additional pay to attract quality people. For example, Mike Toomey earned from $600,000 to $1.4 million as a lobbyist in 2002 before joining the governor's staff. The other side of this argument is that when these people leave office they will be able to command even higher salaries as lobbyists and should not expect additional pay that may compromise their judgments or decisions.

Source: Houston Chronicle, "Political Stipends Sweeten State Pay," 1 February 2004, pages 1A and 14A.

Each governor is going to make different uses of her or his staff. In recent years most governors have used their staff to keep track of state agencies over which the governor has little or no direct control. The staff also gathers information and makes recommendations on changes in policy that impact most areas of state government. A message from a member of the governor's staff to a state agency is taken seriously. A report issued by the governor's office automatically attracts the attention of significant state leaders and the news media. Often the governor must use the information gathered to wage a public relations war with the legislature or state agencies. In Texas the increases in the size, professionalism, and complexity of the governor's staff have become necessary to offset the limited formal control the governor has over state government.

→ ADMINISTRATIVE AGENCIES OF STATE GOVERNMENT

In addition to the office of governor, there are a number of state agencies that make up what might be called the state bureaucracy. The term *bureaucracy* often implies a hierarchy of offices with levels of power leading to a centralized controlling authority. This term does not describe the overall structure of state government in Texas, since there is no overall central governing, controlling authority. Government authority in Texas is much decentralized and resides within many independent state agencies. The structure can best be described as a **plural executive.** That is, the governor is not the only executive; there are other elected officials with whom the governor must share power. In addition there are many independent boards, commissions, and agencies that operate independently of the governor. Power is decentralized among many officials. This decentralized structure of power is in keeping with the traditionalistic/individualistic political culture of the state.

plural executive
System whereby voters elect many statewide officeholders to serve as heads of departments.

Types of Administrative Agencies and Gubernatorial Control

There are three basic kinds of state agencies in Texas. First are the agencies headed by an elected official; second are the appointed single-head agencies; and finally, and the most numerous, are those headed by a multimember appointed board or commission. (See table 8.7.) The governor obviously has little or no authority over agencies headed by other elected officials who are responsible to the voters who elected them. As was indicated earlier, while the Texas governor appoints citizens to these 285-plus state boards and commissions, he or she has very limited removal authority. Each state board and commission operates quite independently from the others, and there is no central controlling authority. Obviously the governor has the greatest authority in the single-head agencies that he or she appoints. Except for the secretary of state, these are of limited significance. Most of the work of state government is conducted by agencies controlled by either elected officials or independent boards and commissions who operate quite independently of the governor. Only the legislature, through oversight and budgetary authority, exercises control over all state agencies.

Agencies with Elected Officials

As indicated earlier, the election of people to head administrative units of government is a concept dating to the 1820s with the election of Andrew Jackson. Known as Jacksonian statehouse government, the belief is that the ballot box was the best way to select

TABLE 8.7

The Administrative Structure of State Government in Texas

Voters in State Elect

Comptroller of Public Accounts
Commissioner of the General Land Office
Attorney General
Commissioner of Agriculture
Railroad Commission (3 members)
State Board of Education (15 members)
Lieutenant Governor

Governor Appoints

Agency Heads
  Secretary of State
  Adjutant General of the National Guard
  Director of Housing and Community Affairs
  Director of Office of State-Federal Relations
  Executive Director of Texas Education Agency
  Commissioner for Health and Human Services
  Eight other minor agencies

Boards and Commissions
  General Government
  Health and Human Services
  Higher Education Boards of Regents
  Other Education
  Business Regulation
  Business and Economic Development
  Regional Economic Development
  Licensing and Professional Examining Boards
  Public Safety and Criminal Justice
  Natural Resources
  Employee Retirement Boards
  Interstate Compact Commissions
  Water and River Authorities
  Judicial

Sources: *Guide to Texas State Agencies,* 9th edition, LBJ School, The University of Texas at Austin, Austin, Texas. Legislative Budget Board, *Fiscal Size Up, 1999–2000 Biennium, Texas State Services.* Legislative Budget Board, Austin, Texas. Some information was supplied by Governor's Appointments Office. The governor makes about 1,000 appointments to task forces or ad hoc advisory committees who make recommendations to the governor or other state officials. They are not governing or policy-making bodies.

administrators and make them accountable to the public. In the aftermath of Reconstruction in the 1870s, the current constitution reintroduced the idea of electing almost all officeholders and limiting the ability of the governor to appoint them.

Office of the Attorney General

This office was created under the 1876 constitution. The **attorney general** serves as the legal counsel to the governor, the legislature, and most of the other agencies, boards,

attorney general
Chief counsel to the governor and state agencies. Limited criminal jurisdiction.

and commissions in state government. Most of the work of the attorney general involves civil law and not criminal law. The attorney general's office, with some 3,700 state employees, is responsible for representing the state in litigation, enforcing state and federal child support laws, providing legal counsel to state officials, and enforcing state laws. Criminal functions of the office are primarily limited to those cases appealed to federal courts. The most common example of these criminal cases are death penalty appeals. Occasionally the attorney general's office may assist local criminal prosecutors when invited to do so. For the most part the functions of the attorney general are civil and not criminal in nature; however, this does not prevent most candidates who run for the office from emphasizing their commitment to law enforcement and getting tough on criminals.

Most of the resources of this office are devoted to collection of child support payments, collection of delinquent state taxes, administration of the Crime Victims Compensation program, and investigation of Medicare fraud. Despite this rather "mundane" list of functions, the office has important political functions. The most important of these is to issue so-called AG opinions on legal questions. Often when the legislature is in session, the attorney general (AG) will be asked for an opinion on a pending piece of legislation. These AG opinions can have an impact on the course of legislation. Often a negative AG opinion will kill a bill's chances of passing.

The office of attorney general is also an important stepping-stone to the governor's office. In recent years several candidates for governor have been former attorneys general (John Hill, Mark White, and Jim Mattox). Dan Morales was the first Mexican American to be elected to the office. He did not seek reelection in 1998, and in 2002 ran and lost a bid to become the Democratic party nominee for governor. John Cornyn, the AG from 1998 to 2002, was elected to the U.S. Senate in 2002.

Comptroller of Public Accounts

comptroller of public accounts
Chief tax collector and investor of state funds. Does not perform financial audits.

Another constitutional office created in 1876, the **comptroller of public accounts** has been assigned many additional duties over the years and currently functions as the chief fiscal and revenue forecasting office. In 1966 the office of treasurer was abolished, and the comptroller is responsible for investing state funds.

In many states and in the private sector, the term is the "controller" rather than "comptroller" as used in Texas. Generally in government the controller has a preaudit responsibility for assuring that funds can be spent for specific functions. In Texas the comptroller not only has the preaudit responsibility, but also serves as the chief tax collector (a function normally associated with the office of treasurer), revenue forecaster, and investor of state funds.

The comptroller is responsible for collecting thirty-one different taxes for the state and collects the sales tax for some 1,169 local governments (1,018 cities, 117 counties, and 34 special districts).[31] The property tax division also conducts annual audits of property appraisal districts in the state to ensure uniformity in appraisals of the value of property across the state. This uniformity is important to improve the equity of state aid to local school districts. (See Chapter 11 on local government.)

Former governor Bob Bullock served as comptroller for many years. During his tenure the office expanded the information and management functions and developed a fiscal forecasting model essential to projecting revenues in a two-year budget cycle. John Sharp, who followed Bob Bullock as comptroller, continued and expanded the information management programs of the office. Also under Sharp the office developed the Texas Performance Review teams to evaluate the effectiveness of government operations and ensure the most efficient use of state funds. These reviews were estimated to have saved the state over $1.3 billion in the 1998-99 biennium fiscal years.

Similar management information and efficiency audits are available to assist local governments. Most of these programs were kept in place by Carole Keeton Strayhorn, who succeeded John Sharp.

The office also provided assistance to the private sector through the provision of information. The State of Texas Econometric Model is used to forecast state economic growth, keep track of business cycles, and generally provide information on the health of the economy of the state. Finally, the office is responsible for investing state funds. This involves investing and securing fund balances that average $8.6 billion during the year.[32]

Commissioner of the General Land Office

Texas is one of only four states to have a **land commissioner.**[33] In Texas the office was created under the 1836 constitution to administer state-owned land. When Texas entered the Union in 1845 the agreement between the former republic and the U.S. government was that Texas kept its public debt and its public land. When Texas became a state most of the land was state owned. Today the state of Texas owns and manages 20.3 million acres of land, including open beaches and submerged land 10.3 miles into the Gulf of Mexico.[34]

land commissioner
Elected official responsible for administration and oversight of state-owned lands and coastal lands extending 10.3 miles into the Gulf of Mexico.

The land commissioner's office is responsible for leasing state lands and generating funds from oil and gas production. The office is also responsible for overseeing the Veterans Land Board and Veterans Land Fund. This fund loans money to Texas veterans to purchase rural land. Finally the land office is responsible for maintaining the environmental quality of the state's open beaches along the Gulf Coast.

Commissioner of Agriculture

The Texas Department of Agriculture (TDA) was created by statute in 1907. A commissioner of agriculture who is elected by the voters in a statewide election heads the department. The TDA has the dual, and sometimes contradictory, roles of promoting agriculture products and production and regulating agricultural practices, while protecting the public health from unsafe agricultural practices. For example, the TDA must both promote cotton production and sales in the state and regulate the use of pesticides.

There are six major functions of the TDA: marketing of Texas agriculture products, development and promotion of agricultural businesses' product production, pesticide regulation, pest management, product certification and safety inspection, and inspection and certification of measuring devices (including gasoline pumps, electronic scanners, and scales).

While the TDA and the agricultural commissioner are not as publicly visible as the other statewide elected officials, it is an important office to a large section of the state's economy—those engaged in agriculture. While the economy of Texas has become more diversified in recent years, agriculture is still a significant player in the state's economy. Major agribusinesses and others in agriculture in the state pay close attention to who serves as the agricultural commissioner.

The Texas Railroad Commission

The **Texas Railroad Commission** (RRC) was created in 1891 under the administration of Governor James S. Hogg to regulate the railroad monopolies that had developed in the state. The commission was also given regulatory authority over terminals, wharves, and express companies. The commission consists of three members elected statewide by the voters for six-year staggered terms with one member elected every two years.

Texas Railroad Commission
State agency with regulation over some aspects of transportation and the oil and gas industry of the state.

The member up for election, by convention, always serves as chair of the Railroad Commission.

In the 1920s when oil and natural gas production developed in the state, the task of regulating the exploration, drilling, and production of oil and natural gas was assigned to the RRC in part because it was the only state regulatory agency in the state at the time. When motor truck transport developed in the state, regulation of the trucking industry was also assigned to the RRC. In part because of federal rules and regulations, the original role of regulating railroads and the later role of regulating trucking have diminished to a minor role of the agency, reduced primarily to concern with safety issues. The regulation of the oil and gas industry is its primary function today.

Many have been critical of the RRC over the years because of close ties between the elected commissioners and the oil and gas industry it regulates. (See Chapter 4 on interest groups.) Large campaign contributions from oil and gas PACs have raised questions about the commission being co-opted by the industry it regulates. Also, like the agricultural commissioner, the RRC has the dual role of promoting oil and gas production in the state and regulating the safety and environmental aspects of the industry (e.g., promoting the development of pipelines to carry petroleum products as well as the safety of such pipelines). A similar conflict may exist between the RRC task of regulating and promoting mining of minerals (especially lignite coal) in the state.

The role of the RRC that most directly affects citizens in the state is that of setting the rates charged by local natural gas companies. Natural gas companies must get the rates they charge residential and commercial customers approved by the RRC. The RRC also regulates the safety of natural gas systems.

The State Board of Education

Unlike the other offices discussed in this section, the governing body for public elementary and secondary education in the state has varied greatly in form and structure over the years. Originally in 1884, an elected school superintendent governed Texas schools. In 1929 an appointed state board was created. In 1949 the Gilmer-Aikin Act created the Texas Education Agency (TEA) with an appointed superintendent of education. In the 1960s an elected state board was added. In 1984 the elected board was reduced from twenty-one members, elected from congressional districts in the state, to fifteen members appointed by the governor. In 1986 the board was again changed from appointed to elected from districts. The current board, called the State Board of Education, nominates a person to the governor to be commissioner of education.

In recent years the authority of the State Board has been greatly reduced by actions of the state legislature. The political battle over the power of the State Board revolved around the Social Conservatives' (Christian Right) success in electing members to the board and the actions taken in setting curriculum standards and textbook selection issues. Public infighting among members of the board diminished its effectiveness. The legislature has removed several functions, most significantly the selection of textbooks, from the State Board in part because of the infighting and control by this faction.

Single-Head Agencies

In some states, a single person, appointed and serving at the pleasure of the governor, heads most agencies. The structure is much like that of the federal government where the president appoints his own cabinet that serve at his pleasure. Only a handful of state agencies in Texas meet this model, and few are of great importance.

Secretary of State

The **secretary of state (SOS)** is a constitutional office, appointed by the governor with approval of the state senate. The constitution and state statutes assign many duties to this office, which can be lumped into three broad categories: elections, records keeping/information management, and international protocol. As the chief election official the SOS is responsible for overseeing voter registration, preparation of election information, and supervision of elections. The SOS issues rules, directives, and opinions on the conduct of elections and voter registration. These duties allow the secretary some latitude in the interpretation and application of the state Election Code. For example the SOS has some latitude in how vigorously they encourage citizens to register and vote.

secretary of state (SOS)
Chief election official and keeper of state records. Appointed by the governor.

A second duty of the SOS is to serve as the official keeper of state records. This includes records on business corporations and some other commercial activities. The office also publishes the *Texas Register,* which is the source of official notices or rules, meetings, executive orders, and opinions of the attorney general that are required to be filed by state agencies. Through the protocol functions of the office, the SOS provides support services to state officials who interact with representatives of foreign countries.

In a few cases the office of secretary of state has been an important stepping-stone to higher office. It is a highly visible office, and the secretary is often in the public eye, especially with the duties as chief election official. It is without doubt the most important single-head agency appointment that the governor makes. The most noted example is Mark White, who became attorney general and later governor. Former Governor Bush picked his secretary of state to become White House counsel in his administration.

Commissioner for Health and Human Services

This office was created in 1991 to coordinate a number of health-related programs and agencies. The governor appoints the commissioner for a two-year term with the approval of the state senate. The commissioner has oversight responsibility over eleven separate health and welfare programs, which are directed by boards, councils, or commissions. The commissioner is not directly responsible for the administration of these programs but has oversight and review functions. Those programs include: aging; alcohol and drug abuse; the blind, deaf, and hard-of-hearing; early childhood intervention; juvenile probation; mental health and retardation; rehabilitation; and departments of Health, Human Services, and Protective and Regulatory Services.

While this office has little direct administrative control, it can and often does have impact on policy. The commissioner serves as a spokesperson for the governor in health and welfare matters.

Office of State–Federal Relations

The governor appoints the executive director of the Office of State-Federal Relations. As the name suggests this office coordinates relations between state and federal officials. The office has existed since 1971 and is the primary liaison between the governor's office and federal officials. To some degree this office becomes an advocate (lobbyist) for the state in dealing with the Texas congressional delegation and federal agencies.

Adjutant General of the National Guard

This office is created by the Texas constitution and is responsible for directing the state military force under the direction of the governor. The governor serves as commander in chief of the Guard. The size of the National Guard (nationwide and in Texas) is determined and funded by Congress as a reserve force to the regular army. The Guard also provides emergency aid and protection of property and persons in times of natural disaster.

In the 1999 November election, the voters of Texas rejected a constitutional amendment that would have allowed the governor to appoint and remove the head of the National Guard. As with other appointees, the governor may appoint the head of the National Guard, but not remove except on approval of the state senate.

Other Single-Head Agencies

The remaining state agencies to which the governor makes a single appointment are not of great significance in terms of policy or politics. This is not to say that they are insignificant, but simply of less importance. These agencies often receive little or no attention from the average citizen or the press. They include the following: Department of Housing and Community Affairs; Department of Commerce; State Office of Administrative Hearings; Executive Director of Health Care Information Council; Insurance Commissioner; Public Utility Commission Council; Fire Fighters (volunteers) Pension Commission Executive Director. In addition, there are five interstate compact commissions governing the rivers in Texas. The governor appoints the executive director of each of these commissions.

Boards and Commissions

state boards and commissions
Governing body for many state agencies; members appointed by the governor for fixed term.

In addition to these elected and appointed officials, the governor also appoints about 2,500 members to 285 **state boards and commissions.** (See table 8.3.) These administrative units carry out most of the work of state government. The board or commission usually appoints the head of the agency (e.g., chancellor of a university or executive director of a state agency) and in varying degrees is responsible for policy and administration of the agency. Most operate quite independently from other agencies of state government, excepting the legislature.

Given the lack of central control and the decentralized nature of state government in Texas, it is surprising that things work as well as they do. For example, there are some eighteen separate agencies that provide health and welfare services. In addition to the Department of Agriculture, the General Land Office, and the Railroad Commission—all having some control over environmental and natural resources—there are at least seven other agencies with independent boards or commissions with some authority in this area. These include the Texas Commission of Environmental Quality, the Texas Parks and Wildlife Department, the Soil and Water Conservation Board, and the Water Development Board.

In this conservative state with a strong belief in the free market there are, nonetheless, no fewer than thirty-eight separate professional licensing and examining boards. Think of a profession and there is probably a state agency that licenses and regulates that profession. Just a few examples are accountants, architects, barbers, chiropractors, cosmetologists, dentists, exterminators, funeral directors, land surveyors, medical doctors, two kinds of nurses, pharmacists, physical therapists, podiatrists, and veterinarians. Most often the professional group asks for regulation by the state. When such groups advocate government regulation and licensing, they claim they are primarily interested in protecting the public from incompetent or dishonest practitioners. This may be partially true; however, regulation also has the added benefit of limiting entry into the profession and the development of rules favorable to the group.

Two good examples are the water well drillers and landscape architects. (See Chapter 4 on interest groups.) Also, professionals always make the argument that the people appointed to the boards by the governor should be knowledgeable of the profession they are governing. While knowledge is one factor, the danger is that these boards and commissions, dominated by members of the profession, will be more inclined to make rules and regulations favorable to that group than to protect the public. Because of this fear, in recent years, the appointment of at least some members of the board from outside the profession has become the norm—for example, nonphysicians on the State Board of Medical Examiners.

There are twelve college governing boards that oversee the institutions of higher education in the state. These boards are required to coordinate their activities and gain approval for some activities and programs from the State Higher Education Coordinating Board. Within these broad guidelines each university governing board is relatively free to set policy, approve budgets, and govern their universities. Once again governance is decentralized, with only a minimum of control from the state and almost none from the governor.

Legislative Agencies

In addition to the previous executive agencies there are also several legislative agencies. These are units controlled by the leadership in the Texas house and senate. Their purpose is to provide legislative oversight of the "executive" agencies and to assist the legislature in its lawmaking functions.

Legislative Budget Board (LBB)   This agency is primarily responsible for preparing the state budget. It is composed of the lieutenant governor, the speaker of the house, four senators, and four state representatives. All agencies that receive state funds from the state budget must submit their requests for appropriations to the LBB. The LBB reviews these requests and proposes a budget to the state legislature. As was indicated before, unlike most other states, in Texas the governor plays a very limited role in budgeting.

Texas Legislative Council   The speaker, the lieutenant governor, four senators, and four state representatives control this agency. They appoint the executive director. This agency was created in 1949 to assist the legislature in drafting bills, conducting research on legislation, producing publications, and providing technical support services. This is a highly professional agency that produces information for the legislature that is made available to the public in various ways.

Legislative Audit Committee and State Auditor's Office   The **Legislative Audit Committee** consists of the lieutenant governor, the speaker of the house, and the chairs of the Senate Finance Committee and State Affairs Committee, and the House Appropriations Committee and Ways and Means Committee. This committee appoints the state auditor, who is responsible for auditing state agencies and assisting the legislature in its oversight functions.

Legislative Audit Committee
Legislative agency that performs audits on all state agencies.

Legislative Reference Library   This organization assists the legislature in doing research and serves as a depository of records for the legislature. The library, located in the State Capitol, is open to members of the public who wish to do research on the Texas legislature.

Judicial Agencies

There are several agencies that can be called judicial agencies and are under the supervision of the State Supreme Court (civil matters). Except for budgeting of money by the legislature, these agencies are relatively free of legislative oversight. The State Bar, which licenses attorneys, receives no state appropriations. The remaining agencies are responsible for court administration (Office of Court Administration), operations of the state law library, and certification of legal licenses and specializations.

Ex Officio Boards and Commissions

There are a number of state agencies that are headed by boards whose membership is completely or partially made up of designated state officials who are members because of the position they hold. Examples of these officials are the statewide elected officials—governor, lieutenant governor, speaker of the house, attorney general, and land commissioner. Examples of these agencies are the Bond Review Board, the Legislative Redistricting Board, and the Budget Execution Committee.

Multiappointment Boards

Finally, there are some state agencies that have governing boards whose members are appointed by more than one elected official. The reason for this is to prevent any one individual from dominating the selection process and the outcome of decisions. Examples of these agencies are the Texas Ethics Commission and the Criminal Justice Policy Council. For example, the Texas Ethics Commission has four members appointed by the governor and two each by the lieutenant governor and speaker of the house.

Democratic Control and Bureaucratic Responsiveness

The concept of democratic control requires that state agencies be responsible to the people—that is, that state agencies respond to demands placed on them by citizens. With Texas state administrative agencies operating quite independently of each other and overall administrative control being absent from state government, agencies are often able to respond only to clientele groups they serve and not the public generally. Thus most state agencies are accountable only to small groups of attentive citizens and not to the public generally. See Chapter 4 on interest groups for a more complete discussion of agency capture.

In other states accountability in a more general sense is ensured by giving the governor broader power to appoint agency heads (rather than independent boards and commissions) that serve at the pleasure of the governor. Also, some states have given the governor broad budgetary control over state agencies. Agencies are required to submit budget requests to the governor, who produces a state budget that is submitted to the state legislature. As indicated previously, in Texas the governor plays almost no role in the budgetary process. The Legislative Budget Board performs this function.

Thus state government in Texas is so fragmented and responsibility so divided that holding anyone responsible for state government is impossible. While citizens may blame the governor when things go wrong, and governors may claim credit when things go right, in truth the governor is responsible for very little and deserves credit for much less than most claim.

Sunset Advisory Commission
Agency responsible for making recommendations to the legislature for change in the structure and organization of most state agencies.

Sunset Review

Given the lack of overall, central control in state government and the limited and weak authority of the governor, in 1977 the Texas legislature created the ten-member **Sunset Advisory Commission** to review most state agencies every twelve years and recommend changes. This commission consists of four state senators, four members of the house of representatives, and two public members.

The sunset process is basically the "idea that legislative oversight of government operations can be enhanced by a systematic evaluation of state agencies."[35] The process works by establishing a date on which an agency of state government is abolished if the legislature does not pass a law providing for its continuance. The act does not apply to agencies created in the Texas Constitution or to some state agencies that are exempt. For example, state universities are not subject to sunset review. Sunset asks the basic question: "Do the policies carried out by an agency need to be continued?"[36]

In the twenty-five years of sunset review in Texas, very few (thirty-one) state agencies have been abolished. Most were minor state agencies with few functions. Most notable were the Boll Weevil Commission, the Battle Ship Texas Commission, and the Stonewall Jackson Memorial Board. More important than abolition is the review process. By forcing a review of an agency every twelve years, the legislature is given the opportunity to recommend changes to improve the efficiency and effectiveness of state government. In many cases functions of state agencies are transferred to other agencies, and agencies are combined or merged. Table 8.8 lists the activities of the Texas Sunset Advisory Commission over the last twenty-five years.

In addition to agencies being abolished or merged and functions transferred, the sunset review process also allows the legislature to recommend improvements in efficiency and effectiveness. Finally, sunset review has also forced public evaluation of many agencies that operate much out of the public's attention. This is especially true of those agencies that license professions. Sunset review resulted in the appointment of nonprofessionals to these agencies in an effort to promote the broader interests of the public over the narrow interests of the agency and its clientele.

TABLE 8.8

Overview of Sunset Actions in Texas, 1979–2003

Year	Session	Reviews	Agencies Continued	Agencies Abolished	Functions Transferred	Functions Merged	Separated
1979	66	26	12	8	1	4	1
1981	67	28	22	2	3	1	0
1983	68	32	29	3	0	0	0
1985	69	31	24	6	0	0	1
1987	70	20	18	1	1	0	0
1989	71	30	25	3	2	0	0
1991	72	30	23	3	3	1	0
1993	73	31	27	1	1	2	0
1995	74	18	16	0	2	0	0
1997	75	21	19	0	2	0	0
1999	76	25	22	1	0	2	0
2001	77	25	23	1	0	1	0
2003	78	26	23	3	0	0	0
2005	79	23	21	6	2	0	0
2007	80	20	18	2	0	0	0
Total		**386**	**322**	**40**	**17**	**11**	**2**

TABLE 8.9

Number of State Government Employees Top 15 Texas Agencies 2007

Ranking	Agency	2006 Number of Employees
1	Department of Criminal Justice	39,339
2	Department of Transportation	14,831
3	Department of Aging and Disability Services	14,607
4	Department of State Health Services	11,807
5	Health and Human Services Commission	9,586
6	Department of Family and Protective Services	8,443
7	Department of Public Safety	7,741
8	Youth Commission	4,959
9	Office of the Attorney General	4,139
10	Texas Workforce Commission	3,500
11	Department of Assistive and Rehabilitative Services	3,126
12	Commission on Environmental Quality	2,990
13	Parks and Wildlife Department	2,961
14	Comptroller of Public Accounts	2,894
15	Texas Department of Insurance	1,845

Notes: Institutions of higher education are excluded. Represents full-time-equivalent positions.

Sources: Legislative Budget Board (*www.lbb.state.tx.us*). *Texas Fact Book* 2006–07.

State Employees

As indicated in Chapter 10 on state finances, most of the funds appropriated by state legislature go to pay for personnel. This is the largest single expenditure item for all state governments. Table 8.9 shows the number of employees for the top fifteen agencies, excluding institutions of higher education. Also, schoolteachers, employed by local school districts, are not included in these figures.

There is no general civil service system or central personnel agency in Texas. Each agency creates its own set of rules and regulations regarding personnel practices and procedures. In most states there is a central personnel system and some form of civil service system that formulates personnel policies and procedures. In keeping with the decentralized nature of state government, the personnel system in Texas is also very decentralized.

Approximately 76 percent of Texas state employees work in the five major functional areas of state government: corrections, highways, public welfare, hospitals, and higher education.

The number of state employees has declined slightly in recent years due in part to the performance review audits conducted by Comptroller John Sharp. Among the fifteen most populous states, Texas ranks tenth in the number of state employees per 10,000 populations. Still, the state of Texas is the largest single employer in Texas.

❖ CONCLUSIONS

Even though governors in most states do not have much formal power, the office has great importance in state politics. In recent years, the importance of the office has increased. Four of the last five U.S. presidents have all been former governors. The office has become increasingly more visible in both state and national politics. The need for strong leadership in this office will continue to increase.

Texas is now the second-largest state in population and one of the leading states in industrial growth. The governor's lack of formal power makes the task of governing this large, diverse, and economically important state both difficult and challenging. Some reform of the powers of the governor is still needed, but it is doubtful that such changes will occur. The political culture of the state does not support increasing the authority of the governor's office. Leadership will have to come from force of will and personality and not from formal changes in structure.

Interest groups are not supportive of transferring power from state agencies they can dominate, to agencies under the control of a single individual appointed by the governor. (See Chapter 4.) While the Sunset Advisory Commission has had a positive impact on some agencies, general reorganization of state government is not likely anytime soon.

INTERNET RESOURCES

Texas Governor's Office: *www.governor.state.tx.us/*
Legislative Budget Board: *www.lbb.state.tx.us/*
  Information on governors' budget proposals.
Council of State Governments: *www.csg.org/*
  Up-to-date information on state governments and governors.
National Governors Association: *www.nga.org/*
  National association of American state governors. This site provides a thorough discussion of each state's

governors and their backgrounds and biographies, powers, offices, and administrative and policymaking duties.
Each of the state agencies has its own Web page. They can be found at the official website for the State of Texas: *www.texasonline.state.tx.us*
  There are also links to other organizations.
Center for American Women and Politics: *www.cawp.rutgers.edu/*

KEY TERMS

acting governor (p. 165)
appointive power (p. 168)
attorney general (p. 181)
budgetary powers (p. 172)
ceremonial duties (p. 159)
chief legislator (p. 159)
comptroller of public accounts (p. 182)
crisis manager (p. 161)
impeachment and conviction (p. 166)
informal qualifications (p. 162)

intergovernmental coordinator (p. 161)
Jacksonian statehouse government (p. 168)
judicial powers (p. 176)
land commissioner (p. 183)
Legislative Audit Committee (p. 187)
Legislative Budget Board (p. 173)
legislative power (p. 174)
line-item vetoes (p. 173)
military powers (p. 176)

partial vetoes (p. 174)
party chief (p. 159)
plural executive (p. 180)
recall of the governor (p. 166)
secretary of state (SOS) (p. 185)
senatorial courtesy (p. 169)
state boards and commissions (p. 186)
Sunset Advisory Commission (p. 188)
tenure of office (p. 167)
Texas Railroad Commission (p. 183)

NOTES

1. Thad L. Beyle, "Governors: The Middlemen and Women in Our Political System," in *Politics in the American States,* 6th ed., eds. Virginia Gray and Herbert Jacob (Washington, D.C.: Congressional Quarterly Press, 2004), 197.

2. Ibid., 197.

3. National Governors Association (*www.nga .org/governors/*).

4. *Book of the States,* 2006, table 4.11, p. 175.

5. Thad L. Beyle, "Governors," in *Politics in the American States,* 4th ed., eds. Virginia Gray, Herbert Jacob, and Kenneth N. Vine (Boston: Little, Brown, 1983), 217.

6. *Book of the States, 1994–95,* 66.

7. Ibid.

8. Bowman and Kearney, *State and Local Government,* 206.

9. Benton, *Texas,* 222–24.

10. Victor E. Harlow, *Harlow's History of Oklahoma,* 5th ed. (Norman, Okla.: Harlow, 1967), 294–315.

11. Daniel R. Grant and Lloyd B. Omdahl, *State and Local Government in America* (Madison, Wis.: Brown & Benchmark, 1987), 260.

12. S.M. Morehouse, *State Politics, Parties and Policy* (New York: Holt, Rinehart & Winston, 1981), 206.

13. Beyle, "Governors: The Middlemen and Women in Our Political System," 230.

14. Ibid., 231.

15. Allan Shivers was elected lieutenant governor in 1946. Governor Beauford H. Jester died in July 1949. Shivers then became governor, and he was reelected in 1950, 1952, and 1954.

16. *Texas Almanac 1994–95,* 519.

17. Beyle, "Governors: The Middlemen and Women in Our Political System," 221.

18. Ibid., 231.

19. Until 1996 the voters also elected a state treasurer. In 1996 the voters approved a constitutional amendment abolishing that office. These functions have been transferred to other state agencies.

20. *Guide to Texas State Agencies* (Austin: University of Texas, Lyndon B. Johnson School of Public Affairs, 1994).

21. Ibid.

22. *Book of the States, 1998–99,* 22, table 2.4.

23. Ibid.

24. Beyle, "Governors: The Middlemen and Women in Our Political System," 234.

25. Ibid., 235.

26. *Book of the States, 1998–99,* 20, table 2.3.

27. Anderson, Murray, and Farley, *Texas Politics,* 122.

28. Deborah K. Wheeler, *Two Men, Two Governors, Two Pardons: A Study of Pardon Policy of Governor Miriam Ferguson.* Unpublished copyrighted paper, presented at State Historical Society Meeting, March 1998, Austin, Texas.

29. Bill Hobby, "Speaking of Pardons, Texas Has Had Its Share." *Houston Chronicle,* 18 February 2001, p. 4c.

30. Beyle, "Governors: The Middlemen and Women in Our Political System," 237.

31. Legislative Budget Board, *Fiscal Size Up 1998–99 Biennium: Texas State Services,* 4–6, Austin, Texas.

32. Ibid., 4–7.

33. *Book of the States, 1996–97,* 33–34.

34. *Fiscal Size Up 2002–03,* 242.

35. Texas Sunset Advisory Commission, *Guide to the Texas Sunset Process, 1997,* Austin, Texas, 1997, p.1.

36. Ibid.

CHAPTER 9

THE COURT
SYSTEM IN TEXAS

Most citizens hold two conflicting views of the appropriate roles of courts in a democratic society. First, citizens think the court system should be above politics. Courts are expected to act in nonpolitical ways. Justice is often portrayed as a "blind-folded woman holding the scales of justice in her hand. Most Americans firmly believe that courts should be blind to political bias: fairness, it would seem, requires neutrality."[1] Second, Americans also want state courts to be responsive to the electorate, "especially if they play prominent roles in molding and implementing public policy."[2] But obviously, courts cannot be both above politics and responsive to the electorate.

Most citizens do not see a conflict between these two ideas. They think that courts should both dispense pure justice and do so according to the wishes of the electorate. Courts are placed in this position because they make decisions on matters ranging from domestic and family law to criminal law and they serve as the final arbitrator of highly political decisions. In playing the dual roles of decision maker and policy-maker, courts function very differently from other institutions.

✦ COURT DECISION MAKING

The courts' approach to decision making is quite different from how the executive and legislative branches make decisions.[3] Courts must maintain a **passive appearance.** Unlike the legislature or governor, who can initiate policy changes, courts must wait for a case to come to them. Most cases do not involve policy questions but deal with controversies between individuals. Courts enforce existing rules and laws; they are arbitrators of conflict, not initiators of laws.

Second, courts have **strict rules of access.**[4] While any citizen may approach the legislature or the governor, courts have rules that limit access to them. Individuals must have "standing." This means that the case must involve real controversies between two or more parties, and someone must have suffered real damage. Courts do not deal in hypothetical or imaginary controversies. In short, they do not play "what if" ("What if I hit this person? What will the court do?").

Courts are governed by **strict procedural rules** that determine when and how facts and arguments can be presented.[5] These rules prevent the introduction of some evidence in a criminal case. For example, evidence gathered by the police in an illegal search may not be allowed.

Generally, a court's decisions affect only the cases being considered by the court and not other cases before other courts.[6] This means that court decisions do not have an effect beyond the specific case being considered. Rarely do trial court decisions have the effect of making general policy. Actions by the legislature do have the effect of making general policy. For example, if a trial court rules that a city ordinance in one city is invalid, this does not invalidate all similar ordinances in other cities. Ordinances in other cities, with slightly different details, might be legal. The court must decide each case separately.

passive appearance
The procedure of courts not initiating cases but waiting for cases to be brought to the court.

strict rules of access
The limited access to courts because of special rules that determine if the court will or can hear the case. Only hears real controversies.

strict procedural rules
The tight rules of courts regarding how cases must proceed and what evidence can be presented in court.

The old restored Texas Supreme Courtroom in the state capital.

There is an exception to this general rule. The rulings of appellate and supreme courts establish rules of law, called *precedent,* which lower courts must follow. Under English law this is called **stare decisis** ("to stand by that which was decided before"). Courts follow principles announced in former cases and diverge from these only when they can show good cause for doing so. In this way, appellate courts affect how trial courts make decisions; however, each case in a lower court might be affected slightly differently.

Courts also differ from other branches of government in that they must maintain the **appearance of objectivity.**[7] Unlike governors and legislators, courts may not appear to be political in their decision making, even though judges might be affected in their decisions by political considerations. Judges must base their decisions on points of law. The result may be quite political, but the process must not appear to be.

Thus, courts differ from governors and legislators in the way they make decisions. They must maintain a passive role, enforce rules that restrict access to the courts, uphold strict rules of procedure, confine their decisions to the **specifics of the cases** before them, and maintain the appearance of objectivity. By doing this, courts help to reinforce the legitimacy of their decisions and their place as the final arbitrators of conflict. This in turn reinforces the concept that the rule of law, and not the rule of arbitrary actions by individuals, governs.

stare decisis
Court decisions depending on previous rulings of other courts.

appearance of objectivity
The appearance that courts make objective decisions and not political ones.

specifics of the case
The fact that court decisions apply only to the case heard in court and not to other cases or issues.

➔ JUDICIAL FEDERALISM

The U.S. Constitution established the U.S. Supreme Court and gave Congress the authority to create other lower federal courts. Article 6 of the U.S. Constitution makes national law the **supreme law of the land.**

States also create state-level courts. This results in a dual court system of both federal and state courts. Federal courts hear cases involving federal laws, and state courts hear cases involving state laws. While there are some cases that might be filed in either state or federal court, most cases go to state courts and not to federal courts. An example

supreme law of the land
The superiority of federal law over state law.

HIGHLIGHT

The Application of Court Rulings

Court rulings in one case do not automatically apply to all similar cases. Two Texas cities (Missouri City and College Station) both had park land dedication ordinances. The Missouri City ordinance was ruled unconstitutional and the College Station ordinance was upheld. Both dealt with park land dedication, but the ordinances were different.

Most cities require land developers to donate land for streets and public rights-of-way when they subdivide land. Missouri City required land developers to donate park land or money for neighborhood park development, but the city could spend the money collected from developers on parks many miles from that development. The development did not directly benefit from the dedication of money by the developer. This ordinance was tried in the Texas courts. The court of appeals ruled the Missouri City ordinance unconsti-

tutional because it took property from developers for which they received no benefit.

College Station also had a park land and money dedication ordinance, but it differed from the Missouri City ordinance in one significant way. Money collected from developers for parks had to be spent in the immediate neighborhood. If the money was not spent within three years, it would be returned to the developer. The Turtle Rock Corporation, a land development company in College Station, refused to pay the park fee, citing the Missouri City case as their reason.

College Station sued, and the Texas Supreme Court upheld the city ordinance. Money spent for parks in College Station benefited the development by providing parks in the neighborhood of the development. This was not true with the Missouri City ordinance (*Turtle Rock Development Corporation v. City of College Station*).

of a case that could have gone to either court system is the case involving the bombing of a federal office building in Oklahoma City. While murder is a crime in Oklahoma, a bombing of a federal facility that results in the death of a federal government employee is a federal crime. Another example is the case of the Unabomber, in which persons were murdered by bombs, most of which were sent through the U.S. mail. Both of these cases were tried in federal court. Initially state prosecutors indicated that they might also file state murder charges against the Unabomber suspect. This did not happen.

Few other countries have dual court systems. Ours developed because of our federal system of government. State courts existed during the colonial period and continued after the adoption of the U.S. Constitution in 1789. State courts act primarily in areas where the federal government lacks authority to act.

✦ TRIAL AND APPELLATE COURTS

trial courts
Local courts that hear cases; juries determine the outcome of the cases heard in the court.

There are two kinds of state courts: **trial courts** and **appellate courts.** They differ in several important ways. First, trial courts are localized. Jurisdiction is limited to a geographic area such as a county.[8] Second, only one judge presides over a trial court, and each court is considered a separate court. Third, citizens participate in trial court activity. They serve as members of juries and as witnesses during trials. Fourth, trial courts are primarily concerned with establishing the facts of a case (such as a determination that a person is guilty). Fifth, trial courts announce decisions immediately after the trial is finished.[9]

appellate courts
Higher-level courts that decide on points of law and not questions of guilt or innocence.

Appellate courts, on the other hand, are centralized, often at the state level. More than one judge presides, citizen participation is virtually absent, and, most importantly, appellate courts decide points of law, not points of fact. An appeal of a murder conviction from a trial court to a higher court is not based on points of fact (Is the person guilty?) but on points of law (Were legal procedures followed?). Trial courts establish guilt, and appellate courts decide whether proper procedures have been followed.

In Texas all death penalty cases are automatically appealed to the Texas Court of Criminal Appeals. The issue is not the guilt or innocence of the person but whether all procedures were properly followed in the trial court.

✦ THE STRUCTURE OF STATE COURTS

Most states provide for three levels of courts: trial courts, appellate courts, and a supreme court. The structure of courts in Texas is more complicated, as can be seen in figure 9.1. Texas has several levels of trial courts and appellate courts. Trial courts are the justices of the peace, municipal courts, county courts, district courts, and special purpose courts such as probate, juvenile, and domestic relations courts. In Texas there are fourteen intermediate appellate courts and two "supreme" appellate courts: one for civil (Supreme Court) and one for criminal cases (the Court of Criminal Appeals). (See figure 9.1.)

Magistrate or Minor Courts

All states provide for some type of minor or magistrate court, usually called the *justice of the peace.* These courts hear cases involving misdemeanors, most often traffic violations and minor civil cases. In Texas there are two courts at this level: justices of the peace (JPs) and municipal courts. Municipal courts hear cases involving violations of city ordinances, most often traffic tickets. In 2003, 85 percent of all cases in municipal courts regarded traffic violations.[10] These courts also have **magistrate functions,** involving preliminary hearings for persons charged with a serious offense. These persons are informed of the

magistrate functions
Preliminary hearings for persons charged with a serious criminal offense.

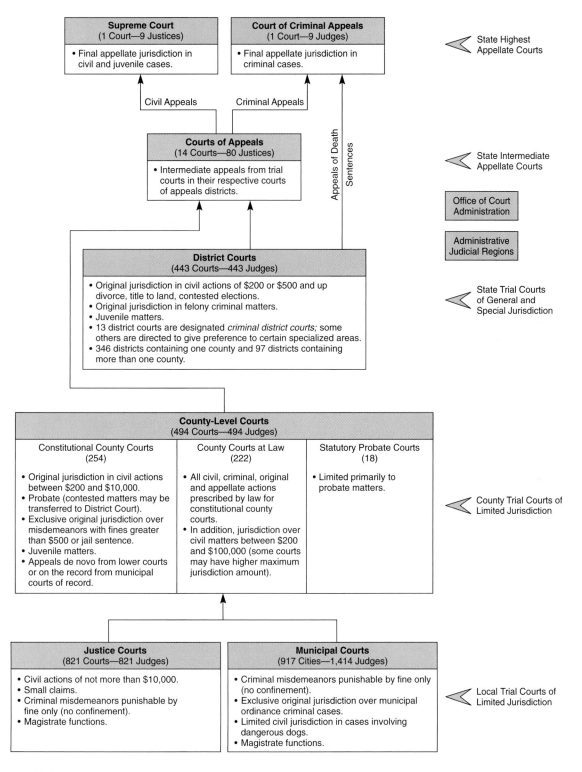

FIGURE 9.1   *Court Structure of Texas, 2008.*

SOURCE: http://www.courts.state.tx.us/

charges against them, told of their rights, and bail is set. As magistrates, municipal judges and JPs can also issue search-and-arrest warrants. JP courts also perform these magistrate functions and hear minor criminal cases, most of which involve traffic tickets issued by the Texas Highway Patrol or county deputy sheriffs. JP courts also serve as small claims courts in Texas. Municipal courts do not.[11] Jurisdiction in small claims is limited to a maximum of $15,000. Ninety percent of the cases in the JP courts are criminal misdemeanor cases; most are traffic cases (66 percent). Only 10 percent are civil cases.

County Courts

In Texas there are two kinds of county courts: constitutional county courts and county courts at law. The state constitution creates a county court in each of the 254 counties in the state and the state legislature has created 209 statutory county courts at law and 17 probate courts. County courts at law are created in large urban counties. In those counties, the constitutional county court ceases to function as a court, and the "county judge" becomes the administrative officer or county executive but retains the title *judge* and some limited judicial functions.

The state constitution determines the jurisdiction of constitutional county courts. The jurisdiction of county courts at law is set by the act passed by the legislature creating the court and varies from court to court. The general levels of jurisdiction are shown in figure 9.1.

County courts primarily hear intermediate criminal and civil cases. Most criminal cases are misdemeanors. Driving while intoxicated (DWI) cases make up a large portion of their docket, as do probate of wills and family law cases such as divorce and child custody. In 2003, there were 1,169,000 cases filed in county courts. Of these, 20 percent were for theft or worthless checks, 18 percent were DWI, 10 percent were assault, 9 percent were for violation of drug laws, 14 percent were traffic ticket appeals from JP and municipal courts, and 29 percent were other criminal offenses.

County courts also serve as appellate courts for cases heard by JP and municipal courts. All JP and most municipal courts in Texas are **trial *de novo* courts** and not courts of record. In trial *de novo* courts, no record of the proceeding is kept and cases may be appealed for any reason. It is a common practice in Texas to appeal traffic tickets to the county court, where, due to heavy caseloads, they get buried. If a person has the resources to hire a lawyer, there is a good chance the ticket will be "forgotten" in case overload.

trial *de novo* courts
Courts that do not keep a written record of their proceedings. Cases on appeal begin as new cases in the appellate courts.

District Courts

In most states, major trial courts are called district or superior courts. These courts hear major criminal and civil cases. Examples of major criminal cases (felonies) are murder, armed robbery, and car theft. Whether a civil case is major is generally established by the dollar amount of damages claimed in the case. In Texas in 2003, there were 420 district courts. These courts are created by the state legislature. Large urban counties generally have several district courts. In rural areas, district courts may serve several counties. The jurisdiction of these courts often overlaps with county courts and cases may be filed in either court. Other cases must begin in district courts. (See figure 9.1.)

Appellate Courts

Ten states do not have courts of appeal, and twenty-three states have only one court of appeals. The other states, primarily large urban states, have several courts of appeal.[12] Texas has fourteen courts of appeal with eighty judges elected by districts in the state. Only California has more judges and courts at this level. These courts hear all civil appeals cases and all criminal appeals except those involving the death penalty, which go directly to the Court of Criminal Appeals. (See figure 9.1.)

Supreme Courts

All states have a supreme court, or court of last resort. Texas, like Oklahoma, has two supreme courts.[13] Oklahoma copied the idea from Texas when it entered the Union in 1907. The highest court in Texas for civil matters is the Texas Supreme Court, and the highest court in Texas for criminal cases is the Court of Criminal Appeals. Each court consists of nine judges elected statewide for six-year overlapping terms.

→ JUDICIAL SELECTION

Under the U.S. Constitution, all federal judges are appointed by the president and serve for life. A lifetime appointment means that a judge continues to serve during good behavior and can be removed only for cause. Among the states, a variety of methods are used to select judges. Seven of the original thirteen states allow some judges to be appointed by the governor and serve for life. Four states, also among the original thirteen, allow the legislature to elect judges.[14] Some states use partisan elections to select some judges. Candidates must run in a primary and general election. Still other states elect some state judges in nonpartisan general elections. Last, some states use the **merit system,** or **Missouri system,** to select some judges. Under this plan, the governor appoints judges from a list submitted by a screening committee of legal officials. After appointment, a judge serves for a set term and is then subjected to a retention election in which the voters decide whether the judge retains the office.

The method of selection also varies between courts within some states. For example, in some states, appellate court judges are chosen by a merit system and the voters elect trial court judges. Table 9.1 shows the number of states using each selection method for appellate and trial courts. Most states have moved away from partisan election of judges and use either a nonpartisan election or a merit system.

merit system, or Missouri system

A system of electing judges that involves appointment by the governor and periodic retention election.

TABLE 9.1

Methods of Selecting Judges

	Number of States Using Method*
Appellate Court Judges	
Legislative election	2
Appointment by governor	3
Partisan election	7
Nonpartisan election	14
Merit plan	24
Trial Court Judges	
Legislative election	2
Appointment by governor	2
Partisan election	11
Nonpartisan election	16
Merit plan	19

Source: Council of State Governments, *The Book of the States 2006* (Lexington, Ky.: Council of State Governments, 2006), 256–258, table 5.9.

*Does not add to 50 because some states use more than one method to select judges. For example, district judges are elected; appellate judges are appointed.

TABLE 9.2

Judicial Selection of State Supreme Court Judges

Partisan Election	Nonpartisan Election	Missouri Plan	Appointment
Alabama	Arkansas	Alaska	Connecticut
Illinois	Georgia	Arizona	Delaware
Louisiana	Idaho	California	Hawaii
New Mexico	Kentucky	Colorado	Maine
Pennsylvania	Michigan	Florida	Massachusetts
Texas	Minnesota	Indiana	New Hampshire
West Virginia	Mississippi	Iowa	New Jersey
	Montana	Kansas	New York
	Nevada	Maryland	Rhode Island
	North Carolina	Missouri	South Carolina
	North Dakota	Nebraska	Vermont
	Ohio	Oklahoma	Virginia
	Oregon	South Dakota	
	Washington	Tennessee	
	Wisconsin	Utah	
		Wyoming	

Table shows how judges are normally selected. Some judges in partisan and nonpartisan systems may get their initial seat by appointment of the governor.

Source: American Judicature Society, *Judicial Selection in the States* (Chicago: American Judicature Society: 2006).

Table 9.2 shows how states initially select judges to the supreme court in that state. As was indicated above, some states use different methods to select appellate court judges and trial court judges.

→ JUDICIAL SELECTION IN TEXAS

partisan election
Method used to select all judges (except municipal court judges) in Texas by using a ballot in which party identification is shown.

In Texas trial court judges are elected in partisan elections for four-year terms and all appellate court judges are elected in **partisan elections** for six-year terms. The only exceptions to this are municipal court judges. Most municipal judges are appointed by the mayor or the city council (812 are appointed and only 18 are elected). In Texas the question of judicial selection has been an issue for the last fifteen to twenty years. In 1995 the Texas Supreme Court established the Commission on Judicial Efficiency to make recommendations on the method of judicial selection, and other issues, to the 1997 session of the Texas legislature, but the legislature took no action on their recommendations. In the 1999 session of the legislature, several bills were introduced to change judicial selections but none passed. In 2001 seven bills were introduced that call for the appointment or **nonpartisan election** of some judges in Texas. None passed. And in 2003, six such bills were introduced and none passed. In 2005 session four bills were filed to move to nonpartisan elections and none passed.

nonpartisan election
Election of judges in which party identification does not appear on the ballot.

Issues in Judicial Selection: Familiar Names

Several events have brought the issue of judicial selection to the forefront in Texas today. The first of these is electoral problems. Although elections are at the very heart of any democracy, they are imperfect instruments for deciding the qualifications of the persons seeking office. This is especially true for judicial offices, for which qualifications are extremely important. The average voter in Texas will be asked to vote for judges for the Texas Supreme Court and the Court of Criminal Appeals, and, in large urban counties, several district judges, county judges, and JPs. Most voters go to the election booth with scant knowledge about the qualifications of judicial candidates, and they often end up voting by **name familiarity.** There are two good examples of this happening in Texas. In 1976 voters elected Don Yarbrough to the Texas Supreme Court. Yarbrough was an unknown attorney from Houston who won nomination as the Democratic candidate and claimed after the election that God had told him to run. Many voters had thought he was Don Yarborough, who had run unsuccessfully for governor. Still others thought he was Ralph Yarbrough, who had served in the U.S. Senate for two terms. Judge Yarbrough was forced to resign after about six months because criminal charges were filed against him. He was later convicted of perjury and sentenced to five years in jail, but jumped bond. He then attended medical school in Grenada, which refused extradition to the United States. He was arrested on St. Thomas, Virgin Islands, while attending medical school classes and returned to Texas, where he was eventually sentenced to five years in prison.[15]

> **name familiarity**
> Practice in Texas of voting for judges with familiar or popular names.

In 1990 there was a similar case of voting based on name familiarity. In that year, Gene Kelly won the Democratic party primary for a seat on the Texas Supreme Court. Some citizens thought he was the famous dancer and film star from the 1950s and 1960s. However, this Gene Kelly was a retired Air Force judge with little nonmilitary experience. Kelly lost to Republican John Cornyn after extensive television commercials questioned his competency. Some have suggested that Justice Sam Houston Clinton may have also benefited from name recognition in his election to the Texas Court of Criminal Appeals.

Straight Ticket Voting

Another electoral problem that has surfaced in recent years is **straight ticket voting.** Texas is one of fourteen states that allow straight ticket voting. Straight ticket voting allows a voter to vote for all candidates in a party by making a single mark. In 1984 many incumbent Democratic judges lost their seats in large urban counties to unknown Republican challengers because of Republican straight ticket voting. Other examples have occurred since 1984. In Harris County in 1994 only one incumbent Democrat was re-elected and Republicans defeated sixteen Democrats because of straight ticket voting. Many of the Republican replacements lacked judicial experience, and one had no courtroom experience. Also in 1994, Steve Mansfield, an individual who had very limited legal experience and no experience in criminal law, was elected to the Texas Court of Criminal Appeals, the highest court for criminal matters in Texas. After the elections, questions were raised about Mansfield's qualifications. In his state bar application, he had failed to acknowledge that he was behind in his child support payments. This raised the possibility that he could be disbarred and therefore ineligible to serve. Some statewide officials called for his resignation. This would have been no loss to the Republicans; if he resigned, then Governor Bush would have made an appointment to fill the vacancy, and he would likely choose a Republican.

> **straight ticket voting**
> System that allows voters to vote for all candidates of a single political party by making a single mark and that has resulted in an increase in the number of Republican judges.

A similar case occurred in the 2002 election. Steven W. Smith, the chief litigant behind the Hopwood case that limited the use of racial quotas in selecting law school students at the University of Texas, won election to the Texas Supreme Court. Despite being a Republican, he had little support from statewide party officials and few endorsements from state bar associations; he still managed to win election due to straight ticket voting. He received about the same percentage of votes as other Republican candidates for statewide judicial office. A study by Richard Murray at the University of Houston

BUT I THOUGHT IT WAS THE OTHER DON YARBOROUGH!

Ignorance about candidates often leads voters to vote by name familiarity.

"Justice for Sale"

Title of a PBS program charging that judges on appellate and supreme courts are under the influence of those who contribute to their campaigns.

demonstrated that about 54 percent of the votes cast in Harris County in both 1998 and 2002 were straight ticket votes. A Republican running for countywide office had a 14,000 vote head start.[16]

In the 2006 elections in Dallas County, the straight ticket voters reversed the tables on Republicans by replacing all countywide elected officials with Democrats. The case was similar to the actions in Harris County in 1994 where people with little judicial experience were elected.

These recent cases of straight ticket voting have caused some to call for nonpartisan election of state judges. In every session since 1995, bills have been introduced that called for the nonpartisan election of district judges and a merit system for appellate judges. Yet another suggestion is to prohibit straight ticket voting in judicial races, which has been considered in past sessions. This would force voters to mark the ballot for each judicial race. Given the recent success of Republicans in gaining control of the legislature and the judiciary, this idea might lack strong support in the legislature.

Campaign Contributions

Another issue is campaign contributions. Under the Texas partisan election system, judges must win nomination in the party primary and in the general election. Two elections, stretching over ten months (January to November), can be a costly process. In 1984 Chief Justice John L. Hill spent over $1 million to win the chief justice race. The cost of this race and other experiences caused Hill and two other Democratic justices to resign from the Supreme Court in 1988. They called for a merit system to replace partisan elections. These resignations, along with other openings on the court, resulted in six of the nine seats on the Supreme Court being up for election. The total cost of these six races exceeded $10 million. One candidate spent over $2 million.[17]

Races for district judgeships can also be very costly. Money often comes from law firms that have business before the judges who receive the money. Other money comes from interest groups, such as the Texas Medical Association, which has an interest in limiting malpractice tort claims in cases before the courts. The Public Broadcasting System's *Frontline* television series recently ran a program titled **"Justice for Sale"** on the Texas courts and money. The Internet site is listed at the end of this chapter. This report details how eight justices on the Supreme Court in 1994 received over $9 million primarily from corporations and law firms. In the 2002 election cycle there were five of nine seats on the court up for election including the chief justice. Close to $5 million had been raised by November of 2002. Many of these contributions came from large law firms that had cases before the court.

The basic question raised by these contributions is their impact on judicial impartiality. Do these contributions influence the decisions made by judges? According to a poll by the Citizens for Public Justice, the average Texan thinks this money influences judges (73 percent). Even court personnel (69 percent) felt that the money influences judges. Lawyers were even more certain (77 percent), and since they contribute about 40 percent of the money, they may be in a position to know. About half of the judges (47 percent) thought the money influences their decisions. When people lose confidence in courts, the respect for law declines. It is this that should be of concern to all citizens.

Limits on Campaign Contributions to Judicial Candidates

Effective 16 June 1995, the Texas legislature passed a law that aimed to reduce abuses of campaign contributions. This law limits the amount of money that individuals, PACs, law firms, and political party organizations can contribute to judicial races. Under this act, corporations are prohibited from making campaign contributions.

The amount of money an individual, PAC, law firm, or party organization can contribute is proportional to the population of the district or county from which the judge is seeking election, and is highest for statewide offices. Unlike state representatives and senators, the number of people in a judicial election unit can vary greatly. Judges in Dallas County must run countywide and appeal to several hundred thousand potential voters. Judges in rural counties might have only a few thousand voters in their district.

The total amount of money a candidate may spend in seeking office is also limited. The limits are as follows:

$2 million for candidates for statewide judicial office
$500,000 for candidates for courts of appeal where the population is more than a million
$350,000 for candidates for chief justice of courts of appeal where the population in the district is less than a million
$200,000 for candidates for district or county courts where the population of the district or county is between a million and 250,000
$100,000 for candidates for district or county courts where the population is less than 250,000

All provisions of this law are voluntary. A candidate may file a declaration of intention not to comply with the provisions of this act. Candidates who file such a declaration must place a notice of noncompliance on all their campaign literature and advertisements. Candidates who comply may state in their literature that they are complying. Noncompliance by an opponent supposedly would become an issue in the campaign, and this is the intent of the act. However, the effect of this act has been marginal at best. Since 1996 when the law went into effect, no one has made an issue of noncompliance. It has had no effect upon campaign contributions or expenditures. Unless these provisions are made mandatory this law will have no effect.

Minority Representation

A fourth electoral issue is **minority representation.** District and county court judges all run for election on a countywide basis. Countywide races for judgeships create the same problem for minorities as multimember legislative districts do. (See chapter 7.) Minority judges have not been successful in races for at-large, countywide offices. The problem is especially difficult in nine urban counties (Harris, Dallas, Bexar, Tarrant, Jefferson, Lubbock, Ector, Midland, and Travis). In 1989 the League of United Latin American Citizens (LULAC) sued, claiming that at-large election of judges in these counties was a violation of the Voting Rights Act. In 1989 the federal district court in Midland, Texas, ruled the Texas system in violation of the Voting Rights Act. On appeal, the Fifth Federal Circuit Court, in 1994, reversed this decision, and the U.S. Supreme Court refused to hear the case, thus upholding the federal circuit court.[18]

Opponents of single-member district elections in urban counties claim that partisan voting was more significant than ethnicity in these judicial elections. The two are obviously related. One could make the same argument that if all twenty-four delegates from Harris County to the Texas house of representatives were elected at large, few minorities would be elected because of straight ticket voting. The issue of minority

minority representation
Election of judges from single-member districts in major urban counties to allow minority judges to be elected.

representation in the state judiciary remains politically active but is judicially dead. Any change would have to come from the legislature.

Conclusions on Judicial Selection

Thus, over the last two decades, several highly political issues have driven demands for change in the way Texas selects its judges. Voting based on name recognition and party label has resulted in the election of persons of questionable qualifications. Campaign contributions from groups with vested interests in cases before the courts have raised the specter of judicial bias or justice for sale. For various reasons the legislature has not acted to correct any of these problems. Last, in large urban counties, minority representation on state district and county courts is biased by at-large elections at the county level.

✦ THE "APPOINTIVE-ELECTIVE" SYSTEM IN TEXAS

appointive-elective system
In Texas, the system of many judges getting the initial seat on the court by being appointed and later standing for election.

Reformers who include some of the best legal minds in the state are calling for change from the current partisan election system. Both nonpartisan and merit systems are being suggested. Some have pointed out that the state already has an **appointive-elective system.** The Texas governor can fill any seat for district or appellate court that becomes vacant due to death or resignation, or any new district court position created by the legislature. Vacancies in the county courts and justice of the peace courts are filled by the county governing body, the County Commissioners Court. Persons appointed to fill vacancies serve until the next regular election for that office, when they must stand for regular election.

Historically, many judges in Texas initially receive their seats on the courts by appointment. The data are not complete for all time periods, but enough is available to show that this is a common practice. Between 1940 and 1962, about 66 percent of the district and appellate judges were appointed by the governor to their first term on the court. In 1976, 150 sitting district court judges were appointed.[19] Table 9.3 shows data on appointments of sitting judges in 2005. As you can see, many judges in all state courts get their appointment to serve.

TABLE 9.3

Texas Judges Serving in 2007 Who Were Appointed to Their Initial Seat on the Court

	Appointed		Elected	
	N	%	N	%
Supreme Court	5	56	4	44
Court of Criminal Appeals	1	11	8	89
Courts of Appeals	42	53	37	47
District Courts	159	38	265	63
County Courts at Law	64	29	157	71
Probate Courts	7	38	11	61
Constitutional County Courts	43	17	210	83
Justice of the Peace Courts	207	25	608	75
Municipal Courts	1,368	99	15	1

Source: Office of Court Administration, Profile of Justices in 2007. See Web site at end of the chapter. Note appellate and district court judges are appointed by the governor. County court judges and JPs are appointed by the County Commissioners.

✦ JUDICIAL SELECTION: IS THERE A BEST SYSTEM?

The debate in Texas over judicial selection will continue in future sessions of the legislature. Judicial selection revolves around three basic issues. Citizens expect judges to be (1) competent, (2) independent and not subject to political pressures, and (3) responsive, or subject to democratic control. Each method used by the states to select judges has strengths and weaknesses regarding each of these issues. (See table 9.4.)

When judicial selection is by appointment by the governor, there is great potential for selection of judges who are competent. However, it does not ensure competence. Governors can use judicial appointments to reward friends and repay political debts. All U.S. presidents, some more than others, have used their judicial appointive powers to select federal judges with political philosophies similar to their own. Governors do the same thing. In such cases, questions of judicial competence are sometimes raised.

Governors are not likely to select unqualified people for judicial appointments; however, governors might not be able to convince the best candidates to agree to serve. The appointive system probably rules out the complete incompetents, but it does not necessarily result in the appointment of the most competent people to serve as judges. Once appointed, judges are not responsive to voters and can exercise great independence in their decisions.

Election by the legislature is a system left over from colonial America when much power rested with the state legislature. It is used only in South Carolina and Virginia. This system tends to select former legislators as judges. In South Carolina, the number of judges who formerly were legislators is very close to 100 percent. Appointment is viewed as a capstone to a successful legislative career.[20]

Nonpartisan elections are one system being given serious consideration in Texas. This system would reduce the cost of campaigns and eliminate the problem of straight ticket voting. Voters would have to base their decisions on something other than party label. It would not necessarily result in the selection of more competent judges, but it would prevent the kind of large-scale changes in judgeships that happened in Harris County in 1994. As indicated before, it has also been suggested that Texas prohibit straight ticket voting for judicial candidates, requiring voters to mark the ballot for each judicial race.

The merit or Missouri plan is also being given consideration as a method of selecting judges. Under this system the governor would appoint judges from a list of acceptable (and, it is to be hoped, competent) candidates supplied by a judicial panel and

TABLE 9.4

Strengths and Weaknesses of Judicial Selection Methods

Method of Selection	Issue		
	Competence	Independence	Responsiveness
Appointment by governor	Strong	Strong	Weak
Election by legislature	Mixed	Strong	Weak
Merit/Missouri method	Moderate	Moderate	Weak
Partisan election	Weak	Weak	Strong
Nonpartisan election	Mixed/Weak	Mixed/Weak	Strong

Source: Ann O. Bowman and Richard C. Kearney, *State and Local Government* (Boston: Houghton Mifflin, 1990), 286–297.

perhaps ranked by the state bar association. Once appointed, the judge would serve for a set term and stand for retention in an election. In this retention election, voters could vote to either retain or remove the judge from office. The system is used by many states; twenty-one states use it for appellate judges, and fifteen for trial judges.

It would seem that the merit plan would be strong on the issues of competency and responsiveness; however, there is little evidence that it results in the selection of more competent judges.[21] There is also evidence that it is weak on responsiveness. In retention elections, the judge does not have an opponent.[22] Voters vote to retain or remove. Several writers have pointed out that it is difficult to defeat someone with no one.[23] In the states that use this system, most judges are retained; less than 1 percent are ever removed.[24] One study showed that between 1964, when the system was first used, and 1984, only 22 of 1,864 trial judges were defeated.[25] When judges are removed, it is usually because of either an organized political effort to remove them from office or gross incompetence.

There are also some variations on these plans. In Illinois judges are elected using a partisan ballot, but they must win 60 percent of the vote in a retention election to remain in office. In Arizona judges in rural counties are elected in nonpartisan elections, but judges in the most populous counties are appointed. These variations might also be considered in Texas.

In short, there is no perfect system for selecting judges. All methods have problems. Also, there is no evidence that compared with the other methods, any one of these

HIGHLIGHT

Money, Campaigns, Conflict of Interest, and Familiar Names

An article in the *Houston Chronicle* covered all the issues in judicial selection:

Texas Supreme Court Justice James A. Baker has removed himself from a drug liability case involving a client of Houston attorney John Hill, a key Baker fundraiser. The court, without comment, announced Friday that Baker had recused himself from deliberations in the Merrell Pharmaceutical Inc.'s appeal of a $3.75 million judgement award to a 14-year-old girl born without fingers on her right hand.

Hill, a former Texas Supreme Court chief justice, urged the court to reverse the judgement in arguments on March 19, one week before signing a fund-raising letter for Baker's election campaign.

A Corpus Christi jury awarded the family $3.75 million in actual damages and $30 million in punitive damages in 1991. The punitive damages were reduced to $15 million because of a limit in state law, and were later thrown out altogether by the 13th Court of Appeals.

The 13th Court upheld the actual damages, which now total $8 million including interest.

Hill admitted the public concern about lawyers writing a fund-raising letter for a judge before whom the attorney has a pending case. He said that is why he

has been trying to convince the state Legislature to change the judicial selection system ever since he resigned from the high court eight years ago.

"I think the system is just absolutely broken," Hill said. "I continue to play by the rules we have, but I do so on a nonpartisan basis."

Hill is a Democrat, and Baker, appointed to the court by Gov. George W. Bush to fill a vacancy last October, is a Republican.

Hill lobbied, without success, for a merit selection system under which judges would be appointed subject to voter review and retention elections.

Baker's Democratic opponent in November is Gene Kelly, a former military judicial official who has been a perennial candidate in recent years for the Texas Supreme Court or the Court of Criminal Appeals.

Although Kelly has no civilian judicial experience, his familiar name has made him a strong opponent of well-established judges in previous campaigns.

Hill and Dallas lawyer, Tom Luce, who also signed the fund-raising letter, urged contributions to enable Baker to purchase television time to overcome Kelly's name identification.

judicial selection methods results in the selection of judges with "substantially different credentials."[26] The only exception to this is that in the states where the legislature elects judges, more former legislators serve as judges.

Removing and Disciplining Judges

Most states provide some system to remove judges for misconduct. Impeachment, a little used and very political system, is provided for in forty-three states, including Texas. Five states allow for recall of judges by the voters.[27] One state, New Hampshire, allows the governor to remove a judge after a hearing. In five states, the legislature can remove judges by a supermajority vote (a two-thirds vote is most common). In recent years, the trend in the states has been to create a commission on judicial conduct to review cases of misconduct by judges and remove them from office. To date, forty-nine states have established judicial conduct commissions. Also, the method of removal of judges can depend on the level of the judgeship—for instance, trial judges versus appellate judges.

In Texas, the state Supreme Court may remove any judge from office. District judges may remove county judges and justices of the peace. The State Commission on Judicial Conduct may recommend the removal of judges at all levels. This twelve-member commission conducts hearings and decides whether "the judge in question is guilty of willful or persistent conduct that is inconsistent with the proper performance of a judge's duties."[28] The commission can privately reprimand, publicly censure, or recommend that the state Supreme Court remove the judge.

The use of review commissions to reprimand, discipline, and remove judges is a good check on the actions of judges. If Texas adopts the merit or Missouri plan, this commission would probably increase in importance as a check on judges.

✦ THE LEGAL SYSTEM

The American legal system can be broadly divided into civil and criminal branches. Civil cases are those between individual citizens and involve the idea of responsibilities and not guilt. Criminal cases are those cases brought against individuals for violations of law—crimes against society. Most (65.9 percent) of the cases heard by the district courts in Texas are civil cases, whereas most (75.6 percent) of the cases heard in county court are criminal.[29]

Under civil law, all individuals who feel they have cause or have been injured by others may file a civil lawsuit. Courts will decide whether the case has validity and should be heard in the court.

Grand Jury

While any citizen may file a civil suit in court, a screening body must review criminal cases. The U.S. Constitution requires the use of **grand juries** to serve as a screening mechanism to prevent arbitrary actions by federal prosecutors. Some states use the grand jury system for some criminal cases, although in recent years the use of a formal hearing before a judge, which is called an **information or an administrative hearing,** has become more common. The judge reviews the facts and decides whether there is enough evidence to try the case.

Texas uses both grand juries and administrative hearings. A citizen may waive his or her right to review by a grand jury and ask that a judge review the charges. In Texas, grand juries consist of twelve citizens chosen by district judges in one of two

grand juries
Juries of citizens that determine if a person will be charged with a crime.

information or administrative hearing
A hearing before a judge who decides if a person must stand trial. Used in place of a grand jury.

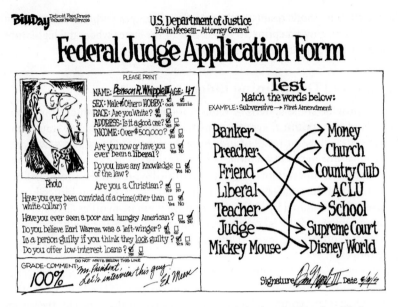

Some methods of selecting judges do not always result in the selection of qualified individuals.

BILL DAY Reprinted by permission of United Features Syndicate, Inc.

ways. The district judge may appoint a grand jury commission that consists of three to five people.[30] Each grand jury commissioner supplies the judge with three to five names of citizens qualified to serve on a grand jury. From these names, the judge selects twelve citizens to serve as a grand jury. In the other method, the district judge can have twenty to seventy-five prospective grand jurors summoned in the same manner used for petit juries. From this group, the district judge selects twelve citizens who are called grand jurors.[31]

Most grand juries serve for six months. They often screen the major criminal cases to decide whether enough evidence exists to go to trial. Grand juries are supposed to serve as filters to prevent arbitrary actions by prosecuting attorneys, but they do not always serve this function. The district attorney often dominates grand juries. Most grand jury members are laypeople who have never served before, and they frequently follow the advice of the prosecuting attorney. Although grand juries may conduct investigations on their own, few do. Those that do conduct investigations are sometimes termed "runaway grand juries" by the media.

A study by the *Houston Chronicle* presented evidence that some judges in Harris County had been given names of citizens for the grand jury by prosecutors from the district attorney's office. The study also demonstrated that many of the same citizens serve on grand juries year after year. Judges justified the repeated use of the same people for grand juries based on the difficulty of getting people to serve. Often, older, retired citizens volunteer to serve.[32]

Thus a grand jury might not always serve the function of protecting the citizen from arbitrary action by prosecutors. For this reason, a person may ask for an administrative hearing before a judge. During grand jury proceedings, the accused may not have an attorney present during the hearing; during an administrative hearing, however, the attorney is present and can protect the accused.

In Texas the prosecuting attorney files minor criminal cases in county courts. The county court judge, who determines whether the case should proceed to trial, holds an "administration" hearing. Criminal cases in the county court are generally less serious than those filed in district courts. They consist of DWI/DUI, minor theft, drug, assault, and traffic cases.

Petit Jury

Both criminal and civil cases can be decided by a petit (pronounced *petty*) jury. **Petit juries** are randomly selected from voter registration lists or, more recently in Texas, lists of licensed drivers. In criminal and civil cases, the defendant has the right to a trial by jury but may waive this right and let the judge decide the case.

petit juries
Juries of citizens that determine the guilt or innocence of a person during a trial. Pronounced *petty juries*.

Very few cases involve jury trials. In 2007 Texas county courts heard 969,443 cases and only 4,211 were jury trials. In district courts, 902,227 cases were disposed of and only 5,568 were jury trials. The lack of jury trials in criminal cases is often the subject of concern to some citizens. Most people charged with a crime plead guilty, often in exchange for a lighter sentence. This process is known as plea bargaining. The person charged agrees to plead guilty in exchange for a lesser sentence agreed to by the accused and the prosecuting attorney. The judge hearing the case can accept or reject the agreement.

If all criminal cases were subject to jury trials, the court system would have to be greatly expanded. Many additional judges, prosecuting attorneys, and public defenders would be needed. In addition, many more citizens would have to serve on juries. The cost of this expanded process would be excessive, and even though citizens support "getting tough on criminals," they would balk at paying the bill.

✦ CRIME AND PUNISHMENT IN TEXAS

Today we hear a lot about crime and the rising crime rate. Political candidates often use the crime issue as a campaign strategy to prove to voters they will be "tough on criminals." It is a safe issue that offends few voters.

In this section we will examine several questions regarding crime and punishment. How much crime is there nationally and in Texas? What factors seem to contribute to higher crime rates? Who commits most of the crimes? What impact does punishment have on crime rates? What is the cost of crime and punishment?

As table 9.5 shows, total violent crime in the United States and Texas from 1990 to 2006 has decreased. Crime has decreased less in Texas than in the United States as a whole. Texas still ranks third among the fifteen most populous states in total crime per 100,000 population.

Many factors contribute to the crime rate. Most crimes are committed in larger cities. If we compare the fifty states, we find that there is a strong correlation between the percentage of the population living in urban (metropolitan) areas and crime rates. This in part explains the crime rate in Texas, since about 80 percent of the population of Texas lives in metropolitan areas.

There is also a strong relationship between age, sex, and crime. (See table 9.6.) People below 25 years of age commit almost 46 percent of the crimes, and males commit almost 82 percent of all crimes. It has been suggested that if society could lock up all men between 18 and 25 years of age, crime would decline tremendously. Race is also a factor in crime. African Americans constitute about 12 percent of the U.S. population, yet, as shown in table 9.6, they constitute almost 30 percent of persons arrested for crime.

In Texas, the number of young men aged 18–24 has decreased in recent years. This has contributed to the reduced crime rate since 1989 in Texas.[34]

TABLE 9.5

Texas and United States Crime Rates, 1990 to 2006

Texas			United States		
Year	Population	Crime Rate per 100,000	Year	Population	Crime Rate per 100,000
1990	16,986,510	7,826.8	1990	248,709,873	5,820.3
1991	17,349,000	7,819.1	1991	252,177,000	5,897.8
1992	17,656,000	7,057.9	1992	255,082,000	5,660.2
1993	18,031,000	6,439.1	1993	257,908,000	5,484.4
1994	18,378,000	5,872.4	1994	260,341,000	5,373.5
1995	18,724,000	5,684.3	1995	262,755,000	5,274.9
1996	19,128,000	5,708.9	1996	265,284,000	5,087.6
1997	19,439,000	5,480.5	1997	267,637,000	4,927.3
1998	19,760,000	5,111.6	1998	270,296,000	4,615.5
1999	20,044,141	5,031.7	1999	272,690,813	4,266.5
2000	20,851,820	4,955.5	2000	281,421,906	4,124.8
2001	21,370,983	5,141.6	2001	285,317,559	4,162.6
2002	21,736,925	5,199.8	2002	287,973,924	4,125.0
2003	22,103,374	5,153.0	2003	290,690,788	4,067.0
2004	22,471,549	5,038.6	2004	293,656,842	3,977.3
2005	22,928,508	4,847.1	2005	296,507,061	3,900.5
2006	23,507,783	4,597.8	2006	299,398,484	3,808.0

Source: www.disastercenter.com/crime/uscrime.htm

TABLE 9.6

Persons Arrested for Crime by Sex, Race, and Age

	Percentage of Arrests, 2006
Sex	
Male	75.0
Female	25.0
Race	
White	65.1
Black	30.1
Others	4.8
Age	
Under 18	19.1
18–24	25.1
25–34	46.3
35–44	5.8
45–54	3.7
55 and over	

Source: Statistical abstract of the United States, 2006, p. 261.

➔ THE EFFECT OF PUNISHMENT ON CRIME RATES

The attitude among most Texans is, "If you do the crime, you should do the time." Juries in Texas give longer sentences than the average nationwide. (See table 9.7.)

However, the average time served in Texas is less than the national average, and the percentage of sentence served by violent offenders in Texas is also lower than the national average, due to the longer sentences imposed by juries. The length of time served has increased in recent years, due to an increase in available prison space. It will probably continue to increase, and the cost of keeping people in jail for longer periods of time will have to be weighed against the cost of other programs that might reduce crime.

Incarceration Rates

Texas has one of the highest rates of incarceration. (See table 9.8.) Rate of incarceration is the number of persons put in prison per 100,000 people. In 2004 Texas incarcerated 649 prisoners per 100,000. Texas ranked third, with Louisiana (861 per 100,000) ranking first, and Mississippi (669 per 100,000) ranking second.

The argument advanced for more incarceration is that it will lead to a reduction in crime rates. Studies of Texas crime show that between 1989 and 1993, when the incarceration rate increased by 4 percent, there was a 1 percent decrease in the crime rate. Even if no other factors affecting crime rates were involved, this is a high cost for such a small reduction in crime. Dr. Tony Fabelo, executive director of the Texas Criminal Justice Policy Council, makes this observation:

> Texans should carefully consider what the cost of continuing to increase incarceration rates means in terms of cost: funding increasingly more adult prison and jail space results in proportionately fewer dollars available for juvenile justice initiatives. Under present policies, most offenders are incarcerated after their criminal career has peaked, limiting the impact of more incarceration on the crime rate. Despite dramatic increases in the incarceration rate in 1993, Texas had the fifth highest crime rate in the country. Perhaps funding meaningful early interventions in the juvenile justice system, ranging from accountable community based programs to residential institutional interventions, will achieve better returns on lowering crime for each new dollar spent.

TABLE 9.7

Average Time Served by Texas Prisoners and Prisoners Nationwide

Type of Offense	Length of Average Sentence (years)		Average Time Served (years)		Percentage of Sentence Served	
	Nation	Texas	Nation	Texas	Nation	Texas
All violent offenses	7.4	12.0	3.6	3.6	48	30
Homicide	12.4	15.6	5.9	5.0	48	32
Rape	9.8	12.9	5.4	4.4	56	34
Kidnapping	8.7	12.1	4.3	4.4	50	37
Robbery	7.9	13.0	3.7	3.4	46	26
Assault	5.1	7.1	2.4	2.0	48	28

Source: Data from Texas Criminal Justice Policy Council, *Testing the Case for More Incarceration in Texas: The Record So Far* (Austin: State of Texas, 1995), p. 13.

TABLE 9.8

Incarceration Rates for the United States

State/Nation	Rate of Incarceration (per 100,000 population)			
	1995	**1999**	**2001**	**2004**
Louisiana	587	776	800	861
Mississippi	464	626	715	669
Texas	636	762	711	649
Michigan	428	472	488	483
Florida	406	456	437	468
California	384	481	453	649
Ohio	377	389	355	574
New York	367	400	310	331
Pennsylvania	235	305	422	329
United States average	387	476	521	486

Sources: Data from Texas Criminal Justice Policy Council, *Testing the Case for More Incarceration in Texas: The Record So Far* (Austin: State of Texas, 1995), 29; data for 1999, Texas Criminal Justice Policy Council Web page; data for 2001 and 2004, *Fiscal Size Up*, table 56; data for 2004, U.S. Department of Justice, Bureau of Judicial Studies, *www.ojp.usdoj.gov/bjs/abstract/p04.htm.*

However, if "you do the crime, you do the time" is the driving correctional philosophy in Texas, then we need to expect that more new dollars will continue to be spent expanding capacity in the adult correctional system to support more incarceration. The paradox of this policy is that more punishment for adults may do very little to continue lowering the state's crime rate, and may actually divert funds that could more effectively impact a decline in crime, if spent on juvenile justice policies or related areas.[35]

Death Penalty

It has often been suggested that the death penalty can reduce crime. The death penalty was outlawed in the United States in 1972 (*Furman v. Georgia*) because it was unfairly applied to many crimes and because of the lack of safeguards in place in many states. In 1976, the U.S. Supreme Court established guidelines under which a state could reinstate the death penalty (**Gregg v. Georgia**). To date, only twelve states *have not* reinstated the death penalty: Alaska, Hawaii, Iowa, Maine, Massachusetts, Michigan, Minnesota, North Dakota, Rhode Island, Vermont, West Virginia, and Wisconsin.

Texas is the leading state in both sentencing people to death and number of prisoners executed. Since the death penalty was reinstated in the state in 1976, and executions began in 1982, Texas has executed 355 of the 1,006 people executed nationwide. (See table 9.9) Texas, with about 7 percent of the total population in the United States, has had 35 percent of the executions. Also, there is no shortage of people in Texas waiting to be executed. In May 2005, there were 413 people on death row awaiting execution in Texas. At the rate of one execution per week, it would take 8 years to execute those persons. In 1995 alone, Texas executed nineteen of the fifty-one people executed nationwide. In 2000 alone, Texas executed forty of the eighty-four people executed nationwide.

Most executions (82 percent; 822 of 1,006) have been in southern states. The death penalty fits well within the dominant traditionalistic culture of the South. In Texas and many other southern states, juries can set the sentence for all crimes, and

Gregg v. Georgia
Supreme Court case that allowed states to reintroduce the death penalty if certain rules were in place.

TABLE 9.9

Executions by State since 1976

State	Total	2005	2006	2007	Executions by Region	
Texas	405	19	23	26	South	961
Virginia	98	0	3	0	West	67
Oklahoma	86	4	4	3	Midwest	127
Missouri	66	5	0	0	Northeast	4
Florida	64	1	2	0	Texas alone	405
Georgia	40	3	0	1		
N. Carolina	43	5	5	0		
S. Carolina	37	3	0	1		
Alabama	38	4	0	3		
Louisiana	27	0	0	0		
Arkansas	27	1	0	0		
Arizona	23	0	0	1		
Ohio	26	4	0	2		
Indiana	19	5	0	2		
Delaware	14	1	0	0		
Illinois	12	0	0	0		
California	13	2	1	0		
Nevada	12	0	1	0		
Mississippi	8	1	1	0		
Utah	6	0	0	0		
Maryland	5	1	0	0		
Washington	4	0	0	0		
Nebraska	3	0	0	0		
Pennsylvania	3	0	0	6		
Kentucky	2	0	0	0		
Montana	3	0	0	1		
Oregon	2	0	0	0		
Colorado	1	0	0	0		
Connecticut	1	1	0	0		
Idaho	1	0	0	0		
New Mexico	1	0	0	0		
South Dakota	1	0	1			
Tennessee	4	2	0–2			
Wyoming	1	0	0			
U.S. Gov't	3	0	0			

Note: 35 percent of all executions since 1976 are from Texas.

Note: Thirteen states do not have the death penalty: Alaska, Hawaii, Iowa, Maine, Massachusetts, Michigan, Minnesota, North Dakota, New Jersey, Rhode Island, Vermont, West Virginia, and Wisconsin.

Source: Death Penalty Information Center, Washington, D.C.

juries might be more inclined than judges to impose the death penalty. As table 9.10 shows, some states sentence many prisoners to death but carry out few executions. For example, California had 648 prisoners on death row in May 2007 but has executed only thirteen since 1976. From 1995 to 2007 California executed only 13 people.

TABLE 9.10

Death Row Inmates by State in 2007

State	Number Waiting to Be Executed
California	660
Florida	397
Texas	383
Pennsylvania	226
Alabama	195
Ohio	191
N. Carolina	185
Arizona	124
Georgia	107
Tennessee	107
Oklahoma	88
Louisiana	88
Nevada	86
S. Carolina	67
Mississippi	66
Missouri	51
U.S. Gov't	44
Kentucky	41
Arkansas	37
Oregon	35
Indiana	23
Virginia	20
Idaho	20
Delaware	18
New Jersey	0
Illinois	11
Nebraska	9
Washington	9
U.S. Military	9
Utah	9
Maryland	8
Connecticut	8
Kansas	9
Montana	2
S. Dakota	4
Colorado	2
New Mexico	2
Wyoming	2
New York	0

Source: Death Penalty Information Center Web page (*www.deathpenaltyinfo.org/FactSheet.pdf*).

The Harris County Factor

While Texas leads the nation in both the number of persons sentenced to death and the number of executions, Harris County contributes a disproportionate share. In fact Harris County (Houston) has contributed more death row inmates than the other large urban

TABLE 9.11	
Death Row Inmates from Selected Counties in Texas*	
Top 5 Counties	**Number of Death Row Inmates**
Harris (Houston)	246
Dallas	78
Bexar (San Antonio)	57
Tarrant (Ft. Worth)	48
Jefferson	24

*There have been 864 total death penalty convictions in Texas since 1977.

Source: *Houston Chronicle,* 5 February 2000, page 11A.

counties combined. (See table 9.11.) Only five states (including Texas) have condemned more people to death (California, Florida, Pennsylvania, and North Carolina). Most counties in Texas contribute very few death row inmates. Of the 245 counties in Texas, 138 have no death row convictions, fifteen have two, and fifty-three have one. Twenty percent of the counties contribute most of the death row convictions. Convictions also come primarily from East Texas, where the traditionalistic political culture is the strongest.

What factors contribute to the large number of death sentences in Texas, and Harris County in particular? First, the statutes in Texas for assigning a death sentence are among the least complicated. A jury must first answer two questions: (1) did the defendant act intentionally and (2) is the defendant a future threat to society? If a person commits murder while committing another crime (rape, robbery) or kills two people, a police officer, firefighter, or child, or is a murderer for hire and did it intentionally and are a threat, the person can receive the death sentence. These standards make it easy for juries to answer yes, and approve a death sentence.

Second, the Texas Court of Criminal Appeals almost never reverses a death sentence. Only 11 of 300 capital cases have been reversed or sent back to lower courts. Recently this court failed to reverse a death sentence when the defense attorney slept during part of the trial. The chief justice of the court, Judge Sharon Keller, in her campaign for election, stated that failure to execute condemned murderers was a violation of human rights.[36] Likewise, the U.S. Fifth Circuit is reluctant to overturn appeals. This court upheld the conviction in the case of the sleeping defense attorney. Thus, the likelihood of winning a case on appeal in Texas is not that great. The purpose of appellate courts is to check on procedures and processes in lower courts and make sure no mistakes are made. Judging by the number of reversals, few mistakes are made in Texas district criminal courts. Those that are found are ruled as not important in most cases. Finally, the Texas Board of Pardons and Paroles, often the final recourse for those with failed appeals, is even less apt to make changes. Since 1990, the Board of Pardons and Paroles has recommended clemency in 10 of 140 capital cases.[37]

Money is also a factor in determining if the prosecuting attorney will ask for a death sentence. Smaller, rural counties often lack the money to prosecute a death sentence case. Even large urban counties often find that death sentence cases will strain their budgets. Harris County is an exception to this and partly explains the reason for so many death sentence convictions. The budget for the Harris County District Attorney's office is $30 million, and it has a staff of 230 assistant district attorneys. Dallas County, by contrast, has a budget of about $20 million. Some of the difference is due to a lower case load in Dallas. Harris County also has a total of twenty-two felony courts (eight in Dallas County). Of these twenty-two Harris

TABLE 9.12

Public Opinion on the Death Penalty

	Texas	Nation
Do you support the death penalty?	69.1%	58.1%
Has an innocent person been executed?		
Very likely	38.9	39.4
Somewhat likely	24.4	24.7
Very unlikely	18.2	17.0
Somewhat unlikely	15.3	15.4
Not sure	3.3	3.6
Is Texas a safer place because of executions?		
Safer	51.5	30.0
Less safe	14.1	27.3
Not sure	34.4	42.7
Is the death penalty a deterrent to crime?		
Yes	58.4	47.7
No	36.6	46.6
Not sure	4.4	5.7

Source: Houston Chronicle, February 4, 2001, pages 24A–25A.

County courts, all but two judges are former prosecutors in the Harris County District Attorney's Office.[38]

One can question the high rate of death sentences in Texas, and the procedures for appeal. Despite these shortcomings, the public heavily favors the death penalty. Table 9.12 provides public opinion data on several aspects of the death penalty. Texas favors the death penalty more strongly than the nation as a whole and thinks the death penalty is a deterrent to crime. Also, Texans feel safer because of the death penalty.

There is little evidence that the death penalty is a deterrent to crime. Endless delays and appeals and the long time span between the sentence and the execution reduce the effectiveness of the death penalty. In Texas the average time from sentence to execution is **9.1 years.** One person, Jerry Joe Bird, spent 16.8 years on death row. No public officials are advocating a return to public executions, but it has been suggested that this might increase the power of the death sentence as a deterrent to crime. However, most crimes are not capital crimes, so the death penalty would do little, even under "ideal circumstances," to reduce the crime rate. Also, the cost to taxpayers for executing felons is quite high.

Additionally, inmates on death row are invariably poor and disproportionately African American or Hispanic. Few middle- and upper-class Anglos are sentenced to death in capital cases. This disparity in sentencing raises questions about equity under the law. Of the 448 inmates on death row in Texas in 2001, 182 were African Americans, 164 were Anglos, 99 were Hispanics, and 3 were of other races. Additionally, most are male—440 males to 8 females.[39]

9.1 years

Average time in Texas between a person being sentenced to death and execution.

✦ CONCLUSIONS

In the twenty-first century, the court system in Texas faces many challenges. Methods of selecting judges will continue to be controversial. Some change in these methods will probably occur. Texans may want to think about their approach to dealing with the high crime rates in the state. While voters seem anxious to approve bonds for the construction of more prisons, they are reluctant to consider other approaches to crime control. The long-term cost of having the highest prison population and the highest execution rate in the world should be weighed against the cost of alternate programs that might more effectively reduce crime.

INTERNET RESOURCES

National Institute on Money in State Politics: *www.followthemoney.org*
Information on campaign finances in Texas judicial races.

Texas Criminal Justice Policy Council: *www.nicic.org*
Good source of information on crime and imprisonments.

Death Penalty Information Center: *www.deathpenaltyinfo.org/*
Keeps track of death penalty in all states.

Office of Court Administration: *www.courts.state.tx.us/oca*
Good source of information on state courts in Texas. Keeps track of court data and serves as a watchdog agency for all state courts.

Texans for Public Justice: *www.tpj.org/*
Advocacy group keeps track of many aspects of state government including information on state courts and campaign contributions.

The organizational structure of state courts can be found at this site: *www.courts.state.tx.us*
You can also find a profile of Texas judges at this site.

For information on the role of money in Texas courts see the Texans for Public Justice Web page: *www.tpj.org/payola/sc_complaint.html*

KEY TERMS

appearance of objectivity (p. 195)
appellate courts (p. 196)
appointive-elective system (p. 204)
grand juries (p. 207)
Gregg v. Georgia (p. 212)
information or administrative hearing (p. 207)
"Justice for Sale" (p. 202)
magistrate functions (p. 196)

merit system or Missouri System (p. 199)
minority representation (p. 203)
name familiarity (p. 201)
9.1 years (p. 216)
nonpartisan election (p. 200)
partisan election (p. 200)
passive appearance (p. 194)
petit juries (p. 209)

specifics of the case (p. 195)
stare decisis (p. 195)
straight ticket voting (p. 201)
strict procedural rules (p. 194)
strict rules of access (p. 194)
supreme law of the land (p. 195)
trial courts (p. 196)
trial *de novo* courts (p. 198)

NOTES

1. Herbert Jacob, "Courts: The Least Visible Branch," in *Politics in the American States,* 6th ed., eds. Virginia Gray and Herbert Jacob (Washington, D.C.: Congressional Quarterly Press, 1996), 254.
2. Ibid.
3. Dye, *Politics in States and Communities,* 8th ed., 227.
4. Ibid.
5. Ibid.
6. Ibid.
7. Ibid., 228.
8. Jacob, "Courts," 253.
9. Ibid., 256–58.
10. Office of Court Administration, Texas Judicial Council, *Texas Judicial System Annual Report* (Austin: Office of Court Administration, 2003).
11. Office of Court Administration, Texas Judicial Council, *Texas Judicial System Annual Report* (Austin: Office of Court Administration, 1994), 31–33.
12. *Book of the States, 1998–99,* 131–32, table 4.2.
13. Ibid., 186–89.
14. Delaware, Maine, Massachusetts, New Hampshire, New Jersey, New York, and Vermont have some judges who are appointed by the governor and can be removed only for cause. Connecticut, Rhode Island, South Carolina, and Virginia have legislative elections. In the other three legislatures using elections, judges serve for life with good behavior. See Jacob, "Courts," 268, table 7.2. Also see *Book of the States, 1994–95,* 190–93, table 4.4. There are

some slight variations between the Jacob table and the table in *Book of the States.* This is probably due to interpretations by the writers. Due to minor variations among states, classification differences are possible.

15. Anderson, Murray, and Farley, *Texas Politics,* 246–47.

16. *Houston Chronicle,* "A Closer Look at Harris County's Vote," 14 November 2002, p. 32A.

17. Anthony Champagne, "Campaign Contributions in Texas Supreme Court Races," *Crime, Law and Social Change* 17 (1992): 91–106.

18. Gibson and Robison, *Government and Politics in the Lone Star State,* 281.

19. Kraemer and Newell, *Texas Politics,* 3d ed. (New York: West, 1987), 281.

20. Herbert Jacob, "The Effect of Institutional Differences in the Recruitment Process: The Case of State Judges," *Journal of Public Law* 33, no. 113 (1964): 104–19.

21. Bradley Canon, "The Impact of Formal Selection Processes on Characteristics of Judges— Reconsidered," *Law and Society Review* 13 (May 1972): 570–93.

22. Richard Watson and Rondal G. Downing, *The Politics of the Bench and Bar: Judicial Selection under the Missouri Nonpartisan Court Plan* (New York: John Wiley, 1969).

23. Dye, *Politics in States and Communities,* 8th ed., 236.

24. William Jenkins, "Retention Elections: Who Wins When No One Loses," *Judicature* 61 (1977): 78–86.

25. William K. Hall and Larry T. Aspin, "What Twenty Years of Judicial Retention and Elections Have Told Us," *Judicature* 70 (1987): 340–47.

26. Craig F. Emmert and Henry R. Glick, "The Selection of Supreme Court Judges," *American Politics Quarterly* 19 (October 1988): 444–65.

27. *Book of the States, 1998–99,* 138–48, table 4.5.

28. Commission on Judicial Conduct, *Annual Report, 1994* (Austin: Commission on Judicial Conduct, State of Texas, 1994).

29. Office of Court Administration, Texas Judicial Council, *Texas Judicial System Annual Report* (1994), 173, 179.

30. Interview with District Court Judge John Delaney, Brazos County Courthouse, November 1995.

31. *Texas Code of Criminal Procedure,* arts. 19.01–20.22.

32. *Houston Chronicle,* "Murder Case Testing Grand Jury Selection," 2 March 2002, pp. 1A and 16A.

33. Texas Criminal Justice Policy Council, *Biennial Report to the Governor and the 78th Texas Legislature,* January 2001.

34. Texas Criminal Justice Policy Council, *Testing the Case for More Incarceration in Texas: The Record So Far* (Austin: State of Texas, 1995), 43.

35. Ibid., 2.

36. *Houston Chronicle,* 9 February 2001, p. 6.

37. *Houston Chronicle,* 6 February 2001, p. 6.

38. *Houston Chronicle,* 4 February 2001, pp. 1A, 24A–27A.

39. Death Penalty Information Center Web page (*www.deathpenaltyinfo.org/*)

CHAPTER 10
❧

FINANCING STATE GOVERNMENT

Today much attention is focused on federal spending, and few citizens realize that state governments also spend large sums of money to supply services to their citizens. In 2007 state and local governments, combined, spent $1.785 trillion. Combined state and local expenditures amounted to $6,821 for each U.S. citizen. During the same year, the federal government spent $6,917 per citizen.[1] Some money spent by state and local government comes from the federal government as grants, but state governments generate about 77 percent of their revenue from their own sources, and local governments generate about 67 percent of their revenue from their own sources.

Because the legislature meets in regular sessions every other year (biennially), the Texas legislature approves budgets for two-year periods. These are called biennium budgets. In May 2007 the legislature approved a budget of $167.8 billion for the fiscal years 2008 and 2009. About 30 percent of the Texas budget comes from federal funds, most of which (60 percent) goes for health and human services (welfare and Medicare).

➜ WHY DO GOVERNMENTS PROVIDE SERVICES TO CITIZENS?

Although there is much discussion about reducing government at all levels, and there are a few who advocate the abolition of government altogether, governments exist and provide services for very practical reasons. Generally, governments provide services (known as **public goods**) when two conditions exist. The first is that it is not practical to exclude

public goods
Those goods provided by government and not by the private sector.

219

citizens from receiving the services for nonpayment (that is, it is not practical to separate payers from nonpayers). Suppose, for instance, that a city tried to charge a fee for fire protection, and that the occupant of one-half of a duplex house paid for fire protection and the occupant of the other half of the duplex refused to pay. The city could not deny fire protection to the person who had not paid because protecting the occupant who had paid could require preventing or putting out any fire in the half of the house occupied by the nonpayer. The same is true for police protection and some other government services. If the city could deny such services, it is called **exclusion.**

exclusion
The ability to exclude services from those who do not pay for them.

The second condition that must exist for a service to be a public good is called **nonexhaustion:** "Any number of people can consume the same good at the same time without diminishing the amount of good available for anyone else to consume."[2] For example, one person's receiving fire protection does not diminish another person's ability to receive fire protection, except in some very marginal way.

nonexhaustion
The fact that one citizen receiving a service does not exclude others from receiving the same service.

Thus, governments provide a service when it is not practical to exclude people for nonpayment, and the use of a service does not exhaust others' ability to use the service. While this explains most government services, it does not explain all government services. Take, for example, public education, for which it would be easy to separate payers and nonpayers. Children who did not pay could be excluded; however, we do not exclude anyone from education for nonpayment. In fact, most states, including Texas, require students to attend school until they reach a certain age. Why do states do this? The answer is that there is a broader public purpose or benefit to having an educated populace. Thus, some government services are provided without charge because there is a benefit to society as a whole—a **collective benefit.** Without government involvement, the collective benefit would not exist.

collective benefit
Goods that are provided with no charge because there is a broader public benefit associated with the good.

For many other government goods, such as toll roads or utilities (e.g., water, sewer, electricity), people are often excluded for nonpayment. Usually there are private-sector counterparts to these "public goods," and governments may provide such goods for a variety of reasons.

Still other government expenditures do not fall into these categories where there is a failure of markets to allocate resources through pricing structures but rather are made for redistributive purposes—**redistributive goods.** Expenditures for welfare purposes are a good example of this. Government, in effect, redistributes wealth from the affluent in society in an effort to correct the deficiencies of the less well-to-do. This redistribution is made out of a desire to see that all members of society have a minimum standard of living, sometimes referred to as the poverty line. In Texas most redistributive funds are from the national government. Very few such funds are from taxes raised at the state level. Also, as we will see later, the tax structure of Texas is very regressive. A progressive state tax structure is necessary in order to redistribute wealth.

redistributive goods
Those goods where government takes money from one group of citizens and gives it to other citizens. Welfare is a good example.

Last, in another class of public goods, the government regulates a good or an activity—**regulatory goods.** An example is the pumping of water from aquifers. Without government involvement, there is no practical way to exclude people from drilling wells, taking water, and exhausting the resource (the aquifer). In Texas, the Edwards Aquifer supplies water to San Antonio, Austin, and many other cities in that area of the state. State government has intervened to regulate the amount of water withdrawn from the aquifer. Similar examples exist in the Houston area, where, when water is withdrawn, the land sinks and the possibility of flooding increases in low areas.

regulatory goods
Public goods where the government regulates the use of resources to prevent overuse. An example is pumping water from an aquifer.

Thus, there are many reasons why governments provide services. Although some citizens think the government provides too many services to far too many citizens, attempts to reduce services will result in protests from those affected. As we all know, everyone favors cutting budgets, but no one wants their favorite program cut. Despite what services one would think could be cut, all services must be paid for, either with tax money or from service charges and fees.

Restored treasurer's office in the State Capitol.

✦ Sources of State Revenue

To pay for the many services a state government provides, revenue must be raised from many sources. For state governments, the primary source of revenue is taxes paid by citizens and not service charges and fees. The amount of tax money available for any given state depends on the wealth of the citizens of that state. Some states, like some individuals, have a higher income capacity than others. The measure of a state's "wealth" is called the state **tax capacity.** This measure is an index of all states, with 100 being the average tax capacity. Most measures of fiscal capacity are based on the median per capita income set to 100. States above 100 have a higher tax capacity, and states below 100 have a lower tax capacity.[3] Texas has a tax capacity of about 97, meaning that it is close to the national average.

 Another measure of fiscal capacity is the **tax effort,** or how close a state comes to its tax capacity. The tax effort in Texas is around 87, meaning that Texas taxes below its capacity. Thus, overall, Texas is a low-tax state; however, it is a high-tax state in terms of its dependency on sales and property tax when compared to other states on these taxes.

Per Capita Taxes

Another measure of state taxes is **per capita tax.** This is a simple measure obtained by taking the total taxes collected and dividing by the number of citizens in the state. While this might be useful to know, it is not very informative about how much citizens actually pay in taxes. The primary thing missed by the per capita tax measure is tax exporting. Sometimes taxes are exported to out-of-state residents. For example, Texas receives

tax capacity
A measure of the wealth of a state or its ability to raise revenues relative to all other states.

tax effort
A measure of how close a state comes to using its tax capacity.

per capita tax
The total taxes raised in a state divided by the number of residents.

TABLE 10.1

State Tax Revenue for 15 Most Populous States, 2005

State	Per $1,000 of Personal Income	Per Capita Personal Income	As % of State-Local Revenue
California	$73.71	$2,722.64	67.1%
Florida	56.11	1,907.62	56.6
Georgia	55.52	1,716.46	57.0
Illinois	57.05	2,069.00	53.7
Indiana	65.81	2,051.38	60.2
Massachusetts	64.37	2,800.19	62.6
Michigan	71.00	2,329.03	66.7
New Jersey	60.12	2,635.14	53.9
New York	65.01	2,598.42	45.2
North Carolina	69.24	2,149.29	68.3
Ohio	65.69	2,092.86	57.5
Pennsylvania	62.90	2,197.68	59.2
TEXAS	**42.34**	**1,429.88**	**47.4**
Virginia	56.11	2,104.46	57.6
Washington	66.48	2,358.53	64.6
UNITED STATES	**63.41**	**2,185.82**	**59.1**
TEXAS AS % OF U.S.	**66.8%**	**65.4%**	**80.2%**

Sources: U.S. Census Bureau, *State Government Finances,* U.S. Bureau of Economic Analysis, *Survey of Current Business.*

about $1 billion in taxes on oil production and natural gas each year. Much of the oil and gas is exported to other states, and the tax paid is exported with the oil and gas and other petrochemical products.

Alaska and Wyoming rank near the top on per capita tax burden. However, much of this tax is from oil in Alaska and coal in Wyoming and is exported to residents of other states—**tax exporting.**[4] Anyone who has ever observed a coal train hauling Wyoming coal to Austin, San Antonio, or Houston has seen tax revenue being exported to Texas from Wyoming. This coal is used to generate electricity, and consumers pay the tax when they pay their utility bills. Thus, per capita tax is not a true measure of the tax burden on the citizens living in the state unless tax exporting is taken into account.

Thus, if you do a ranking of all states on per capita revenues, the data are not very revealing of the actual taxes paid by residents living in the state. A somewhat better measure is to compare the fifteen most populous states on the amount of revenue raised per $1,000 of personal income. This still does not overcome the issues of tax exporting but at least compares the larger states' taxes as a percent of income. By this comparison Texas is the lowest tax state. (See table 10.1.)

tax exporting
The shifting of taxes to citizens in other states. A good example is Wyoming coal, which is exported to Texas to generate elasticity.

State Taxes in Texas

consumer taxes
Taxes that citizens pay when they buy goods and services—sales taxes.

The most common, single sources of revenue for state governments are **consumer taxes,** such as sales and excise taxes on gasoline, tobacco, and liquor. Figure 10.1 shows the breakdown for Texas state tax revenue in 2008–2009, which totaled $81,211.2 billion for the two-year period. As can be seen, most revenue comes from consumer taxes paid by individuals when they make purchases. Over 80 percent of all tax revenue comes from

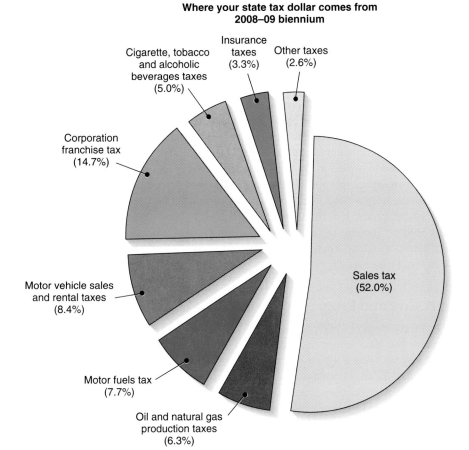

Where your state tax dollar comes from 2008–09 biennium

- Insurance taxes (3.3%)
- Other taxes (2.6%)
- Cigarette, tobacco and alcoholic beverages taxes (5.0%)
- Corporation franchise tax (14.7%)
- Motor vehicle sales and rental taxes (8.4%)
- Motor fuels tax (7.7%)
- Oil and natural gas production taxes (6.3%)
- Sales tax (52.0%)

FIGURE 10.1   Total tax revenue in Texas in 2008–2009 was $81,211.2 billion.

consumer taxes (sales, motor vehicle sales, motor fuels, alcoholic beverages, tobacco taxes).

Because of high sales taxes, most of the taxes in Texas are paid by consumers and not by businesses. There is only a limited tax on businesses, in the form of a corporate franchise tax. When compared to taxes on consumers, business taxes in Texas pale to insignificance. This is discussed later in this chapter.

➔ EQUITY IN TAXES

Many issues are raised when one asks who should pay the taxes. Should those who benefit from public services pay taxes (**benefit-based taxes**), or should those who can most afford it pay the taxes? Some taxes are based more on the benefit a person receives, and others are based more on the **ability to pay.** For example, the excise tax on gasoline is an example of a tax based on benefit received rather than on ability to pay. A large portion of the gasoline tax is earmarked for highway construction. The more gasoline people buy, the more tax they pay and the more benefit they receive from using the streets and highways.

For most taxes, other than the gasoline tax, showing direct benefit is problematic. Benefit received is more applicable to service charges and fees than to taxes. Sometimes

benefit-based taxes

Taxes for which there is a relationship between the amount paid in taxes and services received. Motor fuel taxes are a good example.

ability to pay

Taxes that are not based on the benefit received but the wealth, or ability to pay, of an individual.

the service charge covers the actual cost of providing the service, such as a service charge for garbage collection. In other cases, the service charge might cover only part of the cost of providing the service. College students receive most of the benefit from attending classes, and they pay tuition and fees to attend. In state-supported universities and colleges, however, not all of the cost of a college education is covered by tuition and fees paid by students. Most of the cost is still paid by taxpayers.

Generally, when individual benefit can be measured, at least part of the cost of the service is paid as fees. People using a public golf course pay a green's fee, hunters pay for hunting licenses, and drivers pay a driver's license and tag fee. Often these funds go directly to the government unit providing the service. Taxpayers may pick up part of the cost through money paid in taxes. For example, green fees paid by golfers often do not cover the total capital and operating costs of running a golf course. The difference is paid from revenue from other sources, typically from property tax revenues.

Other taxes, such as the federal income tax, are based more on ability to pay. The higher your net income, the higher your income tax bracket, and the higher the percentage of your net income you pay in federal income taxes. Most taxes, especially at the state level, are not based on ability to pay.

Regressive and Progressive Taxes

Using the criterion of ability to pay, taxes can be ranked as regressive or progressive. A **regressive tax** takes a higher percentage of income from low-income persons, and a **progressive tax** takes a higher percentage from higher-income people. Economists also talk about so-called proportional taxes, in which the tax paid is a fixed percent of each person's income. Examples of **proportional taxes** are difficult to come by but, in theory, are possible. One might argue that some state income taxes that tax each person the same percentage of income are proportional. The proposed "flat federal income tax" might be an example. No taxes in Texas can be described as proportional. The key to understanding this is not the total dollars paid but the percentage of income taken by the tax.

Texas has one of the most regressive tax structures of all the states. The Institute for Taxation and Economic Policy, a Washington, D.C., advocacy group, issued a report in 2002 that ranked the fifty states on the degree of progressivisms or regressivisms of their tax systems. Texas made the **"Terrible Ten" list.**[5] Figure 10.2 shows the percentage of income taken in Texas by income group in 2002, and figure 10.3 shows the U.S. average percentages for each income group. As can be seen, a Texas family in the lowest 20 percent of income will be paying about 11 percent of their income in taxes, while the national average for such a family is slightly less.

What figures 10.2 and 10.3 show is that, while all state tax structures are regressive, the tax structure in Texas is more regressive than average. States like Texas that have no personal income tax have the most regressive tax systems. These states also have the lowest taxes on the rich.[6]

The degree to which taxes are regressive or progressive depends upon many factors. Regressivity/progressivity is affected not only by the mix of taxes used in a state (income, sales, excise, property), but also by taxation rates and what is subject to tax. What is subject to taxation is called the **tax base.** For example, some states tax only unearned income (stock dividends and interest) and not earned income (wages and salaries). Others do the opposite. Some states have a very flat rate (proportional) for state income tax rather than a progressive tax rate.

With the sales tax, the tax base—what is subject to sales tax—is an important factor. If food and medicine are subject to a sales tax, the tax is more regressive. Only seventeen states exempt food items, forty-four exempt prescription drugs, and eleven exempt

regressive taxes
Taxes that take a higher percentage of the income from low-income persons.

progressive taxes
Taxes that take a higher percentage of income from high-income persons.

proportional taxes
Taxes that take the same percentage of income from all citizens.

"Terrible Ten" list
List of states with the most regressive taxes. Texas is on this list.

tax base
The items that are subject to tax; for example, the items subject to sales tax.

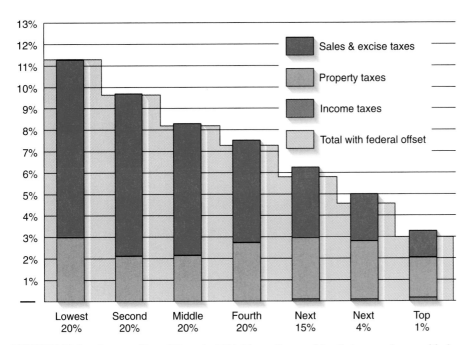

FIGURE 10.2 *State and Local Taxes in 2002, Texas.* Shares of family income for nonelderly taxpayers.

SOURCE: Institute on Taxation and Economic Policy, *Who Pays? A Distributional Analysis of Tax Systems in All 50 States,* 2d ed. January 2003. (*www.itepnet.org*). Reprinted by permission.

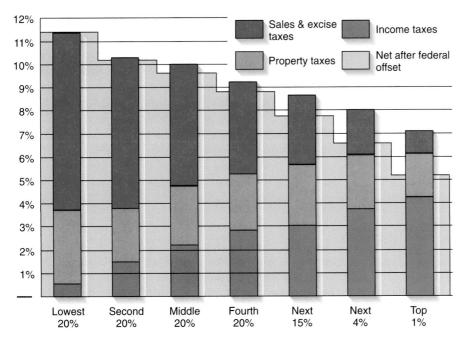

FIGURE 10.3 *State and Local Taxes in 2002, All States.* State and local taxes imposed on own residents as shares of income.

SOURCE: Institute on Taxation and Economic Policy, *Who Pays? A Distributional Analysis of Tax Systems in All 50 States,* 2d ed. January 2003. (*www.itepnet.org*). Reprinted by permission.

TABLE 10.2

Comparison of State Tax Rates on Retail Sales, Cigarettes, and Gasoline: 15 Most Populous States in 2007

State	State Sales	Local	Cigarette Tax (¢ per Pack)	Gasoline Tax (¢ per Gallon)
California	7.25%	2.5	87.0	18.0
Washington	6.50	2.3%	202.5	36.0
Illinois*	6.25	2.5	98.0	20.1
Texas	6.25	2.0	141.0	20.0
Florida	6.00	2.5	33.9	15.6
Michigan	6.00	0	200.0	19.1
New Jersey	7.00	1.0	257.5	14.5
Pennsylvania	6.00	0	135.0	31.2
Indiana	6.00	0	99.0	18.0
Ohio	6.00	2.0	125.0	24.0
Massachusetts	5.00	0	151.0	21.0
New York	4.25	4.5	150.0	24.4
North Carolina	4.25	2.0	35.0	30.1
Georgia*	4.00	3.0	43.0	18.5
Virginia*	4.00	1.0	30.0	17.5

*Georgia also has an additional 3 percent sales tax on gasoline sales. Illinois and Virginia tax food items for home consumption. When food is taxed, the effective rate is higher and more regressive.
Source: Federation of Tax Administrators. (*www.taxadmin.org*).

nonprescription drugs. If services used predominantly by the wealthy, such as legal and accounting fees, are not subject to a sales tax, the tax is less progressive.

Some argue that taxes based on consumption are the "best taxes" because citizens have a choice to consume or not to consume. The less you consume, the less you pay in tax. The degree to which this is true will depend upon what is subject to tax—the base. If many necessities of life, such as food, clothing, and medicine, are subject to tax, the range of choice will be very limited, especially for low-income people who spend most of their income on such items. If, on the other hand, necessities are excluded and nonessentials are included, the choice theory has some validity. For example if golf course fees, country club fees, accounting services, and legal fees are excluded, the argument that choice is a factor takes on a hollow ring. Table 10.2 shows rates of state and local sales taxes in the fifteen most populous states.

Tax Shifting

tax shifting
Passing taxes on to other citizens.

tax incidence
The person actually paying the tax.

Another tax issue is the question of who actually pays the taxes: **tax shifting.** Some taxes can be shifted from the apparent payer of the tax to others, who become the true payers, or the **incidence,** of the tax. For example, a person who purchases something in a store obtains a receipt from the store saying they paid so much in sales tax. It appears that they have paid a tax. They have a receipt that says they paid the tax. Because of high competition from other stores, however, the storeowner might have to lower the prices of goods and thus pay part of the tax in lower profits.

Students who rent apartments near their campus never receive a property tax bill. The landlord pays the tax each year; however, the landlord will try to pass along the property tax as part of the rent. Market conditions will determine when 100 percent of the tax gets passed along to the renter and when the landlord has to lower prices and absorb part of the tax in lower profits.

Except for personal income tax, all taxes can be shifted to others. Market conditions will decide when taxes are shifted. People sometimes argue against business tax increases, advancing the argument that such increases will "simply result in higher prices to the customer." If taxes on businesses could always be shifted forward to customers as higher prices, no business would object to tax increases. Except for the inconvenience of collecting the tax and forwarding it to the government, there would be no cost involved. Obviously, taxes cannot always be shifted to the customer as higher prices, and businesses resist tax increases.

→ LOCAL TAXES

In addition to taxes collected at the state level, local governments in Texas also collect taxes from two primary sources—property tax and local sales tax. Almost all units of local government collect property tax. For school districts, the property tax is the single largest source of revenue, exceeding state contributions. For so-called rich school districts, all of the cost of running local schools may come from the property tax. The property tax is also an important source of revenue for cities and counties. In addition, most cities, many counties, and all local transit authorities collect a local sales tax. In Texas, the local sales tax is fixed by state law at no more than 2 percent of the value of sales. Thus, in most urban areas in Texas there is a 6.25 percent state sales tax plus a 2.0 percent local tax for a total of 8.25 percent total sales tax.

There is effectively no state-level property tax in Texas. All but a small portion of property tax goes to local governments. In recent years property taxes have increased dramatically. In 2005, the most recent year for which data are available, a total of 3,748 local governments in Texas assessed a property tax. The total property tax levy was $33.3 billion, an increase of about 32 percent since 2006. Table 10.3 shows this change. Texas local governments, especially school districts, have become more dependent upon the property tax. Texas is not a low property tax state. It ranks tenth in property tax revenue per $1,000 of personal income among the fifty states. Table 10.4 shows the comparison with the 12 most populous states. Among the top twelve states, Texas has the second highest property tax per $1,000 of personal income. Only New Jersey is higher. Among the fifty states, Texas ranks tenth in property tax.

TABLE 10.3

Property Tax Collections by Local Governments in Texas, in Billions

Type of Government	1990	2000	2005
School Districts	$ 6.6	$13.4	$20.1
City Governments	2.2	3.4	4.9
County Governments	1.7	3.2	4.7
Special Districts	1.4	2.4	3.6
Total Property Tax	$11.9	$22.4	$33.3

Source: Legislative Budget Board, *Fiscal Size Up,* for years indicated in table.

TABLE 10.4

Comparison of Property Tax Revenues per $1,000 of Personal Income: 12 Most Populous States in 2005

State	Revenue	Rank among 50 States
California	$25.27	38
Florida	33.08	20
Georgia	28.93	29
Illinois	40.57	10
Massachusetts	36.78	14
Michigan	39.90	13
New Jersey	50.92	4
New York	43.21	8
North Carolina	24.16	39
Ohio	32.78	21
Pennsylvania	31.01	23
Texas	39.80	17

Source: Legislative Budget Board, *Fiscal Size Up 2008–2009,* table 57, p. 46.

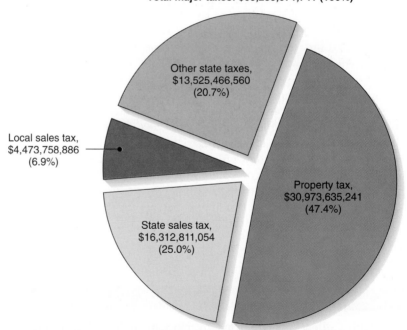

Total major taxes: $65,285,671,741 (100%)

Other state taxes, $13,525,466,560 (20.7%)

Local sales tax, $4,473,758,886 (6.9%)

Property tax, $30,973,635,241 (47.4%)

State sales tax, $16,312,811,054 (25.0%)

FIGURE 10.4   *State and Local Sales and Property Tax and a Percent of Major Taxes in Texas in 2005.*

SOURCE: Texas Comptroller Office.

Comparison of State and Local Tax Revenues

Local taxes often get lost in the focus on state revenues and expenditures. Over the last several decades the legislature has paid for less and less of the cost of local government services, especially school districts. Figure 10.4 shows the total state and local tax revenue picture for the state of Texas in 2005. As can be seen, property taxes in Texas are almost half of all state and local revenues collected (47.4%). If the local sales tax is added to the local property tax, local tax revenues constitute 54.3% of total taxes collected in the state. Thus, local governments collect and pay for over half the total cost of government in Texas.

✧ Nontax Revenue Sources

Service charges and fees are another source of **nontax revenue** for state governments. Governments often charge service charges and assess fees when a person can be excluded from receiving the service for nonpayment. When this exclusion is not possible, tax revenue is usually used to finance the service. Examples of these fees include tuition, driver's license fees, water bills, and fees for garbage collection. Figure 10.5 shows nontax revenue by source for the state of Texas in 2006–2007.

The trend in recent years has been to increase service charges and fees as a way to increase revenue and avoid raising taxes. All students attending state colleges and universities in Texas have experienced these increases as higher tuition and service charges. In terms of total dollars in the state budget, the various service charges and fees provide 15 percent of total state revenue.

The state lottery and interest income generates about 4 percent of all (total) state revenue. (See figure 10.6.) Even though the Texas Lottery has been the most successful lottery in history in terms of total dollars raised, it contributes only a small portion of the state total budget and will never be a significant player in providing revenue. In recent years revenue from the lottery has declined.

Federal aid makes up about 35.5 percent of the Texas 2006–2007 biennium budget. As shown in figure 10.7, the largest part (60.2 percent) of these federal funds goes to health and human services for medical or Medicaid and welfare payments. Education

nontax revenue
Governmental revenue derived from service charges, fees (tuition), lottery, and other sources.

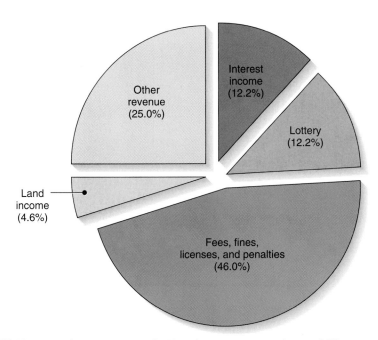

FIGURE 10.5   Total nontax revenue for Texas in 2008–2009 was $27,621 billion.

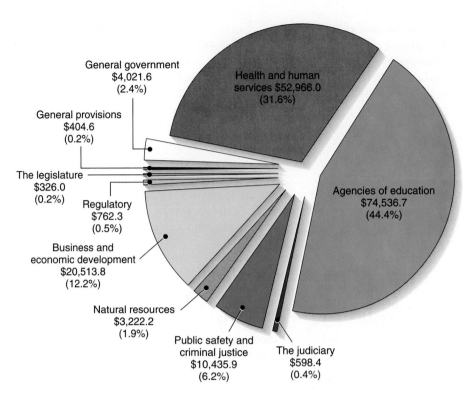

FIGURE 10.6   Total revenue (all sources) for Texas 2008–2009 was $167,787.2 billion.

SOURCE: Legislative Budget Board, *Fiscal Size Up 2008–2009,* p. 4, figure 3.

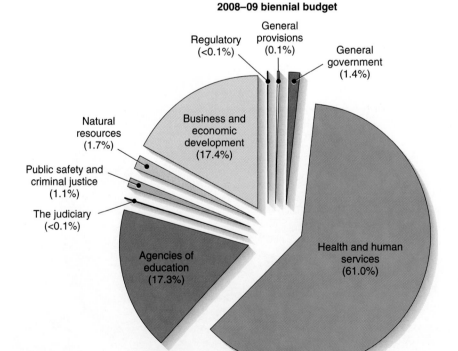

FIGURE 10.7   Total federal funds in 2008–2009: $50,963.0 billion.

gets about 17.4 percent of these funds, about 19.6 percent goes to transportation and highways, and the remainder goes to various other federal programs. Transportation and highway funds from the federal government primarily come from federal gasoline tax paid in Texas and returned to the state.

While state governments obtain only a small percentage of their revenue from service charges and fees, some local governments, especially cities, are heavily dependent upon service charges and fees to finance their services. Cities usually impose service charges or fees for water, sewer, and solid waste collection. Sixty-two cities in Texas also operate an electrical system and receive revenue for providing this service.[7] The largest cities with electrical systems are San Antonio, Austin, Lubbock, Brownsville, Garland, Bryan, and College Station. The trend has been to increase these fees first and to hold tax increases to a minimum.

The Budget "Fix"

The legislature is limited in the amount of discretion it has in spending money. Much of the **revenues are earmarked** for specific items, called fixed revenues. Revenues are fixed in three ways: by constitutional or statutory provisions, by funding formulas, and by federal government rules. While the legislature could change the statutory and funding formula rules, these are often politically fixed by past actions and, except in extraordinary circumstances, are not changed. Interest groups have a strong attachment to these appropriations and will fight to maintain them. Table 10.5 shows how much is fixed in these various categories. These "fixes" primarily are the results of funds being earmarked for specific programs. For example, the proceeds from the state lottery go to education. Motor fuel tax goes primarily to state and local road programs.

The earmarking of revenues obviously limits the ability of the legislature to change budget priorities or to react to emergency situations. If one fund is short, movement of money from another fund may not be possible. Last year's budget becomes the best

earmarked revenue
Tax revenue set aside for specific purposes. In Texas about 80 percent of revenue is earmarked.

TABLE 10.5

Restricted Appropriations in Texas Budgetary Process 2008–2009 (in Millions)

Function	2008–2009 Biennium Appropriation	% of Total Appropriation
Appropriations or allocations of revenue dedicated by constitutional or statutory provisions	$42,171.5	48.9
Appropriations influenced by federal law, regulation, or court decisions	18,920.0	21.9
Appropriations influenced by formulas	10,208.9	11.8
TOTAL RESTRICTED APPROPRIATIONS	**$71,300.3**	**82.7**
Article IX appropriations	$259.4	0.3
Nonrestricted appropriations	14,700.1	17.0
TOTAL, GENERAL REVENUE AND GENERAL REVENUE-DEDICATED APPROPRIATIONS	**$86,259.9**	**100.0**

Note: Numbers may not add due to rounding.

Source: Legislative Budget Board, *Fiscal Size Up 2007–2008,* table 9, p. 5.

predictor of next year's budget. Changes in the budget occur incrementally, in small amounts, over a long period of time.

Table 10.5 indicates that most funds in Texas are fixed, earmarked, or restricted. Only 16.5 percent of the moneys in the general fund are nonrestricted and available for change. This does not give the legislature much leeway in making changes in the budget. Similar patterns are also found in most state budgets. For more detail on this check the Legislative Budget Board's Web site. Except for the Permanent University Fund, which applies only to the University of Texas and Texas A&M, university funding is in the 16.5 percent **discretionary funding.** This is why student tuition has increased in recent years.

discretionary funding
Those funds in the state budget that are not earmarked for specific purposes.

→ EXPENDITURES: WHERE THE MONEY GOES

The pattern of expenditures for Texas differs little from most states in terms of the items funded. In most states, three items consume most of the state budget—education, health and welfare, and transportation. In recent years, an increase in the prison population has greatly increased the amount spent for public safety—which includes prison operations. After these items, everything else pales in comparison. Figure 10.8 shows the major expenditure items in the state of Texas 2006–2007 biennium budget. Table 10.6 shows expenditures for the top fifteen agencies of state government, and table 10.7 shows the top fifteen federal programs in Texas.

While education eats the lion's share of the state budget (39.6 percent), local school districts contribute about 60 percent of the funds for local schools. The state

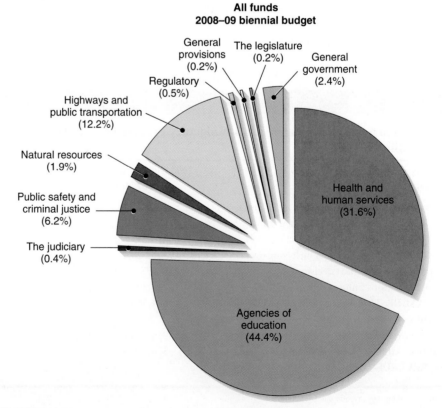

FIGURE 10.8   Total expenditures for 2008–2009: $167,787.2 billion.

TABLE 10.6

Federal Funds—Statewide Summary 2006–2007 and 2008–2009 Biennia

Function in Millions	Expended/Budgeted 2006–2007[1]	Appropriated 2008–2009[2,3]	Biennial Change	% Change
ARTICLE I - General Government	$881.5	$699.1	($182.4)	(20.7)
ARTICLE II - Health and Human Services	29,197.6	31,062.3	1,864.8	6.4
ARTICLE III - Agencies of Education	8,651.0	8,831.6	180.6	2.1
Public Education	8,318.0	8,494.7	176.7	2.1
Higher Education	333.1	337.0	3.9	1.2
ARTICLE IV - The Judiciary	5.4	2.9	(2.5)	(46.6)
ARTICLE V - Public Safety and Criminal Justice[4]	1,327.4	578.7	(748.7)	(56.4)
ARTICLE VI - Natural Resources[4]	328.0	850.8	522.8	159.4
ARTICLE VII - Business and Economic Development	8,798.5	8,858.7	60.2	0.7
ARTICLE VIII - Regulatory	5.4	4.5	(0.9)	(17.2)
ARTICLE IX - General Provisions	0.0	74.4	74.4	NA
ARTICLE X - The Legislature	0.0	0.0	0.0	0.0
TOTAL	**$49,194.8**	**$50,963.0**	**$1,768.3**	**3.6**

[1]Reflects provisions in House Bill 15, Eightieth Legislature, 2007, relating to supplemental appropriations.

[2]Reflects provisions in House Bill 15, Eightieth Legislature, 2007, relating to supplemental appropriations; other enacted legislation affecting appropriations; certain appropriation adjustments made in Article IX of the 2008–09 General Appropriations Act; and the Governor's vetoes.

[3]In addition to amounts indicated, Article IX, Section 19.62 of the 2008–09 General Appropriations Act provides for the transfer of appropriations to agencies for a salary increase for certain state employees.

[4]In addition to amounts indicated, Article IX, Section 19.61 of the 2008–09 General Appropriations Act appropriates funds for Salary Schedule C pay raises for commissioned peace officers.

Source: Legislative Budget Board, *Fiscal note,* table 34, p. 30.

TABLE 10.7

Top 15 Federal Programs in Texas

Ranking	Program	2006–2007 Appropriation in Millions
1	Medicaid	$22,125.5
2	Highway Planning and Construction	6,888.9
3	Title I Grants to Local Educational Agencies	2,305.8
4	Special Education Grants to States	1,799.1
5	National School Lunch Program	1,672.7
6	Temporary Assistance for Needy Families (TANF)	1,136.0
7	Children's Health Insurance Program	1,024.3
8	Special Supplemental Nutrition Program for Women, Infants, and Children	956.1
9	School Breakfast Program	539.6
10	Foster Care Title IV-E	505.4
11	Improving Teacher Quality	497.9
12	Child Care and Development Block Grant	434.9
13	Child Care Mandatory & Matching Funds of the Child Care and Development Fund	373.6
14	Vocational Rehabilitation Grants to States	347.8
15	Child Support Enforcement	343.5

Note: Excludes federal funds for employee benefits and for institutions of higher education.

Source: Legislative Budget Board (*www.lbb.state.tx.us*).

currently finances about 38 percent of the cost of elementary and secondary education. This is a decline in state contributions from a decade ago. The state's contribution has been steadily decreasing, and school districts have been forced to pick up a greater share of the cost of local education, which they are covering by assessing higher local property taxes.

Health and human services, about 35 percent of the state budget, is funded primarily with federal grants to the state. The state of Texas contributes less than most states to the cost of providing these services. The Texas Constitution prohibits spending more than an amount equal to 1 percent of the state budget on welfare. These are the redistributive services discussed previously. Neither tax structure nor the political culture supports such activities. Many students of budgeting have made the point that a budget is a statement of policy in monetary terms. What and how much a state spends money for largely expresses its priorities. The budget becomes a statement of the dominant values in the state. A comparison of Texas with other large industrial states on the primary budget items will tell us something about what Texans value.

As can be seen by examining figures 10.9 to 10.12, of the fifteen most populous states, Texas ranks near the bottom in expenditures for these items. The only exception to this is education, but Texas still ranks below the mean. While Texas spends much money in total dollars, it spends less than the average comparable state in per capita dollars for most items. In recent years, most of the growth in state expenditures has been driven by population increases alone. In terms of per capita expenditures, the state has remained at about the same level over the past decade.

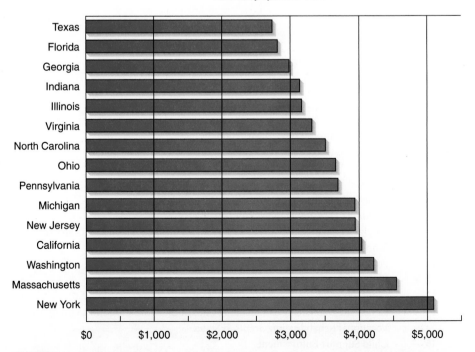

State expenditures per capita 2001
15 most populous states

FIGURE 10.9 Texas spends less per capita than the other most populous states. Fifty-state average is $3,542.

SOURCE: U.S. Bureau of the Census, Legislative Budget Board. *Fiscal Size-Up 2000–2001* (*www.lbb.state.tx.us*).

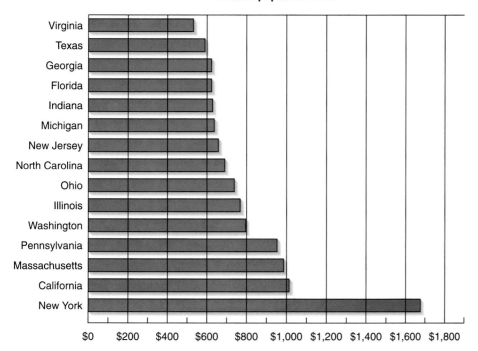

Welfare expenditures per capita
15 most populous states

FIGURE 10.10   Texas has the second lowest per capita expenditures for welfare among the 15 most populous states. Fifty-state average is $710.

SOURCE: U.S. Bureau of the Census, Legislative Budget Board. *Fiscal Size-Up 2000–2001* (*www.lbb.state.tx.us*).

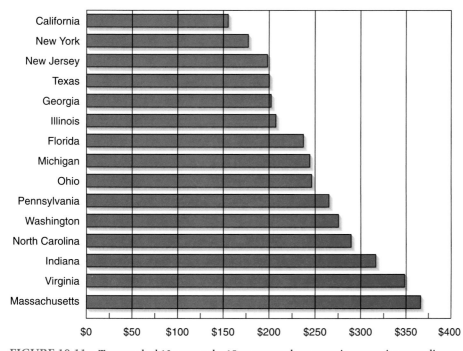

Per capita expenditures for highways
15 most populous states

FIGURE 10.11   Texas ranked 12 among the 15 most populous states in per capita expenditures for highways. Fifty-state average was $285. Highway expenditures are influenced by many factors, including geographic size of the state, climate, and population.

SOURCE: U.S. Bureau of the Census, Legislative Budget Board. *Fiscal Size-Up 2000–2001* (*www.lbb.state.tx.us*).

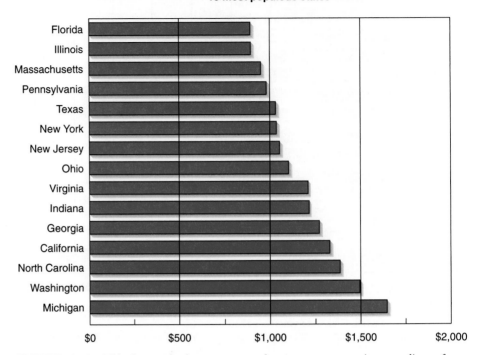

**Expenditures for education per capita
15 most populous states**

FIGURE 10.12   This chart ranks the 15 most populous states on per capita expenditures for higher education. Texas ranks near the mean on this expenditure. On most others, Texas ranks below the mean.

SOURCE: Census of Governments 1999 data.

✦ CONTINUING ISSUES IN STATE FINANCE IN TEXAS

Over the past twenty years Texas has experienced a number of fiscal shortfalls. The legislature has been forced to meet in special sessions to correct these problems. Many of the fixes have been short-term. An examination of several tax issues will help us understand the need for a long-term solution.

Tax Structure

In the past twenty years Texas has experienced many financial problems. During the 1980s there were ten special sessions of the legislature to attempt to correct revenue shortfalls. These shortfalls were caused primarily by a decline in the state economy due to a drop in oil prices from a high of $40 per barrel to a low of less than $10. The fiscal crisis was worsened by the state's tax structure. Texas is very dependent on highly **income-elastic taxes** (85 to 90 percent). An income-elastic tax is one that rises or falls very quickly relative to changes in economic conditions. This means that when the economy is growing or contracting, tax revenue grows or contracts proportionately with the growth or contraction in the economy. For example, as retail sales grow, the sales tax grows. Texas is very dependent upon sales and excise taxes, which are highly income-elastic. The same is true for the tax on oil and gas extracted in Texas. As the price of oil increased on world markets, the economy of the state boomed and tax revenue increased. When the oil bust came, the opposite happened and Texas found itself extremely short of revenue. People quit buying goods and services subject to the sales and excise tax, and revenue fell

income-elastic taxes

Taxes that rise and fall quickly relative to changes in economic conditions. Texas tax system is very income-elastic.

TABLE 10.8

Source of Tax Revenue for 15 Most Populous States (in Percent)

State	Total Sales Tax	General Sales Tax	Selective Sales Tax	License Taxes	Individual Income Tax	Corporation Net Income	Other Taxes
California	38.3	30.4	7.8	6.8	43.7	8.8	2.4
Florida	75.2	56.2	19.0	5.6	0.0	5.3	14.0
Georgia	44.4	33.9	10.6	3.4	46.7	4.5	0.9
Illinois	50.6	27.2	23.3	9.4	30.1	8.3	1.8
Indiana	56.0	38.9	17.1	3.6	32.8	6.4	1.2
Massachusetts	32.1	21.6	10.5	3.8	53.8	7.4	2.9
Michigan	49.0	34.3	14.7	5.7	26.0	8.1	11.2
New Jersey	44.4	28.6	15.8	5.6	35.9	9.7	4.5
New York	32.2	21.9	10.3	2.5	56.0	5.5	3.7
North Carolina	40.9	24.7	16.2	5.9	45.2	6.8	1.2
Ohio	46.4	34.1	12.3	8.3	39.3	5.5	0.4
Pennsylvania	48.5	29.6	18.9	10.0	30.4	6.2	4.9
TEXAS	**78.8**	**49.9**	**29.0**	**13.7**	**0.0**	**0.0**	**7.5**
Virginia	34.4	19.4	15.0	3.9	52.5	3.8	5.4
Washington	78.5	61.6	16.8	4.9	0.0	0.0	16.7
UNITED STATES	**48.1**	**32.9**	**15.2**	**6.6**	**34.0**	**6.0**	**5.4**

Source: Legislative Budget Board, *Fiscal Size Up, 2008–2009,* figure 56, p. 46.

accordingly. As the price of oil declined, oil revenue fell. Depressed oil prices also caused severe economic problems in Mexico and a devaluation of the peso. Fewer pesos flowed across the border, and some border communities experienced severe economic problems and declining local revenue along with the state revenue decline.

Table 10.8 compares the tax dependency of the fifteen most populous states. As can be seen, Texas is far more dependent on sales taxes than most other large states. Only Florida and Washington are about as dependent as Texas on consumer taxes. Washington, like Texas, lacks both a personal and a corporate income tax, and Florida lacks a personal income tax. Heavy dependency on consumer taxes makes for an income-elastic tax structure. In bad economic times the state will face revenue shortfalls.

The Texas tax structure is too dependent upon highly income-elastic consumer taxes (such as sales and gasoline taxes), and a when, not if, there is an economic downturn, the state will again experience revenue shortfalls. The potential for these problems to occur again is quite great. In fact, the 2003 session of the legislature faced at least a $10 billion revenue shortfall due to a downturn in the economy.

Is There a Personal Income Tax in the Future for Texas?

Texas is one of only six states without any form of personal income tax. The other states are Florida, Nevada, South Dakota, Washington, and Wyoming. Alaska, Connecticut, New Hampshire, and Tennessee have a limited income tax on unearned income (dividends, interest, and capital gains). Being in such a limited company of states without an income tax is not troublesome to most Texans. Politically there is great resistance to imposing such a tax. In 1992 the voters approved a constitutional amendment preventing the legislature from enacting an income tax without voter approval. Several legislative leaders felt that without voter approval the tax would never be imposed by the legislature and this amendment forces voter approval.

Texas will face another fiscal crisis so long as it is so dependent on consumer taxes. What recourses are available to the state? During past crises, the problem of revenue shortfall was often solved by raising sales and gasoline taxes and by increasing fees. Can these taxes be tapped again? Texas currently has one of the highest sales tax rates. The state tax is 6.25 percent and local tax is 2 percent, for a total of 8.25 percent. Raising the rate might not be possible. Only four states (Washington, Nevada, Rhode Island, and Mississippi) have higher state (excluding local) sales taxes.

One suggestion, made by former Lt. Governor Bob Bullock, was to expand the base of the sales tax. The base is what is subject to a sales tax. Currently most services are not subject to a sales tax; most notably excluded are legal and financial services. Politically, given the large number of attorneys in the legislature (35 percent), getting such a change through the legislature might be difficult. The proposal was killed in the past several sessions of the legislature including a special session in 2004.

The state tax on gasoline or motor fuel in Texas is currently at 20 cents per gallon, plus 14.5 cents in federal tax. The highest state gasoline tax is in Connecticut, at 29 cents per gallon. There might be room to raise the gas tax a few cents per gallon. If prices at the pump continue to rise, the prospects of this happening is small.

In the last ten years, the tax on oil and natural gas production, which is based on the dollar value of the oil and gas extracted from the ground, has increased. While production has been falling, prices have risen, especially in the past five years. The long-term outlook is for these taxes to rise, with the natural gas tax rising more than the oil tax.[8] In late 1998 the price of oil had fallen to about $11 per barrel, a price not seen since the mid-1980s. In 2008 the price increased to $150 per barrel. Obviously the long-term price of a barrel of oil is very much tied to national and international factors. New oil from Russia, continued war in the Middle East, and many other factors can affect the price of oil and the amount of revenue available.

franchise fee

Major business tax in Texas which is assessed on income earned by corporations in the state.

Texas has a form of corporate "income tax," that is called a **franchise fee.** Organically it was assessed only on corporations doing business in the state. It did not apply to limited partnerships, corporations, limited liability companies, business trusts, professional associations, or business associations. Some businesses and corporations changed their structure to avoid the tax. The legislature was forced to eliminate many of these loopholes in 2007 and apply the franchise fee to most businesses in the state. This tax will begin to be collected in 2008 so the impact is not really known at this time.

In part the legislature was forced to make these changes because of law suits that were filed questioning the constitutionality of the so-called Robin Hood plan for school finance. (See Chapter 11.) Without this threat by the courts to close the school system in the state unless the finances were changed, it is doubtful that the legislature would have acted.

The new franchise fee is rather complicated (for more detail on the tax see *www.window.state.tx.us/taxinfo/franchise/fi_revised.html*), but basically the tax is applied to the gross receipts of most businesses with deductions allowed for some expenses such as wages, salaries, and employee benefits. Taxable entities with revenues of $300,000 or less owe no tax; however, all businesses must file a report. The tax rate is 0.5% for wholesalers and retailers and 1% for most other taxable entities.

This tax is applied to most businesses in the state, and estimates are that it will bring in several billion dollars each year and reduce the growth in property taxes currently used to finance public education.

→ CONCLUSIONS

While the state of Texas spends much money, measured in total dollars, the state still ranks toward the bottom on per capita expenditures. School funding, discussed in the following chapter, will continue to be an issue. Hopefully, the new business franchise fee has addressed the inequities among school districts and the problems created by raising local property taxes to support local schools. Prison funding will become a large problem in the future if the state proceeds on its current path of increasing the number of state prisoners.

State revenue is at or near capacity from most sources, and there is little room to raise existing state taxes. Tax revenue is highly income-elastic, and any downturn in the economy will erase the surplus in state revenues. Perhaps this will force the state to evaluate the current tax system and its impact on the many segments of the state's economy. Politically the prospects for change in the state tax structure are dim. The traditionalistic/individualistic political culture of the state does not support radical change. Without some major crisis, the status quo will probably prevail and the current tax and spending structure in the state will continue.

INTERNET RESOURCES

Comptroller of Public Accounts: *www.window.state.tx.us/*
Information on state taxes and expenditures and rules on taxes. Find out what is subject to sales tax.

Legislative Budget Board: *www.lbb.state.tx.us/*
Budget writing agency for state government. You can get a summary of each state budget. You can find past years' budget reviews in the *Fiscal Size Up* for comparison.

Center on Budget and Policy Priorities: *www.cbpp.org/*
Information on state budgets in general.

Citizens for Tax Justice: *www.ctj.org/*
Liberal group advocating tax reform. Produces studies showing impact of tax changes at the federal level as well as many studies by other advocacy groups. Very useful source for information on taxes and the impact of changes on the average tax payer. This organization has been criticized, but few have found mistakes in the data it releases.

Information on state and local tax rates can be found at the Federation of Tax Administrators Web site: *www.taxadmin.org*

KEY TERMS

ability to pay (p. 223)
benefit-based taxes (p. 223)
collective benefit (p. 220)
consumer taxes (p. 222)
discretionary funding (p. 232)
earmarked revenue (p. 231)
exclusion (p. 220)
franchise fee (p. 238)
income-elastic taxes (p. 236)

nonexhaustion (p. 220)
nontax revenue (p. 229)
per capita tax (p. 221)
progressive taxes (p. 224)
proportional taxes (p. 224)
public goods (p. 219)
redistributive goods (p. 220)
regressive taxes (p. 224)
regulatory goods (p. 220)

tax base (p. 224)
tax capacity (p. 221)
tax effort (p. 221)
tax exporting (p. 222)
tax incidence (p. 226)
tax shifting (p. 226)
"Terrible Ten" list (p. 224)

NOTES

1. *Statistical Abstract of the United States, 2003,* table 421.
2. John L. Mikesell, *Fiscal Administration: Analysis and Applications for the Public Sector,* 3d ed. (Pacific Grove, Calif.: Brooks/Cole, 1991), 3.
3. J. Richard Aronson and John L. Hilley, *Financing State and Local Governments,* 4th ed. (Washington, D.C.: Brookings Institution, 1986), 37–40.
4. Texas Research League, "The Rating Game," *Analysis* 11 (August 1990): 2.
5. Institute on Taxation and Economic Policy, "Texas Taxes Hit Poor & Middle Class Far Harder than the Wealthy," 7 January 2003 (*www.itepnet.org/wp2000/tx%20pr.pdf*).
6. Ibid.
7. Texas Public Power Association, Austin, author's telephone interview with Mike Gibson, 1995.
8. Texas Comptroller of Public Accounts (*www.cpa.state.tx.us*).

CHAPTER 11

LOCAL GOVERNMENTS IN TEXAS

Although the attention of the news media often focuses on state and national government, in many respects local governments have a greater impact on the daily lives of citizens. Many services that local governments provide are taken for granted or expected by citizens, who notice local government only when it fails to properly perform its functions—when the water mains fail, the garbage is not collected, the pothole is not filled, stray animals are not impounded. When things work, local government goes unnoticed.

Citizens depend on local governments for many life support services, such as water, sewers, and police and fire protection. Local governments also help maintain the environment and lifestyles of citizens by protecting neighborhoods through zoning and the regulation of land development. Finally, local governments assume the important, perhaps critical, function of educating children.

While some citizens live in rural areas without services, most people do not find this lifestyle very appealing. Eighty percent of Texans live in urban areas and are very dependent on local governments. Even the 20 percent who live in rural areas expect services from county governments and special districts. Thus, local governments are critical kingpins in modern society. Without the services provided by local governments, modern urban society would not be possible. Understanding how these local governments work and affect our lives is very important.

In Tranquility Park, it is easy to forget the essential government services that are critical to the smooth functioning of a city.

Citizens expect local governments not only to provide services but also to be very decentralized. In this respect, the United States is the most **decentralized nation** in the world. Nationwide there are about 87,525 units of local government; almost 5,000 of these are in Texas. (See table 11.1.) Decentralization allows for local control. In 2002 there were 506,682 local elected officials nationwide and 25,970 in Texas. Many citizens become involved in their local governments, which has the effect of reducing conflict and increasing support for government at all levels. Average citizens feel they can have an impact on their local governments and influence outcomes. It is quite easy to attend a meeting of the school board, city council, or county government and participate in the deliberations, and many citizens do. Unlike local government, participation at the national and state level is difficult, and few citizens have an opportunity to become involved.

decentralized nation
The United States possessing many units of local government controlled by citizens at the local level.

TABLE 11.1

Number of Local Governments and Elected Officials in the United States and Texas in 2002

	United States		Texas	
	Local Governments	Elected Officials	Local Governments	Elected Officials
Counties	3,043	58,818	254	4,491
Cities	19,429	136,632	1,196	7,520
Townships	16,504	125,209	—	—*
School districts	13,506	78,022	1,089	7,423
Special districts	35,052	108,498	2,254	7,187
Totals	87,534	507,179	4,784	26,621

*Texas does not have townships. New England towns in the five New England States are included in township forms of government.

Source: U.S. Department of Commerce, Bureau of the Census, *Statistical Abstract of the United States, 1998* (Washington, D.C.: U.S. Government Printing Office, 2002) (*http://www.census.gov/prod/2003pubs/gc021x1.pdf*).

Thus, local governments, decentralized and locally controlled, are central to the American system of government. Few citizens in other countries have the opportunity to become involved in their local government to the extent Americans do.

→ "CREATURES OF THE STATE"

creatures of the state
The fact that all local governments are created by state government and all powers are derived from the state government.

When citizens become involved in local governments, they do so under the power and authority given them by state governments. All local governments are **creatures of the state,** and whatever power or authority they possess is derived from state constitutions and statutes. Local governments are not mentioned in the U.S. Constitution. They are created under state constitutions to serve the interests of the state.

The amount of local authority granted and the degree to which governments can act independently of state government vary greatly from state to state and within states by type of government. One way to understand this variety is to distinguish between general-purpose and limited-purpose governments. General-purpose governments are those units given broad discretionary authority by the state government. They have the authority to perform many functions and can control their own finances, personnel, and government structure. Limited-purpose governments have very limited authority or control over their finances, and they are governed by a set structure. Personnel decisions are controlled by state law.[1]

A good example of a limited-purpose government in Texas is a school district. It performs only one function (education), has limited revenue sources (property tax and state funds), and is governed by a seven-member school board, and many personnel decisions (such as teacher certification) are controlled by a state agency. Texas counties are also good examples of limited-purpose governments. State laws limit their authority and revenue, they all operate under the same form of government (see subsequent discussion), and state law often dictates personnel decisions.

Texas cities, on the other hand, are excellent examples of general-purpose governments. Under home rule (discussed next), Texas cities have the authority to pass any ordinance not prohibited by state law and have many sources of revenue. The structure of government varies greatly from city to city, and the state exerts limited control over personnel decisions.[2]

Thus, although all units of local government are creatures of the state, some units are granted more discretionary authority and operate relatively free of state control and supervision. Texas cities have very broad authority. Other units of local government in Texas are limited-purpose governments. Next we will examine cities, counties, special districts, and school districts in Texas and the differences among these units of government.

✦ GENERAL LAW CITIES AND HOME RULE

In Texas, city governments are the principal providers of urban services, and they have been granted great authority to act independently from state government. A study in 1982 by the Federal Advisory Commission on Intergovernmental Relations ranked Texas cities number one in terms of local discretionary authority.[3] By comparison, this study ranked Texas counties forty-third of the forty-eight states with county governments. Since 1982 there have been only a few minor changes in state law that affect power and resources of Texas cities.

City governments are technically municipal corporations. The term *municipality* derives from the Roman *municipium,* which means "a free city capable of governing its local affairs, even though subordinate to the sovereignty of Rome."[4]

Texas cities are granted charters by the state government. A city charter is a document, much like a state constitution in that it provides the basic structure and organization of city government and the broad outlines of powers and authorities. In Texas, cities are chartered as either general law cities or home rule cities. **General law city** charters are specified in the state statutes. Cities can choose from seven charters provided in these statutes.[5] These options allow considerable choice as to form of government. There are 938 general law cities in Texas.[6]

general law cities
City charters created by state statutes.

Since the passage of a constitutional amendment in 1912, any city in Texas with a population of at least five thousand may be chartered as a **home rule city**.[7] Most of these cities adopt home rule charters. Of the 309 cities with a population of more than five thousand, only nineteen operate under general law charters.[8] Home rule means that the local citizens may adopt any form of government they want and pass any ordinance not prohibited by state law. For example, state law is silent on the number of members on city councils, but the state constitution limits the term of office to no more than four years. Thus, there is no specific grant of power to cities in the state constitution. Cities can also pass any ordinance (local law) unless there is a prohibition against local governments acting on the matter at issue. Sometimes the prohibition might be only **implied or implicit prohibition on city ordinance power**. For example, there is no explicit prohibition against cities passing an ordinance prohibiting open alcohol containers in vehicles. Several Texas cities passed such ordinances in the 1980s before there was a state law against open containers. However, state courts ruled that the regulation of alcohol was a state function, and by implication (implicitly) Texas cities could not pass no-open-container ordinances.

home rule cities
City charters created by the actions of local citizens.

implicit or explicit prohibitions on city ordinance power
Power limitation of cities, preventing them from passing ordinances that are explicitly prohibited by state law and from passing ordinances that by implication may violate state law.

The home rule provisions of the Texas Constitution allow great latitude in governing local affairs. Once approved, home rule charters may be amended only with the approval of the city voters. Usually the city council or a charter commission proposes changes. While voters are not granted initiative to change the state constitution, 243 home rule charters in Texas allow voters to initiate charter changes.[9]

HIGHLIGHT

The Creation of Impact, Texas

Impact, Texas, is a small city now surrounded by the city of Abilene. It was incorporated in February 1960. The primary purpose of this incorporation was to allow for the sale of liquor. Under Texas law, the citizens of a city may vote to allow the sale of alcohol—so-called wet-dry elections. The city of Abilene is noted for being a center of Christian fundamentalism and is the home of three religious colleges—Abilene Christian (Church of Christ) McMurrey University (Methodist), and Hardin-Simmons (Baptist). Some citizens of Abilene were scandalized at the prospects of liquor sales in this dry corner of the state and attempted to block the incorporation. After several trips to the courthouse,* the

incorporation was allowed and liquor sales took place for many years. Impact was the only place for miles around where liquor could be purchased.

The city of Abilene, using its annexation powers, surrounded the city of Impact, eliminating any chance for it to grow. In 1963, the Texas legislature passed the law creating the Extra Territorial Jurisdiction for all Texas cities and limiting the incorporation of cities within the ETJ of an existing city. The incorporation of Impact was a factor in the passage of this act.

In the 1980s Abilene allowed the sale of liquor within the city limits. The liquor store in Impact is now closed.

*Perkins v. Ingalsbe (1961) 162 T. 456, 347. S.W. end 926.

→ INCORPORATION: THE PROCESS OF CREATING A CITY

incorporation
Process of creating a city government.

The process of creating a city is known as **incorporation** because technically cities are municipal corporations. Creating a city normally involves the following steps. First, local citizens must petition the state and ask to be incorporated as a city. Second, an election is held, and voters must approve the creation of the city. Finally, the state issues a charter.

In Texas the requirements are as follows:

1. There must be a population of at least 201 citizens living within a two-square-mile area (this is a measure of density).
2. Petitions requesting that an election be called must be signed by 10 percent of the registered voters and 50 percent of the landowners in the area to be incorporated.
3. If the petition is valid, the county judge calls an election.
4. If voters approve, the city is created and a general law charter is adopted. A second election is held to elect officials.[10]

extra territorial jurisdiction (ETJ)
City powers that extend beyond the city limits to an area adjacent to the city limits.

While these procedures are not difficult, there are limitations about where cities can be created. Under Texas law, all cities have what is called **extra territorial jurisdiction (ETJ)**.[11] The ETJ extends beyond the city limits of an existing city. General law cities have a half mile of ETJ. The distance increases as population increases, for up to as much as five miles for cities above 250,000 in population.[12] A city may not be incorporated within the ETJ of an existing city unless that city approves. This provision is intended to prevent the growth of smaller cities on the fringe of larger cities and allow existing cities room to grow.

Also, cities may annex land within their ETJ. Annexation is the taking into the city of adjoining land that is unincorporated (not a part of another city). Texas cities have broad annexation powers. The city council, by majority vote, can unilaterally annex land, and the residents living in the area being annexed have no voice or vote in the process. This provision in state law, coupled with the ETJ provisions, provides Texas cities with room to expand. In the 1999, 2001, and 2003 sessions of the Texas legislature there were over twenty bills introduced to restrict the ability of Texas cities to annex land. Some restrictions were placed on home rule cities; however, they still have broad annexation authority when compared to many other states.

✦ FORMS OF CITY GOVERNMENT

There are two basic forms of city government used by cities in the United States and Texas: mayor-council and council-manager. A third form, commission, is not used by any Texas city and is used by only a few cities nationwide. The commission form is discussed in this chapter because it once played an important role in the development of Texas local government.

Mayor–Council Government

Mayor-council government is the more traditional form that developed in the nineteenth century. There are two variations of mayor-council government—weak executive and strong executive. (See figures 11.1 and 11.2.) Under the weak executive or

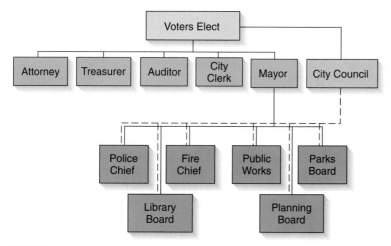

FIGURE 11.1   *Mayor-Council Form of City Government, with a Weak Mayor.*

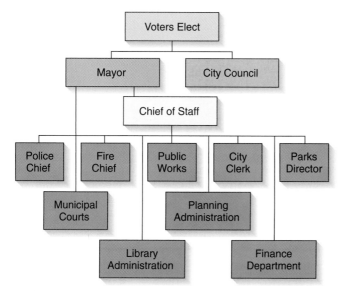

FIGURE 11.2   *Mayor-Council Form of City Government, with a Strong Mayor.*

**weak mayor form
of government**
Form of government where mayor
shares power with council and
other elected officials.

**strong mayor form
of government**
Form of local government where
most power rests with the mayor.

weak mayor form of government, the formal powers of the mayor are limited in much the same way that the Texas governor's formal powers are limited. First, the mayor shares power with other elected officials and with the city council. The weak mayor's executive/administrative authority is limited. Second, the mayor has only limited control over budget formation and execution. Third, the number of terms the mayor can serve is limited. Last, the mayor has little or no veto authority.[13]

Under a strong executive or **strong mayor form of government,** the mayor can appoint and remove the major heads of departments, has control over budget formation and execution, is not limited by short terms or term limits, and can veto actions of the city council.

Only 39 of the 290 home rule cities in Texas use the mayor-council form of government. Houston, El Paso, and Pasadena are the three largest cities using the form.[14] Of these three, only Houston has a strong mayor form. The Houston mayor can appoint and remove department heads and is responsible for budget formation and execution; however, the office has no veto authority, has a short term (two years), and is limited to three terms. In El Paso, the mayor's control over administration is limited by requiring city council approval for appointment of department heads and the chief administrative officer and the lack of veto power. Most Texas cities do not have a strong mayor form.

There are many more mayor-council forms in the general law cities in Texas than in the home rule cities; however, all have formally very weak mayors. Their powers are provided in the state statutes, and no form provided in the state laws can be classified as a strong executive. All are weak mayors.

Council–Manager Government

**council-manager form
of government**
Form of government where voters
elect a mayor and city council. The
mayor and city council appoint a
professional administrator to manage the city.

The most popular form of government among Texas cities is the **council-manager form.** (See figure 11.3.) Except Houston and El Paso, all major cities in Texas use this form. Under this system, the voters elect a small city council (usually seven members), including a mayor. The council hires a city manager, who has administrative control over city government. The city manager appoints and removes the major heads of departments of government and is responsible for budget preparation and execution. The city manager is the chief administrative officer of the city government.

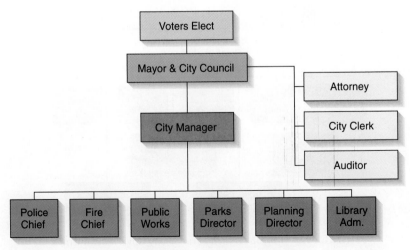

FIGURE 11.3   *Council-Manager Form of City Government.*

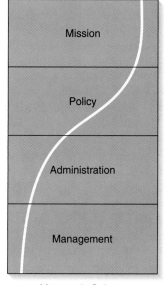

**Mission-Management Separation with
Shared Responsibility for Policy and Administration**

Dimensions of
Governmental Process

Illustrative Tasks for Council	Council's Sphere	Illustrative Tasks for Administrators
Determine "purpose," scope of services, tax level, constitutional issues.	Mission	Advise (what city "can" do may influence what it "should" do) analyze conditions and trends.
Pass ordinances, approve new projects and programs, ratify budget.	Policy	Make recommendations on all decisions, formulate budget, determine service distribution formulas.
Make implementing decisions, e.g., site selection, handle complaints, oversee administration.	Administration	Establish practices and procedures and make decisions for implementing policy.
Suggest management changes to manager, review organizational performance in manager's appraisal.	Management	Control the human, material, and informational resources of organization to support policy and administrative functions.

Manager's Sphere

FIGURE 11.4 *Roles in the Council-Manager Form of Government.* The curved line suggests the division between the council's and the manager's spheres of activity (the council's tasks are to the left of the line, and the manager's are to the right). This division roughly approximates a "proper" degree of separation and sharing; shifts to the left or right would indicate improper incursions.

SOURCE: James Svara, "Dichotomy and Duality: Reconceptualizing the Relationship Between Policy and Administration in Council-Manager Cities," *Public Administration Review* 450 (1): 228, 1985. Reprinted with permission from Public Administration Review © Blackwell Publishing, Ltd.

Administrative authority rests with the city manager, and the council is the policy-making body of city government. The mayor and city council are responsible for establishing the mission, policy, and direction of city government. Their roles in administration and management are greatly reduced. Figure 11.4 shows the roles of the council and mayor on the four dimensions of city government: mission, policy, administration, and management. The council and manager share in each of these areas, with the council dominating in mission and policy and the manager dominating in administration and management.

→ ROLES OF THE MAYOR

The role of the mayor in city governments is often misunderstood. This is due to the variations in the roles of the office in strong mayor, weak mayor, and council-manager governments. This difference often escapes the average citizen.

In the strong mayor-council form, the mayor is the chief executive officer of the city, in charge of the city government. If the mayor possesses a veto authority, she or he can use the threat of a veto to extract some things from the council, just as the governor does with the legislature. There is a separation of powers between the mayor (the executive branch) and the city council (the legislative branch).

In a weak mayor form, the mayor is not the chief executive officer. The mayor might be the first among equals and the most visible member of city government but does not control administrative matters, although the mayor may have some administrative authority. The mayor's control over budgetary matters is limited and generally requires approval of the council even for minor matters such as paying bills. The mayor usually serves as a member of the council and generally lacks veto authority.

In council-manager government, the mayor is not the chief executive officer. The mayor does not control the city administration or budget. These powers rest with the city manager. The mayor is a member of the city council and there is no separation of powers. The mayor serves as a leader of the council, presides over council meetings, usually helps set the council agenda, and serves as the official representative of the city. Some mayors in council-manager cities have been very successful leaders. They rule, not from the formal powers granted in the charter, but from personal abilities or informal leadership traits. Henry Cisneros of San Antonio was one of the best examples of a successful mayor leader in a council-manager city. Cisneros led "by sheer personal magnetism and intellect, facilitating local successes through joint action of the total city council and professional staff."[15] Thus, mayors in council-manager cities are leaders, although the leadership style is quite different. They are not a driving force, as they can be in mayor-council governments, but they can serve as a guiding force.[16]

No matter what the form of city government, the successful mayor must have political support within the community, the support and confidence of community leaders, popular support among the citizens, charisma, and the energy and stamina to lead, mold a coalition, and gain acceptance of his or her programs.

✦ THE CITY MANAGER

city manager

Person hired by the city council to manage the city. Serves as the chief administrative officer of the city.

Because so many cities in Texas use the council-manager form of government, some understanding of the role of the **city manager** is essential. Texas has always been a leader in the use of this form of government. In 1913 Amarillo became the first city in the state to adopt the form. O. M. Carr, the first city manager in Amarillo, strongly influenced the formation of the International City Managers (Management) Association.[17]

Under the council-manager form of government, the voters elect a city council and mayor. Generally these are the only elected officials in city government. The council in turn appoints the city manager and may remove the manager for any reason at any time; managers serve at the pleasure of the city council. In smaller general law cities in Texas, the position might be called a city administrator rather than manager, but the duties are essentially the same.

Most managers are trained professionals. Today many managers have a master's of public administration degree and have served as an assistant city manager for several years before becoming city manager. All but a few city managers are members of the International City Management Association (ICMA) and, in Texas, members of the Texas City Management Association (TCMA). These organizations have a code of ethics and help to promote the ideas of professionalism in the management of local governments. This expertise and professionalism sets city governments apart from county governments in Texas. In county governments, the voters elect most all officeholders and professionalism is often absent.

Because city managers appoint and can remove all major department heads and are in charge of the day-to-day management of city government, they can instill a high level of professionalism in the city staff.

Although the manager's primary role is to administer city government, managers can and do have an impact on the policies of the city made by the city council. Managers provide information and advice to the council on the impact of policy changes in city government. Professional managers attempt to provide information that is impartial so that the council can make the final decision. Councils sometimes delegate this policy-making process to city managers, either openly or indirectly by failure to act. When this happens, councils are neglecting their duty of office and are not serving the citizens who elected them.

Over the last ninety years the council-manager form of government has functioned well in Texas. Texas cities have a national reputation of being well-managed and maintaining a high degree of professionalism in their operations.

⇥ THE COMMISSION FORM OF GOVERNMENT

The **commission form of government** is not used by any home rule city in Texas or by any significant-size city in the United States, but it deserves mention because of its impact on Texas local governments. The city of Galveston popularized this form of government in the early part of the twentieth century. In 1901 a major hurricane destroyed most of Galveston and killed an estimated five thousand people. Galveston was the only major port on the Texas Gulf Coast and a kingpin in the cotton economy of the state. It was in the interests of all Texans to have the city and port rebuilt. A delegation of Galveston citizens approached the Texas legislature for funds to help in the rebuilding. Joseph D. Sayers, the governor then, was opposed to state funding without some state control. The governor proposed that he be allowed to appoint five commissioners to oversee the rebuilding of the city and threatened to line-item veto any appropriations without this control. The legislature balked at the idea of locally appointed officials because of the experiences during Reconstruction under the administration of Edmund J. Davis. John Nance Garner, who served as vice president for two terms under Franklin Delano Roosevelt, was speaker of the Texas house at that time and said that without the threat of a line-item veto you could not have found five men in Galveston who supported the commission form of government. The governor and legislature compromised, and initially the governor appointed three commissioners and the voters elected two. Later all were elected.[18]

The new commission in Galveston worked in a very expeditious manner and quickly rebuilt the port city. This efficiency attracted nationwide attention. Many other cities adopted this new form of government, assuming that the form had caused the efficiency. It was a very simple form (see figure 11.5) when compared to the older weak mayor system and the attendant long ballot of elected officials. In most commission

commission form of government

A form of local government where voters elect department heads who also serve as members of the city council.

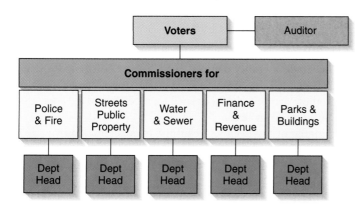

FIGURE 11.5   *The Commission Form of City Government.*

forms, the voters elected five commissioners. Each commissioner was elected citywide by the voters as the head of a department of city government and was also a member of the city commission—the legislative body. Thus, the system combined both executive and legislative functions into a single body of government.

This combination seemed to allow for quick action, but it also created many problems. Between 1901 and 1920, many cities adopted the commission form of government. After 1920 there were very few adoptions, and many cities began to abandon the form. By the end of World War II, few commission governments remained. Even Galveston abandoned the form in the 1950s.[19] These abandonments were caused by several fundamental weaknesses in the form.

The first weakness was that voters did not always elect competent administrators. Citizens voted for people based on apparent qualifications. For example, a failed banker might run for finance commissioner and stress his banking experience.[20] Voters might have no way of knowing that his banking experience had been a failure and vote on apparent qualifications. The bank, where the person worked, might want to see the person depart and not challenge his or her qualifications.

Second, the combination of legislative and executive functions, while efficient, eliminated the separation of powers and its checks and balances. Commissioners were reluctant to scrutinize the budget and actions of other commissioners for fear of retaliation. Logrolling set in: You look the other way on my budget and programs, and I will on yours.

Third, initially the commission had no leader. The commissioners rotated the position of mayor among themselves. This "mayor" presided over meetings and served as the official representative of the city but was not in a leadership position. This lack of a single, strong leader was a major shortcoming in the commission government. One writer describes it as a ship with five captains.[21] Later variations called for a separately elected mayor with budget and veto authority. Tulsa, Oklahoma, one of the last, larger cities to use the form, gave the mayor these powers.[22]

The major contribution of the commission form of government was that it served as a transition between the old weak mayor form, with many elected officials and a large city council, and the council-manager form, with no elected executives and a small city council. Many cities altered their charters, stripping the administrative power from the commissioners and assigning it to a city manager. Many Texas cities retained the term *commission* as a name for the city council. Lubbock retained the five-member commission until the 1980s, when it was forced to increase the size of the council and use single-member district elections.

✦ METHODS OF ELECTING CITY COUNCILS AND MAYORS

The traditional method, used for most of the nineteenth century, to elect city council members was the **single-member district** (see Chapter 7 on state legislature) or ward system. The city is divided into election districts of approximately equal populations, and the voters in these districts elect a council member. There are a few cases of multi-member districts, but none in Texas.

In the beginning of the twentieth century, many cities, led by early commission adoptions, moved away from the single-member district system and began to elect council members at large by all voters in the city. There are several variations on the **at-large election system.**

At-large by place is the most common such system used in Texas. In this system, candidates file for at-large ballot positions, which are usually given a number

single-member district

A system where the city is divided into election districts and only the voters living in that district elect the council member from that district.

at-large election system

System where all voters in the city elect the mayor and city council members.

CITY OF HOUSTON

MAYOR
100% precincts counted

Bell	45,591	16%
Brown (i) (r)	125,187	43%
DeVoy	487	0%
Dutrow	235	0%
Sanchez (r)	115,965	40%
Ullrich	572	0%

COUNCIL, DISTRICT A
100% precincts counted

Lawrence	12,165	43%
Tatro (i)	15,811	57%

COUNCIL, DISTRICT B
100% precincts counted

Cole	1,462	6%
Galloway (i)	16,185	65%
Glenn-Johnson	7,436	29%

COUNCIL, DISTRICT C
100% precincts counted

Goldberg (i)	22,146	68%
Hardy	6,417	20%
Kuhleman	4,096	13%

COUNCIL, DISTRICT D
100% precincts counted

Carter	6,893	17%
Clark	975	2%
Edwards (r)	15,814	39%
McKinney	665	2%
Oliver	3,343	9%
Womack (r)	13,096	32%

COUNCIL, DISTRICT E
100% precincts counted

Jones	4,036	16%
Kish	2,483	10%
Maristany (r)	4,161	16%
Orellana	1,690	7%
Rogers	2,291	9%
Wiseman (r)	10,735	42%

COUNCIL, DISTRICT F
100% precincts counted

Ellis (i)	11,161	76%
Nguyen	3,534	24%
Amadi	117	0%

COUNCIL, DISTRICT G
100% precincts counted

Keller (i)	21,979	58%
Osso	12,212	32%
Varkadoz	3,883	10%

COUNCIL, DISTRICT H
100% precincts counted

Vasquez (i)	11,248	100%

COUNCIL, DISTRICT I
100% precincts counted

Alvarado	9,136	56%
Flores	4,819	29%
Morris	2,397	15%

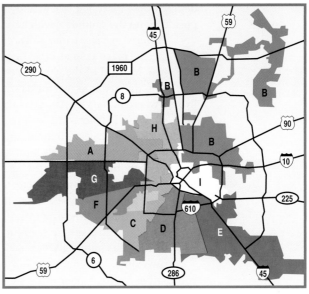

COUNCIL, AT-LARGE POSITION 1
100% precincts counted

Ayres	48,903	22%
Neal	62,762	28%
Parker (i)	114,657	51%

COUNCIL, AT-LARGE POSITION 2
100% precincts counted

Quan (i)	130,371	61%
Terence	84,776	39%

COUNCIL, AT-LARGE POSITION 3
100% precincts counted

Anawaty	9,095	4%
Biggs	15,803	7%
Burks (r)	30,558	14%
Hicks	24,269	11%
O'Brien	20,373	10%
Rodriguez (r)	85,742	40%
Whitehead	26,398	12%

COUNCIL, AT-LARGE POSITION 4
100% precincts counted

Ashley	34,427	17%
Berry (r)	82,088	40%
Griffin	27,961	14%
Lark	9,825	5%
Williamson (r)	49,282	24%

COUNCIL, AT-LARGE POSITION 5
100% precincts counted

Galvan	72,417	36%
Robinson (i)	126,573	64%

CONTROLLER
100% precincts counted

Garcia (i)	202,722	100%

FIGURE 11.6   *Voting Results for the City of Houston Election, November 6, 2001.*

SOURCE: From *Houston Chronicle*, November 8, 2001. Copyright © 2001 Houston Chronicle Publishing Company. Reprinted with permission. All rights reserved.

designation—Place 1, Place 2, and so on. Voters cast one vote for each at-large ballot position, and the candidate with a majority is elected to that place on the city council.

At-large by place with residence wards required is a system by which candidates file for a specific place as in at-large by place; however, these candidates must live in a section, area, or ward of the city to file for a specific place. Abilene, Texas, uses this form. The city is divided into two wards with three council seats in each ward. The mayor can live anywhere in the city. All voters in the city elect them at large.

At-large no place is the least common system used in Texas. Under this system, all candidates seeking election to the council have their names placed on the ballot. If there are ten candidates seeking election and five open seats, each voter is instructed to cast one vote each for five candidates. The top five vote getters are elected. With this method it is not uncommon for a candidate to win with only a plurality (less than a majority).[23]

Last, some cities use a combination of at-large and single-member district systems. Houston is a prime example. (See figure 11.6.) Voters elect nine council members from single-member districts, and five council members and the mayor are elected at large by all voters in the city.[24]

Two other systems are used to elect council members. One system is called **cumulative voting.** Under this system each voter has votes equal to the number of city council seats open in the election. If there are five seats open, each voter has five votes and may cast all five votes for one candidate (cumulating their votes), one vote each for five candidates, or any combination or variation. Several cities have adopted this system as an alternative to going to single-member districts. Since 1991, forty school districts and fourteen cities in Texas have adopted cumulative voting. The Amarillo Independent School District is the largest government body using the system in Texas (160,000 people). (See *fairvote.org/cumulative/texas.html*)

Preferential voting is another system. It allows voters to rank order the candidates for city council. All candidates' names are listed on the ballot, and the voter indicates the order of his or her preferences (first, second, third, etc.). Using a complicated ballot-counting system, the most-preferred candidates are elected. This system was used in Gorman and Sweetwater, Texas, in the past. Neither city uses the system today. The only other city in the United States currently using this system is Cambridge, Massachusetts, which has used the system for almost sixty years.[25]

Supposedly, cumulative voting and preferential voting allow a minority of voters to elect members to city councils without the baggage of single-member districts. There is no evidence that either system results in more minority candidates being elected.

Regardless of the system used to elect city council members, some city charters allow for someone to be elected with a plurality of the vote—less than a majority. In Texas, if the city council term of office is longer than two years, a majority vote is required. This may necessitate a runoff election if no one has a majority.

Since the Voting Rights Act was amended in 1975 and applied to Texas, many cities have changed from an at-large system to single-member districts. Prior to 1975 almost no Texas cities used the single-member district (SMD) system. Most of the major cities have been forced to change to SMD for at least some of the city council seats.

In cities that have changed from at-large to SMD systems, the number of minority candidates elected to the city council has increased substantially. There is some evidence that SMD council members approach their role differently than at-large council members do. A study of council members in Houston, Dallas, San Antonio, and Fort Worth found that council members from SMDs showed greater concern for neighborhood issues, engaged in vote trading, increased their contacts with constituents in their districts regarding service requests, and became more involved in administrative affairs of the city.[26]

cumulative voting
A system where voters can concentrate (accumulate) all their votes on one candidate rather than casting one vote for each office up for election.

preferential voting
A system that allows voters to rank order candidates for the city council.

Partisanship in City Politics

The ballot form might continue to be nonpartisan, but partisanship might become a big factor in Texas city politics. There is already some indication that it is a factor even in smaller cities.

In the mayoral race in College Station, Texas (population 56,000), in 1996, there was an undercurrent of partisanship. Supporters of the winner, Lynn McIlhaney, in door-to-door campaigns, reminded voters that McIlhaney was a Republican and her opponent, Nancy Crouch, was a Democrat. On election day, the chair of the local Republican party was campaigning for McIlhaney at the polling places. Republican voters were telephoned before the election and reminded that Lynn was the Republican candidate. In a city where Republicans dominate national and state elections, often winning up to 80 percent of the vote in such elections, this may have been a critical factor in McIlhaney's very decisive victory.

In 2001 the mayor's race in Houston was openly partisan. The mayor of Houston, Lee Brown, was openly supported and aided by the local, state, and national Democratic parties. Mayor Brown's opponent in that race was Orlando Sanchez, who was openly supported by the Republican party. Brown faced Sanchez in a runoff election. Both national parties supplied resources in the runoff election to increase turnout. The turnout in the runoff primary actually exceeded the first vote. In the end the incumbent Mayor Brown managed to win but not by a large margin. This race indicates the increased role partisanship will play in city elections in Texas.

While SMD council members might view their job as representing their districts first and the city as a whole second, there is no evidence that the distribution of services changes dramatically. District representation may be primarily symbolic. Symbolism is not insignificant, though, because support for local governments can be increased as minority groups feel they are represented on city councils and feel comfortable contacting their council member with problems.

Election of Mayors

The voters of the entire city generally elect mayors at large. During most of the nineteenth century this was the prevailing system. With the coming of the commission form of government, and later the council-manager form, mayors were often selected by the members of the council, from among the members of the council. In recent years the trend nationwide and in Texas has been toward at-large election of mayors in council-manager cities.

In Texas the voters of the city elect most mayors at large. There are thirty-nine home rule, mayor-council cities in Texas. In all of these, the voters elect the mayor at large. Among the 251 council-manager cities, the voters elect 228 mayors at large. The mayors in 23 smaller council-manager cities (9 percent of the total) are elected by the council. Nationwide about 35 percent of all council-manager mayors are elected by the council.[27]

The election of mayors by the voters of the city gives the mayor some independence from the council and therefore the opportunity to function as the leader of the council.

Nonpartisan Elections

Nationwide about 70 percent of city council members are elected in **nonpartisan elections.**[28] In Texas, all city elections are technically nonpartisan. Officially, a nonpartisan election is one where no party labels appear on the ballot. Unlike with the general election ballot used in November, it is not possible for the voter to determine party affiliation by looking at the ballot.

Nonpartisan elections were a feature of the reform movement in the early part of this century and were aimed at undercutting the power of partisan big-city political

nonpartisan elections
Ballot form in which voters are unable to determine the party of candidates for local office by looking at the election ballot.

machines. Reformers said that there is no Democratic or Republican way to collect garbage, pave streets, or provide police and fire protection, so partisanship should not be a factor in city decisions.

Texas cities adopted the nonpartisan system largely because the state was a one-party Democratic state for over a hundred years, and partisanship, even in state elections, was not a factor as long as you ran as a Democrat. It was only natural that city elections used nonpartisan ballots. The Texas Election Code allows for partisan city elections in home rule cities. To date, no city has officially used partisan elections.[29]

However, it should be noted that the use of a nonpartisan ballot does not eliminate partisanship from local politics. Partisanship simply takes new forms and new labels are applied. For decades in several Texas cities, "nonpartisan organizations" successfully ran slates of candidates and dominated city politics. Most noted among these organizations were the Citizens Charter Association in Dallas, the Good Government League in San Antonio, and the Business and Professional Association in Wichita Falls and Abilene.[30] The influence of these groups has declined, but slate making is not unknown today in Texas city politics. Partisanship has been a factor in city elections recently in San Antonio, Houston, and Dallas, especially in mayoral races. There is no doubt that partisanship will be a factor in city politics in the years ahead.

✦ VOTER TURNOUT IN CITY ELECTIONS

Nationwide, voter turnout in city elections is quite low—often lower than state elections. Turnout rates as low as 4 percent are not uncommon in Texas cities, and seldom do they exceed 25 percent. A number of factors contribute to low turnout.

off-year elections
Local elections that are held at another time of the year; not with state and national elections.

The first factor is **off-year elections.** State law provides two dates during the year when Texas cities may hold city council elections: the first Saturday in May, and the first Tuesday after the first Monday in November of odd-numbered years.[31] In Texas most city elections are held on the May date. In the Houston area, many cities follow Houston's lead and use the November date.

The second factor is the lack of contested races. This is so common in Texas that in 1996 a new state law went into effect that allows cities and school boards to dispense with elections if all seats are uncontested. The city or school board declares the uncontested candidates elected. A standard joke often told is that there was a person sitting on a bench by city hall with a sign reading, "Will run for mayor for food."

The third factor is a lack of publicity and interest in city elections. The news media might cover races in the major cities, especially in years when the mayor's office is up for election, but news coverage of suburban city elections in a major metropolitan area is given scant attention by the press. Also, the average citizen does not think local elections are important. The races for president, governor, and other state offices are viewed as more important. These races are also given more attention by the news media.

Off-year elections, a lack of contested races, and low levels of voter interest all contribute to low voter turnout in city elections. Participation is largely class-based; the higher socioeconomic groups vote at higher rates. (See table 11.2.) The 1991 Houston city charter election to increase the size of the city council was aimed at increasing minority representation on the city council. Despite the obvious benefits to minorities, or perhaps because of this benefit, voter turnout was higher in high-income Anglo precincts and lower in low-income precincts.

Thus lower overall voter turnout tends to benefit the high-income, nonminority areas of a city. These groups often dominate city elections and city politics. The use of single-member district systems might overcome the class bias in voting and increase the number of minority members on the council, but there is little evidence that this

TABLE 11.2

Voter Turnout in the 1991 Houston Charter Election to Increase the Number of Single-Member Seats on the City Council from 9 to 16

Group	Percentage Who Voted	Percentage For	Percentage Against
Low-income African American	4.1	64.5	35.5
Middle-income African American	9.1	60.5	39.5
Hispanic	6.9	74.4	25.6
Low-income white	12.2	20.4	79.6
Middle-income white	14.6	11.1	88.9
Affluent	24.4	7.3	93.6

Source: From *Houston Chronicle,* 12 August 1991, 8A. Copyright © 1991, Houston Chronicle Publishing Company. Reprinted with permission. All rights reserved.

produces great changes in policy. Also, SMD elections often lead to council members being elected with very small numbers of votes. For example, in a city with a population of 25,000 and six council seats elected from districts, it is quite common to have someone elected with a few hundred votes.

Low voter turnout can also impact heavily in towns where a large percentage of the population is made up of students. Students generally do not participate in local city elections, even though city governments have a big impact on the student population. For example, in Denton, the home of the University of North Texas, most students live off-campus, and the city provides electrical, water, sewer, and other services, for which fees are charged. These services affect off-campus students just as they do nonstudents. One consequence of students' not voting or participating in city government is that others make decisions that can have profound effects on the cost and the availability of housing.

Finally, while city governments are important providers of local services that are essential to urban living, most citizens pay scant attention to elections. One could argue that this may mean that most citizens are satisfied with the levels and kinds of service they are receiving. The main Texas cities have a reputation of being well run by professionals. This is in stark contrast with county government in the state. Professionalism is often quite lacking in county government. Patronage and politics more accurately describe what happens in county government.

✦ COUNTY GOVERNMENTS

The oldest type of local government in the United States is **county government,** an adaptation of the British county unit of government that was transported to this country. County governments exist in all states except Connecticut, which abolished them in 1963, and Rhode Island (which never needed them). Louisiana calls them "parishes," from the French influence, and Alaska calls them "boroughs." The number of counties varies greatly among the states. Alaska, Delaware, and Hawaii each have three county governments while Texas has 254.[32]

County governments were originally intended to be a subdivision, or an "arm," of state government to perform state functions at the local level. For example, counties in Texas still serve as voter registrar, a state function; voters register to vote with the local county government. In issuing marriage licenses, birth certificates, and automobile registrations, and in operating state courts, county governments are acting as an arm of state government.

county government

Local unit of government that is primarily the administrative arm of a state government. In most states, it does not provide urban-type services.

What's in a Name?

City governments go by a common label—*city government*. But there is no name that is consistently used for the governing body of county governments in the United States. The most common name is *board of county commissioners* or *board of supervisors*. Other examples:

Borough Assembly (Alaska)
Fiscal Court (Kentucky)
Police Jury (Louisiana)
Board of Chosen Freeholders (New Jersey)
Side Judges (Vermont)
Quorum Court (Arkansas)

The name also varies within some states. In New York county governing bodies are known as the board of supervi-sors, the county legislature, the board of representatives, and the board of legislators.

Some county officials feel these differences are confusing to citizens. Most citizens understand the terms *city council*, and *mayor* but don't know the name of county governments. Harvey Ruvin, a Dade County, Florida, commissioner, observed: "If I could wave a magic wand the first thing I would ask of county government would be a change in nomenclature.... If I tell someone in New York I'm a commissioner they think I'm a dog catcher. No wonder the public and the media focus on mayor and council members" (*Governing the States and Localities* [Washington, D.C.: Congressional Quarterly Press, 1989], 42).

Besides performing state functions, county governments also provide local services—in some states they provide many local services. In Texas, however, counties provide only very limited local services. All Texas counties provide road construction and repair and police protection through the sheriff's department. Some urban county governments operate hospitals or health units, libraries, and parks.

Urban and Rural Counties

The distinguishing feature of county government is population. Of the 3,043 counties in the United States, most are rural with small populations. About 700 counties have populations of less than 10,000, and less than 200 have populations of over 250,000. In Texas 56 percent of the population live in the ten largest urban counties. (See table 11.3.) Texas also has the distinction of having the smallest county in the United States. Loving County had a population of seventy in 2000, an increase from eighteen in 1980 due to the oil boom.[33]

In some states, urban counties are major providers of urban services. In Texas, city governments usually provide these services. Urban services include water supply, sewage disposal, planning and zoning, airports, building codes and enforcement, mass transit systems, and fire protection. With a few exceptions, Texas counties cannot perform these functions. Texas counties most closely resemble the traditional rural county governments that perform functions for the state: recording vital statistics, operating state courts and jails, administering elections, and maintaining roads and bridges. Texas counties can also assist in the creation of rural fire protection districts. In Harris County the government may assist in the creation of master water and sewer districts to combine many smaller water and sewer districts.

Urban Texans tend to identify with city governments rather than with county government. People think of themselves as residents of Houston, not Harris County. Some city residents might not be able to name the county where they reside. This stems in part from their identification with a service being provided, such as police protection. Residents of rural areas are more likely to identify with the county rather than the city, for much the same reasons. The county sheriff responds to calls for assistance in rural areas.

TABLE 11.3

The Ten Largest Counties in Texas in 1990 and 2000

	Population	
County and Major City	**1990**	**2000**
Harris (Houston)	2,925,965	3,400,578
Dallas (Dallas)	2,049,666	2,218,899
Bexar (San Antonio)	1,232,098	1,446,219
Tarrant (Fort Worth)	1,208,986	1,392,931
El Paso (El Paso)	614,927	679,622
Travis (Austin)	599,357	812,280
Hidalgo (McAllen)	398,648	569,463
Fort Bend (Richmond)	255,412	313,645
Denton (Denton)	212,792	432,976
Collin (Plano)	234,172	491,675
Total	9,732,023	11,758,288
Total state population	17,655,650	20,851,820
Percentage of population in the 10 largest counties	55%	56%

Source: Texas State Data Center, Texas A&M University (*www.txsdc.tamu.edu*).

The Structure of County Government

All Texas county governments have the same basic structure, regardless of the county's size. This structure mirrors the fragmented structure of state government. It can most accurately be described as weak or plural executive. Voters elect the heads of major departments of county government. (See figure 11.7.) These provisions appeared in the constitution of 1876. The writers of this document distrusted appointive authority and trusted the electorate to choose administrators.[34]

In Texas, the governing body of county government is the **county commissioner's court.** It is composed of the **constitutional county judge** and four county commissioners. The county judge is elected at large, and each commissioner is elected from a single-member district called a *commissioner precinct.* Like most other state officeholders, these officials are elected for four-year terms in partisan elections. Even though this body is termed the *commissioner's court,* it is not a court but a legislative body. Its duties include passing local ordinances, approving budgets and new programs, and oversight of county government.

The county judge presides as the chair of the commissioner's court, participates as a full member in deliberations, and has a vote on all matters. The constitution assigns judicial duties to this office, but the occupant does not have to be a licensed attorney; the constitution states that the constitutional county judge must be "well informed in the law." In seventy-two urban counties, where the state legislature has created county courts of law, the constitutional county judge performs only very limited judicial functions. The judicial functions of constitutional county courts (described in Chapter 9) are transferred to the county courts of law, and the constitutional county judge acts as the primary administrative officer of the county.

Like other legislative districts, commissioner precincts eventually became malapportioned. In 1968 the U.S. Supreme Court ruled that the one-person-one-vote rule applied to these election districts. The Commissioner's Court in Midland County claimed it was a court and not a legislative body, and that therefore the one-person-one-vote

county commissioner's court
Legislative body that governs a Texas county.

constitutional county judge
Chief administrative officer of county government in Texas. May also have judicial duties in rural counties.

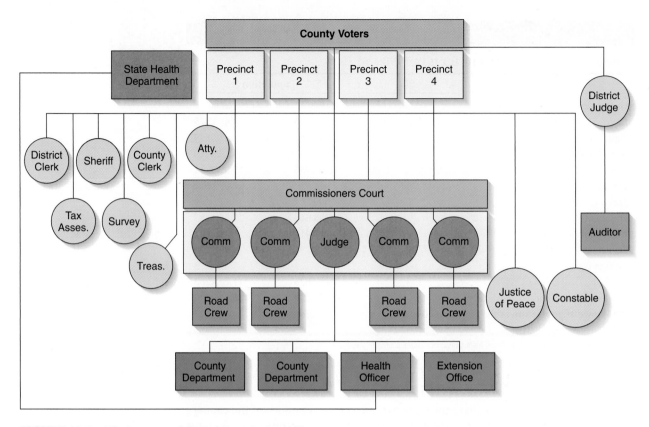

FIGURE 11.7 *The Structure of County Government in Texas.*

SOURCE: John A. Gilmartin and Joe M. Rothe. *County Government in Texas,* issue 2, V. G. Young Institute of County Government. Texas Agricultural Extension Service. Texas A&M University.

rule did not apply. The U.S. Supreme Court disagreed and ruled that it was a legislative body and not a court, and that election districts had to be equally apportioned.[35]

There are seven constitutionally prescribed officers elected by the voters: sheriff, district attorney, county attorney, tax assessor collector, district clerk, county clerk, and county treasurer. These officials act as heads of departments of government. Some counties also have other minor elected officials, such as county surveyor and inspector of hides and wools.

county sheriff
Elected head of law enforcement in a Texas county.

The **county sheriff** is elected countywide for a four-year term and serves as the law enforcement officer for the county. Sheriffs can appoint deputy sheriffs. In rural counties the sheriff may be the primary law enforcement officer. In urban counties city police departments carry out most of these duties, and the sheriff's primary duty may be to operate the county jail. In the smaller counties (below 1,800 residents), state law allows the sheriff to act as the tax assessor collector.[36] Some have suggested that combining sheriff and tax collector is a frightening leftover from Anglo-Saxon law, inspiring visions of Sherwood Forest, the Sheriff of Nottingham, and Robin Hood.

The voters also elect constables, who serve as law enforcement officers. Their primary function is to serve as court officers for the justice of the peace courts, delivering subpoenas and other court orders. Constables may also provide police protection in the precinct they serve.

The county and district attorneys are the chief prosecuting attorneys for criminal cases in the county. Not all counties have county attorneys. In counties with a county attorney, this office usually prosecutes the less serious criminal offenses before county courts and the district attorney prosecutes major crimes before the district courts.

The tax assessor collector is responsible for collecting revenue for the state and county. Before 1978 this office also assessed the value of all property in the county for property tax collection purposes. In 1978 these functions were transferred to a countywide assessment district. There are 180 of these tax assessment districts in the state, and they are governed by a board elected by the governing bodies of all governments in the jurisdiction—counties, cities, school districts, and special districts. While this office still has the title *assessor,* few occupants serve in this capacity today. Most still collect county property taxes, sell state vehicle licenses and permits, and serve as voter registrars. The voter registration function is a carryover from the days of the poll tax.[37]

The county clerk is the chief record keeper for the county and keeps track of all property records and issues marriage licenses, birth certificates, and other county records. Although normally the function of voter registration rests with the tax assessor collector, in some counties this function has been transferred to the county clerk, who in all counties is responsible for conducting elections.

The district clerk is primarily a court official who maintains court records for county and district courts. The clerk schedules cases in these courts and maintains records.

The county treasurer is responsible for receiving, maintaining, and disbursing county funds. In many counties, this office has been eliminated by constitutional amendment because the county auditor duplicates the functions. There is probably no reason to retain the office of treasurer in any Texas county.

The district judge or judges in the county appoint the county auditor. The county auditor's responsibility is to oversee the collection and disbursement of county funds. The auditor reports to the district judge or judges. Not all counties have auditors. Counties with populations of less than 10,000 are not required to have auditors. In larger counties (population above 250,000), the auditor acts as a budget officer unless the commissioner's court appoints its own budget officer.[38]

Weaknesses of County Government in Texas

The **weaknesses in county government** in Texas can be broadly divided into two kinds: (1) inherent weaknesses in the plural executive form of government, and (2) powerlessness of county governments to confront many problems in urban areas.

As we have already seen, the plural executive structure of county government in Texas is a product of the nineteenth century and the general distrust of centralized executive authority. The plural executive structure lacks centralized authority, and the elected officials can, and often do, act quite independently of each other. While the county commissioner's court does exercise some control over these department heads, it is primarily limited to budgetary matters. After a budget is approved, elected officials can make many independent decisions.

Elected officials also hire their own staffs. After each election, personnel at the county courthouse can change dramatically. For example, new sheriffs hire their own deputy sheriffs. The patronage ("spoils") system in some courthouses results in a less professional staff.

As indicated in our discussion of the judiciary in Chapter 9 and in the discussion of the commission form of city government in this chapter, elections are imperfect instruments for determining the qualifications of candidates and do not always select the most competent person to administer departments. The appointment of department heads is more likely to result in the selection of competent persons. A lack of professionalism and competence is a frequently noted problem with county officials in some counties.

weaknesses in county government
The inherent weakness in the plural executive form of government and the lack of power to deal with urban problems in large urban counties.

In most (201 of 254) Texas counties, each county commissioner is responsible for road repair within the boundaries of the commissioner's precinct in which she or he is elected.[39] Basically, this means that there are four road crews, each under the direction of a commissioner. While there is some sharing of equipment, there are duplications and inefficiencies with four separate crews. Commissioners have also been known to use their road crews to reward supporters with more favorable attention to road repairs that affect them directly.

County government was designed to meet the needs of and provide services to a rural population. In rural areas of the state it still functions adequately. However, in large urban counties this form of government has many weaknesses.

The first of these weaknesses is the inability to provide urban-type services. Dense urban populations demand and need services that are unnecessary in rural areas. Usually, county governments are powerless under state law to provide even the most basic services common to city governments, such as water and sewer services. In the 1999 session of the legislature Harris County was given limited authority to assist in the formation of "master" water and sewer districts by consolidating many small suburban districts.

Citizens living on the fringe of cities are forced to provide these services themselves or to form other governments, such as a water district, to provide these services. In recent years, garbage (solid waste) collection and disposal have become a problem in the urban fringe areas. Many citizens must contract with private collectors for this service. Some counties help residents by providing collection centers, often operated by private contractors. In the area of fire protection, counties often help rural residents to establish volunteer fire departments. However, counties are not permitted to operate fire departments. Each rural fire department goes its own way, and there is often a lack of coordination between departments. Training and equipment generally are below the standards of full-time city fire departments. Counties sometimes contract with city governments in the county to provide fire protection for the county, although this practice has declined in recent years.

County governments also lack general ordinance authority. City governments in Texas may pass any ordinance not prohibited by state law, but county governments must seek legislative approval to pass specific ordinances. For example, county governments may not pass ordinances on land use (zoning) or building codes that regulate construction standards. A citizen buying a home in a rural area is largely dependent upon the integrity of the builder.

Even where counties have been given the authority to regulate activities, they often fall short. For example, counties were given the authority to pass ordinances regulating the construction of septic systems. Some counties failed to pass such ordinances, and many failed to adequately inspect the installation of septic systems. This function was transferred to the state health department in 1992.

Last, a related problem with county governments is the inequity of financial resources and expenditures. A few counties have a sales tax, but most rely almost exclusively on the property tax. Most of this tax is paid by citizens living inside cities and not in the unincorporated, rural areas of the county. For example, in the tax year 2000 in Brazos County, the total taxable property was $4.9 billion. Most of this value ($4.2 billion) was located within the cities of Bryan and College Station, leaving only $714 million in rural Brazos County.[40] Thus, most (85 percent) of the cost of county government is paid for by city residents paying county taxes. While county residents pay little of the cost to operate county governments, they receive many services from county governments (such as road construction and repair, police protection) that are not provided to city residents by the county. City residents receive these services from their city and pay city taxes. City residents are paying twice for services they receive only once. This financial inequity goes unnoticed by most citizens.

Possible Reform of County Government

Since the 1930s there have been suggestions to reform county government in Texas. The rhetoric often called for county government to be "brought into the twentieth century." In Texas, apparently all such reforms skipped the twentieth century and have to wait for the twenty-first century. While other states have modernized county governments, Texas has steadfastly refused all efforts for change. One suggestion that has been a frequent agenda item over the past seventy years is to allow for county home rule, which would allow the voters in each county to adopt a local option charter.[41] Voters could then approve any form of government not prohibited by state law; no county would be forced to change their form of government. This might result in the adoption of a strong executive form of government similar to the strong mayor or council-manager forms popular with Texas cities. Even though this suggestion seems quite reasonable, it has been strongly opposed by the many county elected officials in Texas who see this as a threat to their jobs.

The Texas Association of Counties (TAC) is an umbrella organization that represents elected county officials—sheriffs, tax collectors, treasurers, judges, commissioners, and so on. The TAC has opposed granting county governments home rule. This group is politically powerful and has many supporters throughout the state. One group within the TAC, the Conference of Urban Counties (CUC), has shown mild support for home rule. The CUC represents thirty metropolitan county governments in Texas where home rule would have the greatest impact. The CUC is not pushing home rule issues and is more concerned with representing the unique interests of urban counties.

County officials often have very provincial attitudes about the role of county government. The idea of expanding county services is foreign to many county officials. They seem content with the status quo. Prospects are dim for any great change in Texas county government in the short run. Urban counties will continue to face many problems

---

H·I·G·H·L·I·G·H·T

More Books Than Anyone Can Read, Just Do It Right, and Sick Horses

Why should I care if county government is firmly entrenched in the nineteenth century? County officials have traditionally resisted change in their powers to deal with urban problems. They have a very provincial attitude toward providing service, and their view of county government does not extend much beyond that of a ninteenth-century official. This means that urban problems that are outside cities often are neglected. Even simple things like the safety of home construction and septic systems are neglected. This can have an effect on your life and health.

County officials often will not even consider providing things which might enhance community amenities. For example, the city council in College Station once proposed that the city libraries be combined and made into a county library operated by Brazos County. A county commissioner was quoted as saying, "The last thing in the world we need is a bigger library. I was down at the Bryan Library once and they already got more books than anyone can read and every year they ask the county for more money to buy more books." The city council cooled on the idea of a county-run library with this provincial attitude among county officials.

County government was given the responsibility for inspecting septic systems in rural areas. One county never passed an ordinance or put in place an inspection system. When asked why they did not have an ordinance or inspections, a citizen was told, "We just expect you to do it right." The state has since given this authority to the state health department and septic installers must be licensed.

County government is often more concerned with problems of rural residents rather than those living in cities. When the Brazos Animal Shelter confiscated a number of horses that it felt were being mistreated and were malnourished, the county commissioner's court, at the request of rural residents, prevented the animal shelter from doing this in the future and turned this function over to the sheriff who is orientated toward policing in rural areas, but not animal control.

that have only a mild impact on rural counties. Also, proposed changes in Medicare funding could have a great impact on the seven most populous counties that operate hospitals. In the short run, urban counties will have to seek solutions to their problems that do not involve the major structural changes home rule would bring.

Improving the professionalism of the staff might prove difficult since each elected county official can hire his or her own people. Some county officials in some counties place great emphasis on professionalism. Other officials reward faithful campaign workers with appointments. In rural counties, these jobs are often well paid and much sought after by supporters.

→ SPECIAL DISTRICT GOVERNMENTS

special district governments
Form of local government that provides specific services to citizens, such as water, sewage, fire protection, or public transportation.

Special district governments are another form of local government that provides services to local residents. Special districts have been referred to as *shadow governments* because they operate out of the view of most citizens. These governments are created for many reasons and perform many functions. Some districts are single function (e.g., fire) and others are multipurpose (e.g., water, sewer, street repair). Some special districts (such as metropolitan transit districts) cover several counties and others (such as the municipal utility districts) are very small, covering only a few acres.

The primary reason special districts are created is to provide services when no other unit of government exists to provide that service. Sometimes the need extends beyond the geographical boundaries of existing units of government. A good example of this is mass transportation. Dallas/Fort Worth, Houston, San Antonio, Austin, El Paso, and other metropolitan areas have created transit districts that serve several counties. Sometimes the service involves natural boundaries that extend over county lines. Soil and water conservation and flood control are good examples of this. In still other cases, the need for a service may be confined to a single county but no government unit exists to provide the service. An excellent example of this is municipal utility districts (MUDs). These are multifunction districts generally created outside cities to provide water, sewage treatment, and other services. In Texas, these MUDs are created because county governments cannot provide these services. Finally, some districts are created for political reasons, when no existing unit of government wants to solve the service problem because of potential political conflicts. The creation of another unit of government to deal with a hot political issue is preferable. The Gulf Coast Waste Disposal Authority, created to clean up water pollution in the Houston area, is a good example of this.

The Gulf Coast Waste Disposal Authority is a government unit created to deal with water pollution in the Houston area.

Special districts are often an efficient and expedient way to solve a problem, but they can also generate problems. One problem citizens face is keeping track of the many special districts that provide services to them. For example, a MUD, a soil and water conservation district, a flood control district, a fire protection district, a metropolitan transit authority, a hospital district, and a waste disposal district can govern a citizen living in the Houston suburbs. Most citizens have trouble distinguishing among a school district, a county, and a city. Dealing with seven or more units of government is even more complicated.

The governing boards of special districts in Texas are selected in two ways. Multi-county special districts (such as DART in Dallas and METRO in Houston) are governed by boards appointed by the governmental units (cities, counties) covered by the district. Single-county special districts (such as MUDs and flood control districts) usually have a board of directors elected by the voters.

Many special districts have taxation authority and can raise local property taxes. The remoteness of these districts from the electorate, their number, and their potential impact on the lives of citizens raise questions of democratic control.[42] The average citizen cannot be expected to know about, understand, and keep track of the decisions made by these remote governments. The alternatives are to consolidate governments, expand cities through the annexation of land, or expand the power of county governments. None of these alternatives is generally acceptable. Citizens demand and expect local governments to be decentralized. This is true even if they have only limited ability to watch and control the actions of local government and the government is ineffective. Big government is something most Texans want to avoid.

✦ School Districts

Another type of special district government that generally is watched and controlled very closely by citizens is the school district. Because school districts play a very important role in the lives of all citizens, we will distinguish them from other special districts for discussion.

Since 1942 the number of school districts in the United States has decreased dramatically. In 1942 there were 108,579 school districts in the United States. The number had declined to 14,851 by 1982, to 14,422 by 1992, to 13,726 in 1997, and 13,506 in 2002. Texas also experienced declines in the number of school districts: 1,100 in 1992, 1,087 in 1997, and 1,089 in 2002.[43] This consolidation has been driven by several factors. First, there have been demands for improved curriculum, especially in science and math. In many small rural school districts it was not possible to provide the desired range and diversity of curriculum. Second, there has been increased state financial aid to school districts that consolidate. Last, one can point to improved road conditions. For example, Texas developed the farm-to-market road system in the 1950s. This system, coupled with improved all-weather county roads, made possible the busing of students to urban schools.

In the rural areas of Texas there are still many school districts with a small student body that could consolidate with neighboring districts. Sometimes resistance to consolidation is driven by considerations for the school football program and the realization that closing the school will lead to the death of the town. Often the school is the only glue that holds things together. Football and community pride are powerful forces, even if the football team has only six players.

The future will see few additional consolidations. The demand today is not for consolidation but for decentralization with the "open-enrollment charter school." In 1995 the legislature authorized the creation of "up to 20 charters for open-enrollment charter schools. These schools can be operated in school districts or non-school district facilities, by public or private higher education institutions, non-profit organizations or governmental entities."[44] Additional charter schools were authorized in the 1997 and

1999 sessions of the legislature. In 1998–99 there were 89 charter schools operating in the state, and by 2000–2001 the number had increased to 140. The exact implication of these charter schools is not quite clear. Some preliminary reports and data are available from the Texas Education Agency. It is unclear if these schools will produce substantial improvements in student achievement.[45] Thirty-two other states have some version of home rule or charter schools. What is clear from the passage of these laws is that many citizens want to decentralize control over local schools. Further consolidation seems unlikely.

independent school districts
School districts that are not attached to any other unit of government and operate schools in Texas.

All but one of the 1,089 school districts in Texas are called **independent school districts.** This means that they are independent of any other unit of government. In seventeen states, 1,412 school systems are attached, or dependent upon another unit of government, most commonly a city or a county.[46] Most are located in the East and the Midwest. There are few in the West and South. In Texas, the Stafford school district in the Houston suburbs is the only school district attached to a city government. Reformers advocated making the school district independent of city government early in this century. Such independence was supposed to isolate the schools from evil political influences of city government.

A seven-member elected school board governs most independent school districts in Texas. School board elections are often held in May with city elections. Some school boards are elected from single-member districts; most are at large, and all are chosen in nonpartisan ballot elections.

✦ Issues in School Politics

While the creation of independent school districts may have reduced the influence of city politics, school district elections are still quite political. Over the past several decades many issues have dominated school politics.

The first such issue, and perhaps the most difficult to resolve, is school finance. The state of Texas pays for part of the cost of education. Over the past twenty years, the state's share of the cost of education has declined, and local school districts have been forced to pick up a larger part of the cost. Today, the state of Texas pays about 38 percent of the cost of education, and local districts provide the remainder.[47] Because the only source of local financial support is the property tax, some school districts have been better able than others to absorb the higher local share. Some school districts have a high per-pupil property tax base (so-called rich districts) and others have a low per-pupil property tax base (so-called poor districts). While the state does show preference to poor districts with increased funding, this support is still inadequate, and great disparities exist in the amount of money available to school districts on a per-pupil basis.

These inequities became a statewide issue in 1968 when parents in the Edgewood school district in San Antonio filed a lawsuit challenging the financing of schools in Texas (*Rodriguez v. San Antonio Independent School District*). The U.S. Supreme Court found the system of school financing to be unfair, but said that it was a state problem and that its resolution rested with the state. Because of this case, the state did increase aid to poor school districts. However, severe inequities continued. In 1984 another lawsuit brought education finance to the forefront in Texas (*Edgewood v. Kirby*). This case was filed in state district court, and due to efforts of the Mexican American Legal Defense and Education Fund and the Equity Center in Austin, the Texas Supreme Court in 1989 ruled the system of school finance in the state unconstitutional.

Data used in this court case indicate the disparities among school districts. (See table 11.4.) The critical variable in table 11.4 is the *par value*. This is an index of the per-pupil/student value of property in a district compared with the statewide average,

TABLE 11.4

Per-Student Property Tax Value among Selected School Districts in Texas in 1997 and 2002*

School District	Total Students		Market Value per Student		Par Value Index	
	1997	2002	1997	2002	1997	2002
Kingsville	5,136	4,644	$ 79,623	$ 113,995	39	49
Santa Gertudis	263	275	561,398	516,853	277	220
Houston	209,375	210,670	218,539	313,871	108	138
Spring	21,044	24,429	151,327	198,109	75	84
Alamo Heights	4,160	4,493	455,614	611,442	225	261
Edgewood	14,180	13,435	29,893	38,150	14	16
San Antonio	61,361	57,421	94,342	127,469	47	54
Dallas	154,847	163,562	245,753	343,973	121	147
Highland Park	5,483	5,869	740,857	1,116,216	366	476
Plano	40,864	48,944	362,159	523,561	178	223
Harlingen	16,156	16,049	81,171	117,559	40	50
Port Isabel	2,228	2,349	403,515	539,691	199	230
College Station	6,939	7,424	260,347	362,352	128	155
Navasota	3,074	3,049	167,953	201,866	82	86

*Par value is an index of average property values per pupil in the state. An index of 100 is the statewide average, which in 1997 was $202,587 per pupil. If the district is below the statewide average it has an index of less than 100. Above 100 and the district has an above average property tax value per pupil.

Sources: Data for 1997 from Texas Education Agency data set. Data provided by Ken Meier and John Bohte, faculty members at TAMU.

with an index of 100 being average. If a district is above 100, it has more wealth per pupil; below 100, it has less wealth per pupil. Changes in state law have decreased these disparities, but inequities still exist. While state aid does make up for some of these differences, most aid is aimed at providing the basic foundations of education. The rich districts can still provide funds for so-called enrichments.

In an attempt to correct these inequities, the state legislature in 1991 consolidated property taxes within 188 units called *county education districts*. These districts collected property taxes to be used for school operations and distributed it to the school districts in their jurisdiction on a per-student basis. This system became known as the "Robin Hood plan" and was challenged in court by some rich districts. The courts ruled that the plan violated the Texas Constitution. The state legislature proposed a constitutional amendment to make the system legal. In May 1993 the voters rejected this amendment by a large margin (63 percent against).[48]

The rejection of this issue had political implications in the 1995 governor's race. According to the *Dallas Morning News,* the Republican National Committee spent $400,000 to help defeat this amendment and to promote negative views about the governor, Ann Richards. The ads tied Richards to the amendment.[49] Richards was defeated by George W. Bush in 1994. Richards may still have lost even without the ads.

Following the defeat of this amendment, the legislature passed a new law that gave several options to so-called rich districts. This plan was acceptable to the courts. Under this plan a school district's property tax wealth is capped at $305,000 per pupil. At that point a district has several choices. It may send its excess wealth to the state, which will send the money to poor districts. It can also combine its wealth with a specific district. Most send the money to the state. After a district reaches the $305,000 per-pupil cap, it receives very little state money. It still receives some federal funds. Ninety percent of the school districts in Texas are "poor districts." Only 10 percent must give money to the state. This system is also labeled the **Robin Hood plan.**

The 2003 session of the legislature again faced the problem of school finances. A new issue that has grown out of the present system is that school district taxes are capped by state law at no more than $1.50 per $100 of valuation for operations. School bonds can be repaid with additional taxes. Many districts have reached the $1.50 limit and still do not have enough money to operate. A few are suggesting that they may have to close for lack of funds. The legislature will have to find a solution to this problem. The state faced a $10 billion shortfall, and equity in school finance was ignored. The legislature adjourned with no action.

The current system is, at best, a Band-Aid approach that does not address the basic problem of the differences in resources among the school districts in the state. The legislature has had over thirty-five years to address the issues initially raised in *Rodriguez v. San Antonio ISD* and has failed to do so. Equity in education funding is not a value supported by the political culture of Texas.[50]

Governor Bush made education improvement a "cornerstone" of his programs. In the 1995 session of the legislature, he made some progress in getting minor changes that may improve education in Texas. Prior to the 1997 session an interim study group appointed by Governor Bush failed to develop meaningful ideas for improving the financing of state schools. The legislature eventually developed a program to provide for an additional homeowners exemption. While it was billed as the "largest tax decrease" in Texas history, it was not a tax decrease. It was an increase in the amount of money appropriated to schools with the requirement that homeowners be given an additional $5,000 in exemptions in the value on which they had to pay property taxes. In some school districts, most of the property is owner-occupied, single-family property. If the value of each property is reduced by $5,000 the total taxable property is declined; some districts actually had to raise the tax rate. The 1999 session of the legislature gave additional money to schools with the hope that local districts would decrease property taxes. This was also billed as a tax decrease, when in fact it was an increase in appropriations to schools with the hope of tax reductions by school districts. Once again the impact varied from district to district. This required exemption for owner-occupied dwellings has contributed to the problem some districts face of being at the $1.50 tax limit discussed earlier.

The so-called rich districts filed a lawsuit to throw out the Robin Hood plan. The district court ruled the Robin Hood system unconstitutional. This was, in part, upheld by the Texas Supreme Court, which ordered the Texas legislature to redo school finance before September 2006.

Under pressure from a decision by the Texas Supreme Court to close the schools in the Fall of 2006, the legislature met in a special session to consider the changes in school finance. The legislature eventually produced a plan that will provide some modest reduction of property tax for homeowners, additional property tax for businesses, an increase by $1.00 per pack on cigarettes, and an increase in the franchise tax paid by businesses. This act has probably solved the school finance issue for the next year or two. Some estimates are that the state will face funding shortfalls of several million dollars over the next five years.

A second issue is the quality of education given to students. In the early 1980s, Governor Mark White raised the profile of this issue. Working with Lt. Governor Hobby and House Speaker Gib Lewis, a select committee on public education was appointed. Texas billionaire Ross Perot was appointed chair of this committee. The recommendations of this committee led to the passage of House Bill 72, which contained two very controversial provisions. While it provided funding for a teacher pay raise, it also required

ETTA HULME © 2004, reprinted by permission of United Media.

the state's teachers to pass a test to prove their competency. There was great resistance to this test by the teachers, although it was apparently a rather simple test designed to weed out the completely unqualified. Some referred to the test as a literacy test. Despite the easiness of the test, many teachers resented taking it and took it as a personal affront. Many blame this test and the teachers' reactions to it for Mark White's loss to Bill Clements in the 1986 governor's race.

The second controversial provision in House Bill 72 was the no-pass, no-play provision. This new rule prohibited students from participating in extracurricular activities if they were not passing all their courses. Of course, the most important no-play was football. In a state where Friday night football is an institution and in many small towns the premier social event, preventing students from participating simply because they failed a course was viewed as not only un-Texan, but perhaps a little "communistic." Students were also prohibited from participating in band, tennis, soccer, swimming, and cheerleading, but no one really much cared beyond football (although some communities cared about baseball). The no-pass, no-play rule also contributed to Mark White's defeat in 1986. The effects of no-pass, no-play and teacher literacy tests were probably more symbolic than real.

In school board elections in Texas and much of the nation, three curriculum issues have caused much controversy: sex education, **intelligent design (ID),** and bilingual education. Sex education and ID are issues that are driven by the Christian Right or "Social Conservatives," which has a comfortable majority on the state board of education and is attempting to elect local school board members. These candidates often run as "stealth" candidates—not openly revealing their agenda during the campaign. Their aim is to limit sex education to abstinence-based programs and to require the teaching of ID as an alternative to evolution or along with evolution. The extent to which these groups have managed to control school boards is unknown. It is unlikely that the issues will be resolved anytime soon. The Christian Right or Social Conservatives have had an impact

intelligent design (ID)
Faith-based pseudoscience used to counter the teaching of evolution. Also known as creation science.

in choosing the state school board, which is elected by districts in the state. Some authority of this board has been reduced by actions of the legislature in the past ten years. More restrictions are likely in future sessions of the legislature especially in the area of textbook selection.

Bilingual education is a controversy dating to the early twentieth century, when Germans and Czechs in Texas wanted to teach their native languages in the schools. Following World War I, anti-German sentiment in the state killed these efforts, and in the 1920s the legislature prohibited the teaching of languages (other than English). There is an old story in the lore of Texas politics that claims that when Governor Ma Ferguson signed the bill prohibiting the teaching of children in any language other than English, she reportedly said: "If English was good enough for Jesus Christ, it's good enough for the school children of Texas."

Currently the bilingual issue revolves around teaching in Spanish and English to Hispanic children in the elementary schools. Many Anglo Texans object to the use of tax money for bilingual education. Some take the inconsistent position that everyone should speak English but no tax money should be spent to ensure that they can. Governors Bush and Perry both helped soften the resistance to these education programs and reached out to the Hispanic voters in the state.

✦ Conclusions

While local governments do not generate the same degree of interest that national and state governments do, they have extremely important effects on the daily lives of citizens. Without the services provided by local governments, modern urban life would not be possible.

In Texas, city governments are the principal providers of local services. Council-manager governments govern most major cities, a system that has brought a degree of professionalism to city government that is often lacking in county and some other units of local government. In many respects, the contrast between county and city government is remarkable. County governments have resisted change and seem content to operate under a form of government designed by and for an agrarian society. It is a paradox that council-manager city government and plural executive county government could exist in the same state, given the political culture. Economy, efficiency, and professionalism are not values supported by the traditionalistic political culture of the state, yet they are widely practiced in council-manager government.

While many problems of public education remain unresolved, the most pressing is school finance. The current Band-Aid solution does not address the problems of high school taxes in many districts or the degree to which the state finances local government. As we saw in Chapter 10, finding new sources of state revenue to reduce local property taxes seems unlikely.

Internet Resources

Center for Voting and Democracy: *fairvote.org*

City Links: *usacitylink.com/*
> This site has information on cities across the nation. You may be able to locate your home town page and get information on your city government.

Information on state education funding can be found at:
> *teep.tamu.edu/*

International City/County Management Association: *icma.org/*

National League of Cities: *www.nlc.org/*
> National organization representing city governments in the United States.

Texas Association of Counties: *www.county.org/*

Texas Judiciary Online: *www.courts.state.tx.us/*

Texas Municipal League: *www.tml.org/*

Key Terms

at-large election system (p. 250)

city manager (p. 248)

commission form of government (p. 249)

constitutional county judge (p. 257)

council-manager form of government (p. 246)

county commissioner's court (p. 257)

county government (p. 255)

county sheriff (p. 258)

creatures of the state (p. 242)

cumulative voting (p. 251)

decentralized nation (p. 241)

extra territorial jurisdiction (ETJ) (p. 244)

general law cities (p. 243)

home rule cities (p. 243)

implicit or explicit prohibitions on city ordinance power (p. 243)

incorporation (p. 244)

independent school districts (p. 264)

intelligent design (ID) (p. 267)

nonpartisan elections (p. 253)

off-year elections (p. 254)

preferential voting (p. 252)

Robin Hood plan (p. 266)

single-member district (p. 250)

special district governments (p. 262)

strong mayor form of government (p. 246)

weak mayor form of government (p. 246)

weaknesses in county government (p. 259)

Notes

1. Federal Advisory Commission on Intergovernmental Relations, *State and Local Roles in the Federal System: A-88* (Washington, D.C.: U.S. Government Printing Office, 1982), 59.
2. Ibid.
3. Ibid., 59, table 20.
4. Terrell Blodgett, *Texas Home Rule Charters* (Austin: Texas Municipal League, 1994), 1.
5. There are three types (A, B, and C) of cities provided for in Texas state law. However, there are seven variations on the number of council members and their methods of election. See *Vernon's Texas Statutes and Codes Annotated,* vol. 1, 5.001–5.003.
6. Texas Municipal League, *Handbook for Mayors and Councilmembers in General Law Cities* (Austin: Texas Municipal League, 1994).
7. *Vernon's Texas Statutes and Codes Annotated,* "Local Government," vol. 1, 9.001–9.008.
8. Blodgett, *Texas Home Rule Charters,* 4.
9. Ibid., 113–14.
10. *Vernon's Texas Statutes and Codes Annotated,* "Local Government," vol. 1, 7.005.
11. David L. Martin, *Running City Hall: Municipal Administration in the United States* (Tuscaloosa: University of Alabama Press, 1990), 21–22.
12. *Vernon's Texas Statutes and Codes Annotated,* "Local Government," vol. 1, 42.021.
13. James A. Svara, *Official Leadership in the City: Patterns of Conflict and Cooperation* (New York: Oxford University Press, 1990), chaps. 2 and 3.
14. Blodgett, *Texas Home Rule Charters,* 30–31.
15. Ibid., 39.
16. Svara, *Official Leadership in the City.*
17. Richard Stillman, *The Rise of the City Manager: A Public Professional in Local Government* (Albuquerque: University of New Mexico Press, 1974), 15.
18. Bradley Robert Rice, *Progressive Cities: The Commission Government Movement in America, 1901–1920* (Austin: University of Texas Press, 1977), 12.
19. Ibid., 109.
20. Ibid., 85.
21. Ibid., 52.
22. Tulsa City Charter, June 1954, 6.
23. For a good discussion of electoral systems in American cities, see Joseph Zimmerman, *The Federal City: Community Control in Large Cities* (New York: St. Martin's Press, 1972), chap. 4.
24. Blodgett, *Texas Home Rule Charters,* 46–47.
25. Martin, *Running City Hall,* 78. Also see a report on the use of this system in Cambridge, Massachusetts: *Computerizing a Cambridge Tradition: An Analysis of Cambridge's 1991 City Council Election Count Using a Computer Program* (1992), Center for Voting and Democracy, 6905 Fifth St., NW, Suite 200, Washington, D.C.
26. Svara, *Official Leadership in the City,* 136. Also see Lyndon B. Johnson School of Public Affairs, *Local Government Election Systems,* Policy Research Report No. 62 (Austin: University of Texas Press, 1984), 46–55, 145–46.
27. Blodgett, *Texas Home Rule Charters,* 48.
28. International City Management Association, *Municipal Year Book* (Washington, D.C.: International City Management Association, 1988), 17.

29. *Vernon's Texas Statutes and Codes Annotated,* "Elections," 41.003.

30. For a discussion of San Antonio, see David R. Johnson, John A. Booth, and Richard J. Harris, *The Politics of San Antonio: Community Progress and Power* (Lincoln: University of Nebraska Press, 1983). Also see Richard A. Smith, "How Business Failed Dallas," in *Governing Texas: Documents and Readings,* 2d ed., ed. Fred Gantt, Jr., et al. (New York: Thomas Y. Crowell, 1970), 122–29.

31. *Vernon's Texas Statutes and Codes Annotated,* "Elections," 41.003.

32. U.S. Department of Commerce, Bureau of the Census, *1997 Census of Governments: Government Organization,* vol. 1, no. 1 (Washington, D.C.: U.S. Government Printing Office, 1997), 18, table 13.

33. U.S. Census of Population 2000, (*www.census.gov*).

34. Gary M. Halter and Gerald L. Dauthery, "The County Commissioners Court in Texas," in *Governing Texas: Documents and Readings,* 3d ed., ed. Fred Gantt, Jr., et al. (New York: Thomas Y. Crowell, 1974), 340–50.

35. *Avery v. Midland County,* 88 S. Ct. 1114 (1968).

36. Robert E. Norwood and Sabrina Strawn, *Texas County Government: Let the People Choose,* 2d ed. (Austin: Texas Research League, 1984).

37. Ibid., 24. Also see John A. Gilmartin and Joe M. Rothe, *County Government in Texas: A Summary of the Major Offices and Officials,* Issue No. 2 (College Station: Texas Agricultural Extension Service).

38. Norwood and Strawn, *Texas County Government,* 27.

39. Information supplied by the Texas Association of Counties, Austin.

40. Property tax records of the Brazos County Central Appraisal District, 1673 Briarcrest Dr., Bryan, TX.

41. For an extensive explanation of the county home rule efforts in Texas, see Wilborn E. Benton, *Texas: Its Government and Politics,* 2d ed. (Englewood Cliffs, N.J.: Prentice Hall, 1966), 317–81.

42. For a discussion of the benefits and problems of special districts, see Virginia Pernod, *Special District, Special Purposes: Fringe Governments and Urban Problems in the Houston Area* (College Station: Texas A&M University Press, 1984).

43. *2002 Census of Governments,* 2:17, table 3.

44. Texas Legislative Budget Board home page (*http://www.lbb.state.tx.us*).

45. Nancy Frank, *Charter Schools: Experiments in Reform, an Update* (Austin: Texas Legislative Budget Board, Public Education Team, 1995).

46. *2002 Census of Governments,* 2:17, table 15.

47. Texas Legislative Budget Board home page (*www.lbb.state.tx.us*).

48. Secretary of State, State of Texas, *Votes on Proposed Amendments to the Texas Constitution, 1875–November 1993* (Austin: Secretary of State, 1994), 73.

49. *Dallas Morning News,* 12 January 1994, 1A.

50. Secretary of State, State of Texas, *Votes on Proposed Amendments,* 28.

CHAPTER 12

❦

PUBLIC POLICY IN TEXAS

What is public policy? **Public policy** can be any rule or regulation or the lack of rules and regulations that influence how government affects the lives of citizens. When the state legislature passes a law requiring that all students take two political science courses in order to graduate from a public university, this is a public policy. Had the legislature not passed such a rule, most students would not have registered for a course in state and local government. This is a good example of how public policy can affect citizens.

By the same token, the lack of public policy can have an impact on citizens. The fact that the Texas legislature refused to appropriate more money to match federal dollars for the Children's Health Insurance Program (CHIP) is a public policy. The lack of funding for CHIP forces the uninsured to go to public hospital emergency rooms, increasing local property tax. The landlord owner of the apartment where you live may have raised the rent to cover higher county taxes to support medical care for those uninsured children. Any decision or nondecision by government that affects the lives of its citizens is a public policy.

As indicated in the introductory chapter of this book, Texas is a state much influenced by its past and the dominant traditionalistic political culture of the state. Texas is not a state that can be described as innovative in public policy choices. For example, California is a leader in pollution legislation. Their standards for auto emissions have forced the auto industry to reduce automobile emissions nationwide. California is also a state that is leading in efforts to reduce other emissions through the Global Warming Solutions Act. This act will require a reduction of carbon emissions from all sources by 25 percent by 2020.[1] Many Texas public officials deny that global warming is a problem.

One cannot imagine a situation where the Texas Legislature and other state leaders would push efforts to reduce pollution. The nature of Texas politics and political culture

public policy
Any action or inaction by the government that impacts the lives of its citizens.

does not support such actions. In a state where the petrol-chemical and oil industries are a mainstay of the economy, pollution is often viewed as a sign of prosperity. In the past, if someone objected to the smell of oil production, the comeback was often, "Smells like money to me."

Texas is a state that has little concern for the matters of environmental pollution. When George W. Bush was running for president in 2000, Texas ranked as the top polluter among the states. When Karen Hughes, a spokesperson for then Governor Bush was asked about the high pollution ranking of the state, she said, "Governor Bush has done more than any governor in the history of Texas to hold the polluters' feet to the fire and force them to voluntarily comply." The news media reported this statement. No one in the news media asked the obvious question: "How many polluters have complied?" The press simply reported it. To a large degree, state leaders often deal with the problems by denying that they exist and thus foreclosing any need for a change in policy. Former Congressman Tom Delay called the global warming data "political science," meaning that the data is driven by politics and not science.

✦ Steps in the Policy-Making Process

Political scientists have made detailed examinations of the policy-making process for the last several decades. In 1978, James Anderson published one of the first comprehensive attempts to define policy making as a process.[2] The primary stages of this process were defined as Agenda Setting; Policy Formations; Policy Implementation; and Policy Evaluation. Evaluation should lead to feedback on the effectiveness of these policies and possible change in the future.

Not all policies follow all these steps. Most often, there is no Policy Evaluation, which consists of an attempt to evaluate the effect of the policy and make possible changes to the policy. Often policies are passes with no consideration for their impact of need for review and possible change. In some cases reversing a policy would cost a lot of money and no one is interested in the tax increases needed to fund the reversal. An example of this is the tuition increase discussed below. The state legislature in Texas has decided to fund less and less of the cost of education. It is not likely that this policy will be reversed.

Policy Evaluation may also be absent in the Policy Formation stages. Little evaluation is given to the proposed policy change or any alternatives. The legislature often reacts to complaints by constituents. Reacting to constituents' complaints is a time-honored role for legislators. That is what the average citizens expect of state and local decision makers. However, such complaints often lead to changes that are not analyzed and are based on antidotal evidence.

In other cases there is no need for Policy Implementation because in part the new policy is symbolic. As we will see below, many states have imposed bans on gay marriage. This is in large measure more symbolic than it is substantive. Legislators and citizens demand and enact such bans out of genuine concern that allowing such unions is a violation of their religious beliefs. Saying no to gay unions is a symbolic way of supporting their religious beliefs.

✦ Policy Liberalism Index

policy liberalism index
A measure of how liberal or conservative a state is on some state policies.

Table 12.1 is an **index of the policy liberalism** of all the states. This index examines state indicators of policy positions in three areas: gun control, abortion, and tax progressivity. From these four policy areas the index of policy liberalism was constructed for each

T A B L E   1 2 . 1

State Rank on Policy Liberalism Index, 2005

State	Policy	Gun Law	Abortion	Progressive Taxes
California	1	2	1	10
Hawaii	2	4	12	34
New York	3	7	9	19
Vermont	4	27	6	3
New Jersey	5	6	16	21
Connecticut	6	9	3	24
Oregon	7	18	7	6
Massachusetts	8	1	17	18
Maine	9	35	5	5
Rhode Island	10	8	28	27
Maryland	11	3	4	12
Montana	12	50	11	2
Illinois	13	5	20	39
Minnesota	14	17	20	8
New Mexico	15	31	14	26
Delaware	16	21	22	1
Alaska	17	26	10	28
Washington	18	23	2	50
West Virginia	19	29	15	13
Pennsylvania	20	14	47	40
Wisconsin	21	15	32	14
Missouri	22	16	41	20
New Hampshire	23	41	13	43
Iowa	24	10	19	22
Michigan	25	11	43	37
Ohio	26	25	38	11
Kentucky	27	48	49	16
Colorado	28	33	25	33
Nebraska	29	13	36	7
Nevada	30	29	8	47
Kansas	31	32	31	25
South Carolina	32	19	37	4
Indiana	33	24	34	36
Tennessee	34	40	23	48
Arizona	35	29	18	38
Louisiana	36	37.5	50	41
North Carolina	37	20	24	15
Virginia	38	22	40	17
Utah	39	45	42	31
Florida	40	12	27	49
Texas	**41**	**35**	**33**	**44**
Idaho	42	37.5	35	9
Arkansas	43	44	43	23
Alabama	44	49	38	42
Oklahoma	45	39	30	29

(*continued*)

TABLE 12.1 (continued)

State Rank on Policy Liberalism Index, 2005

State	Policy	Gun Law	Abortion	Progressive Taxes
Georgia	46	46	28	30
Mississippi	47	42	43	32
North Dakota	48	43	48	35
South Dakota	49	35	46	45
Wyoming	50	47	25	46

Notes: Each index is ranked: 1 = most liberal, 50 = most conservative. The policy liberalism index also includes right-to-work laws that were not included in this table because the law is a binary variable.

Source: Virginia Grey, "The Socioeconomic and Political Context of States," in *Politics in the American States: A Comparative Analysis,* 9th ed., ed. Virginia Gray and Russell Hanson (Congressional Quarterly Press, 2008). Constructed by the author from data from the Brady Campaign to Prevent Gun Violence (for the gun law index), NAM Pro-Choice America (abortion index), Urban Institute (TAW index), and Institute on Taxation and Economic Policy (tax progressively).

state. If you look closely at this table, you will note that some states rank high on some indicators of policy liberalism and near the bottom on others. For example Washington State ranks number two on abortion rights, but at the bottom on regressive taxes and in the middle on gun control. Many Western states are strongly against gun control. Southern states and Western states rank near the bottom on this index.

Texas ranks low on abortion rights and gun control and even lower on tax progressivity. This ranking is an accurate reflection of the political culture of Texas. Texans oppose gun control, are more often than not pro-life/anti-abortion, and favor regressive consumer taxes (see figures 10.3 and 10.4). The states ranked below Texas are either Western or Southern states.

This policy liberalism index is perhaps an accurate reflection of the kind of policies that can be expected to pass the legislature and be advocated by the governor and other state agencies. This is not intended as a criticism of the state of Texas or its policies but rather is one way of explaining why things are the way they are. Texas ranks 41 because it is anti-gun control, has a very regressive tax structure, and has passed laws restricting the right to abortions, providing no funds for abortions. The average Texan agrees with these policy positions.

→ EXAMINATION OF SPECIFIC POLICY AREAS IN TEXAS STATE GOVERNMENT

An examination of a number of specific policy areas in Texas will help in understanding how these policies impact students. I have chosen several policy areas that should be of interest to college students because they impact their personal lives, and perhaps their pocketbooks as well. Other texts frequently examine such policy questions as welfare reform, business regulation, and regulation of utilities. While these are important areas of policy, they often do not engage students' interest. Often this is also the case for the faculty teaching the courses. The policies examined here also affect other citizens in the state but they affect students more. A few policies are more general and some are what could be described as symbolic rather than substantive.

Tuitions and Fees

For many years the costs of college tuition and fees in Texas were very low and affordable for most people. Nonresidents of Texas often found it cheaper to come to Texas and pay a small out-of-state fee than to attend college in their own state. For many years in each of my classes, I have asked students where their home towns are. For those out-of-state students I ask why they came to Texas. For many years the answer was lower tuition costs. Today the answer is, most often, scholarships. For many years the out-of-state tuition was $200 per semester. The cost to in-state students was about $100 per semester.

In the 1970s the legislature began to gradually increase tuition and tied the amount students paid to semester hours taken. For most of the 1970s the cost was $4.00 per semester hour or about $12.00 per course with a few fees for labs attached to some courses. While this cost was very low, most students did not know what a bargain this was.[4]

Universities approached the legislature for more money during most of the 1980s and 90s. For most of this time the legislature refused to allow universities to set their own tuition rates but did allow the universities to charge additional fees for services provided to students. This included such things as computer access fees, recreational fees, and transportation fees.

Texas A&M and the University of Texas at Austin approached the legislature about allowing the two "flagship" universities to charge a higher rate of tuition. "Flagship" is a term applied by Texas and Texas A&M to define their claimed status as the lead universities in the state. This request to charge higher tuition rates met considerable opposition in the legislature, especially from members of the legislature who were graduates of "non-flagship" universities. Texas A&M and the University of Texas continued to press this issue with the legislature, and in the 2003 session of the legislature, the newly installed Republican majority and Republican Speaker Craddick agreed to allow what was called **"deregulated" tuition** for all state universities. The legislature faced a $10 billion dollar shortfall in revenues, and this seemed an easy solution to part of the problem.

In 2002 the average cost for 15 student credit hours for tuition and fees was $1,685 dollars. After the 2003 session of the legislature about deregulated tuition, the cost per semester increased to $2032, and by 2007–08 tuition had increased to an average of $6,000 per year.[5] After the legislature changed the policy to allow universities to set their own tuition, members began to receive complaints from constituents about the increases. In the next session the legislature held hearings and asked university officials to justify the increases. One wag called the hearings "How dare you do what we told you to do?" hearings.

In Chapter 10 there is a discussion of the **"budget fix."** (See table 10.5.) As was indicated, much of the state budget is fixed by the state constitution and state and federal law. The legislature has very little discretion in how the money is spent. Operating funds for higher education are not part of this budget fix. These funds come from the non-restricted area of the budget. This means that every session of the legislature may find the cost of higher education being funded with tuition and fee increases. Just as the cost of elementary and secondary education has been increasingly funded by local property taxes, which now equal almost half the total taxes collected at the state and local levels in Texas, the cost of higher education will increasingly fall to the individual student and parents, unless there is a drastic change in tuition policy.

Some students might suspect that the tuition increases they have been paying are going to fund faculty salaries. While some of these fees may find their way into the pockets of the faculty, Texas salaries are more comparable with these states today than they were in the past. Table 12.2 shows the average faculty salary in the ten most populous states.

"deregulated" tuition
A decision by the state legislature to allow state colleges and universities to set the rate of tuition charged to students.

budget fix
State laws and constitutional amendments that set aside money to be spent on specific items. The best example is the state gasoline tax being committed to state highways.

TABLE 12.2

Average Faculty Salary in Public Universities in Texas and the Ten Most Populous States (Fiscal Year 2007)

State	Professor	Associate Professor	Assistant Professor	Instructor	Lecturer	Total: Includes All Ranks	Total: Excludes No Rank
New Jersey	$116,21	$84,496	$66,312	$45,113	$53,198	$89,458	$89,700
Pennsylvania	105,812	76,305	61,323	45,000	47,310	75,365	75,830
Michigan	105,794	73,980	61,061	40,783	46,536	77,316	77,965
California	104,816	72,293	62,956	51,333	54,874	82,644	82,658
Florida	100,495	71,363	61,488	45,044	52,223	72,674	73,162
N. Carolina	99,848	72,246	61,810	52,587	42,545	72,202	74,204
Ohio	99,628	69,774	58,371	39,896	42,369	73,758	73,936
New York	98,624	73,656	60,914	47,667	50,538	75,626	75,626
Illinois	98,201	69,383	59,987	37,504	43,349	71,091	71,691
Georgia	95,868	67,102	56,500	40,037	45,593	68,464	68,610
Average: Ten States	102,752	72,593	60,982	42,488	49,763	76,197	76,661
Average: National	97,750	70,359	59,314	41,771	46,932	72,798	73,070
Texas	99,683	69,646	61,159	41,943	45,391	71,608	71,863

Source: Extract from AAUP Survey. Also see *www.Thecb.state.tx.us/Reports* (Texas Higher Education Coordinating Board).

TABLE 12.3

Tuition Costs in 2007–2008 among Major State Universities (Annual Average Cost of Tuition and Fees for Undergraduates)

University	Residents	Nonresidents
Texas A&M	$7,335	$15,675
University of Texas	$8,954	$49,008*
UC Davis	$8,124	$27,744
U of Colorado/Boulder	$6,635	$24,797
U of Illinois/Urbana–Champaign	$11,131	$25,216
University of Iowa	$6,293	$19,465
Iowa State	$8,676	$21,285
University of Michigan	$11,111	$32,400
University of Kansas	$6,600	$16,107
University of Missouri	$8,098	$18,754
Penn State	$12,844	$23,712

*The University of Texas charges different rates for tuition depending on the college. This is an average for undergraduates. Tuitions for other Texas schools were not in this report.

Source: Association of American University Data Exchange, Annual Academic Year Tuition and Required Fees for 2007–2008 Composite Report. Report obtained from Office of Institutional Studies and Planning, Texas A&M University.

Students might well ask why we should care if faculty pay is below or above average. If Texas is not competitive with other states and the salaries are below the norm, it will not be able to attract good faculty members. The tuition increases have helped Texas schools stay competitive with institutions in other states. See Table 12.3 for comparisons of tuition in Texas schools and in other states. There are many colleges and universities that cost less than Texas and Texas A&M.

Curriculum and Degree Requirements

In recent years the Texas legislature has played a more active role in making laws and rules that have an effect on the curriculum choices that students, faculty, and university officials can make. Here are a few examples of these decisions. Some work to the advantage of students and others do not.

- All state universities are required to have a set number of courses in what is called the core curriculum. This cannot be expanded or additional areas or requirements added by colleges and universities. Political Science (6 hours) and History (6 hours) are part of this core. Students must complete these courses before graduating.
- The total number of hours a student can take to complete a degree is limited to 120 hours for most degrees. Prior to this change, most required at least 128 hours. This will go into effect in the fall of 2008. The reason for this policy change is that the legislature wants students to graduate more quickly and reduce the cost to the state for higher education. Also, if a student takes more than 120 hours, the university does not get any money from the state to fund these extra hours.
- Students can receive a rebate of $1,000 if they graduate within three hours of the total hours required for the degree. The legislature forced this policy on universities but did not appropriate any money to cover the cost. This money most likely comes from fees charged to students.
- Undergraduate students are limited to a certain number of total hours in their undergraduate degree in which they will pay in-state tuition. After this number, a student must pay out-of-state tuition.
- The transfer of courses from one university to another has been a source of controversy. If a student takes a course at one school and makes a D in the course, other schools have to accept this course as transfer credit. While this benefits students with a D, some of the major schools feel such credits should not be transferred.
- In addition, there have been a number of proposals that would have an effect on students that did not pass the legislature. Many of these policy changes will return in future sessions of the legislature. The legislature often responds to antidotal evidence. A single complaint from a constituent may result in a legislator responding with legislation to correct the perceived problem.

Higher Education Funds

While the operating budgets for higher education are part of the regular budget, higher education in Texas does have funds for capital projects that are fixed in two funds. The **Permanent University Fund (PUF)** is divided between the University of Texas and Texas A&M University. This fund was established by the Texas constitution of 1876. Originally lands were located in East Texas and were rather good farmland that generated much income. The state legislature later transferred these lands in East Texas to 2.1 million acres of land, primarily in West Texas. In the early part of the twentieth century, oil was discovered on these lands and the income became substantial over time. The current value of the fund is $11.7 billion dollars.[6] The University of Texas and some of its branch campuses receive two-thirds of the money from this fund and Texas A&M and some of its branches and divisions receive one-third of the fund. Most of the money is committed to capital items and not operating budgets.[7]

Needless to say, many of the other colleges and universities in the state were upset that this policy did not give them any portion of these funds. The constitution specifically

Permanent University Fund (PUF)

The PUF is money set aside in the state constitution to benefit the University of Texas at Austin and Texas A&M University.

states that the money could be spent only at the University of Texas and its branch at College Station. The division of the money into two-thirds for the University of Texas and one-third for Texas A&M was an earlier agreement between the two schools.[8]

Due to pressure from other universities for a share in the PUF fund, the Texas Legislature in 1984 proposed a policy change with an amendment to the state constitution, which the voters approved, that created the **Higher Education Assistance Fund (HEAF).** Beginning in 1985 the legislature set aside annual appropriations of $100 million for this fund. This was later increased to $175 million. Today this fund provides about $275 million each year for colleges and universities not included within the PUF.[9]

The original writers of the Texas Constitution in 1876 saw the need for higher education in Texas and created the PUF. Later sessions of the legislature saw the need to fund other institutions of higher education and created the HEAF. These are both examples of public policy having an effect on the education of students in Texas today. While tuition costs have increased and may continue to do so, at least part of the cost of higher education is constitutionally protected.

Access to Higher Education

From the 1950s to the 1970s, access to state colleges and universities in Texas was what could be called "open enrollment," where all students who were high school graduates and Texas residents would be automatically admitted without consideration to high school standing or standardized test scores. Almost anyone could enroll in the university of their choice. In the 1980s many schools, but especially Texas A&M and the University of Texas, began to impose higher standards for being accepted, primarily based on SAT scores and high school class standing.

This action to increase enrollment standards to some degree conflicted with the need to increase minority enrollment in the state colleges and universities. Hispanics and African Americans make up a majority of the state population but only about 20 percent were enrolled in colleges and fewer still in the top two state universities. This was also true of law and other professional schools where minority students were underrepresented.

Many colleges and universities began an affirmative action program to attempt to increase minority opportunities to enroll in colleges and universities. These programs resulted in a lawsuit concerning the admission of minority students to the University of Texas law school. In 1996, the federal courts ended affirmative action practices at the University of Texas law school in the **Hopwood Decision.**[10]

The Attorney General of the State of Texas, Daniel Morales, a recipient of affirmative action programs while a student in Texas higher education institutes, expanded the meaning of the Hopwood case in Texas and effectively eliminated affirmative action admission policies in all colleges and universities in Texas. Morales found that "... Hopwood's restrictions would generally apply to all internal institutional policies, including admissions, financial aid, scholarships, fellowships, recruitment and retention, among others."[11] Thus, under the Morales interpretation, *Hopwood* was extended to prevent the consideration of race in areas beyond admissions.

It should be noted that *Hopwood* was overturned in 2003 by a case originating in Michigan. In June of 2003 the U.S. Supreme Court in *Grutter v. Bollinger,* 539 U.S. 306 (2003), ruled that the U.S. Constitution does not prohibit the tailoring of standards to use race as an admission decision or policy.

Prior to *Hopwood* being overturned, the Texas legislature, in an attempt to solve both the equity of opportunity and the minority representation (affirmative action), changed the standards. They prevented admissions decisions and financial awards from being based primarily on any standardized test score such as the SAT, ACT, or GRE.

Higher Education Assistance Fund (HEAF)
The HEAF is money set aside for use by those universities not benefiting from the PUF.

Hopwood Decision
Decision by federal courts to end affirmative action in Texas schools. These programs had provided for special treatment for minority students in being accepted to colleges and professional schools.

The legislature did allow any student who graduated in the upper 10 percent of his or her high school class automatic admission to any state college or university without consideration of other factors such as SAT scores. This ruling had the most impact on the University of Texas where currently 81 percent of the freshman class is admitted under the 10 percent rule. To a lesser degree this is also the case at Texas A&M University.[12]

This 10 percent rule was supposed to increase minority enrollment by allowing students from inner city minority high schools to attend the top schools in the state. There is some evidence that the 10 percent rule had increased minority enrollment, especially at the University of Texas and to a lesser degree at Texas A&M. It has created a problem for some high performing students in the better high schools in the state. It is not uncommon to see students with 1,500+ SAT scores not making the top 10 percent category in their high school. There are also a few students from small rural schools with very low SAT scores getting accepted under the 10 percent rule.[13]

Limitations on Personal Freedom

In addition to the legislature having an effect on education, both higher and secondary, each session finds bills introduced to limit personal freedom. Some of these bills are more symbolic and do not address problems that are having an adverse affect in the state. The following is a discussion of a few of these policy changes and how they impact the citizens of the state.

Voter ID

In Chapter 3, limitations on voter registration and participation were discussed. The history of Texas until the mid 1970s was one of restrictive voter registration laws and policies. In 1971 the state went from annual registration to permanent. Texas has a very open registration system. Voters can register "off site," meaning they do not have to appear in person at the courthouse or before some public official to register. They can simply fill in a postcard form and mail it, postage paid, to the local voter registrar. This form can be downloaded from the Secretary of State's Web page.

In the past two session of the legislature, bills have cleared the house and stalled in the senate that would have required voters to produce a picture ID with their voter registration card before they would be allowed to vote. The state purpose of this requirement is to reduce voter fraud. The Texas House had an interim committee studying the issue of voter fraud. While their report to the house will not be available until the new session of the legislature meeting in 2009, the committee found that there are problems in the off-site voter registration and mail-out ballots. The committee staff indicated there may be proposals to tighten up off-site voter registration and mail-out ballots.[14] (A voter ID would not solve either of these problems.)

The **Voter ID Bill** is being pushed by the Republican leadership in both the house and senate. The Democrats have opposed the bill and have been able to kill the bill in the senate due to the two-thirds rule discussed in Chapter 7. The Republican argument for this change in policy is that there is a lot of voter fraud in the state. Their position is that the integrity to the ballot needs to be protected. The Democratic opposition to this policy change is based on arguments that many elderly, minority, and low-income people will not be able to produce picture ID. They point out that many older citizens do not have driver licenses because they no longer drive. Many minorities, who strongly support Democrats, would be intimidated by having to go to the courthouse and register to vote and may lack picture IDs. This would be a major change in policy from an open, off-site registration system that has been the policy for many years. It should be noted that the U.S. Supreme Court upheld the picture voter ID requirement in Indiana.[15]

Voter ID Bill

Proposal to require all voters to present a picture ID before they could vote.

HIGHLIGHT

Some states, most notably Georgia, passed a law requiring citizens to get a state-issued picture ID for voting. Georgia charged a fee of $20 for a five-year voter ID card. This law was quickly challenged in federal court, and the court issued an injunction barring the requirement.[16]

The Georgia ID has not been used in any elections. Secretary of State at the time, Cathy Cox, a Democrat who oversaw Georgia's elections said, "There has not been a proven case of voter fraud in the state in nearly a decade.[17] Ms. Cox estimated that some "676,000 otherwise eligible voters lacked a driver's license or state-issued photo ID."[18] For a copy of the requirements in Georgia go to http://sos.georgia.gov/GAPhotoID/default.htm.

Others have argued that the requirement for a voter ID, even a driver's license or other state picture ID, costs money and could be a violation of the 24th Amendment to the U.S. Constitution, which outlawed the poll tax. While it is unclear at this time what actions will be recommended to the Texas legislature in 2009, there is no doubt that such requirements would restrict the right of some citizens to vote.

For most college students, registering to vote and voting in the city where they attend school has been an option since the passage of the 26th Amendment (18-year-old voting) to the U.S. Constitution in 1971, the same year Texas eased voter registration procedures. It is not uncommon to find college Democratic and Republican organizations holding voter registration drives on campus. For most students a picture ID would not pose much of a problem since they are issued one by the school they attend. However, changing the rules for registration from off-site/postcard registration to on-site (perhaps at the courthouse or city hall) might reduce the number of students registering and voting in elections in the place where they attend college.

Gay Rights

Texas was one of the last states that had anti-sodomy laws, which ban private consensual sex between adults of the same sex or the opposite sex. These laws were invalidated by the Supreme Court in 2003.[19] At one time all states had anti-sodomy laws, but in 2003 the number had decreased to 13 states. Today, most Americans agree that such laws should be ended but do not necessarily agree that gay citizens should have the same rights as others.

The 2005 session of the legislature proposed an amendment to ban same-sex marriage. In November of 2005 the voters overwhelmingly approved this amendment (see table 2.2). There is no doubt that this issue, which was primarily symbolic, has the support of most Texans, including many minority voters in the state. Texas joined 38 other states that have bans on gay marriage.[20] Many of these bans follow the same language as the Defense of Marriage Act passed in 1996 by Congress. This act says that states do not have to honor same sex marriage performed in other states. This act goes against the Full Faith and Credit (article IV) provisions of the U.S. Constitution that require states to recognize the acts and judicial proceeding of other states. (See Chapter 2 for a discussion of this.)

One can conclude that Texas is in the company of the majority when it comes to the issue of gay marriage. Most states have such laws. How long these laws will remain on the books remains to be seen. While the idea has much popular support today, the same was true for anti-sodomy laws in the past. Unless Congress passes a constitutional amendment to prevent gay marriage, these bans may not stand the test of time. Just as people have become more tolerant of other rights, the same may happen for these rights.

Also, in the past divorce was very difficult to obtain in most states. A few Western states changed their laws (especially Nevada) and allowed divorce for no reason, the so-called "quickie" divorce. At first some states refused to recognize these divorces, but they were later forced to accept them. Divorce in Mexico was also not recognized by some states that were later forced to accept these legal actions.

In a recent case in New York, a gay couple who were married in Canada filed for divorce in the New York Court system. A State of New York Supreme Court justice recognized the Canadian marriage by the two women and allowed the divorce.[21]

One may ask why gays are demanding such rights. Part of the problem is that without such statutes that allow the recognition of such unions of partnerships, it may be difficult for one of the partners to make decisions for the other if in need of medical care. The same may be true for such things as medical insurance coverage.

In addition, there are many children in need of a stable home, and adoption is one way to achieve this. Texas and many other states make it difficult for same sex couples to adopt children.

To some degree, these actions against gay rights are the results of a generation gap. Many in college today have a tolerant attitude toward gays. Members of the legislature either don't, or are using the issue to appeal to social conservative voters.

Abortion Rights

In 1973 the U.S. Supreme Court in the case ***Roe v. Wade*** decided that the Texas law banning abortions was unconstitutional.[22] This case involved a woman with the fictitious name Jane Doe and the Dallas County District Attorney Henry Wade.[23] This case places restrictions on what states can do to prevent a woman from choosing to have an abortion. Since this case was approved by the Supreme Court, states have tried in a variety of ways to limit and restrict abortions. Texas is no exception. Many attempts have been made to restrict the ability of women to get an abortion. In the last session of the legislature in 2007, a total of 25 bills were introduced to restrict or define abortions and limit abortion rights. Each session of the legislature finds about this same number of bills filed that could have an impact on women's right to abortion. Often these bills restrict the right of a woman to have an abortion unless she has the consent of her parents or the father of the child grants permission. Most bills that have passed primarily affect younger women and parental consent.

The legislature has also altered the rules in the state budget to make it easier for pro-life groups to receive funds for abortion counseling and reduce the availability of funds for organizations such as Planned Parenthood, which support a woman's right to choose.

Many of the legislatures who file these bills do so out of strong religious convictions that abortions are wrong. They have lots of vocal company supporting these actions. At the Planned Parenthood clinic in Bryan/College Station, the local Coalition for Life group keeps a constant vigil in front of the clinic. They have a camera set up to photograph the license plates of everyone who visits the clinic. Parents of students who go to the clinic sometimes get a letter informing them that their daughter has visited the "abortion" clinic.

Given the current makeup of the U.S. Supreme Court, it is possible that *Roe v. Wade* will be overturned. There are state statutes banning abortions that may make their way to the court. If states are given the right to ban abortions, the Texas legislature will have many bills filed to achieve this.

Roe v. Wade
Texas court case that limits what states can legally do to prevent abortions.

Sex Education

The attitude to many citizens of Texas is that it is not the role of public schools to provide sex education, but if they must, teaching total abstinence is as far as it should go. Often the attitude is that teaching sex education will simply encourage students to engage in promiscuous sex. At the beginning of the 2007 session of the legislature, the governor, on very slim authority, issued an executive order requiring all schoolgirls to be vaccinated against the human papillomavirus to prevent cervical cancer later in their life. Several members of the house and senate introduced legislation, which passed, preventing the vaccinations from taking place. Several members expressed concern that if young women were to get the vaccine, it would encourage teen sex because they would not have to worry about getting cancer later in their lives. In part this logic assumed that there is rationality in the behavior of teens when it comes to sex. Other members doubted this.

In March of 2008, the Center for Disease Control and Prevention (CDC) released a study that found that one in four young women was infected with the virus. According to the Houston Chronicle, "Texas Gov. Rick Perry was right. Members of the Texas Legislature who voted last year shot down his plan to require schoolgirls to be vaccinated against HPV were shortsighted. . . . This groundbreaking study shows how pressing is the need for sound public policy based on data and demonstrated best practices rather than emotion."[24]

Some bills involving teen behavior have been known to make the national news. One such bill in the 2005 session, introduced by former Representative Al Edwards of Houston became known as the **"Booty Bill."** This bill would have prevented cheerleaders at high school events, such as football games, from doing dances and moves of the body that were sexually suggestive. Mr. Edwards, testifying before the committee when the bill was given a hearing, was unable to provide the words to describe what constituted such suggestive behavior. Mr. Edwards knew what it looked like when he saw it but could not put it into words. It is interesting to note that while Edwards was unable to describe the sexually suggestive behavior his bill would have prohibited, he expected minors, or cheerleaders, to recognize them.

While the bill gained national attention and resulted in several interviews for Mr. Edwards on national TV, it did not ensure his re-election. In fact he lost his seat in the 2006 election, in part because of the bad publicity from this bill. He did manage to win the Democratic primary in 2008 against the person who defeated him in 2006.

Booty Bill

Proposed bill that would have regulated suggestive body movements of cheerleaders at high school sporting events.

Drinking Age

In 1984, Congress forced all states to raise the age at which people can legally buy alcohol to 21 years of age. If states did not raise the age to 21, they could lose some of their federal highway money. When this law was passed, 30 states had 21 years as the drinking age, 4 had 20 years of age, 13 had 19 years of age, and only 3 had 18 years of age.[25]

Even though this change was made long before most current college students were born, and it applied to less than half the states, if you ask students in class today for an example of the federal government attaching strings to federal money, someone in the class will invariably give this example. It has turned into a sort of a legend on how much better an earlier age was than today's.

✦ LOCAL GOVERNMENTS

Many students attending college in Texas do not live on campus. They rent apartments and houses in the community. The city government in the town where you live can have a great impact on you in a variety of ways.

Local taxes may get passed on to you in the form of higher rents. This may include not only city but county, school, and perhaps a special district. (See Chapter 10 on tax shifting.) You will also pay, as part of the rent or separately, for water, sewer, solid waste, and perhaps other service charges. This has an impact on the cost of your education.

The availability of local housing in your college town can be affected by zoning laws. The city may limit the number of multi-family units (apartments) that can be constructed in the community. Some cities have reduced the number of unrelated people who can live in areas zoned single family from four to two, often making it difficulty for students to afford to live in these areas. Four people splitting the rent is economical. Two is not.

Students' life off campus can also pose problems. Students may have different lifestyles from families living in the same neighborhood. Students' attitudes and taste in music, how loudly the music is played, and how late into the night music is played may be quite different from the lifestyle of a married couple with small children. These differences can result in conflicts that involve the police. Most rules favor a married couple over a student.

Local governments can have an impact on the life of students off campus and the number of units available for rent off the campus. Many colleges and universities lack the resources to provide on-campus housing or the legal clout to make every student live on campus.

✦ Conclusions

What I have tried to show in this chapter is how the government policy-making process can affect the lives of students in the state of Texas. I have provided but a few examples. Earlier in this book an old adage was given: "Neither man nor property is safe so long as the Legislature is in session." The legislature, the governor, and many state agencies, including the board of regents of your college or university, can have a direct effect on your education. New rules regarding admission to schools, tuition, curriculum, and personal freedoms can take place at any time. These new policies may make it easier or more difficult for you to finish your education.

Hopefully, by taking this course, you are more aware of how the government of Texas can have an impact on your life, and you will become more active in both state and local politics.

Internet Resources

Children's Health Insurance Program:
> *http://www.chipmedicaid.com*
> Texas Health and Human Services Commission website provides information about children's Medicaid coverage, costs, qualifications and eligibility.

Permanent University Fund: *http://www.utimco.org/scripts/ internet/fundsdetail.asp?fnd=2*
> Legislative story, financial statements, investment schedule, and annual reports of The University of Texas Investment Management Company.

Higher Education Assistance Fund:
> *http://www.thecb.state.tx.us/reports/PDF/0789.PDF*

Executive summary and strategic plan of the Texas Higher Education Coordinating Board and funding recommendations and allocation formulas.

Centers for Disease Control and Prevention (CDC):
> *http://www.cdc.gov/*
> Discusses environmental and travelers diseases and health conditions and emergency and workplace safety and health preparedness and response.

The Center for Individual Rights and the Equal Justice Society:
> *http://www.cir-usa.org/cases/hopwood.htm*
> *http://www.equaljusticesociety.org/MALDEF.pdf*
> These websites provide information about the *Hopwood v. Texas* and *Grutter v. Bollinger*.

Key Terms

Booty Bill (p. 282)

budget fix (p. 275)

"deregulated" tuition (p. 275)

Higher Education Assistance
   Fund (HEAF) (p. 278)

Hopwood Decision (p. 278)

Permanent University Fund (PUF)
   (p. 277)

policy liberalism index (p. 272)

public policy (p. 271)

Roe v. Wade (p. 281)

Voter ID Bill (p. 279)

Notes

1. Virginia Grey, "The Socioeconomic and Political Context of States," in *Politics in the American States: A Comparative Analysis,* 9th ed., ed. Virginia Gray and Russell Hanson (Congressional Quarterly Press, 2008). Constructed by the author from data from the Brady Campaign to Prevent Gun Violence (for the gun law index), NAM Pro-Choice America (abortion index), Urban Institute (TAW index), and Institute on Taxation and Economic Policy (tax progressively).

2. James E. Anderson, *Public Policy Making* (New York: Praeger Publishing, 1972).

3. *Texas Fact Book, 2006.* See Legislative Budget Board web page. www.lbb.state.tx.gov

4. At Texas A&M University, a student complained to a department head that he did not think he was getting his money's worth in an American government course. The department head pulled out $12 and gave it to him saying he was very busy and did not have time to argue the point.

5. Texas Coordinating Board (http://www.thecb.state.tx.us/)

6. http://www.utimco.org/funds/allfunds/2007annual/puf_overview.asp

7. Some at TAMU have suggested this is the source of the hook'm horns and the gigum Aggies hand gestures.

8. State Constitution, Article 7, sect 18.

9. www.thecb.state.tx

10. *Hopwood v. Texas,* 78 F.3d 932 (5th Cir. 1996), *cert. denied, Texas v. Hopwood,* No. 95-1773 (July 1, 1996).

11. Ibid.

12. *Houston Chronide,* "81% of U.T.'s admissions offers go to top 10% graduates," March 20, 2008, p. i.

13. Personal observation of the author as the Director of Undergraduate Programs in Political Science at Texas A&M University for 17 years.

14. Interview with staff of House Committee on Elections, February 18, 2008.

15. Associated Press, Monday, April 19, 2008.

16. *New York Times,* July 8, 2006 (www.nytimes.com/2006/07/08us08voter.html).

17. Ibid.

18. Ibid.

19. www.cnn.com/2003/LAW/26/scouts.sodomy/

20. http://www.stateline.org/live/ViewPage.action?siteNodeId=136&languageId=1&contentId=1557

21. *New York Times,* March 6, 2008 (www.nytimes.com/2008/03/06gay.html).

22. Tex. Code Crim. Proc. arts. 1191–94, 1196.

23. *Roe v. Wade,* 410 US 113.

24. *Houston Chronicle,* March 15, 2008, p. 68.

25. "Rewriting a Rite to Passage" *Time,* July 2, 1984.

Epilogue

Texas at the beginning of the twenty-first century is quite different from Texas at the beginning of the twentieth century. Many obvious factors will shape Texas government and politics in the twenty-first century. Texas is no longer a rural state with a land-based economy. As the second-largest state in the nation, Texas is very much a metropolitan state, and its economy is no longer dependent on cattle, cotton, and oil, as it was at the beginning of the twentieth century. New economic forces now dominate.

The ethnic makeup of the population is another obvious change that will influence government and politics in the twenty-first century. By 2010, Anglos will be in the minority. (See table 1.1.) This change in the population will have profound impacts on state policies and politics.

Texas is no longer a one-party state as it was for most of the twentieth century. As the Republican party achieved parity with the Democrats, many changes occurred, perhaps most notably in the state legislature. For the last thirty years, both the house and the senate have had nonpartisan leadership. This changed when the Republicans gained a majority in both houses. The 2003, 2005, and 2007 sessions made clear that bipartisan cooperation had ended. The Republicans are in control, and they do not want to compromise. Bills sponsored by Democrats are more often held up in a calendar committee, and few if any points of order made by Democrats are upheld by the speaker.

As was indicated in Chapter 3, Texas ranks very low—(forty-seventh in 2006) among the fifty states on participation by its citizens in voting. Easy access to the ballot box (for instance, motor voter registration) may increase participation by minority groups, especially Mexican Americans. Increased activities by both political parties in the state may lead to increased participation levels in the twenty-first century. Currently Hispanics tend to vote for Democrats. It remains to be seen if this trend will continue or if the Republicans can become successful in attracting the Hispanic vote.

Given these changes, can the leaders of state government meet the challenges they will face? Will Texas continue the process of revising its constitution with biennial amendments proposed to the voters, or will state leaders push for general revision? Will the legislature continue to meet in biennial sessions, with numerous special sessions called to meet new crises, or will it go to annual sessions? Will the pay of the legislature be increased to allow all citizens the opportunity to serve without being dependent on special interest groups? Will Texas continue to elect members of the judiciary in partisan elections, or will some other system be adopted? Can real reform of campaign finance be put in place? With no limitation on individual contributions to candidates, will a few wealthy Texans continue to heavily influence the outcome of elections? Will the state leaders face up to the difficult problem of financing state government, or will the present, exceptionally regressive tax system, dominated by consumer taxes, remain in place? Will the present system of unfair school finances continue, or can real reforms be enacted even when under the gun of a court order? Will Texans be willing to pay for the growing prison population, or will solutions to crime other than "lock 'em up" be considered? Finally, will county government be given the authority to meet the needs of a growing metropolitan population?

The twenty-first century clearly carries many challenges for Texas state government. In an era in which government is viewed by many as the problem rather than the solution, meeting these challenges will be especially difficult. The state leadership, currently controlled by the Republican party, will have to work especially hard to overcome this attitude that government cannot solve the problem. As Paul Burka put it in the February 2006 issue of the *Texas Monthly,* the common flaw of the current leadership "is a desire for power that exceeds a desire for policy—and a complete lack of shame. There is no sense of restraint. There is no impulse to govern. There is only the desire for more power."[1] While the dominant traditionalistic/individualistic political culture that supports the idea of limited government may tolerate this lack of action for a time, the question is, How long will the people of the state tolerate this inaction, especially on the issue of school reform?

---

[1]Paul Burka, "First, Dew No Harm" *Texas Monthly,* February, 2006. p. 16.

Index

Note: Page references followed by *f* or *t* refer to figures or tables, respectively. Page references followed by "n" refer to notes.